The Naked Gaze

Reflections on Chinese Modernity

Harvard East Asian Monographs 308

The Naked Gaze

Reflections on Chinese Modernity

Carlos Rojas

Published by the Harvard University Asia Center
Distributed by Harvard University Press
Cambridge (Massachusetts) and London 2008

Printed in the United States of America

The Harvard University Asia Center publishes a monograph series and, in coordination with the Fairbank Center for Chinese Studies, the Korea Institute, the Reischauer Institute of Japanese Studies, and other faculties and institutes, administers research projects designed to further scholarly understanding of China, Japan, Vietnam, Korea, and other Asian countries. The Center also sponsors projects addressing multidisciplinary and regional issues in Asia.

Library of Congress Cataloging-in-Publication Data

Rojas, Carlos, 1970–

The naked gaze : reflections on Chinese modernity / Carlos Rojas.

p. cm. -- (Harvard East Asian monographs ; 308)

Includes bibliographical references and index.

ISBN 978-0-674-03174-6 (alk. paper)

1. Chinese literature--19th century--History and criticism. 2. Chinese literature--20th century--History and criticism. I. Title. II. Title: Reflections on Chinese modernity.

PL2301.R65 2008

895.1'09005--dc22

2008032984

Index by Casey Lee

♾ Printed on acid-free paper

Last figure below indicates year of this printing

18 17 16 15 14 13 12 11 10 09 08

Acknowledgments

I am very grateful to my parents for their support throughout my studies, even when my decisions may have appeared to them somewhat unorthodox ("You want to go *where* to study Chinese? . . . Do you realize where that *is*?"). Edward Gunn oversaw the birth of this project, and Paul Anderer, Jonathan Crary, Robert Hymes, Rosalind Morris, Shang Wei, and Michael Tsin helped me more than they may realize. I am particularly indebted to David Der-wei Wang, who has been, and continues to be, a mentor nonpareil. An An-Wang post-doctoral fellowship at Harvard and a Cheng She-wo post-doctoral fellowship at Shih-hsin University, Taipei, allowed me to revise this project for publication. Andy Rodekohr provided some invaluable last-minute research assistance while this manuscript was going to press, and Casey Lee prepared the index.

Finally, I owe a special debt of gratitude to Teo, Luodan, and Eileen, for providing continual inspiration and welcome distraction from less important matters.

C.R.

Contents

Reference Matter

Figures

Figures 1–6 and 8 also appear, in color when available, in an insert following p. 90; Fig. 7 appears only in the insert.

Figures 9–20 appear, in color, in an insert following p. 218. Figure 9 and a detail from Figure 17 are also reproduced in the text proper, on the pages shown below.

Credits

An earlier version of Chapter 3 appeared as "The Coin of Gender in *Pinhua baojian*," in David Der-wei Wang and Shang Wei, eds., *From the Late Ming to the Late Qing: Dynastic Decline and Cultural Innovation* (Cambridge: Harvard University Asia Center, 2006), 297–324. Reproduced with permission.

An earlier version of Chapter 4 appeared as "Jin Yong's Martial Arts Picture Manuals," in Ann Huss and Jianmei Liu, eds., *The Jin Yong Phenomenon: Chinese Martial Arts Fiction and Modern Chinese Literary History* (New York: Cambria Press, 2007). Reprinted with permission.

An earlier version of Chapter 7 appeared as "Of Motherlands and Maternities: Spectral Topographies in Li Yongping's *Haidong qing*," in David Der-wei Wang and Carlos Rojas, eds., *Writing Taiwan: A New Literary History* (Durham, NC: Duke University Press, 2006). Reproduced with permission.

An earlier version of Chapter 8 appeared as "Without [Femin]ism: Femininity as Axis of Alterity and Desire in Gao Xingjian's *One Man's Bible*," in *Modern Chinese Literature and Culture* 14, no. 2 (Fall 2002): 163–206. Reproduced with permission.

An earlier version of Chapter 9 appeared as "Wang Shuo and the Chinese Image/inary: Visual Simulacra and the Writing of History," *Journal of Modern Literature in Chinese* 3, no. 1 (Jan. 2000): 23–57. Reproduced with permission.

The photographs of Cixi reproduced on the cover and as Figs. 1, 2, and 3 are reproduced here with the kind permission of the Freer Gallery of Art and Arthur M. Sackler Gallery, Smithsonian. They consist of:

SC-GR-251 The Empress Dowager Cixi. 1903. Photographer: Xunling (1874–1943).

SC-GR-246 Empress Dowager Cixi in the guise of Avalokitesvara. 1903. Photographer: Xunling (1874–1943).

SC-GR-247 Photograph of a portrait of the Empress Dowager painted by Katherine Carl (1865–1938).

The image and details of Su Hanchen's *Lady at Dressing Table in a Garden* in Figs. 4, 6, and 9 are reproduced here with the kind permission of the Museum of Fine Arts, Boston:

Su Hanchen, Chinese, 1120s–1160s
Lady at her dressing table in a garden
Chinese, Southern Song dynasty, mid-12th century
Ink, color, and gold on silk
25.2 × 26.7 cm (9–15/16 × 10–1/2 in)
Museum of Fine Arts, Boston
Denman Waldo Ross Collection, 29.960

The photographs of Eileen Chang from her *Duizhao ji* shown in Figs. 7 and 8 are reproduced here with the kind permission of Huangguan Publishing House, Taipei, Taiwan.

The image from Ye Daying's *Red Cherry* is reproduced from the VCD cover, and the images from Jiang Wen's *In the Heat of the Sun* and Hou Hsiao-hsien's *Shanghai Flowers* are screen captures from VCDs.

The Naked Gaze

Reflections on Chinese Modernity

INTRODUCTION

The Errant Gaze

In a photograph taken late in her life, Empress Dowager Cixi 慈禧太后 (1835–1908) stands in front of her imperial throne, holding a small mirror in one hand and inserting a long-stemmed flower into her hair with the other (see Fig. 1). Positioned above the throne is a banner identifying her expansively as "The Empress Dowager, the sacred mother of the Great Qing Empire, motherly, auspicious, upright, blessed, healthy, dignified, long-lived, respectful, reverend, and worshipful" 大清國當今慈禧端佑康頤昭豫莊誠壽恭欽獻崇熙聖母皇太后, followed by the date the photograph was taken: "Guangxu 光緒 [reign], *guimao* 癸卯 [year]," which corresponds to 1903 in the Gregorian calendar. The empress's contemplative face, dramatically illuminated from the upper right, is oriented in the general direction of the small mirror she is holding in her left hand. Her actual gaze, however, is subtly yet distinctly turned away from the mirror and toward an indeterminate point below and outside the frame of the photograph.

This photograph is one of several that Cixi's court photographer Xunling 勳齡 (1874–1943) took between 1903 and 1905—photographs in which Cixi used carefully staged poses and settings to shape not only how she wished to be perceived but also how she wanted to imagine herself. This particular image is one of a set taken in front of her residence in the Summer Palace's Leshou Hall, where a throne, tripartite screen, pyramids of apples, and other traditional props had been arranged in order to allow Xunling to take advantage of the natural light available there.[1]

Dating from the brief period between the beginning of the twentieth century and the 1911 collapse of the Qing dynasty, Cixi's photographs were taken precisely as China was changing from a "traditional" dynastic system to a "modern" republican one. In this particular image, the moment of historical and political transition is articulated in visual terms through the strategic contrast between the embedded mirror and the meta-representational frame of the photograph itself. As I argue in this book, the mirror and the photograph represent the two paradigmatic visual technologies of the premodern and modern eras, respectively, together with the epistemological and ontological assumptions each presupposes. The schematic opposition in this image between specularity and photography, however, is fractured by Cixi's skewed gaze, which appears to be directed neither at the mirror nor at the camera, nor toward any other identifiable region within the image itself. Cixi's gaze not only originates from the focal point of the image, virtually at the center of the photograph as a whole, but furthermore functions here as an example of what Roland Barthes calls a *punctum*—an incongruous element within a photograph that startles and captures the viewer's attention, disrupting the smooth viewing of the image as a whole.[2]

Cixi's errant gaze simultaneously draws attention to, and disrupts, the schematic opposition proposed here between specularity and photography and, more broadly, between the general historical periods emblematized by these two paradigmatic visual technologies. In this study, I take Cixi's wandering gaze as my own starting point for considering discourses of visuality within three distinct historical moments: the nineteenth-century, late imperial period; the mid-twentieth-century, high modern era; and the contemporary moment. I argue that each period is characterized by a different dominant visual mode—of specularity,

---

1. Lily Kecskes ("Photographs of Tz'u-hsi") notes that this was done in order to avoid the shadows that would have been produced by the artificial light available inside Leshou Hall at that time. For a good discussion of Cixi's interest in photography, see also Cheng-hua Wang, "Presenting the Empress Dowager to the World."

2. Barthes, *Camera Lucida*.

Fig. 1 The Empress Dowager Cixi gazing at a hand mirror. 1903. Photographer: Xunling (1874–1943).

spectatorship, and screened projections, respectively—but at the same time that these historical periodizations reflect not a smooth, unidirectional temporal movement but are bound up in a complex process of retrospection and anticipation. My focus is not so much on visual imagery per se but on the ways in which visuality itself has been perceived and imagined, and their implications for processes of gendered subject formation. I approach these issues primarily through the lens of narrative fiction, using an eclectic selection of nineteenth- and twentieth-century works to identify distinct constellations of visual attitudes for each period.

In the remainder of the Introduction, I analyze Cixi's 1903 mirror photograph to introduce the methodological and theoretical considerations I draw on throughout this study. In particular, I read the photograph through its historical context, focusing on Cixi's attitudes toward photography. I also consider this image through the prism of Lacan's mirror-stage model, especially the model's emphasis on the role of processes of projective identification and anticipatory retrospection in subject formation. Finally, I bring these twin historical and theoretical approaches together by proposing a radical rehistoricization of the mirror-stage model itself—essentially reading Lacan's model against its own textual history—and then using that rehistoricized psychoanalytic model to rethink the historical assumptions on which the concept of Chinese (visual) modernity itself is predicated.

Fractured Mirrors

What is Cixi looking at? Although the object of her gaze cannot be determined, the fact that she is clearly looking away from the mirror in her hand suggests a fracturing of the specular gaze that is the ostensible subject of the portrait. Needless to say, Cixi's act of looking in the mirror was from the beginning precisely that: a mere act, performed for the camera and designed to yield a photograph that would in turn mimic the function of the original mirror image. The resulting substitution of the photograph for the mirror image nevertheless requires the insertion of an external gaze into the original closed circuit of specular reflection. In contrast to the presumptively direct act of seeing one's own reflection in a mirror, the process of viewing a photographic self-portrait involves a complex mediation with several external gazes. In posing for the photographer, for instance, Cixi was literally putting herself on display for an outside observer, and even she herself then had to view the resulting photograph from an external vantage point. Cixi's view of her own photographic image was necessarily mediated through these two external gazes, and it is only by suturing over the perceptual rifts created by this double insertion that the resulting portrait is able to mimic the dynamics of the original mirror scene.

In this image, the subject's negotiation with these putative external gazes also has important implications for the ways in which gender is produced and understood. By the time this photograph was taken, Cixi had, for nearly half a century, been the most powerful figure in the hypermasculine Qing imperial court, repeatedly positioning herself as a surrogate for immature or politically emasculated male emperors. For instance, the reign name used to date the photograph in the overhead banner refers to her nephew, the Guangxu emperor (r. 1875–1908), whom Cixi had placed on the throne 28 years earlier when he was five, and in whose place she had then ruled until he reached maturity. At the time the photograph was taken, the now-adult emperor had been under effective house arrest in the Forbidden City for nearly five years, following his support for the failed Hundred Days Reform movement of 1898, and remained similarly powerless (with Cixi continuing to rule in his place) until his death on November 14, 1908—precisely one day before Cixi herself passed away. Guangxu was not the only infant emperor whose power Cixi had appropriated—he had been preceded by his own cousin (and Cixi's son), the Tongzhi emperor (r. 1861–75), who similarly assumed the throne at the age of five. The Guangxu emperor, meanwhile, was succeeded by China's last emperor, the Xuantong emperor Puyi (r. 1908–12), who was only two years old when Cixi arranged, just hours before her own death, for him to replace Guangxu on the throne.

Against this backdrop of the imperial court—represented metonymically by Cixi's throne and the freestanding wooden screen behind it—Cixi adopted the distinctively feminine pose of adorning herself in front of a mirror, as though in her own private boudoir. This convention of the boudoir mirror scene is a familiar one in late imperial Chinese art and literature, but its gendered implications are complicated by the fact that, although the figure gazing at the mirror is almost invariably a woman, the actual representations were typically created by and for men. Consequently, the genre of the boudoir mirror scene becomes implicitly voyeuristic—insofar as the female subject's intimately specular gaze is figuratively appropriated by the artist's external one. In the case of Cixi's photograph, this gendered inversion of the gaze is redoubled, with Cixi herself appropriating the implicitly voyeuristic gaze as her own and then using it to negotiate her own mediated self-regard.

These contradictory gendered implications of the gaze in Cixi's mirror photograph come together in a visual allusion suggested by the specular image at the heart of the portrait itself. Although invisible to the outside viewer, the image appearing in Cixi's hand mirror is that of her inserting a flower into her hair—or, literally, a flower appearing in a mirror, as in the expression *jinghua shuiyue* 鏡花水月 ([like] a flower in a mirror and [the reflection of] the moon in water). This familiar Buddhist aphorism uses the explicitly feminine symbols of the flower and the moon to suggest the ephemeral nature of both visual imagery and mortal existence, thereby ironically undercutting both Cixi's ostensible act of self-adornment and the fascination with specular and photographic representation that grounds the portrait as whole.

The "flower in a mirror" (*jinghua*) component of this Buddhist aphorism is a synthesis of several different but essentially fungible visual metaphors in early Buddhist texts—metaphors that compare dharmas alternatively to illusions, flames, mirror or dream images, or the reflection of the moon in water. Curiously, however, although these sutras contain many separate references to both flowers and mirrors, the two are rarely if ever explicitly paired in these early texts.[3] Literally invisible in these early discussions of visual ephemera, the figure of the flower in the mirror later comes to function as a nodal point for that entire earlier array of visual tropes. By the same token, the flower in the mirror image nestled invisibly at the heart of Cixi's mirror portrait similarly functions as an empty node at which the contradictory vectors of visuality and gender that inform the image intersect.

---

3. See Chung-Fang Yu, *Kuan-yin*, for a survey of some of these early antecedents of the flowers in the mirror formulation.

If Cixi's 1903 mirror photograph illustrates the conceit of the flower in the mirror, allusions to the parallel moon in water trope can be found in another famous series of photographs for which she posed a few months later.[4] In these photos, Cixi appears in the guise of Guanyin 觀音, the bodhisattva of compassion, seated in the middle of a lotus pond and surrounded by two similarly disguised personal attendants (see Fig. 2). The banners over Cixi's head in these photos identify her as "Guanyin of Putuo Mountain" 普陀山觀音大士. As in the mirror photograph, the visual logic underlying these Guanyin images is clearly one of projective identification—Cixi is producing a visual reminder of how she would like to be perceived. She herself is reported to have remarked:

> Whenever I have been angry, or worried over anything, by dressing up as the Goddess of Mercy it helps me to calm myself, and so play the part I represent. I can assure you that it does help me a great deal, *as it makes me remember that I am looked upon as being all-merciful.* By having a photograph taken of myself dressed in this costume, *I shall be able to see myself* as I ought to be at all times.[5] (Italics added)

In these photographs, Cixi adopted the fictional persona of the bodhisattva in order to see herself as she would like to imagine herself being seen, just as, in the Leshou Hall photograph, she similarly "posed" as the empress dowager in order to accomplish the same purpose. In other words, the patently fantastic quality of the bodhisattva merely underscores the inherently performative and fictional dimension of even those identities that are ostensibly Cixi's "own."

The paradigmatically feminine Guanyin, one of the most recognizable figures within the contemporary East Asian Buddhist pantheon, originated in the masculine figure of Avalokitesvara in Indian Buddhism. Avalokitesvara was introduced into China as early as the third century CE via translations of Buddhist scriptures such as the *Lotus Sutra*, but it was not until several centuries later that artists began representing the deity as androgynous and eventually as unmistakably

4. These photos were taken on July 16, 1903. For a detailed account of the preparations Cixi ordered for these images, see Lin Jing, "Cixi sheying shihua," 84.

5. Der Ling, *Two Years in the Forbidden City*, 225.

Fig. 2 Empress Dowager Cixi in the guise of Avalokitesvara.
1903. Photographer: Xunling.

feminine. One of the earliest examples of this feminine version of the bodhisattva can be found in the "water-moon Guanyin" tradition from the Tang Dynasty (618–907). Although the "water-moon" label refers specifically to the trademark moonlike halo surrounding the bodhisattva's head in this iconographic tradition, its association with the transgendered figure of Guanyin suggests a gendered correlate to the visual skepticism articulated in the Buddhist phrase itself.[6] In other words, the scopic skepticism implicit in the "flower in a mirror / moon in water" aphorism is imbricated over a skepticism of the reliability of gendered appearance—a skepticism particularly appropriate here given that it pertains to a figure whose gendered transformation derived from the evolution of a specifically representational tradition.

Cixi's Guanyin photographs therefore illustrate her projective identification with this paradigmatically feminine icon, together with the connotations of gender fluidity and visual indeterminacy which that icon has historically embodied. By the same token, Cixi's earlier flower in the mirror photograph features her appropriation of the inherently feminine "boudoir mirror" tradition, combined with her implicit affiliation with the voyeuristic gesture of gendered ventriloquism on which that same literary and iconographic tradition is predicated. In both instances, Cixi was using these photographs to assert a specific (feminine) gender identity while simultaneously underscoring the performative and fluid nature of gender identity itself. In other words, in posing for these photos, Cixi was performing not only femininity but more generally the *very possibility of gender performativity itself.*

The allusions to the Buddhist "flower in a mirror / moon in water" formula in these images neatly encapsulate one of the key paradoxes inherent in Cixi's early twentieth-century fascination with photography. Just as the Buddhist aphorism combines a fascination with visual imagery and a critique of the inherent ephemerality and unreliability of

6. The association of this "water-moon" phrase with Guanyin is further reinforced by the later popularity of depicting Guanyin peering at her own reflection in a pool of water. Two examples of this latter tradition may be found, for instance, in Tang Xianzu's seventeenth-century play *Mudan ting* (The peony pavilion), which I discuss in more detail in Chapter 1 (see Tang Xianzu, *Mudan ting*, scene 28, p. 153, and scene 37, p. 200; idem, *The Peony Pavilion*, 158 and 216).

those same images, Cixi's interest in photography similarly joins her captivation with photography's unprecedented verisimilitude and her insistence on using it as a vehicle of fantasy projection. More generally, even as Cixi's 1903 photographs are positioned at a historical watershed between what I will call a specular and a photographic, or spectatorial, visual economy, *both* the premodern and the modern periods on either side of this divide feature a combination of foundational *and* antifoundational attitudes toward visual representation, just as gender identity—which, in any case, is perceived primarily in *visual* terms—in these periods is also simultaneously understood as both an irreducible component of individual identity *and* a performative construct.

"The Age of the World Picture"

Pioneering photographer John Thomson reportedly took Cixi's photograph as early as 1861, in the first year of her virtual reign as empress dowager.[7] Although this claim may well be spurious (and, at any rate, no such photograph exists today), Cixi appears not to have developed a genuine passion for this hyper-mimetic representational medium until nearly forty years later. More specifically, Cixi's (re)discovery of photography took place in the context of the court's increasing concern, around the turn of the century, that she was acquiring a negative image within the foreign community in Beijing and, more generally, among the international community as a whole. As a result, Susan Conger, the wife of the U.S. minister to Beijing and an increasingly close confidante of the empress, decided to use portraiture to help Cixi improve her public image: "For many months I have been indignant over the horrible, unjust caricatures of Her Imperial Majesty in illustrated papers, and with a growing desire that the world *might see her as she really is*, I had conceived the idea of asking her Majesty's permission to speak with her upon the subject of having her portrait painted" (italics added).[8] Conger suggested that her friend, the American painter Katherine Carl, come to Beijing for this purpose.

7. See Sun Yanjing et al., *Wanqing yiying*, 73.
8. Conger, *Letters from China*, 247–48.

Cixi was initially apprehensive about the prospect of being painted, given the associations in Chinese culture between portraiture and postmortem commemoration—associations that must have had a particularly urgent resonance since she was preparing to celebrate her seventieth birthday. Ultimately one of her attendants, the seventeen-year-old Deling 德齡 (1886–1944), helped convince her to proceed. In particular, Deling—whose father, Yugeng 裕庚,[9] was a Manchu official who had recently served as imperial consul to Japan (1895–98) and France (1899–1902)—showed Cixi a portrait of herself (Deling) that Katherine Carl had painted while she was in Paris. After Deling explained to Cixi why she would have to pose for the portraits in person (rather than have someone pose in her place, as Cixi suggested at one point), Cixi finally acquiesced.

Although it was the sight of Deling's oil portrait that helped convince Cixi to have her own portrait painted, an accidental glimpse of a different kind of portrait, also dating from Deling's period abroad, made a much deeper impression on the empress dowager. Prior to Katherine Carl's visit, Cixi wandered into Deling's bedroom in the Summer Palace and saw photographs of Deling taken while she was in France. Deling recalled that the Empress Dowager had been deeply impressed with the verisimilitude of the images, insisting they were much "better" than Carl's oil portrait from the same period. Although still willing to have her portrait painted, Cixi requested that arrangements be made for her photograph to be taken as well. Deling's brother Xunling, an amateur photographer who had brought some photographic equipment back from Paris with him, was recommended for the task. The very next morning, he began taking staged shots of Cixi outside Leshou Hall—including, quite possibly, the mirror photograph.[10]

---

9. Being Manchus, Yugeng and his family would never have used their given name and clan names together. Yugeng's children, however, are sometimes misidentified as having the surname *Yu*, erroneously borrowed, apparently, from the first character in Yugeng's given name.

10. Der Ling, *Two Years in the Forbidden City*, 214–18. Although Deling does not mention the mirror photograph explicitly, her description of Cixi's first set of photographs appears to match that of the mirror photograph closely.

Xunling remained in the palace for the next two years as the court's first official photographer, and his unique position as a figurative lens into court life is represented emblematically by the fact that he was also granted a unique exemption from the rule prohibiting eyeglasses in the empress's presence.[11] During this period, Cixi posed for dozens of pictures for him, including not only the Leshou Hall and Guanyin images but also several series of shots of her and her attendants on the Imperial Barge, in a royal pageant at Kunming Lake, and in other more informal settings.[12] Some of his photographs feature physical settings, such as images of Cixi's empty throne room. There are even photographs of two of the oil portraits that Katherine Carl painted of the empress later that year, including one of the famous portrait subsequently displayed at the 1904 St. Louis World Expo (see Fig. 3). Since Cixi's interest in photography initially developed in anticipation of these portrait sittings, these photographs of the portraits bring this entire cycle of portraiture and photography full circle—yielding a virtual hall of mirrors in which photography and portraiture are recursively embedded within one another. Indeed, Katherine Carl herself was under the impression that Cixi had become interested in being photographed precisely from seeing these pictures of Carl's oil portraits:

> The precedent having been established, the idea of a representation of the Sacred Person of a Chinese Majesty being seen by the world having been accepted, the painting of Her Majesty's first portrait not having been followed by the dire results that the Chinese had prophesied, the traditional prejudice was overcome, and when she saw how quickly the photograph was made of the portrait, and how satisfactory it was, she decided she would have the photographer try one of herself, and she was not to stop at a single trial.[13]

---

11. Kecskes, "Photographs of Tz'u-hsi," 88. Compare the debate years later over whether Puyi should be allowed to wear glasses (as depicted, for instance, in Bertolucci's *The Last Emperor*).

12. The Freer Gallery owns a collection of 44 photo-negatives of these photographs. Reproductions of many of these images, including six in which Cixi appears in the guise of Guanyin, are reproduced in Liu Beisi and Xu Qixian, *Gugong zhencang renwu zhaopian huicui.*

13. Carl, *With the Empress Dowager of China*, 305.

Fig. 3 Photograph of a portrait of the Empress Dowager painted by Katherine Carl (1865–1938).

Breathlessly, Carl insisted that it was her portrait that had whetted Cixi's interest in photography—which in a sense may well have been true, although the inspiration appears to have come not from the St. Louis portrait itself but from Carl's earlier portrait of *Deling* together with the *prospect* of her subsequent portrait of Cixi herself. The inverted chronology of Cixi's interest in photography that Carl (unwittingly) proposes here is symptomatic of the inverted temporality of the historical moment represented by the mirror photograph itself—insofar as the premodern specular visual economy is, I will argue, a retrospective projection of the photographic economy of the "world picture," which remains on the virtual horizon of this particular image.

Just as these meta-representational photographs of Carl's oil portraits underscore the portraits' status as both image and physical artifact, Cixi herself was clearly interested not only in the photographs as images but also in their status as artifacts, particularly their potential reproduction and circulation within a transnational visual economy. She is said, for example, to have kept a photograph of Queen Victoria at her bedside,[14] and in 1904 she sent one of her own photos to the wife of Queen Victoria's grandson, Emperor Wilhelm II of Germany. Furthermore, in a dramatic break from the traditionally strict restrictions on the circulation and display of imperial portraits in China, Cixi permitted her photographs to be enlarged, reproduced, and distributed to officials and visitors; she even allowed some to be published and advertised for sale in a popular newspaper.[15]

Thus, Cixi's encounter with her mirror photograph, although it did not take place until the eve of her seventieth birthday, apparently marks the symbolic beginning of a new awareness of the increasingly hegemonic role of photographic technologies in mediating perceptions of the modern world—an awareness, in other words, of what Heidegger called "the age of the world picture." In his 1938 essay of the same title, Heidegger argued that the "fundamental event of the modern age is the conquest of the world as picture"; by the concept of "world picture," he meant not merely "a picture of the world but the world conceived

14. Cheng-hua Wang, "Presenting the Empress Dowager to the World."

15. See *Shibao* (Eastern times), June 12, 1904; cited in Pang, "Photography, Performance, and the Making of Female Images in Modern China," 64.

and grasped as a picture."[16] Furthermore, according to Heidegger, this modern process of representation has implications not only for how the world is conceived but also for the way in which observers situate themselves as subjects.[17] For subjects to perceive the world as a picture, they must simultaneously picture *themselves* as perceiving subjects. This act of picturing the world effectively positions the observer within the broader model of the "world picture," even as it is predicated on his or her theoretical ability to perceive the world as if from some imaginary Archimedean fulcrum necessarily positioned *outside* the picture being viewed.

Cixi's fascination with photography during the early twentieth century could similarly be seen as part of a broader conceptual shift in understanding of the image(ry) of the world. Xunling's photographs allowed Cixi to see her own image in a new light and also to gain a new appreciation of the visual medium through which these images were produced and disseminated. This new appreciation had important implications both for how the world would be "pictured" and for how subjects like herself would perceive their position within this new "world picture." In these portraits—made possible by photography's unprecedented mimeticism and reproducibility—Cixi actively projected herself into a new economy of visual representation and, in the process, positioned herself as a new kind of viewing subject. Rather than attempting to see herself "directly," as in a mirror, she was instead perceiving herself as mediated through this array of external gazes—gazes she figuratively appropriated as her own even as she projectively identified with the external images associated with those gazes. As a result, the self-image of Cixi that was being perceived, projected, and constituted is itself, in a sense, an artifact of the portraitive process itself.

The Mirror Stage Revisited

In her memoir, Princess Deling recalled that Cixi insisted on watching as the first batch of photographs was being developed (to the point of ruining one print by exposing it to light prematurely); after the

16. Heidegger, "The Age of the World Picture," 130.

17. "That the world becomes picture is one and the same event with the event of man's becoming subjectum in the midst of that which is" (ibid., 131).

photos were finished, she "took the whole of them to her own room and sat down on her little throne, and gazed at them for a long time. She even took her mirror in order to compare her reflection with the photographs just taken."[18]

Cixi's reaction to the photographs reveals not merely a fascination with their inherent mimeticism but also more specifically a displaced and uncanny (mis)recognition of her own image. She appeared to see in these novel images less a reflection of herself and more a plenitude and symbolic power that significantly exceeded her existing self-conception, as represented by her mirrored reflection. As a result of this alienated recognition of the photographic image, Cixi apparently engaged in a process of projective identification, wherein she sought to appropriate the larger-than-life image of herself that she perceived in the photograph and then project it back onto the literal mirror image—and, by implication, onto her own prior self-understanding. This dialectics of (mis)recognition and projective identification operated not merely at the level of the photographic image itself but also at the level of the sociocultural connotations of the photographic medium. Cixi, in other words, appears to have been fascinated less by her image itself and more by her image as embedded within a distinctively modern visual economy. In having her pictures taken, what Cixi was attempting to (re)appropriate visually was therefore a transnational visual embeddedness which did not yet fully exist, but which that seminal moment of photographic recognition helped to begin to make possible.

Cixi's comparison of her photographs to her own mirror reflection could be seen as a transposition and inversion of the moment of alienated recognition that Lacan famously outlined in his mirror-stage essay. Referring to a developmental stage that takes place when an infant is between six and eighteen months old, Lacan described the "startling spectacle of the infant in front of the mirror"—at a point when it still perceives its own body as an amorphous, inchoate mass "in bits and pieces"—"jubilantly" identifying with an external image of a unified body as it appears in the mirror.[19] Given the contrast between the in-

18. Der Ling, *Two Years in the Forbidden City*, 223.
19. Lacan, "The Mirror Stage."

fant's self-perception and the image it perceives in the mirror, the moment of specular "recognition" is really a moment of *mis*recognition (*méconnaissance*), in which the infant actively asserts a relationship of equivalence (between itself and the external image), which is itself ultimately a product of the process of "identification" itself. Cixi's initial reception of her photographs, therefore, could be seen as a second-order mirror scene: she already recognized the image in the mirror as an emblem of her self-conception, and now it was the photographs themselves that became the "startling spectacle" with which she sought to projectively identify.

Like Heidegger in his near-contemporary description of the historical transition into the era of the "world picture,"[20] Lacan proposed an image-based model to describe the infant's entry into subjectivity. Whereas Heidegger located his "world picture" model in geohistorical terms, however, Lacan suggested that the mirror stage's "historical value" lies instead in its identification of a "decisive turning-point in the mental development of the child." Lacan also claimed for his model more universal implications, asserting that it "typifies an *essential* libidinal relationship with the body image" (italics added).[21] The claim to have identified an essential psychological process suggests that the model is, in theory, potentially applicable to any culture or era, and indeed Lacan's mirror stage is routinely invoked to describe a remarkably diverse array of social and cultural phenomena. On the other hand, this same aspiration of universality is also the model's Achilles' heel, inviting the critique that the model elides cultural and historical difference, particularly when it is extrapolated to describe not merely infant development but more general processes of socialization, acculturation, and subject formation.

I will argue, however, that this sort of psychoanalytic approach *is* potentially useful in making sense of culturally and historically disparate phenomena, including Cixi's mirror photograph, and that a rehistoricization of the model suggests a way of appreciating the potential transcultural and transhistorical relevance of the theory itself. To this

20. Heidegger's essay was published in 1938, and, as will be discussed below, Lacan first presented his theory of the mirror stage in 1936 and would have published it in early 1937.

21. Lacan, "Some Reflections on the Ego."

end, I consider the historical implications of Lacan's theory of the mirror stage by, first, reflecting on the way in which the model simultaneously gestures both forward and backward to two crucial transitions in Lacan's career roughly thirty years apart and, then, considering the way in which the understanding of temporality and historicity posited by the model itself is similarly predicated on a continual double gesture of anticipatory retrospection and retrospective anticipation.

Lacan's mirror-stage model is now almost universally known primarily by a few famous lines from his 1949 essay of that title, in which he described how the infant, finding itself supported in front of a mirror, instantly recognizes and identifies with the external image—what Lacan calls the *imago*—of that autonomous and corporally unified self that the infant itself has yet to become:

> This jubilant assumption of his specular image by the child at the *infans* stage, still sunk in his motor incapacity and nursling dependence, would seem to exhibit in an exemplary situation the symbolic matrix in which the *I* is precipitated in a primordial form, before it is objectified in the dialectic of identification with the other, and before language restores to it, in the universal, its function as subject.[22]

The mirror-stage model itself, however, was itself not a static image but an organic concept that evolved throughout Lacan's career. For instance, the first line of the 1949 essay explicitly gestures back to another discussion thirteen years earlier:[23] Lacan's "looking-glass phase" presentation at the Fourteenth Congress of the International Psychoanalytic Association (IPA) in 1936.[24] This 1936 talk was Lacan's debut presenta-

---

22. Lacan, "The Mirror Stage," 2. Originally published virtually simultaneously as "Le stade du miroir: théorie d'un moment structurant et génétique de la constitution de la réalité, conçu en relation avec l'expérience et la doctrine psychanalytique," *Revue française de psychanalyse 1949*, 13, no. 4: 449–55; and, in English that same year, as "The Mirror Stage, Source of the I-Function, As Shown by Psychoanalytic Experience," *International Journal of Psychoanalysis* 30 (1949).

23. "The conception of the mirror stage that I introduced at our last congress [*sic*; it was actually two congresses earlier], thirteen years ago, has since become more or less established in the practice of the French group" (Lacan, "The Mirror Stage," 1).

24. Actually, the French titles of Lacan's 1936 and 1949 presentations at the IPA congresses used the same title, *le stade du mirror*, with the phrases "looking-glass phase" and "mirror stage" appearing only in the translated titles in the *International Journal of*

tion to the IPA and is considered his first formal theoretical contribution (after his dissertation) to psychoanalysis. Consequently it can be seen as a figurative mirror-stage moment marking his entry into the externalized *imago* that was the professional community of the IPA itself. Lacan's most influential revision of the mirror-stage model came nearly three decades later in a series of seminars he gave in 1964, in which he substituted for the proverbial mirror the figure of a screen as a site of cultural projection with which the subject may then either identify or disassociate itself. Known collectively as "Seminar XI,"[25] the lectures in which this model of the screen was proposed were presented on the heels of Lacan's infamous excommunication from the IPA in late 1963.[26]

Just as the model of the screen that Lacan developed in Seminar XI dramatically illustrates the way in which both the mirror-stage model itself and Lacan's own "mirror stage" identification with the IPA continued to evolve and transform themselves throughout his career, similarly the latter screen model is itself concerned with ways in which processes of projective identification continue to inform a subject's self-perception well beyond the precise developmental moment specified in the mirror-stage essay. To this end, the later model stresses a process of mediated identification not with a mirror but with a nexus of culturally produced images, which are then projected onto a space that Lacan refers to metaphorically as a "screen." The subject, then, (mis)recognizes him- or herself within those images while positioning him- or herself in relationship to the socially normative gazes that are inextricably linked with those same images.

In the Seminar XI discussions, the figure of the screen symbolizes the point of intersection between the subject's corporeally localized

---

Psychoanalysis. For simplicity, I use "looking-glass phase" to refer to the 1936 presentation and "mirror stage" to refer to the 1949 version of the essay.

25. "Seminar XI" appeared in English under the title *Four Fundamental Concepts of Psychoanalysis*.

26. This was actually the culmination of a decade-long struggle between Lacan and the IPA, dating back to 1954. The truncated seminar of which Lacan had delivered one lecture when he received the news in 1963 that the IPA was revoking his license as a practicing analyst was, appropriately enough, named "Names-of-the-Father." For a discussion, see Slavoj Žižek and Alain Badiou's special issue "Names-of-the-Father," *Lacanian Ink* 27 (2006).

"look" and a disembodied culturally produced "gaze." That is to say, the figure of the screen represents a fluid, imaginary space wherein the subject identifies with (or against) not only an array of sociocultural subject-models but also the delocalized "gazes" informing the ways in which those models are perceived in the first place. More generally, the figure of the screen functions as the hinge between the decontextualized and presumptively universal "gaze" of psychoanalytic theory itself and the culturally embedded "look" that necessarily conditions the specific subjects (in both senses of the term) which that theory is used to elucidate. As Kaja Silverman argues, the figure of the "screen" represents precisely "the site at which social and historical difference enters the field of vision."[27] This screen, in other words, marks a space of cultural and historical difference—and not merely difference at the level of superficial appearance (e.g., cultural "images") but, and what is more important, difference at the level of the underlying perspectives and epistemologies that make those images meaningful and intelligible in the first place (e.g., a culturally specific "gaze").

Lacan's Seminar XI was presented immediately following the termination of his professional affiliation with the IPA, and it simultaneously marked a figuratively new beginning for him, both personally and professionally. In 1964, for instance, he inaugurated the École Freudienne de Paris. That same year, precisely during the course of his Seminar XI, Lacan first met Jacques-Alain Miller, who not only later became his son-in-law but would subsequently undertake the formidable task of publishing all of Lacan's year-long seminars in written form—starting with Seminar XI. Far more than mere transcription, the process of textual redaction involved taking assorted incomplete and contradictory notes from the seminars and from them reconstructively creating a singular and unitary text that would then stand in for the fragmentary and fleeting oral original.[28] As Miller explained in his introduction to the subsequent publication of Seminar XI, his goal was to "obtain from Jacques Lacan's spoken work an authentic version that would stand, in the future, for the origi-

---

27. Silverman, *The Threshold to the Visible World*, 134–35.

28. Technically, it is not necessarily the oral presentations that were fragmentary and incomplete (although they may very well have been so) but the various written notes from the presentations that happened to have been preserved.

nal, which does not exist."[29] In other words, Miller was seeking to create an external mirror image of the original oral seminar—a unified and stable text that would then substitute for the fragmentary, inchoate, and, in a very real sense, *nonexistent* seminar itself.

Perhaps the most intriguing example of this process of textual transcription functioning as a virtual mirror stage can be found in Lacan's original looking-glass-phase presentation at the IPA congress on August 3, 1936, of which he had previously delivered a preliminary lecture to the Société psychanalytique de Paris on June 6, earlier that same summer.[30] Had that seminal June presentation been an actual child, then the following January it would have been seven months old and entering its own mirror stage.[31] As chance would have it, the June 6/August 3 talk was published, as the editor of the 1977 English edition of Lacan's *Écrits* carefully notes, "in *The International Journal of Psychoanalysis*, vol. 18, part I, January, 1937, under the title, '*The Looking-glass Phase*.'"[32] This meticulously precise bibliographic citation, however, comes across as perhaps a little odd. Odd, not merely on account of the curiously overdetermined use of both italics and inverted commas in citing the essay's title, or because the detailed attention to the publication's date is paired with a failure to provide page numbers for the essay in question. Rather, the chief oddity in this assiduously detailed bibliographic citation lies in the fact that, as Jane Gallop has famously pointed out, the essay in question does not exist.[33] The January issue of

---

29. Jacques-Alain Miller, "Introduction," in Lacan, *Four Fundamental Concepts of Psychoanalysis*.

30. As Elizabeth Roudinesco ("The Mirror Stage," 26) notes, Françoise Dolto took detailed notes of that earlier lecture; for reasons discussed below, these unpublished notes have become the only direct textual record of the "original" version of the mirror-stage essay.

31. "[The mirror stage] can take place . . . from the age of six months" (Lacan, "The Mirror Stage," 1).

32. Lacan, *Écrits: A Selection*, xiii. This abridged translation of Lacan's *Écrits* was published in 1977 and was one of the primary gateways to Lacan's thought for English readers until it was supplanted by Bruce Fink's translation 25 years later (a similarly abridged volume of Fink's translations appeared in 2002, followed by the first complete English translation of the entire *Écrits* in 2006).

33. Gallop, *Reading Lacan*.

the journal indexes only the title of the talk and does not provide the accompanying text. Why, then, did Alan Sheridan, the editor and English translator of the *Écrits*, make such a glaring mistake? Why was the need to posit a specific textual origin for the mirror-stage model so strong that it resulted quite literally in the creation of a nonexistent document?

Ostensibly, Sheridan was attempting to justify his placement of the (1949) mirror-stage essay at the head of his chronologically arranged, abridged version of Lacan's *Écrits*, despite the fact that the essay is not the earliest work included in the translated volume. Sheridan's need to assert the chronological primacy of the *concept* of the mirror stage (as opposed to the actual essay) was so strong, therefore, that he ended up fabricating a redundant and unnecessary textual origin to justify it.[34] This overcompensatory specification of a prior publication date is unnecessary because it presumably would have sufficed simply to have cited the date of the conference presentation, as does the French version of the *Écrits*—though even there, too, the question of origins is rather knotted. The bibliographic guide at the end of the French *Écrits*, for instance, specifies the precise time of the August 3, 1936, presentation down to the minute: 3:40 in the afternoon, though Lacan himself noted in the same volume that this "original" presentation was itself incomplete: "exactly ten minutes into my text" Ernest Jones, then-president of the IPA and chair of the proceedings, halted the talk, ostensibly because Lacan had exceeded his allotted time.[35] Lacan was apparently so miffed by the perceived snub that he left the conference the next day, to attend the Berlin Olympics. In other words, the insistence in the French *Écrits* on specifying the precise time of the 1936 presentation belies the fact that even that oral "origin" was itself aborted and ultimately incomplete.

---

34. As Gallop (ibid.) explains, Sheridan saw the reference to the citation of the *title* of the looking-glass phase in the original French-language *Écrits* and mistakenly assumed that what it was citing as having been published in the *IJP* was the entire article. Since the French *Écrits* was citing the *IJP*'s *English* translation of Lacan's title, that explains why the title appears italicized within the inverted commas. In the context of Sheridan's own *English-language* volume, however, the preservation of the italics becomes oddly redundant.

35. Lacan, *Écrits*, 184–85.

The compulsion to retrospectively posit a temporally stable point of origin for Lacan's mirror-stage model, therefore, appears to be directly proportional to the inherent ambiguity and indeterminacy of that origin itself. In this respect, the history of the model directly mirrors the model's own implicit historicity, insofar as the mirror stage itself is structured around a retrospective positing of origins, and the moment of "recognition" in front of the mirror is intelligible as such only in retrospect, after the infant has already identified with and internalized this external image. Similarly, that original temporal indeterminacy may have helped lay the ground for many of Lacan's subsequent attitudes toward time and temporality. For instance, it is very tempting to see a link between the IPA president's decision to cut off Lacan's presentation precisely at the end of his ten-minute allotment and Lacan's subsequent unorthodox espousal of "variable sessions" of indeterminate length in his own psychoanalytic practice—an espousal that would become the single-most important factor in his subsequent conflicts with, and eventual excommunication from, the IPA. As Elizabeth Roudinesco observes, "All his life, Lacan would struggle with an impossible control over time."[36]

Although Lacan implies that Jones's interruption of his IPA presentation of the looking-glass-phase paper was the reason he subsequently neglected to submit the manuscript for publication, he may also have been distracted during that period by the imminent arrival of his first child, Caroline, who was born on January 8, 1937. In other words, Lacan's daughter quite literally displaced the looking-glass-phase presentation's own figurative mirror stage (as textual publication), and her resulting status as a living stand-in for that figurative *imago* is ironically underscored by the alternative name Lacan gave her: *Image*.[37] Through another uncanny and tragic coincidence, "Image" Lacan, this living embodiment and displacement of the mirror stage's own *imago*, subsequently died in a car accident on May 30, 1973—which also happens to have been the same year in which Lacan's post-mirror-stage theory of

36. Roudinesco, "The Mirror Stage," 25.

37. As Roudinesco (*Jacques Lacan*, 136) explains, Lacan added this second name in accordance with the tradition, in his wife's family, of assigning everyone a "nickname or diminutive."

the screen (developed in Seminar XI) was finally published. The daughter's entire life, therefore, was framed quite precisely by these two paradigmatic mirror-stage moments of her father's own mirror-stage model. The aborted moment of specular recognition between the 1936 oral presentation and what would have been its textual correlate was finally realized 36 years later, when "Image" Lacan's premature death coincided with the publication of the textual transcription of the model's most significant and influential revision.

Just as "Image" Lacan's life was framed quite precisely by Lacan's mirror-stage theory of the image, Cixi's life proceeded in uncanny lockstep with the demise of the dynasty she ultimately came to personify. For instance, two of the pivotal mid-century events that helped set the stage for the ultimate collapse of the dynasty half a century later were the (first) Opium War (1839–42) and the Taiping Rebellion (1850–64). Cixi, born four years before the start of the Opium War, assumed virtual power over the dynasty when her young son was crowned emperor three years before the Taiping Rebellion was suppressed and would go on to retain an almost continual grip on power until her death in 1908, three years before the ultimate collapse of the dynasty itself. These chronological coincidences are, of course, merely another way of saying simply that Cixi's life and career were closely intertwined with the gradual dénouement of China's last formal dynasty. Here, however, I will use these questions of chronology first to return to Cixi's 1903 mirror photograph and then to think through some of the historical implications of the preceding re-historicization of Lacan's mirror stage.

Cixi's mirror photograph was taken in early 1903, on the eve of her seventieth-birthday celebrations later that year. Cixi's seventieth *sui* birthday was actually not until 1904 but, because it had been determined that that would be an inauspicious year for the celebration, she moved everything up to 1903. In planning the actual celebrations, furthermore, Cixi was determined to pull out all the stops, in order to make up for having reluctantly had to cancel her sixtieth-birthday celebrations due to Chinese losses in the Sino-Japanese War (the Chinese calendar was organized around 60-year cycles, and therefore the sixtieth birthday is traditionally a pivotal one). As a result, Cixi's 1903 mirror photograph was positioned at a peculiar juncture in her life—oriented simultaneously toward her forthcoming, and her previous, decadal birthday celebrations. At the same time, these seemingly opposed sentiments of anticipation and nostalgia are intimately bound up with one another, insofar as Cixi looked forward to her seventieth birthday precisely because it would compensate for her aborted sixtieth, just as her recollection of her nonexistent sixtieth was displaced into a compensatory anticipation of her seventieth.

This dialectics of anticipatory nostalgia and retrospective anticipation is, I argue, one that Lacan's mirror stage both embodies and attempts to theorize. Just as the mirror-stage essay implicitly looks forward to its revision in Seminar XI and backward to its origins in the looking-glass-phase presentation, similarly the moment of specular (mis)recognition the model describes is itself one that not only simultaneously looks forward to the unified subjectivity that will follow and backward to the "body in bits and pieces" that precedes it, but furthermore actually *creates* and makes possible both that future unity as well as the past disunity. As Jane Gallop argues:

> The mirror stage is a decisive moment. Not only does the self issue from it, but so does "the body in bits and pieces." This moment is the source not only for what follows but also for what precedes. It produces the future through anticipation and the past through retroaction. . . . What thus occurs in the mirror stage is the formation of what in the future will be an antecedent, what grammatically can be called a "future perfect."[38]

The mirror stage, in other words, not only postulates its own past and future but also simultaneously creates its own identity as a transitional moment mediating between the two. In more general terms, this rereading of the mirror-stage model suggests a model of history grounded not on linear teleologies but on intimately interwoven processes of anticipation and retrospection that simultaneously create the future and the past as dialectically dependent on one another. The past does not exist as a self-evident category; rather, it is a retrospective projection against which the present seeks to distinguish its own future, just as the future has significance only in comparison to a

38. Gallop, *Reading Lacan*, 80–81.

history that is constantly being reconceived from the perspective of the present.

This rehistoricization of Lacan's mirror-stage model, in turn, invites a similar reconsideration of Cixi's 1903 mirror photograph. Cixi's early twentieth-century mirror portrait could be seen as a "decisive moment" in her entry into visual modernity. We may imagine how, like Lacan's swaddling infant seeing its mirrored reflection for the first time, the elderly Cixi may have glimpsed in this photograph an image of how she wished to be publicly perceived, particularly on a global stage. More generally, Cixi perhaps might have also been seeing in the photograph the possibility of an as-yet-unrealized "age of the world picture"—a "world picture" that would increasingly determine not only how the world is perceived but also how subjects like herself understand their position as observers. This age of the world picture, however, is as aspirational for Cixi as is the unified *imago* for Lacan's swaddling infant, and by the same token the premodern "specular" space with which it comes to be contrasted is one that becomes visible only in retrospect.

I have argued that the mirror photograph is positioned within, and itself depicts, a stark transition from a premodern specular to a modern photographic scopic regime, together with the epistemological and ontological implications of each. Now, however, I would go a step further and suggest that the transitional moment represented and embodied by the 1903 photograph inevitably folds in upon itself. Like the mirror stage itself, the historicity of the moment embodied by this mirror photograph is one that, in a sense, is an artifact of that same transitional moment. Just as Cixi herself was simultaneously looking both backward to her cancelled sixtieth birthday and forward to her seventieth, similarly the contrasting premodern and modern scopic regimes posited by this particular image can be seen as figurative projections of this same pivotal historical moment. The ideal of specularity as representing a direct and unmediated perception of the self is arguably one that never existed except as a retrospective projection of a post-photographic age, which, in 1903, still remained on the historical horizon. Conversely, the ideal of a sort of universal photographic transparency (e.g., Heidegger's "age of the world picture") ultimately may have only existed as a phantasmatic anticipation created at a historical moment when photography itself was just beginning to show hints of its current ubiquity.

The Mirrored Screen

Deling, in her description of Cixi's first photo session with Xunling, mentioned that Cixi temporarily interrupted the session after a few preliminary shots in order to receive an official audience. Deling and some of the other attendants hid behind the "exquisitely carved wooden screen" behind the throne and remained there until the visitors had left and Cixi was ready to resume the session. This act of hiding behind the screen appears to have been a common occurrence, since Cixi (according to Deling's recollections) explicitly instructed that Deling hide herself in this manner during imperial audiences, noting that, from behind the screen, "You [Deling] can see all right, but I don't wish that you should be seen."[39]

The tripartite screen was the same one that, after the Empress Dowager's audience that particular morning, was then moved outside along with her throne for the Leshou Hall photo shoot. In the context of the photo shoot, this screen functioned simultaneously as a physical artifact, a visual image, and a locus of a variety of external gazes. First, as a physical artifact, the screen blocked from view what lay behind it while simultaneously serving as one of the visual props (like the throne and the pyramids of apples) within the photograph. Second, in addition to being a visual artifact, the screen contains several embedded images—including what appear to be a pine tree in the center panel and *mei* plum blossoms in the two side panels. These embedded images are then re-embedded within Xunling's photographs, where they are clearly used as symbolic projections of Cixi's own self-identification with Chinese cultural and literati identity. Third, the screen not only contains specific images but also connotes a variety of culturally specific gazes or perspectival orientations, including not only the traditional Chinese cultural perspective against which Cixi seeks to orient herself but also Deling's destabilizing and culturally liminal gaze. That is to say, Cixi's earlier instruction that during official audiences Deling watch from behind the screen—able to see out, but herself invisible to outsiders—implicitly transforms the throne area in front of the screen into a virtual

39. Der Ling, *Two Years in the Forbidden City*, 23, 189.

panopticon, wherein the physical space becomes inflected with the potential presence of Deling's absent gaze. Deling's gaze, moreover, was located quite precisely at the very intersection of China/tradition and foreign/modernity that Cixi is in the process of negotiating with the mirror photograph itself. After all, it was Deling's oil portrait and photographs that inspired Cixi to have her portraits done, just as Deling's experience abroad positions her as part of the target audience for whom these same portraits were created (given that they were undertaken quite explicitly to rehabilitate Cixi's image within the foreign community). The invisible insertion of Deling's latent gaze, via the screen, into the mirror photograph, therefore, precisely mirrors the way in which Cixi's own errant gaze wanders out of the frame of the photo, and part of the function of the image as a whole involves the figurative suturing of the two unrelated gazes.

This study, *The Naked Gaze: Reflections on Chinese Modernity*, takes as its starting point the contested space between Cixi's, Xunling's, and Deling's respective gazes, which is to say, between the figures of the mirror, the camera, and the projective screen. On one hand, Cixi's specular gaze originates from the virtual center of the image but then wanders out of the frame of the photograph. Xunling's photographic gaze is positioned outside the frame of the picture even as it simultaneously frames the picture. Deling's invisible (and, indeed, absent) voyeuristic gaze originates from behind the screen with which Cixi is attempting to frame her own self-presentation and then forcibly reinserts itself into the scene to dominate the photograph as a whole. The intersection of these three gazes is captured in the space of the mirror photograph itself and furthermore constitutes the historical transition point that produced the photograph in the first place. Below, I examine the implications of these shifting understandings of visuality by considering a variety of nineteenth- and twentieth-century texts. I focus in particular on the texts' use of visual tropes as a lens for considering issues of identity and subject formation, particularly the constitution and contestation of gendered identity. In my readings, I attempt both to consider the texts as they see themselves and to mobilize an "outside" gaze in order to read the same texts against the grain. The goal of these readings is to reflect on the significance of Chineseness, modernity, and Chinese modernity, as well as to propose an inverse "reflection" of the naturalized category of "Chinese modernity" itself. I will suggest that this modernity is not an immanent concept in its own right but the product of a continual process of projective identification, anticipatory retrospection, and retrospective anticipation.

This study is divided into three parts, with each part centering around one of the visual components of Cixi's mirror photograph. Part I takes as its starting point Cixi's mirror gaze and reflects on tropes of reflexivity and involution during the nineteenth century. Part II orients itself around Xunling's photographic gaze and looks at issues of observation, spectatorship, and visual mimicry during the mid-twentieth century. Part III takes its inspiration from the figure of Cixi's tripartite screen, which it uses as a prism through which to consider the role of visual imagery as a recurrent site of projective identification during the late twentieth century, particularly the ways in which visual imagery is repeatedly invested with symbolic significance despite an explicit awareness of the ephemerality or impossibility of the images themselves.

In each of these three parts, I address the discursive implications of a distinct visual mode in question, primarily through a detailed examination of a selection of strategically chosen narrative texts. At the same time, I argue that the visual mode in question correlates to dominant sociocultural tendencies of that particular historical period. In Part I, for instance, I focus primarily on two nineteenth-century "literati novels" that revolve around the figure of mirror. I discuss how, in each text, mirroring is used to interrogate conventions of gender differentiation and sexual orientation. More generally, I suggest that the very genre of the literati novel—which explicitly foregrounds a "literati" fascination with literary, linguistic, and cultural allusions—is symptomatic of a tendency in late imperial culture that could itself be described as "specular" or involutive—in which cultural production often came to assume the form of an accumulation of recursive allusions to a common cultural legacy.

During the early to mid-twentieth century, cultural production and intellectual orientation shifted away from a recursive engagement with an existing Chinese tradition to an increasingly self-conscious awareness of how China was being perceived from "outside." During this same period, new representational practices and technologies were introduced into China from the West, such as photography, cinema, and various specific artistic and other mimetic techniques. These two tendencies converge (as they did in the case of Cixi's fascination with photography near the end of her life) in a parallel interest in processes of external observation and in mediated identification with external representations. Here, I focus on the thematization, in works by three influential mid-century authors, of processes of mediated identification with respect to different visual media, including not only photography but also Western art and even traditional Chinese "picture manuals."

In the contemporary period, the unitary category of "Chineseness," together with the presumptive dichotomy between China and an external "foreign" gaze, have become less and less meaningful. "Foreign" and "Chinese" culture and society are ever more intermeshed, even as the category of "China" itself is itself becoming increasingly fractured by political schisms, transnational migration, and the growing visibility of minority groups (ethnic or otherwise) within China, Taiwan, and other Chinese regions. In visual terms, this period is characterized by a shift away from an attention to specular reflections and the observation of external images, to a deconstructive focus on these images themselves. To borrow a cinematic metaphor, images of all kinds are increasingly perceived as screened projections.

Underlying this general diachronic periodization from an early modern culture of reflection to a postmodern culture of screen projections, however, is a synchronic recognition that the three distinct visual modes mapped out above are, at the same time, inextricably intertwined. Just as the specular image, in the nineteenth-century texts, contains within itself a spectatorial and projective dimension, the contemporary skepticism of visual imagery as mere projection comes to function as a site of mediated specular identification.

At the heart of this study, therefore, is a concern with the logic of the gaze, specifically the gaze that is constantly bound up with constructions of gender and articulations of desire. An attention to this "naked" gaze not only permits a reflection on the development of China's modernity but also, by underscoring the underlying continuities of visual logic that extend through the premodern, modern, and postmodern periods, may yield a potentially surprising inverse "reflection" of conventional understandings of that same modernity.

PART I

Specularity

At virtually the precise center of a mid-twelfth-century fan painting attributed to the Song dynasty academy painter Su Hanchen 蘇漢臣 (ca. 1101–63), there appears the back of a lady's head (see Fig. 4). She is sitting in a garden and is in the process of gazing at her reflection in a round mirror positioned on a dressing table in front of her. Like Cixi's 1903 mirror photograph, Su Hanchen's painting features an intersection of three distinct gazes and their corresponding visual surfaces. Triangulating with the lady's specular gaze at the center of the image is a female attendant observing her from behind and a large, free-standing screen positioned in front of her.

The lady appears in a reverse three-quarters profile, facing into the frame of the painting. As a result, her face is largely obscured, although it does appear clearly, and even slightly magnified, in the mirror itself. Not only is the mirror the same basic shape as the fan painting itself, but its orientation (angled slightly upward and along a 45 degree transversal plane as the lady herself) approximates that of an actual fan that a viewer might be holding as she looks at Su Hanchen's fan painting. In other words, Su Hanchen's portrait contains an embedded image (the dressing mirror) that roughly mirrors the fan painting's own shape, content, and even orientation vis-à-vis the painting's viewer—if, that is, she were simultaneously using a replica of the painting as an actual fan. The painting, therefore, contains an image of a mirror that, in turn, functions as a miniature replica of the entire fan painting itself.

Fig. 4 Su Hanchen, *Lady at Her Dressing Table in a Garden.* Fan painting mounted as an album leaf. Photograph © 2008, Museum of Fine Arts, Boston.

The interest of Su Hanchen's painting lies partly in the fact that it deploys the figure of the mirror, one of the oldest and most recognizable technologies of visual reproduction,[1] in a surprising and unusual light. In this section of the book, I similarly take the figure of the mirror as my starting point for examining a specific conjunction of visual, cultural, and epistemological concerns in the late imperial period. More specifically, by the late Qing the mirror not only had become a ubiquitous figure in its own right but could also be seen as a meta-symbol of

1. One of the earliest literary references to a bronze mirror in Chinese writings can be found in the *Zuozhuan*, in a passage referring to events of 672 BCE. Mirrors have been found in archaeological sites dating from much earlier.

the general cultural sensibility of the era. That is to say, the late Qing period can be described as involutive—to borrow a term Clifford Geertz uses to designate a "process whereby a social or cultural pattern persists and fails to transform itself even after it has reached a definitive form."[2] For instance, various late Qing visual genres, from painting to book illustrations, have frequently been described as characterized by an excess of superficial complexity and general lack of "innovation."[3] Eileen Chang has similarly remarked on the "excessive attention to details [that] characterized the Chinese costume of the [nineteenth-century] era."[4] Here, however, I will examine this process of involution by looking, not at visual culture per se, but at the ways in which *tropes of visuality* were deployed within late Qing narrative fiction—which itself has been characterized as having "an introverted tendency, a move that expands and curls in such a way as to turn inward upon itself."[5] I look in particular at how this introverted tendency has developed around the figure of the (bronze) mirror—as both a symbol of traditional Chinese culture in its own right and more generally a meta-symbol of the process of locating one's identity through a recursive appeal to that tradition.

I begin, in Chapter 1, with an overview of different perspectives on visuality during the late imperial period, considering the question of what precisely it means to look at visuality and specularity in their own right. Then, in Chapters 2 and 3, I turn to two nineteenth-century novels that not only exemplify late imperial fiction's involutive tendencies but also use the figure of the mirror to anchor their interrogations of gender and valuation. My goal is to examine how specific regimes of gender differentiation and sexual desire are simultaneously reproduced and undermined. The reflexivity implicit in the "flowers in the mirror" trope provides a model for the social reproduction of gender and sexual norms, while implicitly marking a space for the inversion and transformation of those same norms. By the same token, the reflexive surface

2. Geertz, *Agricultural Involution.*

3. See, e.g., Cahill, "Innovation After 'Progress' Ends," 192; and Hegel, *Reading Illustrated Fiction in Late Imperial China*, 213–14.

4. Eileen Chang, "Chinese Life and Fashions," 66–67.

5. David Der-wei Wang, *Fin-de-siècle Splendor,* 31.

of the mirror emblematizes the tension between self-valuation and external valuation at the heart of each of these novels.

The mirror represents a closed cycle of reflection and involution, yet there is always inevitably an external, spectatorial perspective embedded within that specular gaze. To capture this double perspective, this conjunction of specular and spectatorial gazes, each of these three chapters cites the figure of a mirrored screen (or, alternatively, a stained glass window), which functions both to mirror an external reality and to serve as an object of perception in its own right.

1

Specularity and the Limits of Vision

All symmetry is interrupted between him [the self-portraitist] and himself, between him, the spectacle, and the spectator who he also is. There are now only specters.

—Jacques Derrida, *Memoirs of the Blind*

One of the most famous mirror scenes in Chinese literature can be found in Tang Xianzu's 湯顯祖 late sixteenth-century play *Mudan ting* 牡丹亭 (The peony pavilion). The protagonist Du Liniang has just awoken from a dream in which she meets her dream lover Liu Mengmei, and proceeds to use her mirrored reflection to sketch a self-portrait. The play makes clear, furthermore, that the self-portrait is not a direct copy of the mirror image but a projection of her own idealized self-conception, with which she then attempts to identify. Following the completion of the self-portrait, Du Liniang gradually wastes away while pining after the man she met in her dream. After her death, it is determined that she was predestined to marry Liu Mengmei, and she is sent back to haunt him through her self-portrait. The real-life Liu Mengmei subsequently falls in love with the portrait (it reminds him that he has seen her in *his* dream); as a result of his infatuation with this image, he is able to return her from the underworld and, Pygmalion-like, effectively bring her image itself back to life.

Thus, Du Liniang's original specular gaze leads, via a series of mediated displacements and projective identifications, to Liu Mengmei's subsequent ability to breathe new life into her material image. At the same time, Tang Xianzu's play emphasizes that Du Liniang's perception of her mirror image in the self-portraiture scene is itself neither direct nor transparent; instead, her specular self-regard is already, from the very beginning, overlaid with the sort of external perspective subsequently embodied by Liu Mengmei. For instance, the text specifies that the "haggard" and "thin and frail" image Du Liniang sees in the mirror is quite different from the idealized mental vision she has of herself. Her decision to sketch her self-portrait, therefore, stems from an anachronistic attempt to preserve that idealized youthful visage, whose loss she is already mourning. Du Liniang herself makes this slippage between the specular model and the idealized projection quite explicit when she exclaims, "But it will make a charming picture. Ah, surely my painting promises well, with a sweet appeal *more marked than in the model*!" (italics added).[1]

This mirror scene, therefore, revolves around a paradox: in painting her self-portrait, Du Liniang is actively re/creating her own self-image—a paradox articulated quite concisely in a 1617 wood-cut illustration by Huang Mingqi 黄鳴歧 (see Fig. 5). Huang's print depicts Du Liniang gazing at her reflection in a dressing mirror as she completes her self-portrait. Significantly, the precise moment captured in the engraving does not depict Du Liniang sketching her self-portrait, which sits half-finished on the table in front of her; rather, she is shown raising the brush tip to her mouth to shape it into a sharp point. In fact, the image captures her at the instant at which the tip of the brush reaches the outline of her own face, producing the uncanny illusion that she is sketching, not her image, but literally *her actual face*.[2] The resulting visual pun suggests that the subject is not merely creating her own visual image but simultaneously sketching *herself*, specifically the way in which she would like to see herself and be perceived by others. Moreover, in order to do so, she must first position herself in the space of an imaginary spectator with respect to her own image. In so doing, she implicitly must confront the necessary possibility of her own absence and, by implication, of her own death. Appropriately enough, this specular moment is followed

1. Tang Xianzu, *Mudan ting*, 70; idem, *The Peony Pavilion*, 69.

2. This illustration was first published in the 1617 edition of *The Peony Pavilion* and is reprinted in Chang Bide, *Mingdai banhua xuan chuji*, 10. The image is reprinted, and discussed, in Ko, *Teachers of the Inner Chambers*, 74–75, as well as in Vinograd, *Boundaries of the Self*, 17.

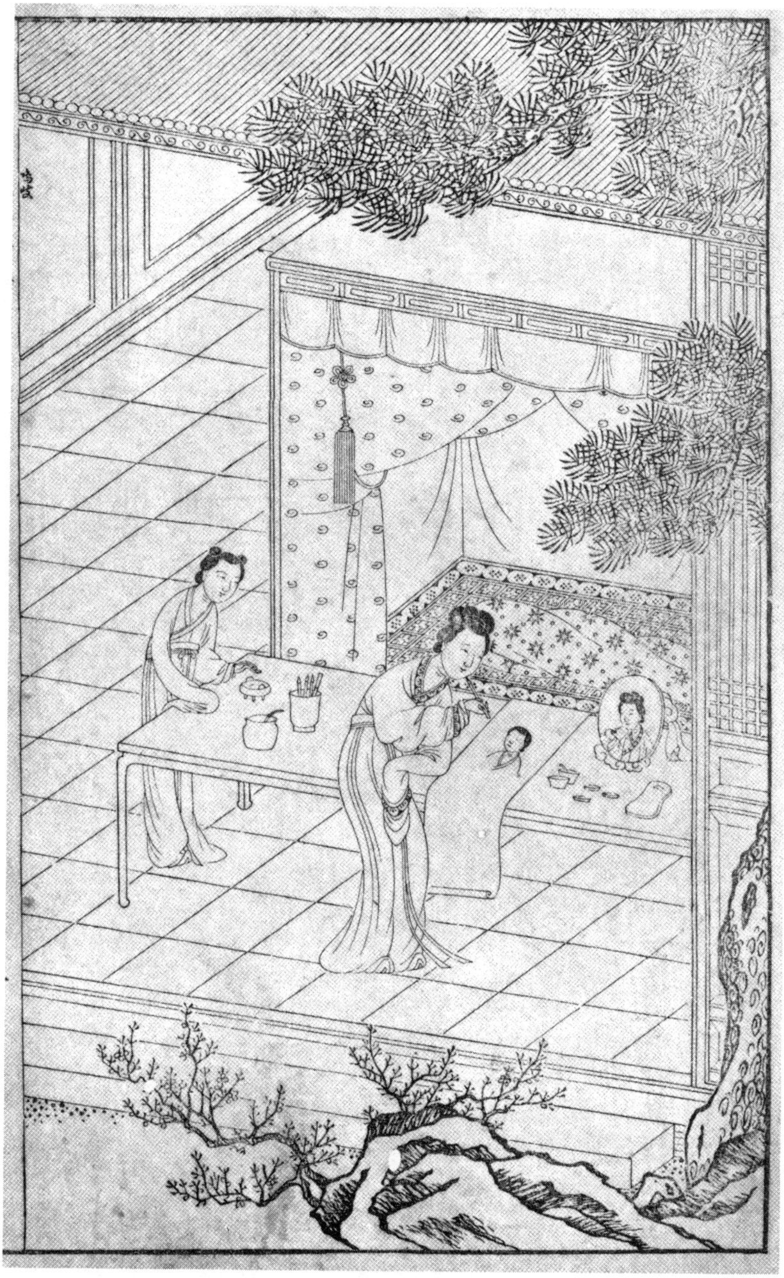

Fig. 5 Huang Mingqi, *Painting the Self-Portrait.* Woodblock illustration of a scene from *The Peony Pavilion* (1617 ed.).

by Du Liniang's actual death, and this same self-portrait mediates between her former existence and her subsequent resurrection.

As noted in the Introduction, there was a strong association in late imperial culture between portraiture and postmortem commemoration. This led to a tendency to see self-portraiture, particularly female self-portraiture, as being what Judith Zeitlin calls a symbolic act of "auto-effigy."[3] This association of self-portraiture and death is not unique to China. In a study of self-portraiture in Western art, for instance, Jacques Derrida similarly suggests that the graphic representation of one's image takes, as one condition of its existence, a moment of figurative blindness, of the inevitable ruins of a prior vision: "At the moment of the autograph, and with the most intense lucidity, the seeing blind man observes himself and has others observe."[4] Derrida is concerned here with the degree to which visual perception is grounded on the necessary possibility of blindness, or the absence of sight, just as self-perception is similarly grounded on the necessary possibility of death, or the absence of self. In the portrait scene from *Peony Pavilion*, not only does the act of self-portraiture prefigure Du Liniang's own subsequent "return as a specter," but the particular woodblock print under consideration here depicts a cycle of "spectral return" inscribed within the very moment of self-portraiture itself. By this logic, Huang Mingqi's print implicitly portrays Du sketching herself *as a specter*, with the inevitable necessity of her own death already inscribed within the self-portrait itself.[5]

The self-portraiture scene anticipates not only Du Liniang's own subsequent return from the dead but also indirectly the virtual reincarnation, four centuries later, of Tang Xianzu's text itself. That is to say, although the work was one of the most popular dramas during the late imperial period and remains a key piece in the *kunqu* 崑曲 operatic canon, only a handful of episodes of the 55-act work are performed regularly. As a unitary, performative text, *The Peony Pavilion* figuratively died not long after it was conceived, and it was not until 1999, just following the work's 400th anniversary, that it finally enjoyed a figurative rebirth. In July of that year,

3. For the term "auto-effigy," see Zeitlin, "Making the Invisible Visible."

4. Derrida, *Memoirs of the Blind*, 57.

5. Cf., e.g., Roland Barthes's famous discussion of how "each photograph always contains this imperious sign of my future death" (*Camera Lucida*, 97).

the U.S.-based Chinese director Chen Shizheng 陳士爭 debuted in New York's Lincoln Center his own version of the 55-act opera in a twenty-hour marathon performance, which aspired to be as faithful as possible to the original text. The program notes emphasized that it was the first complete performance of the work in more than a century.

The 1999 performance was all the more dramatic because, like Du Liniang herself, Chen's performance had, in effect, also recently returned from the dead. Almost precisely a year earlier, the Shanghai Municipal Bureau of Culture precipitated an international uproar when it forced the cancellation of the scheduled impending debut, on the grounds that Chen's interpretation of this Chinese masterpiece was "feudal, superstitious and pornographic." Furthermore, just as Du Liniang's reincarnation was mediated by the visual image of her self-portrait, similarly it was precisely the existence of "self-portraitive" video recordings of the aborted 1998 performance's dress rehearsal that provided the basis for the following year's production.[6] Speaking of the relationship between the stillborn and the reincarnated productions (which were put together and performed by two almost completely different casts of actors and stagehands), Chen emphasized, "This year [the company] is different but essentially, it's the same production. *The vision is still the same*" (italics added).[7]

Cinematic Landscapes

> There was once a painter who one day painted a landscape. It was a beautiful valley with wonderful trees and with a winding path leading away toward the mountains. The artist was so delighted with his picture that he felt an irresistible urge to walk along the path winding away towards the distant mountains. He entered the picture and followed the path towards the mountains and was never seen again by any man.
>
> —Béla Balázs, *Theory of Film*

Although Chen Shizheng, in claiming that the "vision is still the same," was clearly using *vision* in the abstract sense of "creative vision," the specific context of his remark invites a consideration of the status of actual "vision" in different historical and cultural contexts.

6. Smith, "Now the Epic Tale Can Be Told," p. 5.
7. Cited in ibid.

Chen's reliance on the modern technology of video recording in order to re-create an earlier performance that was itself intended to resurrect an "authentic" viewing tradition of a late Ming text raises the question of what it means to see or view something in the first place. Even if the texts/performances were visually identical, would it ever be possible to view a contemporary performance of *The Peony Pavilion* as it would have been seen by Tang Xianzu's contemporaries? How, in other words, do the cultural and historical contexts of a mimetic creation condition the ways in which it is subsequently perceived?

This question of what it means *to see* in different cultural and historical contexts is provocatively posed by a curious series of references in Western film theory to the legend of the Tang dynasty painter Wu Daozi 吳道子 (680–740), who allegedly walked right into a landscape painting he had just completed and was re-absorbed by the mimetic world of his own creation. For example, two giants of early film theory, Béla Balázs and Siegfried Kracauer, cited this legend as an allegory illustrating the ability of cinema to engross and absorb the spectator,[8] essentially finding in Tang landscape painting a figurative *imago* against which film theory may position itself—with Tang dynasty painting representing an idealized vision of the mimetic transparency to which cinema itself aspires. To the extent that both cinema and Tang landscape painting function here as figurative apogees of verisimilitude within their respective representational traditions, contemporary cinema's recurrent appeal to the Tang legend essentially constitutes a mirror-stage moment of mimeticism itself.

One reason for these theorists' fascination with the Tang legend as representing an impossible ideal of mimetic transparency may well have to do with the fact that the anecdote runs in the face of common generalizations about Chinese painting. The generally progressive art historian Norman Bryson, for instance, articulates this conventional view concisely when he postulates that the Chinese and Western painting traditions "bifurcate, *from the beginning*, at the point of deixis" (italics added), with Chinese painting seen as "always" foregrounding deictic

———

8. Balázs, *Theory of the Film*, 48; Kracauer, *Theory of Film*, 164–65. Both of these examples are cited and discussed in Silverman, *The Threshold to the Visible World*, 89.

markers and Western painting attempting to erase them.[9] Setting aside for the moment the fact that this is an absurd claim to make even about Western painting, it is an instructively problematic assertion to make about Chinese painting. Although it is true that, from roughly the Yuan dynasty (1279–1368) on, the literati art tradition that subsequently coalesced around the Ming dynasty artist and theorist Dong Qichang 董其昌 tended to emphasize stylistic concerns over purely mimetic ones, it is nevertheless also true that many other parallel Chinese representational traditions during that same period, not to mention during the pre-Yuan period, continued to value verisimilitude for its own sake. Bryson's claim effectively positions Chinese art within a space of radical alterity with respect to Western art, insisting—in the face of ample evidence to the contrary, not to mention basic common sense—that Chinese art "from the beginning" has positioned itself in opposition to the verisimilitude, particularly the post-*quattrocento* emphasis on perspectival realism, with which Western art came to identify itself.[10] Bryson's claim could therefore be seen as inverse yet parallel to the film theorists' allusions to the legendary Tang landscape painter, in that both comparisons posit a caricatured vision of Chinese art as a mirror image of their own self-conception. Ironically, though, this gesture of reducing Chinese painting to a parody of itself is performed precisely in the interest of reaffirming an ideal of Western mimesis (which ostensibly emphasizes *accurate* representations of external reality).

A similar attempt to view contemporary Western mimeticism through the lens of its Oriental Other also motivated Walter Benjamin's seminal essay, "The Work of Art in the Age of Mechanical Reproduction." In this 1930s essay, Benjamin considered the significance of the work of art in contemporary (Western) society by contrasting it with a premodern (and implicitly Western) art tradition. Benjamin argued that, prior to the development and popularization of modern technologies of visual reproduction, artworks were generally viewed as unique entities inextricably embedded within specific matrices of ritualistic performance and

9. Bryson, *Vision and Painting*, 89.

10. See Clunas, *Pictures and Visuality*, 12–18, for an eloquent articulation of this critique. See also Jay, "Scopic Regimes of Modernity," for a discussion of several alternative "scopic regimes" within the same European tradition.

therefore possessed what he called an "aura." For Benjamin, this auratic quality of the traditional artwork meant that its appreciation implicitly reinforced the social structures within which it was embedded.

The turn-of-the-century popularization of photography, cinema, and related representational technologies, however, made it possible to reproduce artwork and thereby radically transformed its social significance. Although the process of technological development Benjamin described is a long and complicated one, he nevertheless pinpointed the actual moment of transition from premodernity to modernity with considerable precision. "Around 1900," Benjamin specified, pointing to almost precisely the same historical moment in Cixi's mirror photograph, "technical reproduction had reached a standard that . . . permitted it to reproduce all transmitted works of art and thus to cause the most profound change in their impact upon the public."[11] In other words, it was at this juncture that mimeticism essentially folded in upon itself, with art's status as an imitation of nature becoming redoubled by a new emphasis on imitative reproduction of the artwork itself.

Benjamin saw this development as generally positive, allowing, as it does, for the artwork to be severed from its original ritualistic context and reappropriated for new political purposes. In addition to making possible the reproduction of existing works of art, these new technologies of visual reproduction also "capture[ ] a place of [their] own among the artistic processes." That is to say, the technologies of visual reproduction, in Benjamin's account, shifted from merely providing the means of reproducing existing artworks to becoming artistic modes in their own right.

First published in 1936, Benjamin's most-reproduced essay coincided almost precisely with the "original" version of Lacan's best-known essay,[12] and indeed these two seminal works could even be seen as mirror

11. See Benjamin, "The Work of Art," 219–20.

12. Like Lacan's "mirror-stage" essay, Benjamin's "Work of Art" also has a complicated textual history. The first version of the essay was written during the fall and winter of 1935 and then revised during early 1936; an abridged version was then published in 1936 in French as "L'Œuvre d'art à l'époque de sa reproduction mécanisée." Benjamin continued to revise the essay between 1936 and 1939, yielding the version known today (see Caygill, *Walter Benjamin*, 98).

images of each other. In other words, the mirror stage describes how the infant, in a state of bodily fragmentation, finds in the mirror an idealized image of corporal unity with which it may projectively identify, and Benjamin's essay describes how the early twentieth-century subject, on the cusp of an era in which technologies of visual reproduction will lead to an unprecedented fragmentation and disassociation of the artwork, gazes *back* at an idealized premodern era in which the concrete artwork was intimately embedded within its own specific sociocultural matrix. Although Benjamin was generally approving of this modern transformation in the status of the artwork, arguing that it would allow the work to be emancipated "from its parasitical dependence on ritual" and reappropriated for (progressive) political ends, there is nevertheless a distinctly nostalgic overtone to his discussion of the auratic—a nostalgia particularly visible in his emphasis that the auratic, in addition to possessing a "unique phenomenon of a distance," nevertheless is endowed with "the ability to look [back] at us in turn."[13] In other words, it is precisely because of a premodern artwork's uniqueness and social embeddedness that it becomes possible to perceive it as almost another sentient entity and able to return the observer's own gaze.

The implication of this emphasis on the aura's ability to return the gaze is essentially a moment of *double* mirroring. The modern subject looks back to the premodern auratic artwork to see a social unity and totality that no longer exist, while embedded within the auratic itself is an idealized image of specular return, wherein the auratic is able to return the observer's gaze. The catch, however, is that the modern observer perceives that scene of idealized specular return only from the perspective of an external observer—one who can merely peer in on this mirror scene from the outside.

Another parallel between Lacan's and Benjamin's models involves the way in which both presuppose a model of temporality that folds in upon itself. Just as both the "body in bits and pieces" and the unified subject are, in Lacan's mirror-stage model, projections of the paradigmatic mirror-stage moment itself, similarly one might argue that

13. See Benjamin, "The Work of Art," 222–23, 188. For a discussion, see Buck-Morss, *The Dialectics of Seeing*, 194.

Benjamin's auratic represents a state that becomes intelligible only in retrospect, on the eve of its historical disappearance, just as a post-auratic period in which technologies of reproduction truly eclipse the unitary artwork itself was arguably still on the historical horizon at the time Benjamin wrote his essay.

Although Benjamin, at the beginning of his essay, stressed the importance of examining the phenomenon of mechanical reproduction "from the perspective of world history," the narrative he sketched is, nevertheless, a very provincial one. In fact, the only specific reference to a non-European tradition in the entire essay is an elliptical allusion to the proverbial "Chinese painter" who walked into his own painting—although, unlike Balázs and Kracauer, Benjamin cited this painter as an example precisely of what the cinema *is not*, emphasizing a distinction between art forms like Chinese painting that ostensibly invite "contemplation" and those like film that invite "distraction."[14] I, however, take Benjamin's curious elision of China in his essay as a starting point for considering a comparable logic of specularity and mimetic reproduction in a Chinese context, focusing in particular on a novel that is centrally concerned with the question of the relationship between specular images and reality.

Mirrors of Desire

> Fuchun picked up his brush to paint a miniature *gongbi* 工筆 group-portrait; but first he placed the mirror-stand in front of himself and, gazing at the mirror, proceeded to paint his own self-portrait. Only afterward did he turn his attention to painting the portraits of Yiren and Ah Zi.
>
> —Wu Yitang, *Mirror of Romance*

Wu Yitang's 吳貽棠 early nineteenth-century (ca. 1820) novel *Fengyue jian* 風月鑒 (Mirror of romance) describes, at one point, a moment of equivocation between portraiture and self-portraiture. The character Fuchun, before painting a group portrait, first paints his own *self*-portrait on the basis of an image in a mirror, thereby making himself a spectator of his own specular image.[15] This overlapping of specu-

14. Benjamin, "The Work of Art," 238–39.
15. Wu Yitang, *Fengyue jian* (152).

lar and spectatorial gazes represents in miniature the positioning of Wu Yitang's novel with respect to the Qing dynasty classic to which its title alludes: Cao Xueqin's 曹雪芹 eighteenth-century novel *Honglou meng* 紅樓夢 (Dream of the red chamber). The first chapter of that text contains a list of potential alternative titles for the novel, one of which is *Fengyue baojian* 風月寶鑒 (Precious mirror of romance).[16] Wu Yitang dropped the modifier *bao* 寶 (precious)—a deletion that ironically reinforces the general perception that Wu's novel is a perverse parody of Cao Xueqin's classic. Critics, for example, have used the expression *Dongshi xiaopin* 東施笑顰, a figure for specular failure, to express the relationship between these two works; the phrase alludes to the story of how the unattractive Dongshi 東施 furrowed her brows in imitation of the legendary beauty Xishi 西施, but succeeded only in making herself even more ludicrous.[17]

Like the homely Dongshi's unsuccessful attempt to make herself into a living mirror of her beautiful counterpart, the relationship between Cao's and Wu's novels can be seen as one of specular incongruence. The relationship is less one of direct *mimesis* and more a matter of parodic *mimicry*. The two concepts are opposite poles along a continuum of visual imitation: mimesis puts imitation to the service of continuity; mimicry capitalizes on imitation to mark a moment of disjunctive rupture. Moreover, Wu Yitang's specular failure underscores the degree to which *Dream of the Red Chamber* itself is centrally concerned with the question of the limits of specularity and mimetic representation. Composed in the mid-eighteenth century, the novel anticipates the widespread introduction into China of Western representational practices and technologies, although it does occasionally allude to the possibilities they represent. For instance, in one scene Granny Liu observes that, during the Chinese New Year's festival, "we country folk" typically hang a "new year's picture" on the wall and then look at it and

16. One theory of the compositional genealogy of Cao's novel holds that *Precious Mirror* was originally a separate work, which was subsequently inserted into the *Dream of the Red Chamber* narrative. See, e.g., Eileen Chang's discussion of this issue in Honglong meng *yan*.

17. See the introduction to the Taiwan reprint of the novel, Wu Yitang, *Fengyue jian*, 36.

wish "we could get inside it and walk around." In the following chapter, this conceit of being able to step inside a mimetic image assumes an unanticipated irony when Granny Liu mistakes a "foreign-style" portrait of a young woman for a real person and literally runs into it.[18]

By far the dominant technology of visual reproduction in the novel, however, is the traditional mirror, which appears both as a concrete prop and as a symbolic motif. For example, the original name of the novel's Grand View Garden (Daguan yuan 大觀園), in which the majority of the action takes place, is Precious Mirror of Celestial Beings (Tianxian baojing 天仙寶鏡). Similarly, the parallel phrase "precious mirror of romance" (*fengyue baojian* 風月寶鑒)—which uses the character *jian* 鑒 for "mirror," rather than the essentially synonymous *jing* 鏡—not only is listed within the novel itself as one of the work's alternative titles but also is the title of another novel on which Cao Xueqin's famous work is believed to have been partially based.

In addition, this phrase happens to be the name of an actual mirror that figures prominently in the novel, appearing in a famous scene concerning the lovesickness of the licentious Jia Rui. Jia Rui has tried a variety of different remedies but to no avail. Finally, in desperation, he seeks the assistance of an itinerant Taoist monk, who informs him that his only hope for recovery lies in a magical, two-sided mirror with the words "mirror of romance" etched on the "back" side:

> This object comes from the Hall of Emptiness in the Land of Illusion. It was fashioned by the fairy Disenchantment as an antidote to the ill effects of impure mental activity. It has life-giving and restorative properties and has been brought into the world for the contemplation of those intelligent and handsome young gentlemen whose hearts are too susceptible to the charms of beauty. I lend it to you on one important condition: that you must only look into the back of the mirror. Never, never under any conditions look into the front. (1: 171–72 / 1: 251)

The monk's magical mirror mediates between the mortal world and the "world of illusion." One side of the mirror will clear the "impurities"

18. Cao Xueqin and Gao E, *Honglou meng*, 2: 572–73; idem, *Dream of the Red Chamber*, 2: 318–19. Subsequent references to these two works are cited in the text. The first reference is to the Chinese edition; the second to the English translation.

from Jia Rui's mind; the other side contains an image of Wang Xifeng, the object of his desire, beckoning Jia Rui to come and make love to her. Jia Rui, of course, disobeys the monk's injunctions and insists on gazing at the side with the beautiful maiden, with the result that he expires in a pool of his own sweat and semen. Jia Rui's unenviable fate reflects a twin anxiety about the vagaries of specular reflection, on one hand, and of female sexuality, on the other, suggesting that the specular image and female sexuality present a parallel challenge to the perceived self-sufficiency of the masculine subject.

These anxieties about the implications of specular doubling are played out particularly clearly in the protagonist Jia Baoyu's encounter, late in the novel, with his own specular "cousin," Zhen Baoyu (the surname "Zhen" 甄 is a homophone for "true" 眞; Jia Baoyu's surname, 賈, is in turn a homophone for 假 "false"). The first encounter between the two cousins takes place in a dream: Jia Baoyu falls asleep under a large dressing mirror, suggesting that this initial vision of Zhen Baoyu is the product of Jia Baoyu's act of viewing his *own* specular image as if he were "an/Other." Wai-yee Li, in her discussion of this passage, reaches a similar conclusion: "To look into the mirror is also to regard oneself from the perspective of the nonself."[19] The act of looking in the mirror is, therefore, particularly portentous for Baoyu, who, as Li notes in another context, "lacks [in his dealings with the world] a sense of boundary or any awareness of the division of self and other (不分人我)" (206).

Reflections on Origins

> I cannot urge you too strongly to a meditation on optics . . . this strange science which sets itself to produce, by means of apparatuses, that peculiar thing called images, in contrast to other sciences, which import into nature a cutting up, a dissection, an anatomy.
>
> —Jacques Lacan, Seminar I

Jia Baoyu's sense of alienated self-perception from looking *in* the mirror parallels the similarly alienating implications of looking *at* mirrors and other visual technologies explored in a relatively obscure mid-nineteenth-century treatise on optics and visuality entitled *Jingjing*

19. Wai-yee Li, *Enchantment and Disenchantment*, 226.

lingchi 鏡鏡詅癡 (Humble ruminations on specularity; 1846).[20] Written by Zheng Fuguang 鄭復光 (1783–1853) (whose given name, ironically, can be translated literally as "reflected light"), this monograph is neither explicitly literary nor strictly scientific or technological; it therefore challenges the conventional boundaries between these two discursive modes. Although its publication coincided roughly with the invention of photography in Europe,[21] Zheng's text primarily concerns more traditional technologies of visual perception and visual reproduction—including mirrors, pin-hole projection devices, camera obscuras, and telescopes. The work presents a vision of an emergent "modern" scopic regime but at the same time foregrounds the continuing relevance of more "traditional" visual practices.

Humble Ruminations on Specularity begins with a reflection on the difficulty of beginnings—and not just historical beginnings, but equally important methodological and epistemological beginnings:

> Mirrors are used to mirror things, and if you do not illuminate the Origins of the Principle of Things, it will not be possible to acquire the Principle of Specularity.
>
> It is in the Principle of Things that we will find the Origins of Specularity. Herein lies the Illumination of Origins.
>
> 鏡以鏡物不明物理不可以得鏡理物之理鏡之原也作明原

This passage appears as an interlinear commentary (apparently by the author) to the subtitle of the first section of the work: "Mingyuan" 明原 (Illumination of origins). These opening lines explicitly concern the question of beginnings and origins—from the perspectives not only of where to begin the study but also, and more important, of the question of the intellectual grounds for inquiring into Chinese visuality. Zheng's text encourages us to approach visual culture both by considering visual images and by asking what it means to look at images and optical processes in the first place: What can these processes tell us about the underlying principles of the sociocultural order within which

20. Zheng Fuguang, *Jingjing lingchi.* For a discussion and partial translation of this text, see Rojas, "Zheng Fuguang's *Humble Reflections on Specularity.*"

21. For instance, the daguerreotype, a crucial precursor of the photograph, was invented in 1839.

both observer and observed are located? What is the relationship between the ways in which visuality is perceived in different cultural-historical contexts, and the ways in which the observing subjects imagine their own positionality? How, in short, may we view vision itself, and how does this act of perceiving vision position *us* as observers?

The second term of the subtitle of this first part of Zheng's monograph, *yuan* 原, can be used as a verb meaning roughly "to establish the origins or foundations of something," and it is this sense of the term that is used in each of the subsequent section titles: "Yuan se" 原色 (Origins of color), "Yuan guang" 原光 (Origins of light), and "Yuan jing" 原景 (Origins of scenes), etc. In this initial section title, however, *yuan* is itself modified by another term, *ming* 明, which is used here as a verb meaning "to clarify" or "to illuminate." The section title could be read as "illumination of origins," or perhaps, "illumination of the process of establishing origins." To the extent that each of the sections in this opening portion of Zheng's monograph is concerned with exploring the epistemological grounds of a different dimension of visuality, Zheng's commentary on the opening title seeks to specify the ontological foundation of this quest for epistemological grounds itself.

Zheng Fuguang's concern with origins and foundations acquires additional cogency when considered in the context of the specific historical moment in which he wrote his text. Completed in 1846, Zheng's monograph appeared precisely halfway between the end of the Opium War (1839–42) and the beginning of the Taiping Rebellion (1850–64)—two events often regarded as marking the beginning of an increasingly visible encroachment of Western culture and capital into China. Located at this transitional moment between a "traditional" and a "modern" Chinese world-order, Zheng's monograph is a heteroglossic palimpsest of disparate voices, logics, and worldviews. The text uses a vocabulary saturated with Confucian and Buddhist connotations to explain empirical optical phenomena. It discusses visual physiognomy and the etiologies of various visual defects, starting from the traditional view that visual perception is the result of the eye's projection of light rays onto the object being perceived. Furthermore, Zheng's text provides carefully illustrated explications of the mechanics of complicated optical devices, but does so using the ultra-concise and elliptical grammatical structure characteristic of classical Chinese prose.

The hybrid nature of Zheng's text derives in part from the way in which it combines the empiricism of modern physics with the more speculative approach of Neo-Confucian theory. For instance, the "Illumination of Origins" commentary I discuss above uses the term *wuli* 物理, which I have translated literally in its Neo-Confucianism sense of "principle of things."[22] Zheng's use of the term is interestingly indeterminate, however, since it was precisely during this period that the Neo-Confucian term was being reappropriated to translate the Western term *physics.*[23] This ambiguity captures in miniature the degree to which Zheng's entire text is positioned between two distinct epistemological regimes, two distinct ways of approaching the question of the "principle" underlying the material world.

Underlying this dichotomous transition from a Neo-Confucian to a modern scientific *wuli*, however, is a complex series of debates even *within* the Neo-Confucian tradition over how to position oneself with respect to an external reality. A hint of what is at stake in these debates may be glimpsed by looking at the history of another Neo-Confucian term, which, like *wuli*, was being reappropriated during this period to translate the concept of *physics*. The term is *gezhi* 格知, which is an abbreviation of a phrase from the *Great Learning*: *zhizhi zai gewu* 致知在格物, meaning roughly "to acquire knowledge through the investigation of things." The nineteenth-century "translingual" borrowing of this term itself replicates the continual reinterpretation of this deceptively simple concept by successive generations of Confucian thinkers as they struggled to come to terms with the relationship between the external, perceptible world and internal "knowledge." For instance, the patriarch of Song Neo-Confucianism, Zhu Xi 朱熹 (1130–1200), understood *gezhi* to mean "the investigation of things," in the sense that "principle" is inherent in material "things." Wang Yangming 王陽明 (1472–1529), the leading figure of Ming dynasty Neo-Confucianism, by contrast, interpreted the same phrase to mean "to eliminate what is

22. *Wu* 物 refers to "things" or "objects," and *li* 理 means "principle."

23. *Wuli* was used in the sense of *physics* as early as the 1830s (the term was used in this sense as early as 1634, in Johann Schreck and Wang Zheng's 王徵 *Yuanxi qiqi tushuo luzui* 遠西奇器圖說錄最 [Diagrams and explanations of the wonderful machines from the far West]); see Lydia Liu, *Translingual Practice*, 277.

incorrect in the mind so as to preserve the correctness of its original substance"[24]—that is, taking *ge* as "to correct" rather than merely "to arrive at" or "to investigate." In the Qing dynasty, evidential *kaozheng xue* 考證學 scholars such as Yan Yuan 顏元 (1635–1705) used the same formula to express not so much an abstract "study of principle" (Zhu Xi) or the "study of the mind" (Wang Yangming) but a renewed interest in the actual materiality of the perceivable world itself—an interest in materiality that Yan Yuan articulated using strikingly ocular metaphors; for example: "Knowledge has no substance of its own. Its substance consists of things. It is similar to the fact that the eye has no substance of its own; its substance consists of physical forms and colors."[25]

The *gewu zhizhi* formula, in short, is directly concerned with the relationship between the viewing subject and her physical environment. At the same time, the sharp disagreements over the meaning of the phrase underscore the degree to which the understanding of (visual) perception is itself informed by contextual intellectual and cultural considerations. Visuality itself, in other words, is transformed from a transparent window between (observing) subject and (external) object and becomes instead an object of observation in its own right. This miniature genealogy of *gewu zhizhi* is located, like Zheng Fuguang's monograph, within an ambiguous epistemological space between observer and observed, in which the act of seeing is never innocent or transparent and instead is necessarily marked by the specific cultural assumptions that lend it meaning and significance.

It is precisely Zheng's examination of Chinese catotropic traditions and their implications, in other words, that foregrounds the culturally and epistemologically hybrid nature of his own mid-nineteenth-century gaze. In fact, this dialectic of mimicry and alienation is embedded within the title of Zheng Fuguang's monograph itself: *Humble Ruminations on Specularity*. The term I translate as *specularity* is actually *jingjing* 鏡鏡, or literally, "mirror mirror." Or, since the same character is used in Chinese to refer to lenses, another translation of the title could be "mirror-lens." In other words, embedded within the similitude of Zheng

24. Wang Yangming, *Chuanxi lu* 傳習錄 (Instructions for practical living), secs. 7, 85, 174; cited in Wing-Tsit Chan, *A Source Book in Chinese Philosophy*, 655.

25. Yan Yuan, "Learning Through Experience," 707–8.

Fuguang's 鏡鏡 title is precisely the scopic shift in Chinese culture from specularity to (optically mediated) spectatorship that I argue began roughly around the time of Zheng's mid-century monograph. Below, I return to Zheng's text to reflect on the relationship between these gestures of looking *in* and looking *at* a mirror, and specifically their implications for this figurative insertion of external gazes into the specular act of regarding oneself.

Opaque Windows

> When glass is used for a window, one can see outside from within the room, and a dark room can be illuminated—these are its advantages. However, when colored glass is used for a window, it becomes more difficult for people outside to peer in and see what is going on, but the window is nevertheless brilliant to look at. Therefore, one of its uses lies in the beauty of its exquisite decoration.
>
> —Zheng Fuguang, *Humble Ruminations on Specularity*

In a discussion of windows near the beginning of his study, Zheng noted the concatenation of transparency and opacity that one encounters when viewing a stained-glass window. More specifically, the semitranslucent aperture of the window stands at a figurative chiasmus of three distinct gazes. The first gaze treats the stained glass as a conventional transparent window and seeks to look *through* it at the scene outside. The second gaze focuses on the semiopaque surface of the stained glass itself and treats the "brilliance" of the window as an object of observation in its own right. Finally, there is simultaneously a third gaze that remains invisible in Zheng's passage, but that practical experience would lead us to expect to find in a semiopaque glass surface of this sort: namely, while the observer is looking *through* the window at the scene outside and also gazing *at* the window as an object in its own right, she may at the same time also glimpse a reflection *of her own image* in the opaque surface of the stained-glass window itself.

A similar concatenation of gazes can be found in the self-portraiture scene of *Peony Pavilion*. I argue above that Du Liniang can draw her self-portrait only by first perceiving her mirror image as that of an alienated other, and that it is precisely this alienated self-perception, Tang Xianzu's play implies, that anticipates her subsequent death. The simultaneous external and projective gazes implicit in Du Liniang's ostensibly specular gaze are made explicit by her maid, Chun Xiang, who remarks to herself as Du uses the mirror image to sketch her self-portrait: "Easy enough to sketch her aspect in hues red or dark; harder to portray *the true colors* of the rare individual self, *when the image reflects the reality like flowers seen behind closed lids, or the moon in the water*" (italics added).[26] In this remark, Chun Xiang uses a variant of the Buddhist aphorism *jinghua shuiyue* (like flowers in the mirror, or the reflection of the moon in water) to articulate the gulf separating ("mere") visual mimicry and ("true") internal fidelity. In other words, it is easy to perceive one's true surface "aspect," but in order to perceive one's own "true colors," it is first necessary to recognize and come to terms with the inherent ephemerality of those visual appearances themselves.

The intersection of three separate gazes found in Zheng's figure of the stained-glass window, as well as in Du Liniang's self-portraiture scene and Cixi's mirror photograph, in turn, neatly encapsulate my approach toward vision and visual imagery in this study. That is, I stress the degree to which visual images (and, more abstractly, visuality itself) provide a glimpse of an external reality, while constituting objects of observation in their own right. Equally important, however, I am interested in the way in which these same visual images may also function as specular foils through and against which viewers may come to perceive themselves. In the following chapters, I propose a new way of seeing visuality, as well as the processes of (gendered) subject formation for which it serves as a powerful metaphor.

26. Tang Xianzu, *Mudan ting*, scene 14, p. 70; idem, *The Peony Pavilion*, 69; translation adapted.

2

Li Ruzhen and Laughing at the Gibbon

The Fairy of a Hundred Grasses said, "That the Star of Literature now appears in feminine form is undoubtedly a female sign. . . . This suggests that there will appear not just one or two daughters from good families, but rather a large number of female talents."

"That may be true," the Fairy of a Hundred Flowers replied. "Still, even if that which is recorded is indeed about women . . . would it not then be like admiring flowers in the mirror and the moon's reflection in water?"

— Li Ruzhen, *Flowers in the Mirror*

A central image of Li Ruzhen's 李汝珍 early nineteenth-century novel *Jinghua yuan* 鏡花緣 (Flowers in the mirror) is precisely contained in the title. In context, however, this figure is not so much an actual image as an anti-image—a potent symbol of the inherent limits of visual imagery itself. To begin with, the flowers in question are not literal flowers but transparent symbols for women and femininity. By the same token, one might ask whether the female characters in the novel are what they appear to be, or whether they are merely symbols of issues or concerns that have nothing to do with women at all.

Like the proverbial flowers reflected in a mirror, Li Ruzhen's novel is grounded on a general logic of inversion. It takes as its historical backdrop the reign of China's only female to rule in her own right, Wu Zetian 武則天 (r. 684–705), and opens on a celestial plane with the empress peremptorily ordering her celestial counterpart, the Fairy of a Hundred Flowers, to arrange for all the flowers on earth to bloom together in the middle of winter. These parallel inversions of political authority and of celestial order, combined with the subsequent appearance in female form of the conventionally masculine "Star of Literature" (*kuixing* 魁星), are believed to herald the arrival of some extraordinary "literary event." It is the significance of this "literary event," and by implication of the novel as a whole, that the Fairy of a Hundred Flowers calls into question in the epigraph to this chapter when she asks whether their viewing of the event might turn out to be just a case of admiring "flowers in the mirror and the moon's reflection in the water" (*jinghua shuiyue* 鏡花水月).

One could even take the Fairy's rhetorical question quite literally and suggest that the novel is not so much about women as about actual mirrors, together with the abstract processes of reflection and inversion they connote. This is true, for instance, with respect not only to the carnivalesque inversions of political and cosmic order that frame the novel as a whole but also to the way in which the novel is constantly reflecting on a pre-existing linguistic, literary, and philosophical cultural tradition.[1] In the following discussion, I attempt to take the Fairy's framing question quite seriously and develop a reading of the novel that seeks to bridge these concerns with flowers and mirrors on one hand and with gender and visuality on the other by focusing on the fulcrum of value and identity. In particular, I look at the ways in which both value and identity are informed not only by a specular moment of self-perception but also by the circulation of those mirror images within a broader symbolic economy.

Representing Woman

A sign we are, without meaning
Without pain we are and have nearly
Lost our language in foreign lands,
For when the heavens quarrel
Over humans and moons proceed
In force, the sea
Speaks out and rivers must find
Their way . . .
. . . .

1. Hsia, "The Scholar Novelist and Chinese Culture."

> Not everything
> Is in the power of gods. Mortals would sooner
> Reach toward the abyss. With them
> The echo turns. Though the time
> Be long, truth
> Will come to pass.
>
> —Hölderlin, "Mnemosyne"

In spatial terms, the novel's interest in questions of reflection and inversion manifests itself through a thematics of exile—that is, through a substitution of the familiarity of home with the unfamiliarity of exile. For instance, the work opens with the protagonist, Tang Ao, leaving China with a small group of traveling companions after having been falsely accused of participating in a rebellion against Empress Wu Zetian (although she herself subsequently exculpated him), and embarking on a long ocean voyage. Meanwhile, on a celestial plane, the Fairy of a Hundred Flowers and her 99 flower fairies have been banished to the earth because the Flower Fairy obeyed Empress Wu Zetian's transgressive command that they make all the world's flowers bloom in the middle of winter. Twelve of the flower fairies are reincarnated as young women scattered among various fantastic island-countries outside the borders of the Kingdom of the Earth (i.e., China) itself, and the Fairy of a Hundred Flowers herself is reincarnated as Tang Ao's daughter, Tang Xiaoshan. Within this space of double exile, the novel describes a quest for identity—a quest with startling implications for the understanding of gender and subjectivity during the period in which the novel was composed.

Li Ruzhen completed *Flowers in the Mirror* around 1820, several decades before the dramatic twentieth-century transformation in the status of women in China—a transformation that would include the abolition of footbinding, the vocal critique of arranged marriages, the large-scale entry of women into the non-household workforce, and even the granting to women of limited suffrage.[2] Part of the reason for the novel's modern appeal lies in the way it appears to anticipate these reforms decades before the fact. In particular, the novel is currently best known

---

2. The work was completed around 1820; the first-known printed version is a woodblock edition dated 1828; see the discussion of the novel's publishing history in Kao, *Li Ju-Chen*, 25–27.

for its infamous description of the Country of Women—a topsy-turvy realm where women occupy the social positions traditionally reserved for men, and vice versa. The notion of a "country of women" is not original to this particular text; Li Ruzhen was drawing on a long tradition of literary precedents, including a rather cryptic reference in the early mythological text *Shanhai jing* 山海經 (Classic of mountains and oceans), as well as the more detailed discussion in the classic Ming dynasty novel, *Xiyouji* 西遊記 (Journey to the west). What is distinctive about Li's description is that it not only places women in positions of power and authority but subjects male visitors to such painful and humiliating "female" practices as footbinding and concubinage.

Modern readers, therefore, are tempted to read Li Ruzhen's Country of Women as an early critique of the misogynist and patriarchal tendencies in traditional Chinese culture—a reading of the novel articulated memorably by the American-educated reformist scholar and critic Hu Shi 胡適 during the reformist May Fourth period in 1920s China.[3] The inverse of Hu Shi's reading, however, can be found in C. T. Hsia's argument that, despite the novel's show of a carnivalesque inversion of gender positions and stereotypes, the work reinforces underlying Confucian notions of patriarchal privilege—as illustrated, for instance, by the fact that the various "flower fairies" (or young girls, as they appear in their mortal incarnations) walk with the same "willowy" steps indicating bound feet, and by the end of the novel several of them have followed the conservative practice of taking their own lives in order to "protect their virtue."[4]

To the extent that Li's novel uses mirrors as a figure for the strategic inversion of conventional gender relations, these twentieth-century debates over the "feminist" implications of the novel invite us to extend the trope of the mirror to the work itself—to consider how the novel itself may be seen as a figurative "mirror" of the external social realities upon which it appears to reflect. Hu Shi suggested that Li Ruzhen used the novel to reflect on gender relations in nineteenth-century China,

3. Hu Shi, "*Jinghua yuan* de yinlun."

4. Hsia, "The Scholar Novelist and Chinese Culture." For a more detailed discussion of this twentieth-century debate over the novel's "feminist" implications, see Qingyun Wu, *Female Rule in Chinese and English Literary Utopias*, 84–87.

and Hsia implies that these same gendered themes betray the degree to which Li Ruzhen had internalized many of the same gendered attitudes that Hu Shi believed Li was attempting to critique. If anything, Hsia suggests, Hu Shi's reading of the novel should be seen as more a projection of the reformist May Fourth critic's *own* feminist sensibilities than a reflection of the novel's social perspective.

In a more recent discussion of the work, Stephen Roddy develops an interesting twist on this question of the gendered implications of the novel, locating the novel within nineteenth-century debates between speculative Neo-Confucian philosophy and the mid-Qing revival of "Han learning," also known as the philological "evidential studies" (*kaozheng xue*) movement.[5] Roddy suggests that, in this context, Li Ruzhen's work illustrates a "feminization of literati knowledge" and uses the girls in the novel as idealized embodiments of the Han learning movement. In particular, he argues that the novel approvingly presents the girls' enthusiasm for literary and linguistic "gaming" as an end-in-itself and holds this up as the model against which male literati's concerns with social recognition and material gain might be critically evaluated.[6] For Roddy, therefore, the representations of women in the novel function neither to critique (Hu Shi) nor to reaffirm (Hsia) the status of women in Chinese society; rather, they are used as symbols within a philosophical debate that, as the Fairy of a Hundred Flowers might say, ultimately has nothing to do with women at all.

My own reading of *Flowers in the Mirror*, by contrast, proposes that we may extend and complicate the reading of the novel's use of the mirror as a figure for gender inversion by turning instead to a related visual trope mentioned in an anonymous commentary appearing at the end of the first chapter of a late nineteenth-century edition of the novel. This commentary compares the novel to the act of

> placing a crystalline screen at the interstices between inner and outer; the observer need not step corporally into the [outer] space in order for the scene and objects to completely enter his/her eye.

---

5. For further discussion of these two movements, see Elman, *From Philosophy to Philology*.

6. Roddy, *Literati Identity and Its Fictional Representations*, 171–206.

水晶屏風於內外交界之所關著不必身踏其地而個中景物已了了在目矣。[7]

Here, a figurative "crystalline screen" (*shuijing pingfeng* 水晶屏風) placed between the observer and an external scene allows the observer to perceive on the screen's translucent surface a projection of an external scene. Like Zheng Fuguang's stained-glass windows—discussed in Chapter 1—this trope of the crystalline screen similarly not only functions as a figure for reflective specularity but also connotes a paradoxical conjunction of transparency and opacity. More specifically, I use this figure of the crystalline screen to examine the representation of gender in Li Ruzhen's novel, arguing that it would be an oversimplification to view the novel as merely a straightforward critique or reaffirmation of the social position of women in late Qing dynasty China. Instead, I suggest that the novel operates simultaneously on three distinct levels of representation: (1) it represents "women" directly; (2) it uses the trope of "women" as a metaphor for other sociocultural concerns; and (3) it implicitly comments on the process by which the signifier "woman" is itself used discursively within the novel itself. When this third level of meta-representation is used to reread the other two levels of "direct" and "metaphorical" representation, it becomes possible to see the novel as making a quasi-feminist statement about the discursive uses of tropes of women, even as it simultaneously uses apparent feminist allegories within a satirical frame.

Inverse Homesickness

> "When one becomes sick, but then recovers upon leaving one's home region, this is what is called 'homesickness.' This is a very strange illness, and although I just now came up with it, her father had already said much earlier that this girl was destined to travel to foreign lands, and only by doing so could she survive."
>
> —Li Ruzhen, *Flowers in the Mirror*

If *Flowers in the Mirror*'s interest in gender issues is most memorably reflected in its famous description of the Country of Women, the literati novel's parallel interest in linguistic and literary concerns is illustrated most evocatively in its discussion of the Country of Fork-

7. Li Ruzhen, *Huitu Jinghua yuan* 1.3b (originally published in 1888).

Tongued People (Qishe guo 歧舌國). The Fork-Tongued are described as a polyglot nation who possess a highly prized "rhyme scheme" (*yinyun* 音韻) that allows them to learn any foreign language with ease by breaking new words into their constituent phonemes. This "rhyme scheme"—a version of which is printed within the novel itself—was clearly of considerable importance to Li Ruzhen, who had published a six-volume treatise on Chinese phonetics, entitled *Yinjian* 音鑑 (Mirror of rhymes), in 1805, about five years before beginning work on *Flowers in the Mirror*. At the same time, it also represents an example of precisely the sort of scholarly erudition that makes the novel so challenging for many modern readers.

Rather than dividing the novel into those portions with gendered implications and those featuring scholarly erudition, I will instead begin by considering a third episode, which intervenes, both geographically and textually, between the descriptions of the countries of Fork-Tongued People and of Women. The scene in question begins in the Country of Fork-Tongued People, where the voyagers are asked to help cure the young daughter of their interpreter there—another of the fallen flower fairies by the name of Melody Orchid (Lanyin)—who is suffering from a mysterious debilitating illness. Ever since she was a little girl, her malady has "caused her abdomen to become swollen and tight as a drum" (*dufu pengzhang* 肚腹膨脹).[8] Tang Ao diagnoses the illness as a case of "worms" and prescribes medicinal herbs. As the travelers are preparing to leave, the girl's father rushes to inform them that two of the herbs cannot be found in their island-country. The father asks Tang Ao and his companions to take Melody Orchid with them, on the grounds that "a stranger once told [the father] that Melody Orchid's fate lies abroad, and that if she should meet an Immortal named Tang, she should go with him in order to prolong her life" (251/103). Tang Ao accedes to the father's request, and the voyagers, together with Melody Orchid, leave the Country of Fork-Tongued People.

8. Li Ruzhen, *Jinghua yuan*, 247; idem, *Flowers in the Mirror*, 102. Subsequent references to these two works are given in the text. The first number cited refers to the Chinese edition; the second to the corresponding passage in the English translation (many of which have been modified or retranslated).

The travelers soon find the herbs to cure Melody Orchid's illness, but when they attempt to return her to her father, she suffers a relapse as soon as they cross back into the waters of her home country. They then conclude that her illness is caused not by worms but by a peculiar kind of "homesickness":

> Lin said, "This girl, in my opinion, is suffering from 'homesickness' (*lixiang bing* 離鄉病)."
>
> Tang Ao replied, "What is this 'homesickness'?"
>
> Merchant Lin explained, "When one becomes sick, but then recovers upon leaving one's home region, this is what is called 'homesickness.' This is a very strange illness, and although I just now came up with it, her father had already said much earlier that this girl was destined to travel to foreign lands, and only by doing so could she survive. . . ."
>
> When Melody Orchid learned the details of this, she had no choice but temporarily to put aside her affections for her father. (257/105)

In this scene, the sexual connotations of Melody Orchid's original illness (the swelling of her abdomen), combined with the explicit discussion of her need to leave both her home and her father, suggest that her inverse "homesickness" may be read as an implicit commentary on the dominant kinship structure in traditional China in which women were figuratively exchanged exogamically between male patrilines.

This exogamic theme of (inverse) "homesickness" is, moreover, not unique to Melody Orchid; indeed, this circulation of "feminized" individuals functions as one of the driving forces behind the novel's own production of meaning. Not only are most of the characters in *Flowers in the Mirror* (including Tang Ao and his companions, Little Hill and the other mortal incarnations of the celestial flower fairies) presented as having been displaced from their original homes, but the novel at various points foregrounds the literal exchange of women between men. In the waters of the Country of Gentlemen, for example, the voyagers run across a fisherman who is holding a young girl, Flowering Maple, captive on his boat. The three voyagers use several different lines of argument to try to convince the fisherman that he must let the girl go, but ultimately they have no alternative but to buy her from him:

> Old Tuo said unhappily, "We offered you money with good intentions; how can you tell us to mind our own business? You don't believe that just because

this thousand-tael young girl happened to fall into your net, she is therefore yours to dispose of as you please?"

Lin added, "I tell you, you may dispose of the fish in your net as you please. But today's catch is a person, not a fish, and don't pretend you are blind and can't tell the difference. . . . What if we say that we don't let *you* go until you let *her* go?" (94–95/63).

Ironically, even though Tang Ao and his companions adamantly insist that Flowering Maple be recognized as an autonomous human being, they nevertheless find it necessary to "buy" her freedom, thus implicitly reinforcing the very "exchange value" they are ostensibly attempting to deny in the first place.

This scene near the Country of Gentlemen is followed by two more instances in which Tang Ao uses his financial resources to "liberate" other female or effeminate characters. In the first instance, superficially very similar to that of Flowering Maple, Tang Ao runs across some fishermen who have caught several "overseas mermaids" (*haiwai yuren* 海外魚人) and, taking pity on their predicament, decides to purchase them out of captivity (116/73). Several chapters later, the voyagers reach the Country of Scholars and find a young girl, Marsh Orchid, who is essentially being held captive by a matchmaker because all the eligible bachelors in the country are too stingy to want to "buy" her, and her relatives dare not come to her assistance because they fear reprisal from the royal son-in-law. Once again, Tang Ao draws on his own financial resources in order to remedy the situation. To express her gratitude, the woman subsequently insists on referring to Tang Ao as her "master," but Merchant Lin advises her to regard Tang Ao "as your godfather; we shall have none of this master-and-servant relationship here" (198/84–85).

Despite the fact that, in each of these instances, Tang Ao is ostensibly purchasing women precisely in order to liberate them from the system of commodity exchange in which they find themselves, in each case the act of "liberation" functions to reinforce the same economy it is being used to negate in the first place. That is, by a textual law of supply and demand, each act of exchange (even seemingly emancipatory ones) establishes a precedent for subsequent "purchases," thus buttressing the economic system that Tang Ao's emancipatory acts were intended to subvert while at the same time transposing the attendant relations of indebtedness from a strictly economic plane to a sociocultural one. For example, although Tang Ao sets Marsh Orchid free, she still feels compelled to think of their relationship in master-and-servant terms. Similarly, although the mermaids have been granted their freedom, they nevertheless later feel obliged to return and rescue the travelers when they are in need.

The social circulation of Melody Orchid, Marsh Orchid, and the mermaids reproduces in miniature the exogamic kinship structure of traditional China, in which the bride typically left her natal household and married into the groom's family. Indeed, Li's interest here in symbolic variants on exogamic relations may have stemmed from the fact that he himself, while composing the novel, was in an implicitly "feminine," uxorilocal position within his own marriage: he spent most of his adult life in his wife's hometown in Jiangsu and was financially dependent on his in-laws during much of that period.[9] In an influential discussion of the sociocultural implications of kinship structures, Claude Lévi-Strauss suggested that this exogamic circulation of women between patrilines can be thought of as "a kind of language, a set of processes permitting the establishment, between individuals and groups, of a certain kind of communication."[10] Like language, Lévi-Strauss argued, this circulation and exchange of women help to cement intersocial bonds between different families or social collectives by allowing them to be "communicated" and thereby reinforce implicit relations of social indebtedness.

One implication of this model, however, is that it might appear to reduce actual women to the status of abstract signifiers. Lévi-Strauss himself was not unaware of this problem and at one point attempted to sidestep it by suggesting that women are never totally reduced to the status of a "mere" sign, because they are always something "more," existing simultaneously as *both* sign and value.[11] What Lévi-Strauss failed to address, however, is how "value" is constituted, and what is the exact nature of its relationship with the semiotic function to which it is implicitly opposed. Elizabeth Cowie has observed, for instance, that the practice of exogamic exchange itself has the effect of undermining woman's ostensible "value" by reinscribing the sociocultural system

9. See Kao, *Li Ju-Chen*, 25.
10. Lévi-Strauss, *Structural Anthropology*, 51.
11. Lévi-Strauss, *The Elementary Structure of Kinship*, 496.

within which "woman's" status is always already that of a mere token of exchange: "The form of the sign—the signifier in linguistic terms—may empirically be woman, but the signified is not 'woman.'"[12] More generally, Cowie takes issue with Lévi-Strauss's contention regarding the fundamental "'neutrality' of exchange as a concept." Noting that Lévi-Strauss assumed that the subordination/oppression of women can be analyzed independently of their use as elements within a system of exchange/communication, Cowie responds:

> In arguing the "neutrality" of exchange as a concept, Lévi-Strauss overlooks the fact that while in his theory the principle of exchange itself does not define or "value" the items of exchange, which must always be equivalents although different, the terms or items of exchange must *already* be constituted, in a hierarchy of value, in order to be available to a system of exchange. (59)

Exogamic exchange itself, as Cowie argues, serves as a "putting into place—of culture, and crucially, of sexual relations," which is to say, it amounts to the "establishment/re-establishment of kinship structures or culture" (59). These issues of circulation and value are, in turn, directly relevant to Li Ruzhen's *Flowers in the Mirror*, in that we may read the novel's interest in the figurative exchange of both women and signs as itself a commentary on the ways in which "value" is itself an *artifact* of this same process of symbolic exchange. In Li Ruzhen's novel, the structures being implicitly established or re-established are not merely cultural or social ones; they are also structures of semiotic and textual representation itself. In particular, the novel implicitly comments on ways in which the semiotic structures used to signify gender difference are themselves modified and reaffirmed through processes of signification.

Uncanny Returns

> This uncanny is in reality nothing new or alien, but something which is familiar and old-established in the mind, and which has become alienated from it only through the process of repression.
>
> —Sigmund Freud, "The 'Uncanny'"

---

12. Cowie, "Woman As Sign," 59. A revised version of this essay appears in idem, *Representing the Woman*, 15–35. Subsequent references to this work are cited in parentheses in the text.

In the preceding discussion, I suggest that the Melody Orchid "homesickness" passage can be seen as providing a bridge between two paradigmatic descriptions, those of the Country of Fork-Tongued People and the Country of Women, thereby underscoring several evocative parallels between the two longer accounts. Both passages revolve around processes of defamiliarization—the "familiar" in the first case being ordinary language, and in the second case accepted sociocultural gender stereotypes. Furthermore, in both instances this defamiliarization is achieved through an implicit focus on the signifying process itself. For example, the Country of Women passage points to the arbitrariness of the relationship between biological sexuality and sociocultural conventions of gender, just as the rhyme scheme of the Fork-Tongue People itself foregrounds the arbitrary relationship between the phonetic and semantic elements of the Chinese language.

In the novel's discussion of the rhyme scheme, the defamiliarization consists of a shift from an illusion of semantic transparency to an attention to the physicality of the sign and to the apparent opacity of the linguistic medium itself. When the travelers finally succeed in obtaining the rhyme scheme, for example, they discover that it yields not so much an increased understanding of their own language as a distinct defamiliarization of the language they had previously assumed to be "their own." In fact, so complete is the resulting defamiliarization that Merchant Lin initially thinks that they have been tricked and not been given the desired document after all. Tang Ao, however, quite reasonably points out that if the king of the Fork-Tongued People had been trying to trick them, he would have chosen more difficult and unfamiliar ideographs for the rhyme scheme.

The moment of recognition in the discussion of the rhyme scheme occurs frequently throughout the rest of the novel as well. For example, the travelers periodically have experiences in the countries they visit that cause them to regard previously familiar idioms in a new light. In one case near the beginning of their journey, Tang Ao sees a bird carrying pebbles in its mouth and dropping them into the ocean. This causes him to remark, "I always thought that 'trying to fill up the ocean by dropping stones' was just an expression" (52/46). Shortly afterward, they run across a special kind of rice, with enormous grains; this inspires Merchant Lin to come up with a spurious etymology for another familiar expression: "No wonder when an important official shoots with bow and arrow, the subordinates always say, 'Missed by a grain of rice' when the official misses the target by at least a couple of feet . . . . They must mean this kind of rice" (55/47). In similar passages throughout the work, the travelers marvel at the sudden strangeness of the language they had previously regarded as their own.

This issue of linguistic unfamiliarity also has implications for Melody Orchid's "homesickness" and, by implication, not only for our understanding of the commodified status of the individuals and symbols being exchanged but also for the way in which this figure of the "home" is itself subsequently understood and imagined. From a gendered perspective, the figurative space of the home occupies a rather contradictory position in Chinese culture. On one hand, it is frequently gendered as feminine and is associated with the figure of the wife or mother. On the other hand, it is regarded as the space of the patriline and consequently falls under the symbolic purview of the father. In an exogamic society, therefore, the space of the "home" would presumably come to assume a paradoxical quality of familiar unfamiliarity—representing a quintessentially intimate space, but one in which the bride always remains, at some level, an outsider. Below, I consider this quality of familiar unfamiliarity, specifically its relationship to the space of the home, by turning to Freud's discussion of the "uncanny."

In his influential essay of the same title, Freud suggested that the "uncanny" may be defined as "that class of the frightening which leads back to what is known of old and long familiar." He then proceeded to strategically defamiliarize the "old and long familiar" (German) term for "uncanny," *unheimlich*, noting that it literally means "unhomely" but is semantically equivalent to its apparent inverse: *heimlich* ("homely"). Proceeding from this etymological insight, Freud argued that the "uncanny" is located at the knotted intersection of the "homely" and the "unhomely," of the familiar and the unfamiliar.[13] The uncanny, for Freud, marks a figurative "return of the repressed"—the disconcerting reappearance of that which was not only familiar but perhaps even *too* familiar.

13. Freud, "The 'Uncanny,'" 220–21.

This moment of uncanny recognition of the familiar in the unfamiliar, and of the unfamiliar in the familiar, constitutes an important theme in Li Ruzhen's novel. For instance, at a sociocultural level, the travelers' experiences in foreign countries also allow them (and the reader) to perceive their own culture and society through the prism of difference of the foreign country. The most familiar example of this kind of insight occurs in the Country of Women, where the male travelers are treated as "women," thus ostensibly allowing them to reflect on women's oppressed condition in contemporary society. A similar insight is expressed in the Country of Gentlemen. There, Tang Ao asks one of the first inhabitants they encounter whether it is true that all members of the country are in fact "gentlemen." The inhabitant is unable to comprehend the question, much less respond, because he simply does not understand the meaning of the word "gentleman." In a country where everyone is supposedly a "gentleman," there is presumably no need for the concept of *gentleman* in the first place (74/58).

An exception that supports this rule of the recognition/construction of identity through difference can be found in a scene in which Little Hill and her friends meet an Immortal disguised as a nun dressed in ragged clothing. Whereas all of Little Hill's friends see the nun only as a hideous old woman, Little Hill is nevertheless able to perceive that she is an Immortal. By way of explanation, the nun observes:

> "In the *Shijing* 詩經 (Book of odes) it says, 'How does one distinguish between a male and female bird?' This phrase indicates that if one does not belong to a certain species, he can not distinguish between males and females of that species. He who is not a bird himself cannot make the distinction."
>
> "But if they are of the same species, why should they not be able to distinguish; they should be able to tell the difference at a glance," said Little Hill.
>
> "Since this is so, then Immortals should recognize each other at a glance. In the *Yijing* 易經 (Book of changes) it says, 'Only those who are benevolent can recognize benevolence. Only those who are wise can recognize wisdom.' From this the Bodhisattva should recognize my meaning." (374–75/144)

These passages quoted by the nun from the *Book of Odes* and the *Book of Changes* suggest that identity is the product—not of difference and unfamiliarity—but rather of equivalence. At the same time, however, it is significant that this assertion of the relationship between equivalence and identity is posited by a paradigmatically uncanny figure—an old woman who is not at all what she initially appears to be, and who seems eerily knowledgeable about Little Hill herself.

This sense of the "uncanny" is elaborated further in the passage that immediately follows the one cited above:

> When Little Hill heard the words 'hundred flowers,' she was quite astonished, "I wonder if I have already heard these two words 'hundred flowers' before? . . . Perhaps they have something to do with my hidden destiny?" She thought to herself. . . .
>
> Before she [the nun] finished talking, Little Hill asked, "Whom are you looking for?"
>
> "I am looking for the incarnate of the Fairy of a Hundred Flowers."
>
> When Little Hill heard this, she became dazed. It was as though she were half drunk and half awake, and felt an indescribable turmoil in her heart. She was lost in a stupor for a few moments. (375/145)

As we know, Little Hill is herself the mortal incarnate of the Fairy of a Hundred Flowers for whom the nun is searching, even though at this point Little Hill remains unaware of her own identity. Her sense of stupor and turmoil upon hearing the nun's answer, therefore, represents a partial recognition of her own repressed identity.

This uncanny dynamic of familiarity and unfamiliarity is repeated in another passage several pages later, when Little Hill and her friends arrive at the island of Little Penglai in search of Little Hill's father, Tang Ao (who has disappeared from the mortal world after becoming a Taoist immortal). The women finally arrive at the Peak of Flowers in the Mirror, and a village called "Village of the Moon in the Water." What follows is a kind of uncanny textual treasure hunt, in which the women find a series of odd, inscribed texts—none of which makes complete sense to them, but each of which leads them to another, equally mysterious text. First, they meet an old woodcutter, who gives Little Hill a letter from her father informing her that he will not see her until she has passed the imperial examinations and become a "Talented Lady." Little Hill's response is one of bewilderment: "Why? When I am here already and it would be so easy for us to meet? And why does he call me 'Daughter of Tang'?" (400/159). Next, they arrive at an old tomb, where they find the words "Tomb of the Flowers in the Mirror" carved into the stone. Again, their reaction is one of puzzlement: "They did not know what this meant, and were sorry that they could not ask the woodcutter about it" (400/160). Finally, they arrive at a pavilion, textually marked by the characters for "Village of the Moon in the Water" carved in white jade. Within the pavilion they find a large plaque, a jade altar, and a tablet of white jade; all three objects similarly have textual inscriptions. Most important, the tablet contains the names of a hundred girls, including "Tang Guichen," which is to say, "Daughter of Tang."

Furthermore, the ideographs used for the girls' names are perceived differently by Little Hill and her friend Flowerlike. For Flowerlike, the ideographs appear as archaic and unintelligible "seal-script" characters, whereas for Little Hill they instead appear as "perfectly ordinary characters." As with Little Hill's ability to perceive the true identity of the nun in the preceding scene, her ability to read the engraved tablet appears to reinforce the nun's implication that only "like can recognize like." The irony, however, is that this moment of recognition results not in a confirmation of identity but in a process of internal questioning and doubt. Even though Little Hill is able to read the characters, she is nevertheless initially at a loss as to their significance.

For example, following the list of the hundred names inscribed on the jade tablet, Little Hill finds the following verse:

> Vast, vast the wilderness,
> Incredible, incredible the destinies involved;
> If Tang meets Tang,
> Carry the news back to the kingdom on Earth.

> After giving it some thought, Little Hill decided, "The first Tang must refer to the Tang dynasty. The second Tang must mean me, since my surname is Tang. Does it mean that since this is the Tang dynasty, my surname is Tang, and I have seen this tablet, I must therefore take the messages written here back to the Kingdom on Earth?" (410/164–65)

Just as with the green nun and the seal-script ideographs, Little Hill locates difference within the identity affirmed in the relationship between "Tang" and "Tang." Furthermore, there is an apparent continuity between this passage and Lévi-Strauss's discussion of the creation of meaning and communication through the literal and symbolic exchange of women. Here, Little Hill must become an envoy, and it is only *through* her that the significance of her father's text can, in a sense, be realized. That is, she herself occupies an uncanny liminal position with regard to the text of her father: she is close enough to the text to be able to partially understand it, but she herself also represents a figurative displacement of that same text. It is only through her position as Othered Self that the "word of the Father" is able to be made intelligible to the outside world.

This theme of the daughter occupying a liminal position between the figures of the Father and of the external "Other" is reiterated a few pages later when Flowerlike recommends that Little Hill give up trying to find her father and instead merely jot down the inscriptions in her copybook and return home. As Little Hill is considering this advice, she suddenly notices a stone wall on the side of the road with the following inscription:

> The love of father and daughter is human nature,
> How can you forget?
> But you'll look for me in vain though you go to
>   The edge of the sky.
> For us to meet, you must first recall the past,
> Home awaits you on top of [Mt.] Penglai.
>
> It was dated and signed, "Tang Yiting, in view of immediate circumstances."
>
> When Little Hill read the last two lines, *she was stunned. It seemed as if there were something in her past which she could not remember, but she could not think of what it was. She stared at the stone wall as in a stupor.* (412/165–66; italics added)

In this passage, the treatment of Little Hill's past as something eliciting a sense of "stupor" is clearly reminiscent of Freud's discussion of the uncanny as a "return of the repressed." More specifically, the inscription on the jade tablet represents not only the voice of Little Hill's father as well as the celestial "home" from which she has been forcibly displaced but also her own identity and "destiny."

The "uncanniness" of this passage revolves around Little Hill's alienation not only from her own origins but also from her own identity. In particular, Little Hill is unaware of her own status as a figurative intermediary—a status that positions her within the more general textual-cultural structure within which she is figuratively embedded. In the following section, I examine how the novel develops a similar uncanny dialectics of identity and textual dissemination via, not the figure of Little Hill herself, but her own spectral double—a "fairy gibbon" who ultimately steals the inscribed jade tablet from her and subsequently comes to stand in a figuratively meta-textual position with respect to the novel itself.

"Laughing at the Gibbon"

> For several very primitive peoples in the Malay Archipelago the supreme sin, unleashing storm and tempest, comprises a series of superficially incongruous acts which informants list higgledy-piggledy as follows: marriage with near kin; father and daughter or mother and son sleeping too close to one another; . . . laughing at one's own face in the mirror; and, finally, teasing animals and, in particular, dressing a monkey as a man, and making fun of him.
>
> —Claude Lévi-Strauss, *Elementary Structure of Kinship*

In Li Ruzhen's text, the message inscribed on the jade tablet can be seen as complicit, to borrow Cowie's terms, in the "establishment/re-establishment" of the social positions of each of the flower fairies/girls in the novel, insofar as the inscription contains their names and their respective "destinies." However, by the time this "message" reaches the fairies/girls whom it describes, it has already undergone multiple processes of displacement and transformation. First, since the jade tablet on which the message was inscribed cannot be transported directly, it is necessary for Little Hill to transcribe the text of the message into a copybook. Then, by the time Little Hill is finally reunited with the other fairies/girls to relate to them their destinies, the copybook itself has been stolen by a mischievous gibbon, and Little Hill is forced to try to reconstruct its contents from memory (602–3/238). In this way, the "message" is internalized by its original "messenger" (Little Hill)—opening up a wide range of possibilities for the message itself to become altered through a process of repetition and displacement. Furthermore, this scene represents a moment in which the dissemination of the message is bifurcated between two separate messengers (Little Hill and the gibbon), a division suggesting that we may see the figure of the gibbon as a mirror image of Little Hill herself.

The position of this white fairy gibbon is crucial to an understanding of how individual agency can be created through, and in spite of, the cultural/discursive construction of subjectivity. The gibbon (*yuan* 猿)

can be seen as a figurative Other of the Other, a doubly displaced feminine.[14] That is, if it is true that women, in Li Ruzhen's late imperial Chinese society, were on the whole devalued in comparison to men, then the gibbon can be seen as occupying a doubly subordinate position, since it is looked down upon and mocked not only by men but also by women. This particular gibbon first appears in the novel just before Tang Ao reaches Little Penglai and is described as "a white gibbon with red eyes and red spots all over its fur, which stood two feet tall, and was holding some rock fungus in its hands" (329/129). The travelers capture the gibbon in order to obtain the fungus it is carrying and then carry the animal back to the ship, where one of the girls "secured the gibbon with a piece of string, and played with it with Melody Orchid and Flowerlike" (329/130). In this initial encounter, therefore, the gibbon is perceived as a mere animal, to be chased, caught, and played with.

Later, after Tang Ao has departed from the mortal world, the gibbon reappears, again functioning as a mediating element within a system of symbolic exchange. The scene occurs at the beginning of Chapter 43, when the gibbon pulls some bedding out from under a certain Mistress Jiang's bed:

> "What a mischievous gibbon!" said Little Hill. "First he took Wanru's scroll and leafed through it, now he has taken Mistress Jiang's guest bedding and made a mess of it. . . . But why have you put a perfectly good pillow under your bed?" she asked Mistress Jiang.
>
> She then took the bundle away from the gibbon, gave it a closer look, and recognized it as belonging to her family. She lifted the bed curtains and discovered a bundle under the bed. . . . When she had a good look at it, she recognized it to be her father's things. She was going to ask Mistress Jiang for an explanation when her mother walked in and saw her husband's things lying on the floor, and the frightened expression on Mistress Jiang's face. Sensing that this could not mean anything good, she broke into loud wails. (362/138–39)

14. Although the figure of the gibbon may be an allusion to what is almost certainly the most famous simian in Chinese literature, Sun Wukong in *Journey to the West* (a text to which *Flowers in the Mirror* bears many obvious resemblances and even explicitly alludes to in several places), at the same time the origins of the figure of Sun Wukong himself are, at the same time, a matter of considerable dispute. For a discussion of these debates, see Jing Wang, *The Story of the Stone*, 221–50.

Here, the gibbon's handling of Tang's Ao's possessions places the gibbon in the position of a messenger bringing Little Hill a cryptic message about her father's disappearance. Subsequent passages elaborate the process whereby the role of "messenger" shifts from the daughter to the fairy gibbon. After Little Hill has copied down the list of prophecies from the jade tablet, the white gibbon snatches the copybook away from her and appears to express great interest in it. Little Hill responds by joking: "I have seen you abstain from meat and you meditate too. But how can you recognize the writings on this tablet? Why do you want to take it to look at? Maybe after a few hundred years you will acquire the Dao 道 [the Way], and then you will help me find a writer who will record all the events for us?" (423/170). Somewhat later, Little Hill's joke about the gibbon's apparent ability to read the text is repeated, although this time Little Hill begins to suspect that it might not be a mere joke after all:

"Can the white gibbon read?" asked Melody laughing.

"I wouldn't know," said the Daughter of Tang. "When I was copying the notes on board the ship overseas, the white gibbon stood beside me and watched. At that time I said to it in fun, if there was man who could record the history of the lives of the people whose names are carved on the jade tablet for posterity to enjoy, would it please go and find him, and do us all a great service? I wonder if the gibbon intends to do so?"

"No wonder he is reading it so intently!" said Red Lotus, joking, and then asked the gibbon, "Are you going to undertake the job?"

The white gibbon gave a snort and nodded and, taking the notes with it, leaped out of the window, and from below, made a funny face at them. The three of them stared out the window at the gibbon in amazement. (465–66/188)

Considerable emphasis is placed in the novel on the question of who can or cannot read certain texts, and therefore it is significant that the gibbon appears to be able to read the text in the Daughter of Tang's copybook, when none of the girls except the Daughter of Tang is able to make any sense of it. The Daughter of Tang rationalizes the gibbon's behavior by recounting her joke when the gibbon first appeared to express interest in the text of the copybook. The gibbon responds by grabbing the notes and running away and then, from a safe distance, making a "funny face" at the girls. Here, the hierarchical relationships between the girls and the gibbon are inverted—with the gibbon, which had previously merely been the butt of the girls' jokes, here actively taking the copied text from the girls, and then proceeding to laugh at *them*.

In the end, the gibbon does indeed have the last laugh, as the text Little Hill copied from the jade tablet at the Pavilion of the Flowers in the Mirror (the text containing the "destinies" of all of the flower fairies) becomes conflated with the text of the novel itself, in turn becoming subsumed within an outer, meta-textual frame. The structure of this frame effectively mirrors the general dynamics of signification I have sketched above in anthropological/psychoanalytic terms, and which, I have argued, constitutes one of the primary narrative forces of the novel. In this outer frame of the novel, the gibbon ultimately assumes this position of the figurative exogamic "daughter" and, in the process, becomes the bearer of a message that will ultimately serve both to bridge and to reaffirm this figurative gap between Self and Other. This is most evident, for instance, in the last paragraph in the novel:

> As for the white gibbon, it was a fairy gibbon who had lived in the cave of the Fairy of a Hundred Flowers for many years. When the Fairy of a Hundred Flowers was ordered to earth, it had come, too, with the intention of waiting for Daughter of Tang and returning to the cave with her. However, when Daughter of Tang told it to take the record of what was written on the jade tablet in the Lament for the Beauty Pavilion, and go find a scholar or historian to write about it, the gibbon then proceeded to go in search of him. (892–93/290)

In this way, the gibbon ultimately comes to occupy a position figuratively transcending the text of the novel.[15] The gibbon not only displaces the figurative "daughter" as a conveyer of the father's text but also, as a bearer of the text of the novel itself, ultimately assumes a position transcending even that of the "father" himself.

To the extent that the fairy gibbon comes to stand as a figure for textual production, it is mirrored within the novel by an uncanny reflec-

15. It is ironically appropriate, furthermore, that, precisely at this point when the novel is most explicitly concerned with issues of authorship and textual transmission, it tropes most directly on its eighteenth-century literary "model," *Dream of the Red Chamber*, and particularly the Taoist Vanitas's search, at the end of the novel, for a suitable "author" to copy out the text and publish it.

tion of itself. This mirror image of the fairy gibbon can be found embedded at a point in the novel before the fairy gibbon has even made its first appearance at Little Penglai. In particular, I am thinking of an odd-looking fantasy animal known as an "indeed" (*guoran* 果然), described as "in appearance resembling a gibbon" (*xingxiang ru yuan* 形象如猿). Simultaneously like and unlike the fairy gibbon (both are white in color, but the indeed is covered with black marks [*wen* 紋], whereas the fairy gibbon has red spots), the indeed occupies a position in the text that simultaneously affirms and questions concepts of identity and representation.

I quote the passages describing the indeed at length because my analysis hinges on a close reading of how this enigmatic creature is represented and misrepresented within the novel:

> A strange-looking animal appeared on a hill. It resembled a gibbon, with a white coat with black lines on it, and was about four feet long, with a tail which was almost two feet long after it was wound around the body. Its fur was fine and long, and there were black whiskers under its chin. They saw that it was guarding the dead body of another indeed and crying very hard.
>
> ". . . Is that an 'indeed'?" asked Lin.
>
> "It is indeed," said Old Tuo. "It is also called the indeed animal. It has a fierce loyalty to its own kind, which is why this particular indeed is crying. . . . I suppose the dead indeed has been left there as a lure by a hunter. Soon, he'll come along and catch the live one without any trouble, because an indeed will always stop to weep over a dead one." . . .
>
> When the large hairy tiger suddenly appeared from out of a high peak, the indeed shuddered with fright, but still did not leave the carcass of its dead companion. The tiger let out a blood-curdling screech, and opened its huge mouth and started to clamp its jaws on the indeed. But an arrow flew out from the side of the hills, and pierced it precisely in the eye.

The fact that the tiger is struck precisely in the eye is not coincidental, since Old Tuo, in his subsequent rationalization of the scene they have just witnessed, proceeds to stress the issue of the tiger's *vision*, and more specifically its ostensible ability to *see through* the indeed's outer appearance and perceive its inner virtue:

> "Seeing the tiger attack the indeed has made me think," said Lin. "I have heard it said that when a man meets a tiger, whether the tiger eats him or not depends upon destiny, and if it isn't in one's destiny to be eaten by a tiger,

the tiger will not harm him even though he comes face to face with it. Is that true?"

"No, indeed," said Old Tuo, shaking his head. "Actually, tigers don't want to eat people at all. It is best put this way: if a tiger eats a man, it is because it mistakes him for a beast, because the man is like a beast in some way. Actually, tigers and leopards are afraid of human beings. The reason why some people are mistaken for beasts by tigers is this: we men all have a radiance over our heads, and a tiger will shy away from it when it sees it. But if a man's light is dimmed through evil-doing, the tiger will mistake him for a beast, for beasts don't have any radiance. The brightness of a man's light depends on his goodness, and a good bright light will not only keep tigers away, but all kinds of evil spirits as well. That is the difference between human beings and animals. But take the indeed, for instance, who would not abandon its dead friend. Indeed, it may be said to have a beast's face, but a human heart. How are we to know that it does not have a radiance over its head, too, for did not the tiger ignore, and not harm it? By the same token, when a tiger sees a man with a human face and a beast's heart, why would it not eat him? People hate tigers for injuring people, but they really don't know why they do it." (62–70/51–55)

The contradictions in the way the indeed is textually represented underscore tensions characteristic of processes of signification and communication in general, particularly with respect to the representation of women in Chinese society during this period. To begin with, the gibbon is represented as being both human-like and, at the same time, not quite human, just as women are perceived as being inscribed with a mark of difference or "lack" of some sort—simultaneously linking them to, and distinguishing them from, the presumptive standard of (male) humanity. Second, Old Tuo's and Merchant Lin's description of the indeed's "fierce loyalty to its own kind" is also characterized by this kind of ambivalent self-interested use of the figure of the Other, in that this valorization of the indeed's virtue is used to justify and naturalize the possibility of *human* virtue. Thus, it is clear that Old Tuo's allegory is not really about tigers or indeeds but about trying to create and justify a position for people themselves.

Old Tuo not only elaborates the fable of indeed loyalty in order to justify *human* virtue, but even goes so far as to distort the actual circumstances that ostensibly serve as the basis for his own parable in the first place. Specifically, the crux of this miniature morality tale comes down to Old Tuo's contention that the reason the tiger ignored, and *did not* try to devour, the indeed was precisely because it recognized that the indeed actually possessed an "aura" indicative of its inherent morality (despite its superficial, beast-like features). This certainly makes for a good story, but it conveniently contradicts the fact that not only did the tiger *not* ignore the indeed but would almost certainly have devoured it, had it not been for the fortuitous appearance of a girl named Red Lotus, who was in the process of exterminating all the tigers on the mountain as an act of filial piety to avenge her mother, who was killed by tigers.

The reason the travelers are able to encounter (and consequently comment and pontificate on) the indeed's virtue in the first place is precisely because they happen to see the indeed mourning the corpse of one of its fellows. Furthermore, Old Tuo himself matter-of-factly points out that hunters, familiar with the indeeds' distinctive behavior, generally set traps for them by leaving behind the body of a dead indeed to serve as a lure. In fact, Old Tuo speculates that this same scheme might itself have been responsible for the death of this particular indeed as well. The way in which the indeed's own supposed virtue functions to trap it within a variety of systems of oppression is, in turn, reminiscent of the ways in which discourses of female virtue in China have themselves traditionally been complicit in the effective oppression of women (as is arguably the case, for instance, with the Neo-Confucian emphasis on widow chastity and its attendant idealization of suicide as a means of protecting that chastity). The indeed's liminal status at the margins of human subjectivity makes it, like women, an ideal vehicle for negotiating the construction and bridging of the boundary between Self and Other. Insofar as this negotiation of the boundary between Self and Other is intricately intertwined with the communicative process, the indeed can be read as a trope for signification in general: a *tabula rasa* onto which people like Old Tuo can inscribe their moralizing narratives,[16] just as the indeed's spectral reflection, the fairy gibbon, is

16. The indeed is described as being covered by black lines, or *wen* 紋—a term homophonic with, and etymologically related to, the term *wen* 文, which may be translated as "text" or "culture." The indeed, therefore, is described as being physically covered in "text/culture," just as rhetorically it provides a site for others to inscribe their own moralizing narratives.

also presented as being, at a meta-textual level, a figurative embodiment of language itself.

Both the indeed and the fairy gibbon are positioned at the margins of the human image, evoking a distinctly uncanny combination of familiarity and unfamiliarity. Both gibbons simultaneously embody tensions between the human and nonhuman, male and female, Self and Other, equality and oppression, signifier and signified, and communication and miscommunication. In short, they symbolize a return of a repressed rupture lying behind the construction of truth and identity on the back of nontruth, nonidentity, and the feminine. For further insight into the status of the gibbon in Li Ruzhen's text, we may return briefly to Lévi-Strauss's *Elementary Structures of Kinship*, the same study in which he developed his theory of the semiotic dimensions of exogamic exchange. In a discussion of the kinds of cultural prohibitions found among some "very primitive" peoples of the Malay archipelago, Lévi-Strauss presented a view of language that seems to overlap very suggestively with the kind of uncanniness embodied by the figure of the gibbon in Li Ruzhen's text:

> For several very primitive peoples in the Malay Archipelago the supreme sin, unleashing storm and tempest, comprises a series of superficially incongruous acts which informants list higgledy-piggledy as follows: marriage with near kin; *father and daughter* or mother and son *sleeping too close to one another*; . . . laughing at one's own face in the mirror; and, finally, teasing animals and, *in particular, dressing a monkey as a man, and making fun of him*. . . . All these prohibitions can be reduced to a single common denominator: *they all constitute a misuse of language*, and on this ground they are grouped together by the incest prohibition, or with acts evocative of incest. What does this mean, except that *women themselves are treated as signs*, which are *misused* [italics in original] when not put to the use reserved to signs, which is to be communicated?[17] (Except as noted, italics added)

Drawing on his earlier semiotic reading of exogamic exchange, Lévi-Strauss suggested that, in the Malay culture described here, the ultimate taboo lies in failing to distinguish objects that resemble each other *too* closely—mistaking a monkey for a man, or a mirror reflection for an actual face. Under this view, figurative incest ("father and daughter . . .

17. Lévi-Strauss, *The Elementary Structure of Kinship*, 494–96.

sleeping too close together"), or in other words a breakdown of the exogamic imperative, represents a confusion of near-likenesses—namely, a failure to effectively distinguish close kin from the available mates whom they otherwise resemble.

Its own name ironically suggesting self-evidence, the simian indeed stands paradoxically as both an assertion and a subversion of similitude. Like Lévi-Strauss's figures of the monkey and the mirror image, the indeed marks a fault line in the orders of similitude and difference that structure the social world of Li Ruzhen's novel. More generally, I argue that *Flowers in the Mirror* can be seen as an uncanny play, a process of simultaneously remembering and repressing the realization that the use of language is necessarily grounded on the possibility of its *mis*use. In other words, the very possibility of representation itself necessarily contains, and is in fact grounded on, the possibility of misrepresentation.

Avian Specularities

> "In the *Book of Odes* it says, 'How does one distinguish between a male and female bird?' This phrase indicates that if one does not belong to a certain species, he cannot distinguish between males and females of that species. He who is not a bird himself cannot make the distinction."
>
> —Li Ruzhen, *Flowers in the Mirror*

The argument that representation and subjectivity are grounded on a sublimated moment of specular misrecognition is also one of the central claims of Jacques Lacan's influential "Mirror Stage" essay, which contends that the infant's conception of self is grounded on its seminal moment of *misrecognition* of its own external mirror image. Near the middle of the essay there is a rather peculiar piece of ornithological errata, in which Lacan draws attention to a

> biological experimentation that is itself so alien to the idea of psychical causality that it cannot bring itself to formulate its results in these terms. It nevertheless recognizes that it is a necessary condition for the maturation of the gonad of the female pigeon that it should see another member of its species, of either sex; so sufficient in itself is this condition that the desired effect may be obtained merely by placing the individual within reach of the field of reflection of a mirror.[18]

18. Lacan, "The Mirror Stage," 3.

Mirroring the specular dynamics of the mirror stage, Lacan cites the example of the pigeon's maturation—a biological example that initially strikes him as profoundly "alien to the idea of psychical causality"—and then he himself proceeds to "identify" with the model of psychic formation it appears to suggest. This ornithological excursion ironi-cally reinforces some of the methodological and epistemological questions that persistently haunt Lacan's famous essay as a whole. That is, although he cloaks his argument in an air of empirical objectivity, his model often appears to be most useful when interpreted metaphorically—*not* as describing a specific moment in child development but as gesturing to a more abstract process of the subject's interaction with culturally created externalized images.

Lacan's account is oddly reminiscent of another avian anecdote, one that appears in Lévi-Strauss's famous anthropological travelogue, *Tristes Tropiques.* The anecdote concerns the French-Corsican "B____ brothers," who, before becoming garage proprietors, made a living hunting egrets. Their technique "consisted in placing cornets of white paper on the ground in such a way that when the tall birds, *fascinated by the immaculate whiteness similar to their own*, thrust their beaks into them, they became hoods which blinded the birds and made them easy to capture" (italics added).[19] This anecdote of the hooded egret can be seen as a concise allegorical description of Lévi-Strauss's own anthropological project—in which the anthropologist implicitly finds himself so fascinated by the apparently "immaculate" pristineness of the "primitive" peoples he encounters, particularly insofar as he sees them as a reflection of his own culture's past (and future?), that he metaphorically thrusts his analytical beak into them and is, in turn, blinded to his own complicity in the process.

I have argued in this chapter that critics interested in the issue of the apparent "feminism," or lack thereof, of Li Ruzhen's *Flowers in the Mirror* run a similar risk of being "blinded," like the egrets, by the *images* of women circulating throughout the text and of failing to pay sufficient attention to the mechanisms through which those representations are produced. Both Li Ruzhen's novel and many of the twentieth-century

19. Lévi-Strauss, *Tristes Tropiques*, 206–7.

debates over the significance (positive *or* negative) of the novel's apparent feminist implications were produced in cultural climates in which the sign of "woman" was frequently used as a figurative screen for the projection of a multitude of other sociocultural concerns, many of which were quite unrelated to actual women. For this reason, I would suggest that the gendered significance of Li Ruzhen's novel lies not so much in the work's actual representations of flowers/women but in the ways in which the text as a whole reflects on the nature of these representational processes themselves. To lose sight of this is to run the risk of sharing the symbolic fate of the pheasant, described in the novel as living at the Phoenix and Unicorn Mountain. Like Lévi-Strauss's hooded egrets, whose capture is made possible by their specular obsession with their own sublimated image, Li Ruzhen's pheasant is depicted as being obsessed with its visual similarity with the highly esteemed phoenix, despite the fact that the pheasant lacks all of the phoenix's inner virtues. The pheasant's specular obsession yields it the fate of an avian Narcissus condemned to eternal, uncanny repetition:

> "That's the pheasant," said Old Tuo, "which is very vain about its looks, and often drowns in the water, *dazed from admiring its own reflection.* It has all the phoenix's outward appearance, but none of its virtues, and is sometimes called the dumb-phoenix." (162–63/78; italics added)

3

Chen Sen and the Coin of Gender

> Making prices, assessing values, thinking out equivalents, exchanging—all this preoccupied the primal thoughts of man to such an extent that in a certain sense it constituted *thinking* itself.
>
> — Friedrich Nietzsche, *Human, All Too Human*

Near the beginning of Chen Sen's 陳森 1849 novel *Pinhua baojian* 品花寶鑒 (Precious mirror for evaluating flowers), several maidservants gather in the bedroom of one of the novel's protagonists, the opera patron Mei Ziyu, and are admiring the exquisiteness of its decoration. The newly arrived maidservant Ba, in particular, is fascinated by the portrait of the

> young beauty painted on the mirrored screen (*jingping* 鏡屏). He had a powdered face and rouged lips, refined elegance and blinding splendor (*guanghua yaomu* 光華耀目), and she felt as if she had never seen with her own eyes (*jue yanzhong cong wei jianguo* 覺眼中從未見過) such a beautiful person.[1]

Ba asks maidservant Sun who the subject of the portrait is, and Sun replies with a smile, "This is our future 'uncle'; isn't it a perfect resemblance (*zhen huade xiang* 真畫得象)!"

The emphasis on the visual quality of Mei Ziyu's portrait in this early scene is significant, since his position in the novel is explicitly linked to his status as a patron and observer of *kunqu* opera, and particularly his relationship with Du Qinyan, a male *kunqu* performer specializing in *dan*

1. Chen Sen, *Pinhua baojian*, 66. Subsequent references to this work are cited in parentheses in the text. All translations from this work are my own.

旦, or female, roles. It is significant that the emphasis in Mei Ziyu's initial appearance is precisely on his own private "mirrored screen." The mirrored screen carries connotations not only of Ziyu's *self-regard* (i.e., in the mirror) but also of processes of external perception (the screen as symbol of voyeuristic observation). Within the novel itself, mirrors are used as symbols of the social reproduction of gendered norms, as well as of the potential inversion of those same norms. The *precious mirror* in the novel's title refers specifically to a "flower selection" (*huaxuan* 花選) competition, in which the novel's elite *dan* performers are evaluated and publicly ranked by their (male) admirers. The contest is a parodic hybrid of the processes by which (male) viewers established the literal worth of female courtesans and opera performers and by which the male scholars were themselves externally evaluated through, for instance, the civil service examinations (on which the "flower selection" competition was partially modeled). More generally, however, *precious mirror* connotes the logics of specular valuation that underlie the work as a whole.

In this chapter, I take the figure of Mei Ziyu's mirrored screen as my starting point for considering the intersecting themes of gendered identity, sexual desire, and axiological valuation in Chen Sen's novel. More specifically, I argue that the novel initially holds up the figure of the mirror as a model for a kind of reflexive transparence of appearance and identity but then complicates it with the figure of the screen, which cuts across these neatly dichotomous relations and marks a space for the projection of assumptions and fantasies. Gender, as a result, becomes not a function of equivalence but the product of a complex circuit of fantasy and perception, continually re-established as it is circulated between representations and gazes.

Precious Mirror and the Price of Passion

The flower on its stem does not feel for Man, but sometimes the
reflection of love is better than the reality.
Perhaps I should put myself into the mirror's realm and forget
the flower and self of the world outside!

—Zhong Xing 鍾惺

Completed in 1849, Chen Sen's *Precious Mirror for Evaluating Flowers* dates from a period when China's political and cultural identities were increasingly coming under attack, as a result of growing Western influence following the Opium War, an increasingly acute silver drain, and a weakened imperial center. It was also precisely during this period when these same identities began to be asserted most emphatically in fictional narratives such as *Precious Mirror*. Like *Flowers in the Mirror*, *Precious Mirror for Evaluating Flowers* features an abundance of the esoteric discussions and literary parlor games typically associated with the late imperial genre of the literati novel. Furthermore, Chen Sen's novel not only builds on Li Ruzhen's attention to issues of gender performativity but also extends them to include an exploration of issues of romantic and sexual desire. The main plot of *Precious Mirror* follows the melodramatic courtship of two pairs of male lovers, with each pair consisting of a *dan*-role-playing opera performer and his male benefactor.[2] The presentation of these two couples is quite idealized and platonic, although considerable attention is given to the specific financial relationships that bind the actors both to their original opera masters and to their subsequent patrons. At the same time, these idealized romance narratives are contrasted with several intersecting subplots involving an assortment of secondary characters whose sexual predilections are described in considerable detail. As such, the novel represents a cross between idealized *caizi jiaren* 才子佳人 (talented scholar and beautiful woman) romances such as *Dream of the Red Chamber*, on one hand, and the late imperial tradition of erotic fiction best exemplified by the mid-Ming novel *Jinping mei* 金瓶梅 (Plum in the golden vase), on the other.

Although Chinese discourses and practices of homoeroticism have enjoyed a surge of visibility since the 1990s, this attention stands in sharp contrast to the comparative invisibility of homoeroticism in China during most of the twentieth century, particularly under the Communist and Nationalist regimes in China and Taiwan during the post-1949 period. Historically speaking, however, allusions to same-sex desire in pre-twentieth-century China were quite common, with examples ranging

2. Of these two pairs, one—that of the *dan* performer Du Qinyan and his patron and lover Mei Ziyu—is generally regarded as merely fictitious, but it has long been recognized that the second pair—Su Huifang and Tian Chunhang—was modeled on the historical figures Bi Qiufan 畢秋帆 (a governor-general of Hunan and Hubei) and Li Guiguan 李桂官, his lifelong partner. For a discussion, see David Der-wei Wang, *Fin-de-siècle Splendor*, 63.

from laborers in all-male communities to elite men and their social inferiors. In fact, such classic romances as *Peony Pavilion* and *Dream of the Red Chamber* include explicit discussions of male same-sex desire. Chen Sen's novel represents a fusion of discourse and practice, insofar as it was based on an actual same-sex couple and represents a logical extrapolation of the familiar genre of same-sex romance. Although it was probably not until the twentieth century that the figure of the homosexual emerged as a distinct *identity* in China, this process arguably originated during the mid-Qing, at a time when legal codes began to refer specifically to same-sex relations.[3]

In the discussion of *Flowers in the Mirror* in Chapter 2, I took Melody Orchid's departure from the Country of Fork-Tongued People as marking a point of intersection of the novel's interests in issues of gender and linguistics. Here, I similarly open my discussion of *Precious Mirror* by considering a parallel point of intersection between the novel's linguistic/literary and gendered/sexual concerns. More specifically, at various points *Precious Mirror* uses literary or linguistic arguments to legitimate male-male desire. For instance, near the beginning of the work, a character by the name of Zhong Qing advances a detailed etymological argument that certain compounds like *meiren* 美人 (beautiful woman/person) and *jiaren* 佳人 (exemplary woman/person)—both frequently regarded as having specifically feminine connotations—have a long textual tradition of being applied to individuals of *either* sex. To support his claim, Zhong Qing cites a series of passages from classical texts dating as far back as the *Book of Odes* (compiled ca. 400 BCE), all of which use the adjectives *mei* and *jia* to refer to men.

Zhong Qing's etymological argument is echoed by a subsequent discussion of whether the word *se* 色—"passion" or "sexual attraction"—does or does not specifically connote a "heterosexual" attraction between men and women. Here, Tian Chunhang (another female-role-playing *kunqu* actor, who parallels Mei Ziyu as one of the novel's four main protagonists) advances his argument in no uncertain terms:

> What I find most incomprehensible is why contemporary people regard love for a woman to be common/normal (*chang* 常) and love for a man to be

3. Sommer, *Sex, Law, and Society in Late Imperial China.*

> unusual/deviant (*yi* 異). After all, since both are instances of passion (*se*),[4] what need is there to distinguish between man and woman? To love women but not men is lust (*yin* 淫) rather than passion. To be lustful cannot be considered passion, and we dare not regard passion as mere lust. (135)

This passage is frequently cited in contemporary discussions of the novel's homoerotic themes. Much more rarely discussed are Chunhang's subsequent remarks, in which his focus shifts from the *objects* of desire to the nature of desire itself:

> What I also find most incomprehensible is when people value equally the two terms wealth (*cai* 財) and passion (*se*); when they not only treasure passion [for people], but at the same time stingily hoard their wealth. They try to exchange a rotten and decayed clod of dirt and dung for a miraculously fragrant precious flower. Which is negligible and which is important? It would be splendid to be able to distinguish between the two! (135)

On a moral, didactic plane, the rhetorical positions Chunhang adopts in these two passages seem roughly parallel: true "passion," he advocates, should be distinguished both from mere heterosexual "licentiousness" and from monetary avarice. However, in a sense the two claims implicitly contradict each other: the first position holds that one should value passion itself, irrespective of its object; the second contends that the object *does* matter and that certain foci of libidinal attachment are valued more than others.

Although this reading of Chunhang's distinction might appear to involve a pedantic logical quibble over the nature and object of desire, I argue that the novel explores the interrelationship between different forms of (material) attachment and (libidinal) transference. In particular, I examine the ways in which these issues are developed in some of the novel's minor subplots—subplots that thematize a series of libidinal transferences to and from fetishized objects such as pieces of jewelry, which may be seen as quintessential instances of the wealth to which Chunhang argues one must remain unattached.

4. *Se* 色 is sometimes translated "lust," but since it is being explicitly contrasted in this passage with the more pejorative *yin*, it seems appropriate to interpret it here as having a more neutral connotation.

Boys and Bracelets

She threw a quince at me;
In requital I gave a bright girdle-stone.
No, not just in requital;
But meaning I would love her for ever.

—*The Book of Odes*

Two of the novel's more prominent secondary characters, who stand as comical foils for the two idealized pairs of pure and virtuous protagonists, are the drinking buddies Xi Shiyi and Pan San. Even when these two characters do not appear together, their respective narratives proceed in uncanny synchronicity. Below I discuss a couple of instances of this sort of narrative parallelism between these two minor characters—the first involving a double exchange of bracelets; the second, a recurrent anxiety about the significance of the anatomical penis. In each case, I suggest that these fortuitous parallels at the level of the work's narrative structure help to underscore the relationship, in the novel itself, between processes of circulation and the creation and affirmation of different kinds of value.

The first example of this sort of narrative parallelism occurs in a pair of minor subplots recounted in Chapters 36 and 40. The first subplot begins with a description of Xi Shiyi's infatuation with the actor Du Qinyan, specifically his decision to "borrow" a jadeite bracelet from his concubine Ju Hua in order to give it to Qinyan as a token of his affection. When Ju Hua asks him why he is taking her bracelet, he invents an excuse: "I just want to compare its color with someone else's, after which I will bring it right back."[5] When Xi Shiyi attempts to give the bracelet to Qinyan, however, Qinyan politely refuses it. Xi Shiyi mistakes his gesture of refusal for one of acceptance and places the bracelet onto Qinyan's outstretched wrist. Qinyan immediately removes it and, in the process, drops it to the ground, shattering it into three

5. The reference to "comparing color" (*biyibi yanse* 比一比顏色) of the bracelet (which itself serves as a fulcrum between Xi Shiyi's heterosexual and [desired] homosexual attachments) appears to pun on the Chapter 12 discussion of the gender specificity (or lack thereof) of the concept *se* (which I have provisionally translated as "passion" in the preceding discussion, but which is also the same character used to mean "color" in the Xi Shiyi passage).

pieces. The chapter concludes with one of their acquaintances, Ba Yingguan, attempting to make light of the situation by joking that "if the bracelet was originally worth one thousand strings of cash, then these three bracelet pieces together must now be worth three thousand strings!" (410). After a brief digression, this subplot resumes at the beginning of Chapter 40, when Ju Hua asks Xi Shiyi about the bracelet, and he tells her that he has misplaced it. Shortly afterward, however, she discovers the truth and becomes rather upset. At this point, the narrative focus abruptly shifts to another subplot involving Pan San—one that, with its own parallel reference to three bracelets, could be seen as a symbolic realization of Ba Yingguan's joke at the end of the earlier installment.

The second subplot begins with an account of Pan San's (Pan the Third) relation with a well-built sixteen-year-old lad in his shop by the name of Xu *laosan* (Old Xu the Third). Pan San has long been sexually attracted to him. Xu *laosan* happens to have a weakness for alcohol, and Pan San gets him so drunk that he passes out. Pan San then rapes him and afterward inserts bundles of human hair into Xu *laosan*'s anus, thus producing an acute itch that can be relieved through sodomy. Xu *laosan* is naturally rendered quite distraught by this turn of events but initially is powerless to do anything about it. However, he happens to have an older sister, referred to as Zhou *xiaosan* (Missy Zhou Number Three) and San *jie* (Third Sister), who is described as being "only nineteen years old and extremely beautiful, humorous, eloquent, and exceedingly intelligent. If she were a man, she would surely be an extremely accomplished one, but as it turned out she was only a woman" (451). This older sister comes up with a plan to avenge her brother's abuse by seducing Pan San and then arranging for him to be caught with his proverbial pants down.

The first time that San *jie* seduces and subsequently entraps Pan San, she settles for merely having him discovered and embarrassed. The second time she demands his gold bracelet as blackmail. It is not until the third time, however, that she explains to him that she is seeking revenge on behalf of her brother. Comprehending at last, Pan San asks her in distress how much money she wants. She replies that she merely wants him to give her two more gold bracelets worth eight *liang* each. In addition, she exacts further revenge by inserting the bundle of hair into Pan San's anus.

In the end, San *jie* relieves Pan San of three bracelets, which are then sold for precisely three hundred strings of cash. This repetition of threes is apparently not coincidental, since the names of all the major participants in this little vignette contain the character for "three," or *san* 三: Pan San, Xu *laosan*, Zhou *xiaosan* / San *jie*. At one level, this trifecta of threes can be seen as simply another instance of the sort of wordplay that pervades the novel.[6] At the same time, the juxtaposition of this play of names with the related discussions of the tripled bracelets (viz., Xi Shiyi's three bracelet fragments and Pan San's three gold bracelets, with the latter being symbolically divided and reapportioned into three hundred strings of cash) suggests the possibility of an alternative reading, one that unifies the novel's interests in gender and wordplay. Specifically, the bracelets are used as intermediaries between different values (e.g., monetary values) or libidinal loci (witness Xi Shiyi's revealing decision to use his own concubine's bracelet as a gift for Qinyan, on whom he has designs). Moreover, the positions of these values or libidinal loci do not exist independently of the sort of intermediary exemplified by the bracelet; rather, they are created dialectically through the process of exchange itself. One implication of this argument is that the bracelet not only stands as a figure that mediates between independent, isolated points on the linguistic and libidinal topographies but also can be seen as contributing to the constitution of these same topographies even as it circulates through them.

Building on this reading of the two sets of bracelets, I would suggest that Chen Sen's novel presents a parallel between the circulation of bracelets and other jewelry, on one hand, and the circulation and exchange of the young opera performers, on the other. Both jewelry and actors are presented as functioning as tokens of exchange (when they are reduced to their presumptive monetary value) and also as unique, irreplaceable objects that necessarily transcend monetary valuations. Like the pieces of jewelry, the young boys also enter into circuits of exchange in which they mediate between different libidinal and monetary

6. In fact, a few chapters earlier, in Chapter 36, various characters play a word game which is explicitly described as "making 'one' into 'three'" (416; *wo you ge 'yi' zi zuowei 'san' zi de ling* 我有个'一' 字作为'三'字的令).

loci of value. For instance, an evocative parallel to the figure of Xi Shiyi's bracelet can be found at the beginning of the Xi Shiyi / Du Qinyan subplot described above, when Qinyan is told by another actor that his "master" (*shifu* 師父), Chang Qing, has passed away and that Qinyan must therefore return to Chang Qing's hometown in order to pay his respects. This announcement is, in turn, embedded within a series of events and discussions concerning Qinyan's own status as a commodity.

Some ten chapters earlier, the wealthy Lord Hua (Hua *gongzi*) had expressed an interest in purchasing Qinyan out of his state of apprenticeship to Chang Qing, but he and Chang were unable to agree on a price. While the proposed purchase is still under consideration, Xi Shiyi makes his first appearance in the novel and immediately sets his lecherous sights on Qinyan. In order to shield Qinyan from Xi Shiyi, Chang Qing decides to have Qinyan provisionally move to the Hua mansion but without having Lord Hua purchase him outright. In this way, Qinyan enters into a complicated arrangement in which he has simultaneous, and somewhat conflicting, financial *and* social obligations to *both* Chang Qing and Lord Hua. In Chapter 36, these conflicting obligations come to the fore when Qinyan has to request a month's leave from Lord Hua to pay his respects to the deceased Chang Qing. This journey precipitates another chain of events that ultimately results in Qinyan's formal emancipation from both sets of obligations. When Qinyan returns to his master's home, his master's widow informs him that she expects him to either continue paying his monthly maintenance fees or arrange to be purchased outright (Chapter 43). Qinyan and his friends opt for the latter, after realizing that the purchase has the ancillary effect of emancipating Qinyan from his "social" obligations to the Hua mansion as well.

This question of Qinyan's social and financial obligations to Chang Qing and Lord Hua build, in turn, on a series of detailed discussions about the relationship between Qinyan's monetary value, on one hand, and his status as a potentially autonomous individual, on the other. For example, at one point Qinyan's friends, Wei Pincai and Ye Maolin, discuss with Chang Qing the proposed purchase of Qinyan at great length:

[Chang Qing:] "You know, in half a year, he [Qinyan] has earned more than ten thousand [taels]; so you can just imagine how much he would be able to

Fig. 1 The Empress Dowager Cixi gazing at a hand mirror. 1903. Photographer: Xunling (1874–1943). Photograph courtesy Freer Gallery of Art and Arthur M. Sackler Gallery, Smithsonian Institution, Washington, DC.

Fig. 2 Empress Dowager Cixi in the guise of Avalokitesvara. 1903. Photographer: Xunling. Photograph courtesy Freer Gallery of Art and Arthur M. Sackler Gallery, Smithsonian Institution, Washington, DC.

Fig. 3 Photograph of a portrait of the Empress Dowager painted by Katherine Carl (1865–1938). Photograph courtesy Freer Gallery of Art and Arthur M. Sackler Gallery, Smithsonian Institution, Washington, DC.

Fig. 4 Su Hanchen, *Lady at Her Dressing Table in a Garden*. Fan painting mounted as an album leaf. Photograph © 2008, Museum of Fine Arts, Boston.

Fig. 5 Huang Mingqi, "Painting the Self-Portrait." Woodblock illustration of a scene from *The Peony Pavilion* (1617 ed.).

Fig. 6 Su Hanchen, *Lady at Her Dressing Table in a Garden* (detail). Photograph © 2008, Museum of Fine Arts, Boston.

Fig. 7 Eileen Chang, "Turquoise photograph" and "Silk-shirt photograph," from Chang's *Mutual Reflections* (1994). © Eileen Chang Estate.

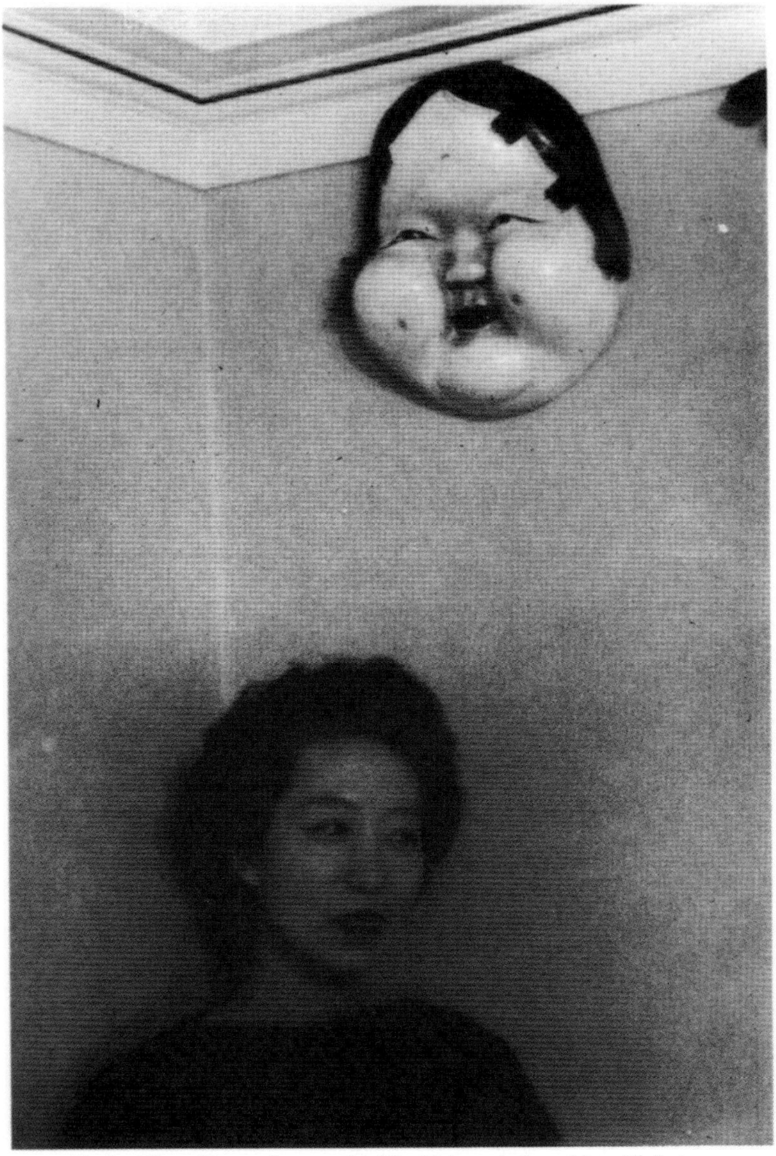

Fig. 8 Eileen Chang, photograph with a Noh mask, from *Mutual Reflections*.

earn in five years. I couldn't even begin to speculate as to how much that might be. In any case, all that I ask is that Lord Hua think it over, that is all."

Ye Maolin then consulted with Pincai. Pincai shook his head and said, "This is hard to talk about. You are proposing to sell a young boy for ten thousand taels of silver; but, after all, he isn't an extraordinarily precious object. From my perspective, four or five thousand taels would be perfectly adequate." (292)

Here, as in numerous other scenes throughout the novel, Qinyan's friends essentially fall into the same trap observed in *Flowers in the Mirror*, insofar as their attempts to purchase Qinyan's freedom inevitably reaffirm the same systems of economic commodification they are ostensibly attempting to subvert.[7] Qinyan's purchase out of apprenticeship, in other words, is possible only through an explicit acknowledgment of his own monetary value.

In discussing *Flowers in the Mirror*, I suggested that economies of exchange, instead of being formally negated, often might simply be translated from an overtly "economic" to an implicitly sociocultural level. In *Precious Mirror*, we may observe a similar phenomenon: the repeated attempts to purchase Du Qinyan out of apprenticeship not only function to reinforce the actual monetary economies within which he is embedded but also repeatedly resurface at an imaginary level in Du Qinyan's fascination with his own relation with a variety of spectral "doubles." Toward the end of the novel, for instance, when Qinyan discovers that he is the reincarnation of a certain "female immortal Du," he decides to change his name to "Qinxian," or "Immortal Qin." He then embarks on a quest to find the gravesite of his former incarnation. He ultimately succeeds, with the help of an unnamed "woman by the lake," and when he places some offerings on the tomb, the unnamed woman inquires:

"Why don't you perform obeisance [to the tomb]?"

Qinxian responded, "I am she, and she is I."

The woman laughed as she answered, "What are you talking about? What idiotic talk! Because there is you, therefore there is no she; and if there were she, then there would be no you."

7. See, e.g., the discussions in Chapters 26 and 43 of the novel.

> Qinxian heard this and realized that her words betrayed a certain degree of insight. He watched her, and she, in turn, watched him. (626)

Although this unnamed woman initially functions primarily as a foil for Qinyan's own displaced encounter with his former incarnation, she gradually comes to play a parallel role as Qinyan's mirror double in her own right. This specular relationship is initially hinted at, for instance, in the moment of mutual observation at the end of the passage quoted above ("he watched her, and she, in turn, watched him") but is then developed more explicitly in an intriguing dream Qinyan has a couple of days later.

In the dream, Qinxian sees a beautiful woman who looks just like himself in his stage-dress. The woman holds up a mirror, and she and Qinyan see their respective reflections appearing together in the mirror. These two reflected images are nearly identical, spurring the woman to remark: "A single mirror separately reflects two people, making it impossible to distinguish sentiment from reality." Qinxian takes a closer look and discovers that he has now become that same nameless woman who previously directed him to the grave of his former incarnation. Qinxian also sees several other people's reflections in the mirror and realizes that they correspond to actors in his opera troop. He turns the mirror over and sees reflected on the obverse side images of his other acquaintances, such as Wei Pincai and Xi Shiyi. The mirror then starts spinning, and a blue hand reaches out and grabs it, whereupon Qinxian wakes up with a start and realizes that it was only a dream (645–46). Troping explicitly on the linkage between specularity and desire in Jia Rui's famous "mirror of romance" in *Dream of the Red Chamber*, this passage in *Precious Mirror* adds an additional twist—the first thing Qinxian sees in the dream-mirror is *himself* cross-dressed as the woman beside the lake.

These moments of specular encounter between Qinyan and his various figurative doubles—including the "female immortal," the nameless woman by the lake, and the dream-woman who is perceived as doubly cross-dressed (appearing in Qinyan's own transvestite attire)—are then repeated at the end of the novel, when Mei Ziyu marries a woman who looks just like Qinyan. In each of these three instances, Qinyan's self-perception is developed in relationship to the figures of women, each of whom is an exact replica of himself. In this way, sexual difference is not presented as being situated at the level of visual appearance; rather, it is constituted by the inevitable *remainder* produced by these series of mirrored processes of exchange.

These parallel concerns with commoditized circulation and specular encounter come together most suggestively in a poignant scene at the beginning of Chapter 36, when Qinyan is informed by a fellow performer by the name of Lin Shanzhi, that "your" (Qinyan's) master, Chang Qing, has passed away. Qinyan subsequently remarks on the fact that Shanzhi (also a former apprentice of Chang Qing) had referred to Chang Qing as "your"—rather than as "our"—master. This makes Qinyan wonder whether Shanzhi believes that, just because Shanzhi has already been "released from apprenticeship" (*chushi* 出師), he therefore no longer recognizes Chang Qing as his master (401). Qinyan's rhetorical aside here is particularly interesting because Shanzhi is not just a random fellow actor. Rather, he and Qinyan have a very specific relationship. Lin Shanzhi had also been one of Chang Qing's apprentices, and Chang Qing had subsequently traded him for another actor by the name of Xiu Fang. When Xiu Fang was purchased out of apprenticeship, Chang Qing used the money to purchase Qinyan. In this sense, Qinyan can be seen as an indirect replacement of Shanzhi, or as a material embodiment of Shanzhi's exchange value.

Therefore, in this little exchange between Shanzhi and Qinyan concerning the death of their mutual master, we see two roughly equivalent nodes of value regarding each other through the symbolic mirror of autonomous identity and commenting on each other's relationship to their shared point of (valued) origin. This encounter precipitates Qinyan's struggle to emancipate himself from the literal economies of exchange binding him to that same master, even as his status as a figurative token of exchange is figuratively re-established at the level of his relationship with his various visual doubles.

The Circulation of the Phallus

> All of these propositions merely veil over the fact that the phallus can only play its role as veiled, that is, as in itself the sign of the latency with which everything signifiable is struck as soon as it is raised (*aufgehoben*) to the function of signifier.
>
> The phallus is the signifier of this *Aufhebung* itself which it inaugurates (initiates) by its own disappearance.
>
> —Jacques Lacan, "The Meaning of the Phallus"

I began the preceding discussion with a consideration of two separate subplots in *Precious Mirror* involving minor characters and the circulation of bracelets—subplots that, when considered together, suggest an evocative parallel between the positions of "bracelets" and those of "boys" as situated within the novel's symbolic circuits of exchange. Within these symbolic economies, there is a recurrent tension between the status of the bracelet/boy as a mere commodity of exchange, on one hand, and as an irreducible kernel of autonomous identity, on the other. Similarly, in my discussion of *Flowers in the Mirror*, I suggest that Li's novel thematizes a comparable symbolic economy wherein women enter symbolic circuits of exchange, producing an explicit tension between the status of the "women"[8] as both exchangeable commodities and autonomous individuals. More specifically, I noted Elizabeth Cowie's critique of Lévi-Strauss's reliance, in his discussion of exogamy, on the fundamental "'neutrality' of exchange as a concept." For its part, Chen Sen's novel can be seen as developing further this question of the relationship between circulation and value, while also pointing to an important ambiguity in Lévi-Strauss's original gendered model itself.

Although Lévi-Strauss's model emphasizes the exchange of *women*, other critics have noted that this focus on an exogamic exchange of women should be seen merely as a historically contingent condition, not a structurally necessary one. In other words, nothing in the theory itself would necessarily preclude the possibility of social/ideological structures being grounded on the exchange of men, or even of both men *and*

8. Here, and in the following discussion, I use the term "woman" in a broad sense to embrace not only actual "women" but also girls, fairies, mermaids, and even disempowered men as well.

women. Similarly, I have suggested that one apparent implication of *Flowers in the Mirror* is the potential mutability of gender, just as *Precious Mirror* illustrates that, under certain circumstances, disempowered men may be commoditized and exchanged as easily as women. One consequence of this approach to gender and signification in *Precious Mirror* is that even as "biological" sex is replaced by a focus on inherently fungible sociocultural gender attributes, the possibility that these gendered trappings of "masculine" power might ultimately be grounded on some sort of anatomical "maleness" continues to occupy a subterranean presence in the work, erupting occasionally into bursts of anxiety and melancholia. These cases make it clear that sexual difference has *not* been banished from the novel's consciousness; rather, it has been sublimated into the sphere of culturally determined gender attributes itself.

This rearticulation of the novel's disjunction of "sex" and "gender" in the form of an anxiety about the biological primacy of "masculine privilege" can be seen most clearly in a second instance of narrative parallelism between the accounts of Xi Shiyi and Pan San. This second synchronicity begins in Chapter 47, when Xi Shiyi is given a canine penile implant to restore his sexual potency after having contracted a venereal disease. A Buddhist monk, identified as "Monk Tang," introduces Xi Shiyi to the idea, saying that he knows a certain Zhang Xiaomei, who, in turn, has a relative specializing in prosthetics:

> Zhang Xiaomei has a relative from Suzhou who specializes in precisely this kind of operation. He supplies people with prosthetic eyes, prosthetic noses, prosthetic teeth—but all of these are merely artificial. Only when it comes to grafting "that" kind of thing is it necessary to first apply anesthesia, then cut "it" open into four sections and insert a dog's member. Then, one must apply medicinal dressings, and one month later it will be as good as new. This canine member must be obtained when two dogs are coupling—the two animals must be stabbed to death with a knife, and then the member may be extracted from the female dog's pudendum. Only when this procedure is followed will the member be serviceable and not be some sort of "seal kidney." (533)[9]

9. The term used here is *shen* 腎 (literally "kidney") is as an abbreviation for *waishen* 外腎 (outer *shen*), which is a medical term for testicles. The context, however, makes it clear that even *waishen* is here being used metonymically for the penis itself. The term "seal kidneys" (*haigoushen* 海狗腎) may be a double pun on the original abbreviated

Ironically, even as this passage is explicitly concerned with processes of corporeal dismemberment and rearticulation, this passage is itself grounded on a similar process of textual dismemberment and suture. Specifically, the passage as a whole is an obvious borrowing from Li Yu's 李漁 (1610/11–80) notorious novel, *Roupu tuan* 肉蒲團 (The carnal prayer mat). Chen Sen has figuratively extracted the "canine penile grafting" passage from the earlier work, modified it slightly, and then reinserted it into his own novel. In the following discussion, therefore, I take this moment of textual "grafting" and use it to reconsider the assumptions that Chen Sen's text appears to make about male corporeality.

After hearing about this proposed operation, Xi Shiyi asks Monk Tang to have his relative Yang Shanxiu come over for a consultation. After hearing the problem, Yang explains:

> All grafting methods are different, and first we must consider the individual's "source" (*benyuan* 本源), and then we must consider the individual's "goods" (*hanghuo* 行貨). For example, those old men whose energy has been exhausted cannot accept grafts, and to give them grafts would be in vain. If someone's source is good, but their organ has just rotted away or been half cut off, then as long as they still have a good stump, we can give them a penile graft. But first we must see the individual's capital (*benqian* 本錢), and only then we can discuss grafting methods. (533)

This discussion of the operation focuses on the relationship between the "natural" and the "artificial," the "original" and the "supplement." One effect of the scene is to dereify the status of the phallus as a determinant of masculinity. The penis is represented as being a mere appendage susceptible to rotting, severing, grafting, and replacement. The determinant behind this contingent penile epiphenomenon is, instead, the subject's more abstract and intangible "source" (*benyuan*) of "energy." However, this symbolic dereification of the phallus/penis is accomplished through language that ironically further reinforces the

metonymy. That is, the Chinese term for "seal" is *haigou*, or "sea dog," but if one deletes the middle *gou*/dog from *haigoushen*, one is left with *haishen*, which is a close homophone of *haishen* 海參, "sea cucumber / sea slug"—a culinary delicacy in China whose physical appearance and texture connotes very aptly the state of sexual impotence with which Xi Shiyi was apparently stricken.

penis's material status. The euphemism used for the penis in this passage, for instance, is *hanghuo*, which suggests a commodity produced by a less-than-perfect production process. However, the passage emphasizes that the true determinant (*benyuan*) of the value of this "commodity" is not the use-value of the commodity itself but the abstract store of energy/value it represents. Furthermore, there is a clear parallel in the passage between this originary store of energy/value (*benyuan*) and the etymologically similar originary store of monetary capital (*benqian*), in that both are presented as being determining conditions for the success of the operation.

Therefore, the transplant passage begins by pointing to the epiphenomenality of the penis—the most obvious physical instantiation of the symbolic phallus. The passage goes on to postulate the existence of an originary store of energy/value, an invisible, ontological ground undergirding the contingencies of external penile health. Nevertheless, the clear parallel in the passage between the subject's "virile source" (*benyuan*) and his "capital source" (*benqian*) suggests that even the former is not necessarily inherent to the subject himself but subject to the same sorts of circuits of exchange and transference as is the metaphorical "commodity" (*hanghuo*) of the penis itself.

These doubts and anxieties concerning the determining conditions of masculinity are not developed further in this passage, but they do make an uncanny reappearance in another, otherwise unrelated, scene, in which a flash of self-doubt uncharacteristically intrudes into a moment of homoerotic intimacy between Pan San and his male attendant, Tian Xiang. Instead of allowing Tian Xiang to minister to him, as is their custom, Pan San decides instead to fondle Tian Xiang's own organ. He is surprised to discover how underdeveloped it is and is frustrated that it does not respond to his attentions. Tian Xiang laughs and asks him, "Why is Third Uncle (*san ye* 三爺) angry with me today? I didn't need this sort of attention; why is it that Third Uncle has found the wrong portal today?" (539). Tian Xiang then begins to fondle Pan San but finds that Pan San is not as sexually responsive as he usually is. Later, Pan San asks Tian Xiang what pleasure he can derive from ministering to others, and Tian Xiang replies that the pleasure lies precisely in waiting on others and giving them pleasure.

Although the ostensible reason for Pan San's sudden, uncharacteristic need to fondle Tian Xiang's member lies in his desire to have Tian Xiang penetrate him (generally, Tian Xiang, not Pan San, would have been in the receptive position in their relationship) and, in this way, help Pan San to alleviate his own rectal discomfort (resulting from the bundle of hair San Jie had previously inserted into his anus). In a broader sense, however, Pan San's sudden interest in Tian Xiang's member could also be seen as reflecting a moment of insecurity regarding the significatory relationship between his own physical penis and the "phallus" of social privilege he otherwise enjoys. It is therefore not surprising that Pan San's concern for the underdeveloped state of Tian Xiang's male member quickly shifts to a curiosity about the nature of the pleasure Tian Xiang is able to derive from "passively" providing pleasure to others. Even though this moment of sexual self-doubt is experienced by one of the work's most licentious antiprotagonists, it nevertheless allows us to reconsider some of the novel's assumptions about desire in general and about homoerotic desire in particular. More specifically, the question is whether the novel portrays homoerotic relationships purely as sites of performative evocations of femininity, or whether they are perhaps rather more complicated sublimations and re-reifications of one's own biological sex.

A similar instance of apparent insecurity concerning the relationship between maleness and masculine privilege can be found in another scene a few chapters later, in Chapter 51, in which a minor character by the name of Yuanmao employs a "seamstress" (*fengqiongpo* 縫窮婆).[10] The sequence of events that ensues from this encounter helps to reinforce the way in which the sign of "femininity" in the novel has the potential to plant a seed of self-doubt within the presumed self-sufficiency of the masculine position itself.

The scene begins when Yuanmao has the seamstress mend a garment for him and then decides to hire her to stay on to perform some additional services. Yuanmao's friend, Sun Sihui, has secretly been

10. The term is a conventional euphemism for "prostitute," but, as the context here makes clear, this particular woman of the cloth is actually *both* a seamstress *and* a prostitute.

observing the entire scene. The next day, Sihui hires the same seamstress to do some sewing for him and follows Yuanmao's example in keeping her on for additional services. Afterward, Sihui tries to pay her the same 400 cash that he saw her accept from Yuanmao the previous day. As Yuanmao himself secretly eavesdrops on them from his own room, he hears the seamstress respond indignantly:

> "This is for me? Tze, Tze, Tze! This is some offer! And you call yourself a "lord" (*laoye* 老爺)? This is not my price."
>
> When Sihui heard this, he answered, "But I saw you accept this price yesterday; I haven't underpaid you. How is it not four hundred cash?"
>
> . . . Then he [Yuanmao] heard the seamstress say, " Quick, quick! Pay up! Don't waste my time!"
>
> Sihui answered, "Why is this? I am the same kind of person [as Yuanmao]. So why do I have to pay extra?"
>
> The seamstress answered, "The same kind of person? He is an ordinary person, but you are a *laoye*! And furthermore, yesterday we didn't even take off our clothes, but today I have had to go to two or three times as much trouble. And you have the gall to only give me four hundred cash? As a *laoye*, you're a joke!" (582–83)

Sihui asks her how she knows that he is a *laoye* and Yuanmao wasn't. Sihui has a black dot on his penis, and he tells her that if she can correctly identify how many portions of his body are "precious," he will happily pay the price that she is asking. She correctly identifies the black stain on his phallus but then takes offense at his insinuation that she is trying to blackmail him (582–83).

This scene presents, in an unusually clear way, the same sort of tension visible in the penis-grafting scene—namely, a tension between the physical corporeality of the penis and the more abstract status of the phallus as a symbol of social privilege. This phallus is, moreover, a performative construct essentially coterminous with the cluster of sociocultural attributes associated with gender. The facility with which men performatively assume feminine social positions in *Precious Mirror* is an obvious illustration of this general principle. Equally important, however, is the recognition that the phallus derives much of its significatory potential from the fact that it, like women's femininity, *can* be detached from its original "source" and permitted to circulate within larger symbolic economies.

In this scene, therefore, Sihui takes the practice of prostitution, with its explicit reduction of effeminate bodies to the status of mutually interchangeable commodities, and tries unsuccessfully to reflect this process of reductive valuation back onto *himself*, saying, in effect: "I am functionally equivalent to Yuanmao and therefore the cost of providing me with sexual services should be the same." The seamstress, however, takes Sihui's own implicit sign of social privilege and turns it against him—using it as a justification for *her* to assign *him* a monetary/social value—and thus inverting what might be assumed to be the typical prostitute-client relationship in which it is the client who evaluates the commodity value of the prostitute. Furthermore, Sihui reacts to this implicit challenge to his naturalized masculinity by falling back onto the concrete specificity of his physical penis—and specifically his rather peculiar fantasy that his *laoye* social status is instantiated by the black dot(s) on his male member.

As with Pan San's unconsciously defensive obsession with Tian Xiang's male member in Chapter 47, Sihui's fascination with the concrete physicality of his own penis in this passage can be seen as presenting an additional challenge to the naïve naturalization of sexual difference—a challenge that effectively takes us beyond even the straightforward gender/sex dichotomy I pointed to at the beginning of this chapter. Specifically, I initially indicated that both *Flowers in the Mirror* and *Precious Mirror for Evaluating Flowers* suggest a contrast between biological sex and socioculturally assumed gender attributes. However, Xi Shiyi's, Pan San's, and Sihui's obsessive interest in their respective genitals implies that, in these cases, even the "innate" physical attributes of sexual difference are subject to a psychic reinvestment that effectively brings them into the fold of culturally and psychically determined gender attributes as well.

Contemporary Returns

> The *objet a* is something from which the subject, in order to constitute itself, has separated itself off as organ. This serves as a symbol of the lack, that is to say, of the phallus, not as such, but insofar as it is lacking. It must, therefore, be an object that is, firstly, separable and, secondly, that has some relation to the lack.
>
> —Jacques Lacan, Seminar XI

I opened Chapter 1 with a discussion of the late Ming *kunqu* opera *Peony Pavilion*, noting the way in which that work's theme of self-representation and spectral return is itself mirrored in the text's own recent transhistorical spectral return in the form of a contemporary performance of the opera aspiring to hyper-authenticity in relation to the original work. Given that *Precious Mirror* itself takes as its subject the interactions between different troops of *kunqu* opera performers, it is therefore appropriate that Chen's novel contains several prominent allusions to this *kunqu* classic. For instance, at the beginning of the novel, when Du Qinyan is first introduced, he is explicitly compared to Bridal Du, the protagonist of Tang Xianzu's earlier work: "His surname is Du, and perhaps he is the reincarnation of Du Liniang" (17). This initial suggestion of Du Qinyan's doubling of one of *kunqu* opera's most famous characters is, in turn, later reinforced by Du Qinyan's explicit attention to his doubled relationships with a variety of other characters (e.g., the relationship between Qingyan as "female immortal Du" and his fellow-actor Lin Shanzhi). In each case, these specular doubles provide Du Qinyan with sites of displaced identification, against which one may develop a better understanding of his own identity.

More recently, in 1996, Du Qinyan made a figurative double-return when the Taiwan author Wu Chi-wen 吳繼文 used Chen Sen's narrative as the explicit model for his own debut novel, *Shijimo shaonian ai duben* 世紀末少年愛讀本 (Fin-de-siècle reader of young love).[11] *Fin-de-Siècle Reader* opens with a preface stressing the importance of paying attention to the minor, frequently nameless secondary characters in classical novels; the text then turns to an imaginative retelling of Chen Sen's literati novel about opera cross-dressing and male homoeroticism. Unlike Chen Sen's original novel, which is narrated by an omniscient narrator, *Fin-de-siècle Reader* is narrated in the first person by precisely one such secondary character—one who remains nameless and, from the perspective of the original *Precious Mirror*, identityless.[12] Wu's novel

11. For a more detailed discussion of this work, see Rojas, "Wu Jiwen and the Ruins of Representation."

12. Actually, only half of the novel is narrated in this manner; the even-numbered chapters are narrated by an omniscient, third-person narrator and frequently depict

retells Chen Sen's story largely from the perspective of this new narrator, beginning with an account of his close personal relationship with Du Qinyan himself. Not only does this personalized narrative voice lend Wu's text a certain autobiographical quality, but the nameless narrator is inextricably bound to many of the other characters through a vast symbolic economy of displacements and transferences, with the result that even the narrator's portraits of other characters frequently come to assume a quality of displaced autobiography.

I conclude this chapter by turning to a scene in Wu Chi-wen's novel in which the fellow opera performer Lin Shanzhi describes to Qinyan and the narrator the events following his purchase by his new patron, Lord Hua. Shanzhi relates that his initial mixed feelings about the prospect of physical intimacy with the older man were changed by the sight of Hua's flaccid and entirely unimpressive penis:

> In the deepest recess of that thick mass of pubic hair, at first I couldn't believe what I was seeing, thinking that it was my blurred vision (*yanhua* 眼花 [literally, "flowers in the eyes"]) or an optical illusion in that deepest mystery of mysteries, there was a purplish-red phallus (*fenshen* 分身). It looked like the viscera of some animal, listlessly laid out there on display. . . . It looked like a not-yet-mature pear, exceedingly . . . comical. Maybe when it is standing tall, it might assume a different appearance altogether, but I already had no interest in knowing. (201)

Interestingly, however, it is precisely the phallus's own pathetic appearance that makes it so endearing for Shanzhi: "I loved (*aishang le* 爱上了) him because I had the power to pity (*lianmin* 怜悯) him [Hua], because I knew that in the end we were equal, because I knew that he, too, had his own fears" (201).

This scene inverts, on multiple levels, the Freudian primal scene in which the young boy sees the mother's penisless body and develops, in turn, an anxiety about the possibility of the potential loss of his own phallus. In Wu's novel, by contrast, it is the symbolically castrated Shanzhi ("castrated," in the sense that he not only is expected to occupy the passive position in male-male sexual relations, but also is him-

---

events that neither Qinyan nor the personal servant provided by Wu Chi-wen had a chance to observe personally.

self exchanged between men like a mere commodity) who catches a glimpse of a "de-auraticized" phallus. The significance of this flaccid penis, as it echoes Shanzhi's own social position at the margins of the sphere of male privilege, can be seen in terms of what Michèle Montrelay calls the "ruin of representation"—or the process whereby the psychic representations of castration become unmoored from their original psychic groundings and instead begin to circulate emptily, having lost both their "castrating effects" and their "power of turning the subject away from *jouissance*." As Montrelay argues, "The penis produces *jouissance* because it incarnates a finitude. Sublimation always implies a deidealization. The phallic signifier, detached from the terrifying representations of the superego which revolve around the imaginary phallus, must appear as an object of not-much-meaning."[13] Similarly, Shanzhi's glimpse of Hua's phallus effectively detaches the "phallic signifier" (i.e., the actual penis) from the "terrifying representations" that accrue around the "imaginary phallus" (as an instantiation of patriarchal power) and redirects it as a symbol for his own disempowerment, his status as an "object of not-much-meaning."

As Shanzhi continues his description of the scene (from which both Qinyan and the narrator clearly derive an immense vicarious pleasure), he relates how this ability to pity Hua's phallus leads him to want to love it and restore it to its former glory:

> I tenderly (*lian'ai* 憐愛 [literally "pityingly and lovingly"]) used an ointment to gently cover his phallus (*fenshen*), and that formerly limp and cold thing gradually was restored to its former vitality. My hand could feel its reawakening, together with the warmth occasioned by that reawakening. After passing through my hand, that warmth permeated my entire body. . . .
>
> Its enormity vastly exceeded what I could have imagined, and the base was so thick that its girth could not be grasped with a single hand. Enormous, hard, and burning hot. Its color changed from date-red to purplish black, and the oil made it resemble the blinding light given off by a newly polished bronze ornament. . . .
>
> This was the first time that I was able to carefully observe and touch a body, one which was completely open to me, and receptive to my pity, and which could use love to respond to my love. . . . I let my hand move faster,

13. Montrelay, "Inquiry into Femininity," 245.

and felt as though the person lying there was myself, and as though it were my own phallus (*fenshen*) in my hand. (201–2)

The specific term used for the phallus in these passages, *fenshen*, is unusual in this context, and very revealing. Composed of two characters meaning "partial/parted" and "body," respectively (echoes, perhaps, of the penile-grafting scenes in Chen Sen's original novel), the term is also the precise inverse of the binome *shenfen* 身分 (identity).[14] This fortuitous parallel between the binomes for "partial body" and for "identity" suggests, in turn, an evocative deconstructive reading in which identity itself is necessarily grounded on the possibility of its own failure or fragmentation.

Originally Buddhist in origin (*ātmabhāva-nirmita*, in Sanskrit), the term *fenshen* conventionally refers to the separation and reduplication of the body of the Buddha.[15] The classic sixteenth-century Chinese "Buddhist" novel *Journey to the West* adds an additional dimension to this term, which it uses to the describe how the novel's irascible protagonist, Monkey (Sun Wukong), is able to use hairs from his own body to create a multitude of alternative Selves, miniature replicas of himself who obediently perform his bidding.[16] Wu Chi-wen's text borrows this Buddhist trope of multiple selves and applies it to the relationship between the individual and the phallus, implicitly commenting on how the phallus stands as a displaced double of the individual's own self-identity.

The use of *fenshen* in this passage from *Fin-de-siècle Reader* to refer to the phallus suggests, moreover, a compelling link to Lacanian psychoanalysis. For Lacan, the phallus is an example of a kind of psychic entity that he calls an *objet petit a*, or "partial object," which can become figuratively disassociated from the body and enter into circulation within a

14. The Chinese term for "identity," *shenfen*, can be written either 身分 or 身份.

15. For instance, a *locus classicus* for this term is Chapter 11, "The Emergence of the Treasure Tower," of the Buddhist scripture *The Lotus Sutra* (precise origins unknown; first translated into Chinese in 255 CE), where it is used to refer to the "various Buddhas who are emanations of my [the Buddha's] body" (Watson, *The Lotus Sutra*, 172).

16. The first instance of this term in the text can be found in Chapter 3, in which the protagonist, divine Monkey, resorts to the "magic of bodily division" (*fenshen fa* 分身法) to transport a large armory of weapons he has found (Anthony Yu, *Journey to the West*, 1: 101).

psychic liminal realm in which it comes to function as "causes of desire." The quintessential *objet petit a*, for Lacan, is the mother's missing phallus, which the child (of either sex) identifies with in order to compensate for the mother's apparent castration:

> The *objet a* is something from which the subject, in order to constitute itself, has separated itself off as organ. This serves as a symbol of the lack, that is to say, of the phallus, not as such, but insofar as it is lacking. It must, therefore, be an object that is, firstly, separable and, secondly, that has some relation to the lack.[17]

For Lacan, the *objet a* stands as both a symbol of this potential "lack" and a symbolic displacement of that which is lacking in the first place. Similarly, in the scene here, we can see Shanzhi clearly, and in some ways quite literally, identifying with Hua's dephallicized penis, with that penis functioning for him as a doubly-displaced "partial object."

The use of the term "parted/partial self" (*fenshen*) in this passage to refer to the phallus also encapsulates particularly neatly the dynamics of vicarious voyeurism that characterize the scene as a whole. To recapitulate: Shanzhi, in his symbolically emasculated social position, clearly derives a paradoxical pleasure from identifying with Hua's flaccid, dephallicized phallus. Subsequently, Shanzhi describes his sense of identification with both the actual male body and the phallic "partial/parted body" that lie before him. Furthermore, this entire account is then retold for the listening pleasure of Qinyan and the narrator. Moreover, as noted above, Qinyan and Shanzhi are themselves displaced reflections of each other, since Qinyan stands as a mediated replacement of Shanzhi after Shanzhi was traded by his former master, Chang Qing.

Just as in the earlier scene in *Precious Mirror for Evaluating Flowers*, in which we observed Qinyan and Shanzhi observing each other across the corpse of their mutual master, similarly in this scene from *Fin-de-siècle Reader* we have the same two characters symbolically observing each other across the emasculated body of their mutual patron (Lord Hua). Finally, the passage as a whole ends with a hint of yet another potential turn of the vicarious screw, when Shanzhi remarks to Qinyan

---

17. Lacan, *Four Fundamental Concepts of Psychoanalysis*, 103.

that, "I hope that someday, someone will be able to relate to me his own secrets, the same way I have just done for you" (203)—suggesting that he himself has derived a vicarious pleasure from identifying with the pleasure that he imagines Qinyan and the narrator themselves to have derived from listening to his account of pleasuring Lord Hua.

Lin Shanzhi's concluding remark not only evokes an image of a dizzying hall of mirrors reflecting not actual images but rather abstract desires, but also reflects back ironically on the textual status of Wu's novel itself. The sense of anticipatory retrospection in Lin's hope that "someday, somebody will be able to relate to me his own secrets" repeats a narrative trope found in a wide array of late imperial fiction (including both *Dream of the Red Chamber* and *Flowers in the Mirror*), in which the texts of those works are imagined to be circulating through future eras, searching for an "author" willing to tell their respective stories. Lin's sense of future-perfect anticipation also reflects back on the status of Wu Chi-wen's own text—which has already, in effect, placed itself in that same position of "future author" with respect to Chen Sen's mid-nineteenth-century novel. Circulating between these various texts is the coin of gender, which lacks an absolute value but is constituted through the circuit of exchange itself.

Chen Sen's and Wu Chi-wen's novels, in other words, are positioned as mirror images of one another, even as they simultaneously underscore the processes of transformation and transvaluation that inevitably intrude within the specular condition itself. In the following chapters, I examine how concerns with the reliability and self-evidence of visual imagery and gendered appearance anticipated in late imperial novels like *Flowers in the Mirror* and *Precious Mirror for Evaluating Flowers* are further developed and complicated in a variety of mid- and late twentieth-century works.

PART II

Spectatorship

The maid in Su Hanchen's fan painting discussed at the beginning of Part I is positioned at a discrete distance behind and to the left of the mirror-gazing lady. Like Chun Xiang in Huang Mingqi's illustration of the *Peony Pavilion* mirror scene, the maid in Su Hanchen's fan painting introduces an external, spectatorial perspective into the specular mirror-gazing scene at the center of the painting. The maid's embedded gaze not only helps direct the viewer's gaze toward that mirror-gazing scene but also simultaneously challenges and even displaces the centrality of that specular scene by pulling the viewer's attention back toward the maid herself (see Fig. 6).

If we trace the lady's presumptive line of sight, as we did for Cixi in the mirror photograph, we find that her specular gaze is actually an impossible one. The lady's pupils, distinctly visible in the mirror, are oriented toward the upper left-hand corner of the painting. Given, however, that her face is itself positioned *above* and oriented *to the left* of the mirror, she would therefore have to be looking *downward and toward the right-hand side of the painting* in order to be able to see her own reflection, and consequently her eyes as they appear *in the mirror* would *also* have to be oriented *downward and toward the right-hand side of the painting.* By having the mirror-face appear to be gazing instead *upward toward the left-hand side of the painting,* Su Hanchen precisely inverted the orientation the lady's gaze *should* have in the mirror reflection and as a result creates the illusion that the mirror-face is actually an independent entity gazing back up at the lady herself.

Fig. 6 Su Hanchen, *Lady at Her Dressing Table in a Garden* (detail). Photograph © 2008 Museum of Fine Arts, Boston.

Or, alternatively, depending on the precise spatial configuration of the scene, the mirror-face might appear to be gazing *past* the dressing table lady at the maid standing off to her left. In fact, there would appear to be an almost precise eye-line match between the gaze of the mirror-face and that of the maid. That is, within the carefully constructed three-dimensional space of the painting, the face in the mirror appears not as a reflected image of the lady's (impossible) specular gaze but as an independent visage that seems to be returning the gaze of the maid observing from off to the side. As a result, the mirror-face is transformed into an independent entity, the maid is translated from the margins of a specular scene to the center of an observational one, and the lady at the dressing table is transposed into a mere spectator of the displaced version of her own original (and impossible) mirror scene.

This translation of Su Hanchen's mirror scene into a spectatorial one is symbolic of the shift I propose here from a late nineteenth-century visual and cultural economy grounded on a logic of reflection to an early twentieth-century one grounded on a logic of representation and external observation. That is, in contrast to the late imperial period's attempts to locate its own identity through an involutive return to a prior Chinese cultural tradition, by the early twentieth century China became increasingly concerned with how it was perceived in the eyes of foreigners, a concern that contributed to a mood of what Lin Yü-sheng calls "totalistic antitraditionalism," or a determination to radically rethink many of the conventional aspects of Chinese culture and society.[1] Reinforcing this concern with the abstract Western gaze was the parallel introduction into China of a variety of "Western" technologies and practices of visual representation, such as photography, cinema, and Western art. Together, these technologies and practices heralded the prospect of what Rey Chow describes as the "all-encompassing force of the visual image in modern and postmodern culture, when entire nations, histories, and peoples are to be exposed, revealed, captured on the screen, made visible as images; when visuality is to become the law of knowledge and the universal form of epistemological coercion."[2]

In Part II, I consider these themes of spectatorship and visual reproduction as they are developed in the works of three mid-twentieth-century authors—Wumingshi, Eileen Chang, and Jin Yong—all of whom were born within a seven-year period at the height of the May Fourth era (in 1917, 1920, and 1924, respectively) and began their respective writing careers during the socially and politically tumultuous decades of the 1940s and 1950s. Even though each of these authors was writing at a time when not only photography but also cinema had become familiar elements in Chinese visual culture, each nevertheless remained peculiarly fascinated by the mimetic dimension of these images, particularly their ability to function as vehicles of an external gaze.

Wumingshi's 1949 *Golden Night of the Serpent*, for instance, opens with a detailed description of a portrait of a courtesan and enters into a

---

1. Lin Yü-sheng, *The Crisis of Chinese Consciousness.*
2. Chow, *Primitive Passions*, 10.

meticulous discussion not only of the male protagonist's obsession with the woman depicted in the painting but also of his sense of being the object of her own inscrutable gaze. Although Jin Yong's five-volume martial arts novel *Tianlong ba bu* is set not in the contemporary era but in the thirteenth-century Northern Song dynasty, it nevertheless features a cluster of visual texts similar in function to Wumingshi's painting. These visual texts are martial arts picture manuals, and not only do they provide the viewer with a visual model for learning specific forms of martial arts practice but one of them in particular features a female image that evokes in the fictional male viewer a similar conjunction of obsessive gazing and a self-conscious awareness of being the object of another's gaze. Finally, I conclude this part by turning to the works of Eileen Chang, looking not only at the thematics of visual observation in several of her mid-century writings but also at the theme of anticipatory nostalgia developed in the *Mutual Reflections* photo album she compiled at the end of her life. This "auto-effigial" text illustrates how Chang viewed her own life, as well as how she hoped to be recalled after her death.

Whether presented in a modern, premodern, or even quasi-postmodern setting, the visual imagery in these works not only provides gendered subjects with a site of projective identification and carries embedded within it a variety of external gazes but also becomes an object of fetishistic investment in its own right, entering a space of fantasy that far exceeds the concrete representational status of the image itself.

4

Wumingshi and Pictorial Fetishism

And because these illusions function as a screen between one person and another, as well as between people and things, we can therefore live in a fairly relaxed and comfortable fashion; and it is only in this way that life's feeling of beauty can be produced. Sometimes, a person whose soul is as clear as a bright mirror will actually need a little mistiness and ambiguity.

—Wumingshi, *Siren of the Sea*

Near the beginning of Wumingshi's 無名士 (1917–2002) 1949 novel *Jinse de sheye* 金色的蛇夜 (Golden night of the serpent), the protagonist Yin Di views an ominous Western-style painting by his friend Lin Suzi entitled *Shijie mori* 世界末日 (The end of the world). The painting purports to depict the final moments of the "destruction of Pompeii," although in reality it consists of an orgiastic, bacchanalian scene featuring "one naked, flowery female body after another, each swaying and trembling like red opium poppies as they rise up."[1] Yin Di is shocked by the work: "This is not an image of the destruction of Pompeii. Rather it represents the destruction of the painting's observer (*guanhuazhe* 觀畫者). You are simply destroying the painting's viewers (*kanhua de ren* 看畫的人)!" (15). Standing quietly off to one side, Lin Suzi's student Ma Erti concurs with Yin Di: "Actually, this painting shouldn't be called *End of the World* or *Destruction of Pompeii* but *Our Era* (*Women de shidai* 我們的時代)." Lin Suzi agrees: "What I was basically trying to paint was our

1. Wumingshi, *Jinse de sheye*, 14. Subsequent references to the constituent volumes of *Wuming shu* are cited in the text.

own era: this China on the brink of its own 'destruction of Pompeii,' this world that is in the process of repeating Pompeii's fate" (16).

Although obviously not literally the end of the world, the era in which Wumingshi wrote this volume was certainly a pivotal one. Published in early 1949, the first volume of *Golden Night of the Serpent* appeared at the end of more than a decade of warfare (including the Sino-Japanese War, World War II, and the ensuing civil war between the Nationalists and the Communists) and was followed by the establishment of the People's Republic of China in October of that year. The *Our Era* painting therefore poses precisely the question of the position of the observer in this mid-twentieth-century era. The claim that this painting represents the "destruction of the painting's observer . . . [of] the painting's viewers" suggests the figurative destruction of a certain perceptual mode. Within the terms of this study, what is being challenged by this Western-style painting is a late imperial specular mode of seeing and what is being created is what I call a spectatorial mode, which foregrounds the necessary gap between viewer and scene. In other words, what Yin Di describes here as the destruction of the observer represents, in reality, the symbolic creation of a *new* observational mode—one that is always grounded, however, on its own necessary impossibility.

In the following discussion, I examine the way the multivolume work that comprises *Night of the Serpent*, Wumingshi's (Anonymous) *Wuming shu* 無名書 (Anonymous book) (composed between 1945 and 1960), explores this figurative transition from a specular to a spectatorial visual mode by focusing specifically on its treatment of women. The novel uses the figure of woman to reflect and embody many of the same social concerns associated with the mid-century period in which the novel is set—even as this same female figure becomes an object of fascination in its own right, functioning as a figurative screen shielding the viewer from the historical realities lying behind it. For Yin Di, the work's idealistic protagonist, woman is situated at the figurative limits of visual perception but at the same time is imagined as possessing a powerful and all-encompassing gaze. Woman, in this reading, simultaneously marks the necessary limits of the male gaze and represents the symbolic domain of the visual gaze itself. I take this linkage between the figure of woman and the workings of the gaze as my starting point for reflecting more specifically on the way in which Wumingshi's work reflects on the nature of vision itself.

The Figure of Woman

> Woman and Revolution—neither exists merely as an image; rather, both are also a kind of higher truth. But when I made an effort to excavate their foundations and found that at their center there was a fissure, the disappointment I felt was simply unrepresentable.
>
> —Wumingshi, *Golden Night of the Serpent*

Wumingshi literally means "anonymous," and is the pen name the Shanghai-born author Bu Ning 卜寧 (also known as Bu Naifu 卜乃夫) selected for himself at the beginning of his writing career in the early 1940s. Although two early works published under this pen name were popular romances—*Beiji fengqing hua* 北極風情畫 (Arctic romance; 1943) and *Tali de nüren* 塔裏的女人 (Woman in the pagoda; 1944)—Wumingshi could not have anticipated at the time that the work he himself would regard as his masterpiece, *Anonymous Book*, would ironically confirm the very "anonymity" that his pen name inadvertently presaged.

Begun in 1946 during the tumultuous transition from imperialist aggression to civil war and completed in secrecy fourteen years later, at the height of the famine wrought by the disastrous Great Leap Forward, Wumingshi's signature work, *Anonymous Book*, is a provocatively "untimely" meditation. Wumingshi wrote and published the first two and a half volumes of this six-volume work during the late 1940s, with the first half of the third volume being published only two months before the founding of the People's Republic of China in October 1949. The latter half of volume 3 and the remaining three volumes were composed in secret over the course of the next decade. During the 1970s, Wumingshi began sending the unpublished pages of the manuscript to his brother in Hong Kong disguised as personal letters and, in this way, was finally able to have the complete text published in Hong Kong and Taiwan.[2]

2. For an overview of Wumingshi's life and work, see Chen Sihe, "Shilun *Wumingshu*"; and Rojas, "Wumingshi."

Anonymous Book takes as its starting point the failure of the first Communist revolution of 1927, and most of the narrative is set during the political and social turmoil that subsequently enveloped China in the 1930s. Against this tumultuous backdrop, the work's idealistic protagonist, Yin Di, turns to a variety of different philosophical, religious, and aesthetic traditions as he persistently seeks the meaning of life and the truth of existence. More generally, Wumingshi's work builds on the late imperial genre of the literati novel—with its unapologetic fascination with philosophical, literary, and aesthetic issues. In fact, Wumingshi's novel even has its own version of the lengthy banquet scenes (complete with detailed descriptions of wordplay drinking games and elaborate, allusive jokes) for which both Li Ruzhen's and Chen Sen's nineteenth-century novels are so notorious.

The relationship between the contents of Wumingshi's novel and the historical circumstances under which it was composed is therefore both quite direct and curiously mediated. That is, the historical setting of the novel closely mirrors that of the mid-century period in which it was written, and Yin Di's idealistic search for truth and meaning is similarly mirrored by the author's idealistic investment in this philosophical and introspective literary creation. At the same time, however, that same idealism places the novel so curiously out of step with its own historical circumstances. In fact, the philosophical abstraction of *Anonymous Book*, combined with its rather ambivalent portrayal of communism, was so starkly at odds with the contemporary orthodoxy of socialist realism that Wumingshi had to complete the latter half of his mammoth project in complete secrecy.

This tension between issues of philosophical transparency and historical opacity is developed in the work through the twin metaphors of the mirror and the screen. For instance, the passage cited in the epigraph heading this chapter borrows the familiar Taoist metaphor of the soul being like a "bright mirror" and inverts its significance—suggesting that sometimes this idealized transparency is actually *not* to be desired, and indeed mistiness and illusion may instead be needed to intervene as figurative "screens" between one person and another. Wumingshi's pairing in this passage of the figures of the mirror and the screen draws on a rich tradition of mirror imagery in late imperial literati fiction; it can also be seen as a metaphorical commentary on the historical position of Wumingshi's work itself. Wumingshi's *Anonymous Book* reflects many contemporary political and social concerns, even as its highly erudite fascination with esoteric aesthetic and intellectual issues can be seen as constituting a figurative screen intervening between the text itself and the more sobering historical conditions of the period.

Anonymous Book follows the spiritual journey of a single protagonist, Yin Di. Each of the six volumes has a different thematic focus, ranging from revolution (vol. 1) to romance (vol. 2) to religion (vol. 4). Volume 1, *Yeshou, yeshou, yeshou* 野獸 野獸 野獸 (Beast, beast, beast), centers around Yin Di's attempt to find this meaning or truth through political activism, particularly through his participation in the 1927 Communist uprising. In volume 2, *Haiyan* 海艷 (Siren of the sea), Yin Di shifts his attention from revolution to romance and looks to a seemingly ideal young woman, Lin Meili, for the key to his search for the meaning of existence. In volume 3, *Jinse de sheye* (Golden night of the serpent), the focus shifts again, this time to a prostitute by the name of Sha Kaluo who represents the decadent antithesis to Lin Meili's pristine innocence. Volume 4, *Si de yanceng* 死的岩層 (The stone strata of death), details Yin Di's turn to organized religion for possible answers to his questions. Although Wumingshi himself was agnostic, this volume draws eclectically and eruditely from both Buddhism and Christianity. Volume 5, *Kaihua zai xingyun yiwai* 開花在星雲以外 (Blooming flowers beyond stars and clouds), perhaps the most philosophical and self-reflective volumes in the series, describes Yin Di's departure from the stifling urban environment of Xi'an and Chongqing (where he had resided in the previous volume), and his turn to a reclusive existence at Mount Hua. Finally, volume 6, *Chuangshiji da puti* 創世紀大菩提 (The great enlightenment of the creation of a new era), describes Yin Di's marriage to his cousin, Qu Ying. The account of their connubial bliss is layered with complex discussions of axiological realization, or the process of realizing one's own subjectivity through a dialogical interaction with another autonomous individual.

A recurrent theme in the work is Yin Di's attention to his relationships with various women in his life in an attempt to come to terms with the political, social, and intellectual transformations taking place around him. In fact, throughout the novel as a whole, women are consistently located at the limits of visual representation—with the result that the beautiful woman's "figure" comes to signify the limits of figuration. Whether it be Yin Di's romantic infatuation with Lin Meili in volume 2, his carnal obsession with Sha Kaluo in volume 3, or his eventual matrimonial bliss with Qu Ying in volume 6, much of the work revolves around Yin Di's attempt to come to terms with women, either as autonomous individuals or as figurative nodal points of imaginative identification.

Sigmund Freud once famously remarked that "throughout history people have knocked their heads against the riddle of the nature of femininity"[3]—a sentiment explicitly echoed at one point in *Golden Night of the Serpent*, when Yin Di observes that "the most difficult thing to understand in the universe is woman" (2: 152). For both Freud and Yin Di, the enigma of "woman" results not from her literal invisibility but from her exorbitant *visibility*—a visibility that, by virtue of its very excess, paradoxically makes "woman" appear all the more impenetrable. Despite a prominent rhetorical tradition equating women with visual imagery and surface adornment, Yin Di nevertheless stresses—in the passage cited in the epigraph above—that neither "woman" nor "revolution" exists solely as "visual image" (*xingxiang* 形象); rather, both can also be seen as "a kind of higher truth" (1: 51). This linkage points to the paradoxical way in which both "woman" and "revolution" represent necessary "fissures" (*liehen* 裂痕) within (masculine/patriarchal) civilization—fissures that, in turn, provide the requisite ground on which that same civilization is based. This symbolic ambivalence may be perceived, for instance, in "woman's" idealized status as demarcating the symbolic boundaries between different patriarchal lineages, as well as in the role of "revolution" in marking the temporal boundaries between different eras. Although these twin themes of revolution and femininity are directly relevant, in different ways, to each volume of Wumingshi's *Anonymous Book*, they are perhaps developed most explicitly in the third volume of that work, *Golden Night of the Serpent* (whose composition straddled the 1949 Communist Revolution). I begin therefore by considering the way in which

3. Freud, "Femininity," 113.

this thematic linkage of revolution and femininity is developed in *Golden Night*'s opening discussion of a portrait of the courtesan Sha Kaluo and then look at the novel's treatment of the figure of Sha Kaluo herself.

The novel opens with a consideration of two Western-style paintings both entitled *End of the World*. The first of these is Lin Suzi's *Our Era* painting discussed above; the second is by his student Ma Erti and depicts a hauntingly beautiful woman. Yin Di quickly becomes obsessed with this image, to the point that the female subject of the portrait—the courtesan Sha Kaluo—becomes the object of his fervent pursuit. After nearly half a year's pursuit, he finally encounters her at a bar one evening (although he initially fails to realize who she is). In implicit contrast to the apocalyptic connotations of the figure in Ma Erti's portrait, Sha Kaluo in the flesh initially impresses Yin Di as an image of prehistoric antiquity:

> As she hid in the darkest recesses of that corner, she resembled a female statue left behind on a cave wall in prehistoric Europe, both indistinct and solid. The shadow of a tapering column outlined in gold completely covered her; and as a result he couldn't see her head, face, eyes and could only discern the form of her body, black as ebony. . . .
>
> He walked over to the counter to get a glass of whisky, and it was then that he grasped the basic image of this woman.
>
> From the instant that he grasped her image, he was reminded of the world's earliest famous female image: that painting of the Egyptian queen Nefertiti, symbolizing eternal death, standing erect in front of the mausoleum gravestone. Her mysterious black eyes bore a compelling resemblance to the famous black eyes of that painted statue. (1: 236–37)

Yin Di feels an instant attraction to Sha Kaluo, but she rejects his advances. What is curious about this passage is that, even as Yin Di in effect visually reifies Sha Kaluo as a material object ("she resembled a female statue"), he simultaneously reduces her image to a pair of autonomous "mysterious black eyes"—eyes that not only answer Yin Di's gaze but also reflect his obsessive, reifying gaze *back at him.*

The next night, Yin Di attends a costume ball, where he runs into a woman disguised as a Tibetan "death mask" dancer (*kulou wuzhe* 骷髏舞著). Although he cannot discern her face, Yin Di is immediately attracted to this dancer, just as he was previously drawn both to the woman in black and to the woman in Ma Erti's painting. He approaches her and suggests that they must have met before:

> "Do you believe that we have known each other a long time, like one transparent mirror (*touming jingzi* 透明鏡子) made out of a chromium and gold alloy knowing another such transparent mirror? . . .
>
> "Do you believe . . . that I could rip off your mask with one hand, making you instantly reveal your original form?" (1: 253–54)

It is not until this mysterious woman has left the party, however, that Yin Di learns that she is the infamous Sha Kaluo; it is only then that he realizes that the "woman in black" from the previous night must have been Sha Kaluo as well.

Each of these encounters between Yin Di and Sha Kaluo revolves around a dialectic of visibility and invisibility, form and content. Ma's portrait of Sha Kaluo, for instance, reduces her to her own visible form, and it is her physical presence that Yin Di craves; but in the subsequent two encounters, her visible image (as well as her "true" identity) is hidden from him. Particularly revealing in this regard is Yin Di's comparison of both Sha Kaluo and himself to a pair of "transparent mirrors" facing each other. This simile not only reinforces the explicitly visual dimension of his relationship with her but also returns us to the issues of commoditization and exchange value that I developed in my discussions of *Flowers in the Mirror* and *Precious Mirror for Evaluating Flowers*. More specifically, the trope of the mirror functions as a figure for gendered or sexual inversion, while simultaneously signaling the antinomies of exchange value produced by the process of circulation itself. It is therefore quite appropriate that, in *Golden Night of the Serpent*, this figure of the mirror is repeatedly used to reflect Sha Kaluo's status as a courtesan, particularly insofar as the courtesan functions quite literally as a commodity for masculine exchange and consumption.

This focus on the circulation and exchange value of the courtesan brings us back to the earlier discussion of the relationship between the exogamic circulation of women and the parallel semiotic circulation of tropes of women and other signifiers. In an influential response to Levi-Strauss's discussion of exogamic exchange, the French feminist theorist Luce Irigaray draws on a similar combination of tropes of mirroring and anti-mirroring to describe the ways in which both commodities *and women* may become paradoxical embodiments of value:

> *In other words, for the commodity, there is no mirror that copies it so that it may at once be itself and its "own" reflection.* One commodity cannot be mirrored in another, as man is mirrored in his fellow man. For when we are dealing with commodities, the self-same, mirrored, is not "its" own likeness, contains nothing of its properties, its qualities, its "skin and hair." . . . *Commodities, women, are a mirror of value of and for man.* In order to serve as such, they give up their bodies to men as the supporting material of specularization, of speculation. They yield to him their natural and social value as a locus of imprints, marks, and mirage of his activity.[4]

One of the most explicit instances of this sort of commodification of women, Irigaray suggests, can be found in the figure of the prostitute—who, she explains, is "implicitly tolerated" by the "social order" on the grounds that "the break between usage and exchange is, in her case, less clear-cut" (186). Alternatively, however, we might instead suggest that the prostitute can actually be seen as posing a *greater* threat to the "social order" precisely because she represents a potential category crisis within the process of commoditization itself.

As a prized courtesan, Sha Kaluo can be seen as a quintessential commodity. At the same time, however, she also represents the potential negation of the same economic/symbolic order that ostensibly grants the commodity its meaning and value in the first place. We are told, for example, that Sha Kaluo has absolutely no respect for either money or private property ("She had always despised money. . . . Actually, she didn't even understand the concept of private property"; 1: 263). Nor, ironically enough, does she appear to have any respect for sexual relations or even for sexual difference. As the narrator observes, "Sexual intercourse, to her, was comparable to simply shaking hands; and she had long ago lost the concept of sexual difference. When in front of a man, she never thought of herself as a woman" (1: 262).

At one point, Yin Di draws explicitly on the metaphorics of optical illumination to illustrate Sha Kaluo's status of radical negativity with respect to established axiological and epistemological value systems:

4. Irigaray, "Women on the Market," 176.

> Even in the darkest depths of my despair, there would still occasionally be a miraculous flash of light. This is also the part of me that Sha Kaluo would never be able to completely understand, because with her, there was never any such flash of light. She was a dark entity constituted by absolute darkness, which is different from those dark entities that still stand to benefit from an occasional flash of light. (2: 83)

This characterization of Sha Kaluo as representing an absolute absence of light as well as the radical negation of the very possibility of visual perception ironically reinforces the earlier description of her as a "transparent mirror," in the sense that a mirror's ability to reflect light is premised on its own *opacity*.

Sha Kaluo's dual status as an embodiment both of the radical absence of light and of specular plenitude is already explicit in the account of Yin Di's first face-to-face meeting with her, when the narrator exclaims:

> Oh, it is black night again, black night again. It is piles upon piles of incompletely painted blackness. Gradually, two deep-black circles emerge out of the blackness; it is an Egyptian painted statue, a hoarse female voice. Yes, this is truly a statue of the age! Everything pertaining to the dark side of the age, all accumulates on itself. This is a simple woman, but is also a complex light-reflecting mirror. (1: 272)

In this passage, Wumingshi used the redundant phrase "light-reflecting mirror" (*huiguang jing* 迴光鏡) to describe Sha Kaluo's status as an absolute *absence* of light—comparing her to two black circles emerging out of a sea of "incompletely painted blackness." Similarly, the earlier linkage of Sha Kaluo's image with issues of temporality (as in Ma Erti's *End of the World* painting) recurs in this passage as well, although here this gendered temporality is presented more as a *negative* presence: "the *yin* side of the era" (*shidai yinmian* 時代隱面). The term *yin* here is, of course, drawn from the foundational *yin/yang* (隱/陽) dichotomy in Chinese cosmology, with *yin* connoting not only darkness and being hidden from view but also, and most explicitly, femininity itself.

This association of Sha Kaluo with the quality of feminine *yin* recurs throughout the volume; one of the most interesting instances comes in the discussion of her home. This residence is initially described as "a foreign building in the style of a medieval castle" (2: 178), and in the ensuing discussion it is repeatedly characterized as being "dark" (*yin'an*

隱暗). The narrative then draws on a striking ocular metaphor to characterize Sha Kaluo's relationship to this ironically "unhomely" environment:

> This old building constituted a sort of general symbolic embodiment of the emotional state of its female protagonist. As for her, her relation to the residence was, to borrow the familiar expression, that of an "eye added to a painted dragon." Ever since the old building reached the end of its first sixty-year cycle (*huajia* 花甲), it had lacked this sort of a pair of "eyes," and after Sha Kaluo arrived, she was able to constitute precisely this sort of "addition" (*dian* 點). (2: 180)

The expression "adding eyes to a painted dragon" (*hualongdianjing* 畫龍點睛) refers to the act of adding a finishing touch to a work of art or other creative project. It derives from a Tang dynasty anecdote about the verisimilar continuity between representation and reality (in the anecdote, as soon as the eyes are added, the painted dragon comes to life and flies away). This conventional expression comes to have an unexpectedly literal resonance when used to describe Sha Kaluo, since she herself is referred to metonymically throughout much of the novel in strikingly ocular terms—"a pair of eyes from an Egyptian sculpture," "two deep-black circles emerg(ing) out of darkness," etc.[5] Rather than positioning Sha Kaluo as a figure of visual transparency, however, these ocular metaphors instead present her as a metaphor for *the limits* of Yin Di's own sight.

In the following section, I build on the linkage between truth and illusion suggested in the "dragon-eye" expression, specifically with regard to its reference to the figure of the eye itself. In particular, I examine how Wumingshi used mimetic representation to reflect on the

---

5. Wumingshi draws on a rather similar optical metaphor in a discussion of the War of Northern Expedition at the beginning of the first volume in the series, *Beast, Beast, Beast*, one that resonates ironically with the allusion to "dragon-eye flowers" a few lines earlier:

> This was a beautiful night in May. A typical Southern night. *White dragon-eye flowers* (longan flowers) *opened in the night*. The souls of each of these young people also bloomed like fragrant flowers. . . . *This war is like the eyes of the statue of the great revolution; it is only with the addition of eyes that the revolution can come to have a form and spirit.* (113; italics added)

nature of vision, including the ways in which we perceive—perceive not only the nature of our own visual perception but also, by implication, the way we perceive *ourselves* as well. The visual process becomes a metonymic representation of the Self, and the resulting fragmented and decentered perception of the visual process also becomes a figure for the constructed nature of the subject as perceived vis-à-vis that same visual process.

True Illusions

> A face reflected in one of our contemporary [glass] mirrors is very different from that same face as seen reflected in an old bronze mirror of antiquity, even though the two would of course still have a few attributes in common.
>
> —Wumingshi, *Blooming Flowers Beyond Stars and Clouds*

In the preceding discussion of Yin Di's relationship with Sha Kaluo in *Golden Night of the Serpent*, I argue that his perception of her image is frequently folded back onto an attention to the dynamics of visual perception itself—with Sha Kaluo typically represented alternatively as either two autonomous black eyes or a mirror that reflects Yin Di's own gaze back at him. These themes of the gaze and of mutual reflection are in turn central concerns throughout *Anonymous Book*. Wumingshi frequently reflected on the practical and theoretical implications of various visual technologies and representational practices, as well as of the workings of the human optical system. The passage from *Blooming Flowers* cited in the epigraph to this section, for instance, uses the differences between traditional Chinese bronze mirrors and modern (Western) glass ones to comment metaphorically on the site of difference that intrudes into the ostensibly "reflective" moment of a face gazing at its own mirror image. The optical contrasts between the two types of mirrors in this passage become a metonym for the specular gap between the observer herself and her own reflection in each mirror.

The focus on the two *End of the World* paintings at the beginning of *Golden Night of the Serpent* is just one of the many instances in *Anonymous Book* in which painting is explicitly thematized. Throughout the work there are detailed discussions of the relationship between traditional Chinese painting practices and the gauntlet of modernist European styles such as cubism, surrealism, fauvism, and futurism. This linkage between Chinese and Western artistic traditions is reinforced by the particularly close connection between the fictional character of Lin Suzi (the painter of the first of the two *End of the World* paintings) and recent trends in modern Chinese art history. More specifically, it is well known that Lin Suzi—whom Wumingshi's biographers Wang Yingguo and Zhao Jiangbin suggest "represents Yin Di's own reincarnation at an artistic level"[6]—was inspired by the contemporary painter and Wumingshi's close personal friend Lin Fengmian 林風眠 (1900–1991). Lin Fengmian, about whom Wumingshi published an essay in 1947, was one of modern China's most influential artists. He studied abroad in France from 1918 to 1926 and subsequently headed the Beijing and Hangzhou art academies. In the process he helped to train a generation of Chinese artists interested in synthesizing Chinese and Western artistic traditions.

This attention in Wumingshi's novel to traditions of Chinese and Western painting practice is paralleled by a tendency to view human existence itself as a figurative painting. For instance, near the end of *Blooming Flowers Beyond Stars and Clouds,* the painter Qiao Junye suggests that human existence can itself be regarded as the figurative artistic product of a higher consciousness:

> "Now I finally understand: people are . . . a pile of oil paints and grinding stones, which are constantly being painted and molded by another black hand. I am a painter, but there is another being who is constantly painting me, and who, furthermore, is painting me not in accordance with my own ideas but following his own opinions."

A similar metaphor is deployed with radically different implications in the final volume of the work, *The Great Enlightenment of the Creation of a New Era*, when Yin Di remarks to Qu Ying shortly after their marriage, "Can you believe it? What I would really like to be is a painter, so as to be able to paint your body in a myriad of different images and postures" (88). Both Qiao Junye's and Yin Di's remarks point to two separate concerns developed with increasing urgency throughout the work: namely, the status of visual perception as a key sensory portal to the material world and the status of visuality within axiological processes of mutual realization.

---

6. Wang Yingguo and Zhao Jiangbin, *Wumingshi zhuanqi*, 265.

The figurative inverse of this use of artistic metaphors to articulate the subject's own self-conception is a close attention in *Blooming Flowers Beyond Stars and Clouds* to the physiology of visual perception. One of the most detailed discussions of the relationship between visual perception and reality, for instance, can be found in a passage from the middle of *Blooming Flowers*:

> In reality, there is no blue, green, red, or other color; these are only forms of light, which has many different colors, and which occasionally comes into contact with our crystalline lens, the iris, the pigments in our arterial membranes, cornea, aqueous fluid, vitreous body, optic nerve, and central cerebrum. Only through the reciprocal interaction of all these different elements are we able to call something red, green, blue, etc. . . . These three colors are merely hypotheses, hypothetical colors; and they require our vision for their confirmation. Not only do they not exist solely at the level of light, but they also do not exist solely at the level of the eyeball or of the eye's aqueous fluid, or the iris, or the optic nerve either. If you were to use a scalpel to cut open these optical organs, you would not find any reds, greens, and blues. These three colors are only a momentary illusion, and the memory of these colors constitutes only an inverted reflection of that same illusion. (415–16)

Here, Wumingshi sketched a rather modern-sounding theory of perception—one grounded not on a simple stimulus-response model but on the principle that sight only becomes possible, to paraphrase the turn-of-the-century neurologist Charles Sherington, "through the reciprocal interaction of all these different elements" of the optical system.[7] The visual image, in this approach, is not a direct correlate of some external object or scene; rather, it is a contingent and somewhat arbitrary creation of the human optical and nervous systems.

Whereas the discussion of the fundamental contingency of visual perception is articulated through explicitly "modern" discourses of optical physiognomy (with references to the iris, aqueous fluid, optic nerve, etc.), Wumingshi also deliberately and pointedly translated a similar ocular skepticism into the "indigenous" traditions of Chinese art theory and Buddhist thought. For instance, the *Blooming Flowers* passage on colors, cited above, concludes with the following reflection:

---

7. For a discussion, see Crary, *Suspensions of Perception*, 349.

> These three colors are nothing more than a momentary illusion, and the memories of these colors are nothing more than the inverted reflection of that illusion, like the reflection of a pavilion in water. At this moment, we can enjoy only our instantaneous illusion.
>
> Our entire life is merely an illusory life. (415–16)

On one hand, this allusion to the pavilion's reflection in water evokes the "flowers in the mirror, and the moon in water" (*jinghua shuiyue*) aphorism, the connotations of which are further reinforced by the similarly Buddhist observation that "our life is merely an illusion." On the other hand, the reference to the pavilion's reflection also suggests one of the most recognizable visual motifs in Chinese art: the single pavilion beside a lake in the foreground of many of the minimalist landscape paintings by the Yuan dynasty painter Ni Zan 倪瓚.

This evocative juxtaposition of allusions to Ni Zan's art and the "flowers in the mirror" formula is made even more explicit in another passage later in the same chapter:

> [The expression] "flowers in the mirror and the reflection of the moon in water" is not [a reference to] life's true flower and true moon, but it is nevertheless still an apparent flower and an apparent moon. An apparent object is not an original object, "resemblance" (*si* 似) is not "truth" (*zhen* 真); but it is only not the "truly true" and remains "apparently true." In the eyeball's cornea and the conjunctiva, flowers in the mirror still retain the form and appearance of flowers, and the reflection of the moon in water still retains the form of the moon; the former has color, and the latter has illumination. And even if it is the case that this color and illumination are neither true nor originary color and illumination, then we must still ask to what extent true moon and flowers themselves can be said to have true light and color? (437–38)

The irony of this passage is that this traditional Buddhist insight into the unreliability of sensory perception and the ephemerality of human existence is yoked to a highly skeptical reading of the visual epistemology underlying modern medical understandings of visual perception. In this way, the passage suggests that *all* visual perception is necessarily located at the level of the merely "apparently true," rather than that of the "truly true."

This passage returns to the theme of Chinese painting, specifically addressing Ni Zan, who was implicitly alluded to in the earlier passage:

> A painting by Ni Yunlin 倪雲林 [Ni Zan] is, after all, a painting; a Qing dynasty imitation (*fang* 仿) of one of his paintings is false (*jia* 假), yet similarly it is still a painting. This latter work is not the original color, but it is still a true painting by the Qing dynasty painter. Ni Yulin would say that it is a forgery (*jia*), yet the Qing dynasty painter would say that it is "true" (*zhen* 真). (438)

Wumingshi's emphasis on Ni Zan is significant insofar as Ni Zan was one of the four "Yuan masters" whom the late Ming dynasty painter and theorist Dong Qichang singled out in his influential advocacy of artistic innovation through subtle variations on established stylistic models (with Ni Zan's own style constituting one of those models), as opposed to an emphasis on issues of mimeticism and reference. In a well-known observation about his own artistic practice, Ni Zan once noted: "What I call painting is no more than free brushwork done sketchily*; it does not aim at formal resemblance* and is merely done for my own amusement" (italics added).[8] Wumingshi's observation, however, deals not so much with Ni Zan's antimimetic tendencies as with the artistic practice (increasingly prevalent during the late imperial period) of *fang*, or "creative imitation." The act of modeling one's own work after the style of an established master such as Ni Zan was generally seen not as an act of "plagiarism" but as a form of creative production. Thus, the Qing dynasty practice of *fang* is "false" only if seen as an attempt to replicate the Ni Zan original; it is actually "true" or "authentic" (*zhen*) if viewed as an artistic creation in its own right.

Following this discussion of Ni Zan's paintings, Wumingshi makes a similar point about the relationship between copying and authenticity in a suggestive discussion of counterfeit coins:

> A counterfeit coin, until it is discovered to be counterfeit, has the same value as a real coin. Moreover, even after it has been found to be a counterfeit, it still retains the same true value as an actual counterfeit coin. Now, assume that it is a coin created in imitation (*fang*) of the past, even though it won't have the aesthetic beauty or monetary value of a real coin, it nevertheless still has its modeled (*fangzao* 仿造) beauty and value. (438)

8. Ni Zan, *Qingbige ji* in *Changzhou xianzhe yishu*, comp. Sheng Xuanhuai (Wujin: 1899), 10.5a; cited and translated in Bush, *The Chinese Literati on Painting*, 135.

It is quite appropriate that Wumingshi concludes with a discussion of the counterfeit coin, since the coin is an example par excellence of a class of object that derives its value, and indeed its meaning, from the process of being reproduced and exchanged. Although counterfeiting, at one level, challenges the coin's orthodoxy of value, the coin's very nature is, at the same time, grounded on the possibility of the controlled production of identical replicas of itself. This double figure of the (counterfeit) coin, furthermore, allows us to expand further on the discussion of the "coin of gender" in Chen Sen's *Precious Mirror for Evaluating Flowers*, insofar as Wumingshi's discussion suggests that not only is value created through a process of exchange, but so are perceptions of identity and authenticity.

Whereas the discussions of visual representation and perception in *Blooming Flowers* tend to revolve around epistemological issues of perception and knowledge, in *Great Enlightenment of the Creation of a New Era*, by contrast, the focus tends to be more on axiological issues concerning the ways in which one individual relates to another. For instance, almost immediately after Yin Di's marriage to his cousin Qu Ying at the very beginning of the novel, there is a scene in which the two newlyweds find themselves in a beauty salon, where Qu Ying watches Yin Di's reflection in a large mirror positioned in front of her. The narrator remarks: "This transparent pane of glass was like a transparent language, and through it they were able to communicate with each other" (58). A few chapters later, the figure of a dressing mirror intrudes into another intimate scene between Yin Di and his new bride:

> You certainly can't place a bureau or cabinet, or even a large chest, with a full-length mirror in your bedroom, because if you do, your entire imaginative disposition will be doomed. A large dressing mirror is sufficient to cause you to flicker day and night like a specter or ghost. A person's entire soul will become concentrated in their image, and they will forget the beauty of the external universe. At the same time, the mirror's excessively bright reflection has the capacity to destroy a person's thought and imagination. (106)

Although this passage might appear to signal a return to the sort of specular skepticism found in the previous volume of Wumingshi's work (with its concern with mimicry and imitation), its significance is specified in the following paragraph. The figure of the mirror is redeployed to bring it into alignment with *Enlightenment*'s more axiological concerns with the nature of interpersonal recognition and valuation: "We have another, even more beautiful, mirror—namely, all sorts of fresh flowers and evergreen plants, and they reflect back to us our own spirits" (106). Here, Nature itself is viewed as a sort of mirror writ large, against and through which the subject becomes able to perceive herself.

This "mirror of nature" metaphor is developed more explicitly a few pages later, when a lake is described as a figurative spiritual mirror: "Gradually, the lake ceased being a lake and instead became a silvery mirror for reflecting all sorts of thought projections: shadows of mountains, of embankments, of trees, of stones, of clouds, of pagodas, of buildings, of walls, of flowers, of grass, of birds, of people, . . . ; of all these, there was none that was not merely a thought shadow" (137). The same figure of this specular lake recurs about halfway through the novel, with an even more explicit emphasis on axiological recognition. In this scene, Yin Di is speaking with Qu Ying and quotes a fragment from a Tang dynasty lyric poem to describe the feeling the lake inspires in him: "This entire lake is a boudoir mirror, and we are all about to become young women, inserting flowers into our hair in front of the mirror." Qu Ying immediately recognizes this literary allusion and quietly recites the relevant poem by the (male) poet Wen Tingyun 温庭筠: "Inserting flowers in front and in back of the mirror / the flower and the face mutually reflect each other" (528). In this exchange, Wumingshi takes the trope of the lake-as-mirror and gives it a gendered twist, whereby Yin Di implicitly sees in the lake/mirror not his "own" reflection but himself *as a young woman*. Whereas Yin Di's original remark suggests the surreptitious intrusion of the specter of femininity into a narcissistic moment of male specularity, Qu Ying's subsequent echo of his quote suggests the opposite: namely, how, under the male (poetic) gaze, a woman's moment of specular *recognition* becomes instead a symbol of her reduction to the status of mere figuration.[9]

---

9. Along these lines, it is significant that the genre of *ci* 詞 lyric poetry, to which this particular Wen Tingyun poem belongs, is itself (in)famous for the practice of having male poets poetically ventriloquize women's voices, particularly those of female courtesans. For further discussion of this issue, see Fong, "Engendering the Lyric."

Wumingshi later brought the fascination with the physiological basis of visual perception developed in *Blooming Flowers* and the concern with axiological ethics developed in *Great Enlightenment* together in an essay, "Dongti ningsi" 胴體凝思 (Meditations on the body), which itself developed out of the passage in *Blooming Flowers* discussed above. This essay points to the invisible disjunction intervening between raw visual stimuli and the higher-order mental processes that enable the observer to make sense of them:

> If you cut open the cerebral membrane and the central nervous system, you won't find these lines and curves inside, nor will you find these complex myriad manifestations of nature. No camera will be able to photograph the internal sensations of curvature, of straightness, and of myriad forms, which they generate when they move. And even if you were to photograph them, you would still not be able to capture that highest determining and ultimate deciding power that resides in the central nervous system. You would be even less able to capture those exceedingly complex and internal forms of the circulation of our ideas. What, in the end, is it that is determining and deciding? How do those passive organs and dynamic physiological processes communicate and come together with those ultimate judgments and news? (392)

In this passage from "Meditations on the Body," as well as in the passage on visual physiognomy from *Blooming Flowers*, there is an implicit critique of the modernist confidence that *direct observation* (combined with mediated perception via an assortment of prosthetic visual devices) of the structure and functioning of the human body necessarily leads to a more accurate understanding of the body's physiological processes. The fact that the physiological process in question is itself specifically an *optical* one serves to further compound the resulting optical skepticism.

This line of reasoning anticipates (or, in the case of the "Meditations" essay, perhaps even echoes) more recent "postmodernist" arguments that objects and events do not exist independently of the concrete physiological process by which they are perceived in the first place. For instance, the opening of the "Meditations on the Body" essay articulates this polemical postulate with surprising directness:

> Human corporeal bodies are, perhaps, mere signifiers (*fuhao* 符號). After this corporeal signifier has been developed (*xianying* 顯影) and fixed (*dingying* 定影)

on a roll of Kodak film, it becomes a dark shadow (*heiying* 黑影). On a sheet of wove paper that has been exposed to sunlight, it becomes a cluster of lights and shadows, with washes of ink and color added to lines and curves. In Eastern ink and wash paintings, it mainly displays the mood and flavor of the component calligraphic strokes, to which are added compositional components, coloring, the technique of baked dyes, etc. With Michelangelo, it becomes a stone statue; and with the cubists, it can sometimes take the form of a pile of toy bricks, a violin, or any other of a wide assortment of utensils. In the eyes of the Dadaists, it becomes mere grains of sand, black dots, or other markings. (389)

Although this passage articulates a skepticism as to whether the "reality" of the human body can be disarticulated from the various visual signifiers used to represent it, another passage a few pages later articulates a similar skepticism toward the physiological and epistemological status of the visual image itself:

> Life stares at life. Faces stare at faces. Eyes stare at eyes. How can this eye remain within that eye? How can one eye walk into another? How can an eye climb into someone's hair, skin, cervical vertebra, body hair, and fibrous tissue? How can it make out which is this eye, and which is that eye? When they are inextricably bound up with each other, how can one eye know that there is another eye? How does one vitreous body know that there is another vitreous body? How does light recognize light? How does color recognize color? How does a face's roundness, a mouth's polyhedral shape, or an eyebrow's straightness manage to take form within the perceiving pupil? And how about the convexity of a nose? Is life's most secretive and most mysterious inner space merely the product of an initial cluster of circles, lines, and polyhedrons? (391)

This remarkable passage starts from the psychoanalytically seminal moment of "specular" recognition—in which one face perceives another, and one eye stares at another—and then proceeds to radically defamiliarize this scene by breaking it down into its individual physiological components ("How does the vitreous body know that there is another vitreous body?"). The passage simultaneously breaks down the visual image itself into its separate geometrical components: "a cluster of circles, lines, and polyhedrons." The question posited here is not only how we perceive sight itself but—more important—how we perceive the necessary gap between raw sensory data and the additional processes by which we are able to make sense of that data.

This theme of "eyes star(ing) at eyes," in turn, touches on what is arguably one of the central concerns of *Anonymous Book*. Above, I discuss Wumingshi's use of the trope of mutually reflective mirrors to describe Yin Di's relationship with Sha Kaluo; here he uses a similar metaphor to interrogate the relationship between vision and reality itself. At issue in both of these cases is not only the question of how we may perceive and understand visuality, but also the more abstract issue of how vision and specular reflexivity are perceived as intersecting within modern structures of consciousness. For instance, this notion of having become the object of a figurative "returned gaze" is explicitly associated with the "auratic" in Walter Benjamin's famous essay on "The Work of Art in the Age of Mechanical Reproduction":

> Experience of the aura thus rests on the transposition of a response common in human relationships to the relationship between the inanimate or natural object and human beings. The person whom we look at, or who feels he is being looked at, looks at us in turn. To perceive the aura of a phenomenon means to invest it with the ability to look at us in turn. (188)

Benjamin associated the modern period with the gradual loss of a sense of the auratic, although, ironically, it is during this same modern period that the aura first becomes intelligible as such. The aura, with its dimension of the returned gaze, therefore becomes, to paraphrase Benjamin, a sort of "love at last sight"—a structure of identification that can be appreciated only when it is on the verge of being lost.

More recently, Jacques Lacan developed a similar conceit of the inanimate world gazing back at the observer in his well-known discussion of the "sardine can" in Seminar XI. Lacan recounted that, during a fishing trip, a friend had joked with him, "You see that can? Do you see it? Well, it doesn't see you." Lacan later reflected to himself that the sardine can "was looking at me, all the same. It was looking at me at the level of the point of light, the point of light, the point at which everything that looks at me is situated—and I am not speaking metaphorically."[10] In this rather cryptic passage, Lacan is drawing attention to the way in which the subject is not only the possessor of a localized and

10. Lacan, *Four Fundamental Concepts of Psychoanalysis*, 95.

embodied "look," but also, necessarily, the figurative object of a more abstract, disembodied "gaze."

One of the interesting implications of Lacan's discussion of the sardine can is that it represents a move away from the inherently *dyadic* model of perception and subject formation found in his earlier "mirror stage" model to a more complex *triadic* model, in which the viewing subject is positioned as the direct object, not of the sardine can's imagined gaze, but, to borrow Martin Jay's description of this passage, of the "screen in an impersonal field of pure monstrance."[11] That is, the subjectivity of the viewer, in this model, is perceived as being split between the physical location of the embodied subject, on one hand, and the figurative "screen" against which the subject perceives herself as the *object* of an array of abstract sociocultural gazes, on the other. In the context of Wumingshi's novel, this idealized moment of narcissistic self-reflection is interrupted not so much by the objectifying gaze of the "voice of the father" as by (e.g., in the Wen Tingyun passage discussed above) the implicitly "female," *self-objectifying* gaze of absent presence.

Philosophies of Commoditization

> Each woman is simply a cigarette, the only difference between them simply being at the level of their respective brand names.
>
> —Wumingshi, *Golden Night of the Serpent*

The linkage, which Wumingshi develops in *Anonymous Book*, of "woman," commoditization, and epochal transition is illustrated particularly clearly in the genre of the calendar poster, which first appeared in China as early as 1895 and became increasingly popular during the first decades of the twentieth century. Essentially a synthesis of the traditional genres of the "New Year's poster" and the "beautiful woman" prints, these modern pictures typically featured a combination of a printed calendar and a visually striking image of a person or scene. Even though it eventually became common to produce the posters without the calendars, they nevertheless continued to be referred to as "calendar posters." Similarly, even though these posters featured a wide variety of historical or fictional scenes, they came to be most stereotypically associated with

11. Jay, *Downcast Eyes*, 365–66.

their illustrations of "beautiful woman"—in which the women appeared dressed either in traditional or in modern attire.

The practical and aesthetic appeal of the posters (viz., the inclusion of the calendars and the colorful images) were ultimately merely strategic elements to facilitate the posters' primary objective of advertising specific commodities. Furthermore, although the posters were used to promote a wide array of different products, they were associated primarily with cigarettes. The resulting stereotypical image of the "beautiful woman" calendar poster advertising specific brands of cigarettes was, therefore, grounded on a crucial paradox—the visual association of women with cigarettes stood in ironic contrast to the fact that the vast majority of cigarette smokers in the early twentieth century were actually men (as remains the case in China today, although to a somewhat lesser extent). Presumably, the typical male viewer was expected not to identify with the women depicted in the posters but to make an imaginary linkage between the figurative "consumption" of beautiful women and the actual consumption of cigarettes. At the same time, underlying this parallelism between the consumption of women and of cigarettes was a process of displaced *identification* between the commoditized women depicted in the posters and the (typically male) viewers, who were thereby interpellated into the commodity logic of the poster (a displaced identification rendered more ironic by the fact that many of the "beautiful women" in these posters were *men*, because of the general taboo in China at that time against live women models).

This evocative parallel between the commoditization of women and the consequent reductive reification of male viewers as they are interpellated into that same commodity system is developed particularly clearly in the 1930s short story "Luotuo, Ni Cai zhuyizhe yu nüren" 駱駝, 尼采主義著與女人 (Camel, Nietzschean, and woman), by the "new perceptionist" author Mu Shiying 穆時英. The narrator of the story opens with an explicit linkage between Nietzsche's metaphor of the camel in *Thus Spoke Zarathustra* and Camel cigarettes. He then proceeds to become infatuated with a "modern woman," who instructs him about "373 brands of cigarettes, 23 kinds of coffee, and 5,000 formulas for mixed drinks."[12]

12. Mu Shiying, "Luotuo, Ni Cai zhuyizhe yu nüren," 195.

In this story, the figure of the modern woman comes to occupy a double position—her own reified status mirrors the general system of commodity fetishism within which she is embedded, and the erotic power she has over the male narrator similarly mirrors his own subjected status within a regime of postmodern commodity culture.

Mu Shiying's short story can be seen as an attempt to bridge the separate discourses of aesthetics, philosophy, and commodity capitalism, particularly by playing on the convenient coincidence between the Camel brand name and Nietzsche's famous foregrounding of the figure of the camel in the opening of *Thus Spoke Zarathustra*. The latter half of Wumingshi's *Golden Night of the Serpent* from approximately a decade and a half later contains a strikingly similar reference to the commoditizing "philosophy" that can be associated with (Camel) cigarettes. Sha Kaluo at one point is described as "stuff[ing] a Camel cigarette into [Yin Di's] mouth [and saying to him:] 'Come and enjoy a cigarette; all philosophy has its origins in the green/blue smoke of a cigarette'" (2: 261). This passage is not an isolated example; it is located within a complex web of allusions to cigarettes throughout Wumingshi's volume as a whole.

One of the most direct comparisons of Sha Kaluo and cigarettes can be found near the beginning of the second half of *Golden Night*. After Sha Kaluo points out to Yin Di that she is the same young woman who caused him considerable anguish fifteen years earlier (when she went by the name of Guo Shaojia), he then informs her: "In my life, you are that kind of a cigarette butt. My entire past spiritual conflagration, right up to the ashes of the present, is all the result of that single tossed cigarette" (2: 42). In the context of the present discussion of *fin-de-siècle* consciousness, this fiery metaphor of the cigarette carries obvious connotations of an end-of-the-world conflagration, together with the suggestion of a symbolic phoenix rising from the ashes to herald the arrival of a new era.[13] This linkage between actual cigarettes and Sha Kaluo's conflagrational sexuality is developed equally explicitly a few pages

13. Although the myth of the phoenix is of Egyptian rather than Chinese origins, it was a familiar myth in Wumingshi's twentieth-century China, as exemplified by Guo Moruo's 郭沫若 famous poem "Fenghuang niepan" 鳳凰涅盤 (Phoenix nirvana). Wumingshi himself integrated many explicit Egyptian references into his text as well.

earlier, when Sha Kaluo remarks sarcastically to Yin Di, "God only knows that sleeping with a woman is equivalent to simply smoking a cigarette. Each woman is merely a cigarette, the only difference between them simply being at the level of their respective brand names" (2: 36). Here, the use of individual brand names to illustrate the reification associated with commodity fetishism suggests a systematic divergence between loci of individual identity and the ways in which those identities (in the form of their brand names) come to circulate within a larger socio-symbolic environment.

Wumingshi's association of woman with cigarettes in this passage underscores the degree to which women, in Wumingshi's works, are not only presented as objects of addictive fascination, but also constitute a hazardous presence that constantly threatens to destabilize the integrity of the (male) gaze that is ineluctably drawn to them. Like cigarettes, furthermore, women in the novel constitute figures of temporal specificity, while at the same time also symbolizing a perennial chain of substitution that implicitly stretches from the darkest recesses of primeval history to the end of time itself. Composed at a pivotal moment in modern China, *Anonymous Book* itself similarly reflects a historically specific cluster of anxieties about perceptions of both gender and the visual gaze, while simultaneously bridging the late Qing and contemporary concerns, as explored in Parts I and III of this volume, with the reliability of visual imagery and gendered identity.

5

Jin Yong and Picturing Nationalism

Traditionally, it has always been graphic artists that have provided illustrations for authors, but in antiquity or in the present, in China or abroad, it seems as though there has never been a case in which a novelist has used stories to "illustrate" an album of drawings.

— Jin Yong, *Thirty-Three Images of Chivalrous Swordsmen*

Standing in stark contrast to the virtual anonymity of the aptly (pen-)named Wumingshi, the Hong Kong martial-arts novelist Jin Yong 金庸 (1924–) is quite possibly the most widely read Chinese-language author in the world today. Not only did his novels become mega-bestsellers in China and throughout the Chinese diaspora, but many of them have been adapted into a variety of other media, including film, television, comic books, and video games. Recent polls repeatedly place Jin Yong within the top echelon of modern Chinese writers, and the extent of his cultural influence is reflected in the common observation that his works constitute "the common language of Chinese around the world."[1] Although I take Jin Yong's extraordinary popularity as my starting point, I begin here by considering one of his lesser-known works. In January and February 1970, Jin Yong "illustrated" a small album of drawings of famous "chivalrous swordsmen" by the early nineteenth-century artist Ren Weizhang 任渭長, who, Jin Yong notes, "is commonly regarded as our nation's last great master of [woodblock] engravings. All subsequent engravings were influenced by Western aesthetics, resulting in a style quite different from that of traditional

1. For a discussion of this expression, see Hamm, *Paper Swordsmen*, 49.

China."[2] While *Sanshisan jianke tu* 三十三劍客圖 (Thirty-three images of chivalrous swordsmen), Jin Yong's "illustration" of Ren Weizhang's drawings, is a minor work within the Jin Yong canon—more a series of sketches than a coherent novel—it nevertheless marks three crucial transitional moments crucial to an understanding of Jin Yong's significance.

First, the work's composition in early 1970 positions it precisely at the end of the fifteen-year period during which Jin Yong composed and serialized all fifteen of his major fictional works and at the beginning of the decade from 1970 to 1980 during which he would systematically revise and "rewrite" each of his novels for publication as independent (nonserialized) volumes.[3] By the same token, Jin Yong's gesture of taking Ren Weizhang's text and reframing it as a literary volume ironically mirrors Jin Yong's subsequent attempt to "reframe" his own earlier works, stripping them from the specific historical context within which they were originally composed and re-presenting them as ideally timeless contributions to the Chinese literary canon.

Second, Jin Yong positioned Ren Weizhang at a symbolic watershed between two representational regimes, as the "last great master of woodblock engravings" to have been untainted by Western aesthetics. In locating Ren at this symbolic watershed of representational practice, Jin Yong notes that Ren was working on the cusp of the large-scale Western cultural imperialism in China following the Opium War. Jin Yong, meanwhile, finds himself straddling a similar historico-technological divide. He relies on modern technologies of mass reproduction (including not only printing but also television, cinema, and, increasingly, the Internet) to disseminate his works to a readership throughout the global Chinese diaspora, but his novels typically deal with issues and themes from China's own "traditional," imperial past. Third, Jin Yong's act of "textually illustrating" a graphic work underscores the degree to which *all* his works are positioned at the interstices of the textual and the visual, insofar as the genre of martial-arts fiction is arguably driven by the attempt to render inherently visual

2. Jin Yong, *Sanshisan jianke tu*, 701.

3. Li Yijian, "Canonically 'Rewriting' Jin Yong's Novels."

action into narrative—which then inspires the inverse gesture of translating it back into visual media.

Here, I consider one of Jin Yong's best-known and most ambitious works, his multivolume *Tianlong ba bu* 天龍八部[4] (serialized in Hong Kong between 1963 and 1967). Specifically, I use discussions of visual imagery in Jin Yong's works to examine social and psychic processes of identification with "imaginary" communities of various sorts.[5] In these works, the visual image becomes one of the paradigmatic means for accomplishing this process of imaginary identification. I focus on the figure of the illustrated martial-arts "picture manual" (*tupu* 圖譜) in that work and specifically argue that these manuals paradigmatically function by enabling viewers to establish a visual and corporeal identification with the externalized image of an "Other." In this sense, the picture manuals in *Tianlong ba bu* replicate in miniature one of the functions of Jin Yong's fiction itself, insofar as they provide an external cultural model, or screen, against which readers in China and throughout the Chinese diaspora can position themselves.

The Image of Jin Yong

> Every novel is an ideal plane inserted into the realm of reality. Cervantes takes pleasure in confusing the objective and the subjective, the world of the reader and the world of the book.
>
> —Jorge Luis Borges

Comprising five volumes and about two thousand pages in many of its contemporary reprints, *Tianlong ba bu* is one of Jin Yong's most elaborate works. The novel follows the intersecting paths of three main protagonists (Duan Yu, Xiao Feng, and Xu Zhu) together with a multitude of minor ones. It is set against a backdrop of the complex political and ethnic structure of China and East Asia during the late Northern Song (960–1127). At the time, "China" was a highly contested

4. Jin Yong's text offers "Demi-gods and Semi-devils" as the English translation of the title, but since this translation is not widely used and does not seem satisfactory, I use the transliteration of the Chinese title here.

5. I am borrowing Benedict Anderson's concept of *imaginary* as developed in his analysis of modern nationalist identity in *Imagined Communities*.

conceptual entity, with a number of ethno-political powers asserting varying degrees of sovereignty over territory to the north, west, and south of that controlled by the (Chinese) Song dynasty. As a character in the novel observes at one point:

> In the contemporary world, the five nations of the Great Liao 大遼, Great Song 大宋, Tufan 吐蕃, Western Xia 西夏, and Dali 大理 stand side by side; and except for the nation of Dali, remotely located on the southern border and therefore not in conflict with anyone else, the other four nations are hopelessly interlocked with one another. (1573)

The political geography alluded to here can be summarized as follows: in the first half of the eleventh century, two Central Asian empires had established enough power to force the Song dynasty to sign two unfavorable treaties. The first of these treaties was with the Liao empire of the Khitans 契丹, located in what is today northern Hebei and Shanxi provinces; the second was with the Western Xia kingdom of the Tanguts 黨項 to the northwest. In addition to the Song, Liao, and Western Xia, there was also the Tibetan kingdom of Tufan to the west, and finally, in modern-day Yunnan, the modest kingdom of Dali, which enjoyed political sovereignty from 902 until 1253, when it was destroyed by the Mongols.

Beyond these five empires and kingdoms, several other ethno-political groups make appearances in the novel. For example, there are occasional allusions to the Jürchens 女眞, the founders of the Jin dynasty, which overthrew the Liao dynasty and then occupied north China in 1126; as well as to the kingdom of Yan, already defunct for more than half a millennium by the time the events of the novel take place, which makes a spectral appearance via two of its descendents who endeavor to resurrect the ancient kingdom's glory. Finally, a fictional, multiethnic brigade known as the Beggars' Gang (*gaibang* 丐幫) also plays a central role in the work. Although its members hail from various different ethnicities, in political terms it is adamantly pro-Song and anti-Liao.

Each of the work's three main protagonists represents a different ethno-political entity. For example, the novel opens with an account of Duan Yu—who, it is later revealed, is ostensibly the crown prince of the kingdom of Dali.[6] In addition to allowing him to inherit his father's throne, Duan Yu's bloodline also becomes an issue near the beginning of the novel, when he becomes infatuated with three young women—only to come to believe (mistakenly, it turns out) that they are his half-sisters. The second protagonist, Xiao Feng, is the leader of the Beggars' Gang. Although this leadership position (unlike Duan Yu's) is non-hereditary, Xiao's ancestry becomes an important factor when he discovers roughly halfway through the novel that, although he was raised as a Han Chinese, his biological parents were Khitans.[7] The third major protagonist is Xu Zhu, a Han Chinese whose attempt to pursue the ascetic life of a Buddhist monk is stymied by his receipt of what would otherwise be enviable honors—including marriage to a daughter of the emperor of the Western Xia. In addition to these three protagonists, two of the more prominent secondary characters are Mu Rongfu and You Tanzhi. Mu Rongfu, believing himself to be a descendent of the ruling house of the Later Yan kingdom (defunct for more than five hundred years), tries to re-establish the kingdom by marrying a princess from the Western Xia empire. You Tanzhi spends much of the novel pursuing Xiao Feng to seek retribution for Xiao's role in the deaths of You's parents. At the same time, You also becomes infatuated with Duan Yu's half-sister, Ah Zi, who is in love with Xiao Feng.

The novel ends on a stunning chord of desolation and compounded misery of Sophoclean proportions. Having been forced to betray his native Liao dynasty in order to protect the "Chinese" Song dynasty, Xiao Feng commits suicide by stabbing two arrows into his heart (1967). After his suicide, as Ah Zi is mourning his corpse, she is approached by the now-blind You Tanzhi (he donated his eyes to Ah Zi earlier in the novel), and Ah Zi immediately proceeds to gouge her "own" eyes out of their sockets and fling them back at him. When the proverbial dust clears, Duan Yu—who has recently learned that, with the death of his (ostensible) father, he has become emperor of Dali—

6. Actually, it is ultimately revealed that Duan Yu's father is actually not the emperor of Dali but another man with the same surname; but this discovery is not made public and everyone continues to view Duan Yu as the crown prince.

7. In recognition of this discovery of his "true" ethnicity, he promptly changes his surname from Qiao to Xiao.

returns home with his entourage. One of the first scenes they observe upon reaching Dali is of a crowd of children paying obeisance to the "emperor." Just as Duan Yu is wondering how the children could have learned so quickly that he had assumed the throne, he realizes that they are genuflecting not to him but to the now-insane Mu Rongfu, the self-proclaimed "Emperor of Yan," who is rewarding them with candy for their tribute.

As even this highly schematic plot summary makes clear, a central concern in Jin Yong's novel is the relationship between visual appearance and identity, including gendered, ethnic, political, and genealogical (familial) identities. For instance, the novel explores the tension between appearance and identity through the theme of cross-dressing, as when Xiao Feng's quest for filial vengeance goes awry when he unwittingly kills his beloved, Ah Zhu, because she happened to be disguised as her own father. Jin Yong's work also develops this issue of visual identity through an attention to the themes of masking, corporeal inscriptions, the rediscovery of blood ties, and the like. The theme of masking is developed most strikingly in the case of You Tanzhi, whose head is encased in an iron mask. When he finally succeeds in removing it, he discovers that his face was so badly scarred by the molten iron that he has to fashion himself another mask made out of human flesh. Similarly, tattoos and other visual marks are frequently used as clues to an individual's "true" identity—as in Chapter 23, when Ah Zi finally realizes her true paternity because of the "Duan" 段 ideograph tattooed on her shoulder. In each of these cases, visual markers of identity are frequently at variance with other assumptions about the subject's identity and may indeed come to function as the basis for a new understanding or re-imagining of those same identities. Even in cases in which the external markers correspond to an individual's "real" identity (as in the case of Ah Zi's "Duan" tattoos), they nevertheless illustrate the degree to which even "real" identity is itself ultimately constructed or imagined.

Furthermore, in addition to these various interrogations of the relationship between external appearance and intrinsic identity, there is a parallel theme of the relationship between these sorts of intrinsic identity and the more socially constructed identities produced within the martial-arts social space each character inhabits. For instance, a recurrent theme in Jin Yong's work concerns the relationship between various characters' actual paternity (their relationship to their biological "father" [*fu* 父]), and their "social" paternity (their relationship to their martial-arts "master" [*shifu* 師父]).[8] These surrogate kinship relations come to serve as a model for the social constructivity of other, more naturalized, forms of identity (familial, gendered, ethnic). This theme of martial-arts identity as a performative social construct comes full circle to the theme of visual appearance via the figure of illustrated martial-arts "picture manuals."

These picture manuals in *Tianlong ba bu* complement the many other instances of visual imagery in Jin Yong's works, but they may also be compared to other precedents in Chinese culture of using illustrated manuals for instructional purposes. For example, China has a long tradition of "sex manuals" (*chungong hua* 春宮畫); originally they appear to have served a hygienic, instructional function (e.g., for newlyweds), but increasingly came to be used as a means of voyeuristic sexual titillation.[9] A related tradition can be found in the illustrated painting manuals, which first appeared during the Song dynasty and became increasingly popular during the Yuan and Ming dynasties.[10] These manuals typically contained models of how to paint stereotypical literati imagery such as bamboo and plum blossoms and, as such, implicitly reinforced the literati identity on which they were premised. At the same time they implicitly challenged the limits of that social identity itself because, in theory, the manuals made it possible for anyone to learn "literati" representational techniques. An important characteristic of both of these pictorial/textual traditions is that the picture manuals functioned both as orthodox interpellative devices introducing the subject into certain pre-established social structures and as transgressive challenges to the very identity of those social structures themselves. In the following discussion of the picture manuals in Jin Yong's text, I similarly examine their simultaneous interpellative and transgressive potentials.

8. See Song Weijie, *Cong yule xingwei dao wutuobang chongdong*, 97–107.

9. Van Gulik, *Sexual Life in Ancient China*, 168, 268. For a detailed discussion of this genre of text, see Wile, *Art of the Bedchamber*.

10. For a detailed discussion of this genre, see Sungmii Lee Han, "Wu Chen's 'Mo-Chu P'u,'" chap. 3.

There are three prominent instances of martial-arts picture manuals in *Tianlong ba bu*, each of which ostensibly provides a different character in the novel with a visual model for the acquisition of martial-arts mastery. The first such manual, *Lingbo weibu* 凌波微步 (Walk with dainty steps as if treading the waves), is initially discovered by Duan Yu in Chapter 2. Although the discussions of the text are concentrated in Chapters 2 through 9 (at which point Duan Yu realizes that he has accidentally destroyed the manual), allusions to the actual martial-arts practice by the same name continue to recur periodically throughout the rest of the novel. The second manual is You Tanzhi's *Yijin jing* 異筋經 (Classic of the shifting tendon), references to which are concentrated in Chapters 27–28. Finally, in Chapter 39, Xu Zhu discovers the final such "picture manual"—although the text in this last instance takes the form not of a bound volume, as in the previous two examples, but of a series of images inscribed on the stone wall of a cave. Below, I briefly discuss each of these three texts and then proceed to a more general consideration of some of the issues of identity and representation they raise.

The *Dainty Steps* manual first appears when Duan Yu visits the cave of the Sister Goddess Immortal and finds the picture manual, together with written instructions from the goddess telling him to practice diligently the martial arts it contains.[11] When Duan Yu opens the manual, the nude images of the goddess inspire in him a sense of excitement and shock:

> With his left hand, he slowly opened the silk scroll, and suddenly gasped "Ah!"—His heart started pounding, his face and ears instantly turned red, and his entire body became feverish.
>
> He was startled to see a painted image of a reclining nude woman appear on the silk scroll: her entire body was completely bare and her visage was identical to that of that jade figure [a statue which he had just encountered in the cave and initially mistaken for a real person]. Duan Yu felt that to continue to look would constitute an act of blasphemy against the Goddess Immortal, and therefore he

11. Given this injunction to observe, and model himself on, the images of the Goddess Immortal contained in the manual, it is intriguing to note that the manual's name, *Lingbo weibu*, coincides with the Chinese name for the narcissus flower, *lingbo xianzi* 凌波仙子, or "dainty-stepping immortal."

quickly slammed the scroll shut and turned away. After a long pause, he once again started to reflect, "The Goddess Immortal instructed me: 'You must carefully practice [the martial arts techniques illustrated in] the following images.' Therefore, I must follow her instructions so as not to be disrespectful." (61)

When he initially views the manual, Duan Yu finds himself conflating the printed images with the imagined naked body of the goddess herself. Although the resulting slippage of image and referent might appear to imply that the images are highly mimetic, the passage specifies that the naked figures in the manual are overlaid with schematic symbols denoting such things as the locations of the body's acupoints and "vital energy veins."

References to either the illustrated scroll or its specific martial-arts techniques recur on a regular basis over the next several chapters. In Chapter 5, for instance, Duan Yu suddenly remembers the Goddess Immortal's injunction that he study diligently from the scroll—but even the mere thought of its contents is enough to set his pulse racing and make him blush in embarrassment (180). He tries to reassure himself that because the Goddess herself instructed him to study from the scroll, his viewing images of her naked body would not constitute a blasphemy. Nevertheless, he still attempts to focus only on the written text on the reverse side of the illustrations, together with his own *memory* of the images themselves:

He didn't dare to look too long at the nude female images in the illustrations, and therefore, having memorized from the illustrations the locations of the acupoints and *jingmai* [vital energy veins], he proceeded to practice the martial arts in question relying only on this memorized information. (180)

In Chapter 9, however, Duan Yu seeks the scroll in the stone chamber where he had stored it, only to find that it has been mutilated almost beyond recognition. After a moment of initial confusion, he realizes that he must have been the one who had destroyed the scroll:

When he was locked up in the stone chamber by Qingbao Guaike, he felt unbearably hot and, as a result, tore off all his clothes and ripped them up; and later, when he was deliriously running around back and forth, he continued ripping his clothes up and, in the confusion, must have accidentally ripped up the silk scroll as well. (345)

This destruction of the *Dainty Steps* scroll represents a form of psychic closure for Duan Yu. The same sorts of feverish restlessness the nude images in the scroll had originally inspired in him are ultimately also responsible for the scroll's destruction. The sexual dynamics that had caused him such acute embarrassment upon viewing the Goddess Immortal's nude image are, in effect, sublimated as the image of the figurative "Other" is destroyed; at the same time, the axiological perspective of the Other has been internalized by Duan Yu himself.[12]

The quality of self-destructive madness that characterizes Duan Yu's shredding of the *Dainty Steps* scroll is even more pronounced in the introduction of the second "picture manual" passage, some twenty chapters later. The *Classic of the Shifting Tendon* consists of an illustrated Sanskrit document Ah Zhu had originally retrieved from the Shaolin temple, which eventually ends up in You Tanzhi's possession. After You Tanzhi's confrontation with Xiao Feng in Chapter 27—in which Xiao Feng forbears from killing him and You Tanzhi is unable to carry out his filial vengeance against Xiao Feng—You ends up a prisoner of the Khitan, poisoned and delirious. Under these precipitous circumstances, he enters into a rather peculiar sadomasochistic relationship with Ah Zi—including a particularly bizarre scene in which he becomes entranced by her naked feet and proceeds to suck uncontrollably on her toes as two Khitan soldiers observe impassively. Ah Zi arranges for You Tanzhi's head to be encased in an iron mask—on the grounds that this will protect him from being recognized and killed by Xiao Feng—and then condescends to let him become her "companion."

One day, Ah Zi announces to You Tanzhi that she wants to try a new kind of martial arts techniques and needs his assistance. What she needs him to do, it turns out, it to allow himself to be stung by poisonous centipedes. He accedes and proceeds to become violently ill, with bodily fluids of all sorts seeping out of the tiny apertures in his mask. Fortunately, he happens to fall face forward onto the *Shifting Tendon* volume, and his various bodily fluids (blood, drool, vomit, etc.) saturate

12. This partial internalization of the perspective of the Other can be seen from the fact that Duan Yu continues to practice the Goddess's "dainty-step" martial arts techniques throughout the novel.

the pages of that text. To his astonishment, on the pages that previously contained only indecipherable (Sanskrit) scribblings, there abruptly appear pictures of a naked Buddhist monk whose body is contorted into a variety of bizarre positions. Already in mortal agony, You Tanzhi decides to imitate the monk's postures and discovers to his astonishment that the unbearable itching with which he had been afflicted is suddenly relieved. After a while, Ah Zi returns and expresses surprise at the fact that You Tanzhi is still alive. After he explains to her the secret of the *Shifting Tendon* images, she gleefully decides to collect an even greater assortment of poisonous insects to feed on You Tanzhi's blood and, in the process, serve as ingredients for her own *wugong* 武功 (martial arts) concoctions. In the following chapter, You Tanzhi comes to his senses and, realizing that Ah Zi is merely using him for her own purposes, decides to leave her.

In this description of the *Shifting Tendon* manual, the *wugong* technique contained in the manual is specifically designed for combating and neutralizing various sorts of external poisons. Furthermore, You Tanzhi discovers and develops the manual's potential during a bizarre sadomasochistic incident. Both You Tanzhi's masochism as well as the theme of bodily poisoning are instances of what Julia Kristeva calls "abjection." Kristeva uses the term to describe the psychic constitution of the "Self" through the systematic expulsion of elements perceived to be "foreign" and "unclean."[13] At the same time, however, Kristeva emphasizes that this expulsion of the Self's "Other" is itself intimately related to the Self's expulsion of "it-self": "I expel *myself*, I spit *myself* out, I abject *myself* with the same motion through which 'I' claim to establish *myself*. . . . During the course in which 'I' become, I give birth to myself amid the violence of sobs, of vomit" (3). The *wugong* manual itself—the contents of which You Tanzhi must himself mimetically recreate in

13. Kristeva, *Powers of Horror*. Also relevant to this argument is the connection Kristeva draws between abjection and the processes of mimetic identification on which Jin Yong's picture manuals are ostensibly grounded: "In this struggle, which fashions the human being, the *mimesis*, by means of which he becomes homologous to another in order to become himself, is in short logically and chronologically secondary. Even before being *like*, 'I' am not but do *separate*, *reject*, *ab-ject*. Abjection, with a meaning broadened to take in subjective diachrony, *is a precondition of narcissism*" (ibid., 13).

order to regain control over the poisons that have entered his body—is itself presented as symbolizing a sort of cultural alienation (it is written in Sanskrit characters, rendering the text completely meaningless to You Tanzhi).

Both of these themes of poisoning and abjection involve a sense of self-alienation, a quality You Tanzhi subsequently discovers is related in a very specific way to the *Shifting Tendon* manual itself. As he later reflects:

> "This *Shifting Tendon* is truly one of *wuxue*'s unsurpassable treasures. Only, its method of practice is extremely difficult *and requires first the dissolution of distinctions between self and other*. Furthermore, one must not contain in one's heart the slightest desire to learn the *wugong* in question." (1111; italics added)

This passage stresses the degree to which this process of identification with the picture manual images is itself premised on both a cleavage of desire from the object of desire itself and a "dissolution" of perceived distinctions between Self and Other. The term I have translated as "dissolution" in this passage is *kanpo* 看破, which literally means "to read through" or "to analyze." This sense of "reading through" is important here because the ideal mode of engagement with the *wugong* picture manuals is precisely one of "reading through" their surface appearance, to grasp the martial arts principles that lie beneath.

The third prominent instance of visual mimeticism in *Tianlong ba bu* can be found at the beginning of Chapter 39, when Xu Zhu is shown a "stone room," the walls of which are covered with an assortment of graphic images and textual inscriptions, including "human images, animal images, incomplete blocks of text, and other codes and diagrams" (1506–7). These images are explicitly referred to as *tupu* (1508), the same term used to refer to the picture manuals discussed above. In the following discussion, however, I am less concerned with these wall paintings themselves and consider instead two other representational artifacts—a portrait scroll and a miniature sculpture of a human figure—discussed in the same passage.

The passage describes how Xu Zhu has with him a portrait scroll he obtained from his *wugong* master, Wu Yazi, before he died. The portrait is assumed to be a representation of Li Qiushui, who, like Xu Zhu, is also an apprentice of Wu Yazi. However, when Li eventually sees the portrait for herself, she notices a dimple and a black mole and realizes that the portrait actually depicts her younger sister. Li Qiushui then proceeds to relate to Xu Zhu the story of her own relationship with her former master:

> At the time, I lived with your master [Wu Yazi] in a stone cave on the shore of the Jian Lake at Wuliang mountain in Dali. Our happiness and freedom surpassed even those of the spirits and immortals. I bore him a lovely daughter. The two of us collected *wugong*-secret books from all different schools and divisions, but we ourselves aspired only to create a new school of all-encompassing, marvelous *wugong*. That day, he [Wu Yazi] found an enormous piece of beautiful jade in the mountain and proceeded to carve it into a figurine using my own image as a model. But afterwards, he would spend the entire day just staring at the jade sculpture and eventually ceased paying any attention to me altogether. When I spoke to him, he would give answers unrelated to the original questions or would listen without hearing—his entire attention being completely absorbed by that jade figurine. Your master's craftsmanship was extraordinarily skilled, and as a result that figurine was, in fact, quite beautiful. Nevertheless, it was, after all, inanimate; and *how could it be that, while I—on whom the statue was modeled—stood at his side, he could still ignore me in favor of staring infatuatedly at the figurine?* With his eyes full of that expression of being conquered by love? Why was this? Why was this? (1456; italics added)

In an ironic reversal on the Pygmalion theme of the artist who succeeds in bringing a female image to life through the strength of his love, the artist's attentions are instead deflected from the living woman he ostensibly desires back onto the *mimetic artifact*. The representation, therefore, comes to function as a substitute for another desire, which has not even been explicitly acknowledged by the subject himself.

One of Li Qiushui's strongest resentments stemmed from her inability to engage Wu Yazi in a dialogue and consequently feeling that he was ignoring her in favor of the jade figurine. It is therefore ironically appropriate that, at precisely this point in her narrative, Li Qiushui subtly shifts from a third-person to a second-person narration. Grammatically speaking, her interlocutor ceases to be Xu Zhu and becomes the imaginary reapparition of Wu Yazi himself:

> *Shige* 師哥,[14] you were extremely intelligent, but you nevertheless were also extremely infatuated; how could you have fallen in love with a jade figurine that you had carved with your own hands? How could you fall in love with her while forgetting that mortal *shimei* 師妹 at your side, someone who [unlike the figurine] is able to talk, to laugh, to move, and to love you? In your heart, you regarded this statue as my own little sister, isn't that right? I became jealous of this statue and as a result quarreled with you and went out in search of attractive young lads, whom I would bring back and flirt with in your presence. Thereupon you left in a fit of fury and never returned. *Shige*, actually, you needn't have gotten angry, because in the end I killed all those handsome young men, and sank their corpses in the lake. Didn't you know? . . .
>
> *Shige*, when was it that you painted this portrait? You knew that it was a portrait of me, so you had your apprentice bring this picture with him to Wuliang mountain in search of me. But, without your being conscious of it, you had actually painted my younger sister—didn't you ever realize this? All along, you assumed that it was I that you had painted. *Shige*, in your heart the one that you really loved was actually my younger sister; and about that infatuated way you had of staring at that jade figurine—why was that? Why was that? Now I finally understand. (1456–57)

This episode points to the way in which an image can oscillate uncertainly between being a subject of representation and a cathected object of desire. Wu Yazi created, with his own hands, both the jade figurine and the portrait scroll and was initially under the impression that the portraits were in fact representations of the person who had ostensibly modeled for them: Li Qiushui. In fact, however, he had actually (and unwittingly) been using Qiushui as an intermediary model for her younger sister, the person he truly desired.

In each of the three passages discussed above, the picture manuals (together with the other representational artifacts, such as statues and portraits, with which they are juxtaposed) circulate through the social world of *Tianlong ba bu*—simultaneously consolidating and fracturing social relations as they are passed from hand to hand. Similarly, the visual signifiers also circulate through the representational and psychic worlds in which they are embedded. Complex logics of displacement,

14. The terms *shige* and *shimei*, below, both borrow kinship nomenclature to address fellow *wugong* practitioners.

condensation, and sublimation ensure that the relationship between visual signifier and signified is inevitably volatile and contested. The circulation of picture manuals through Jin Yong's novel underscores a double symbolic economy of graphic and textual signifiers by means of which individual and collective subjectivities are constituted and reconfigured.

Of Manuals and Mimicry

They found a set of twenty-four pictures representing the pleasures of love and endeavored to reproduce in real life the joys depicted in the pictures.

—*Plum in the Golden Vase*

I have suggested that the various picture manuals in Jin Yong's novel function as models for more general processes of subject formation and ideological interpellation. More specifically, I argue that the manuals provide the viewing subject with an external point of identification, allowing her to identify not only with the actual visual images contained in the manuals but also with the social or ideological "gaze" that implicitly lies behind them. In the novel, for instance, the circulation of texts between characters often provides a serendipitous and causal glue holding the larger narrative together. On a more subjective level, these sorts of representational media within the novel can be seen as a sort of Lacanian *objet a*, mediating between the "subject" and the various "partial objects" that escape its embodiment and enter into symbolic circuits of exchange outside the Self. This cluster of theoretical reflections on the circulation of images and the role of the *objet a* as a "relay point" between the Self and exterior "partial objects" (or bodily appendices) has several clear dimensions of potential applicability to *Tianlong ba bu*.

The *Shifting Tendon* text consists of images drawn in a sort of invisible ink (which needs to be exposed to bodily fluids in order to be made visible), and its *wugong* secrets specifically concern tactics for detoxifying external poisons. Both invisible ink and poison are recurrent elements in Jin Yong's works,[15] although in this particular scene they are inter-

15. See, e.g., Jin Yong's *Liancheng jue* (translated as "A deadly secret"), which features a *wugong* manual written in invisible, poisonous ink, which will kill any reader who licks

related in a particularly interesting way. Specifically, You Tanzhi's tears, mucus, vomit, and the like—all of which are quintessential exemplars of Kristeva's notion of the "abject"—render the images of the manual visible. Moreover, it is precisely the mediated return of these partial objects, in the now-symbolic form of the *objet a* of the *wugong* manual, that permits the expulsion of the "abject" poison from his body.

At the level of corporeal integrity, the paradigmatic mode in which the picture manuals function is one of corporeal identification with the externalized image of the "Other." This model of subject-formation, or social interpellation based on an externalized image, is comparable to Lacan's notions of the "mirror stage" or the "screen" as mediating between the subject's individualized "look" and a decentered "gaze" of sociocultural assumptions. In Jin Yong' s novel, the "screen" of the picture manuals stands as a clear portal into the socio-symbolic world of martial arts mastery, and the process of apprenticeship with the manuals necessarily entails an internalization of the culturally recognized "gaze" of authority lying behind them.

Complementing this theme of portraits and *wugong* picture manuals is the related theme of corporeal identification with, and disassociation from, certain socially codified norms of gendered or ethnic identity. Throughout the novel, many different characters—Duan Yu, Xiao Feng, Ah Zhu, among others—attempts to rediscover their "true" parentage and ethnic roots. At issue are not only the "face" they present to the outside world but, more important, the subjective "gaze" (and the contextualized subject position it implies) with which they perceive the social world around them.

One of the most memorable examples of this dialectics of social representation and visual perception can be seen in the tragicomic relationship between You Tanzhi and Ah Zi. As discussed above, Ah Zi "de-faces" You Tanzhi by encasing his head in an iron mask. You then assumes a new social identity (of sorts) through the corporeal imitation of the *wugong* picture-manual images. The two former lovers subsequently part ways, and when, after several intervening adventures, they

his fingers to turn the pages (this borrows from an old, apocryphal anecdote that the pornographic Ming dynasty novel *Jinping mei* was written with a similar purpose in mind).

ultimately re-encounter each other, You discovers that Ah Zi—whose destructive gaze had literally cost him his face—is now blind. For a period, Ah Zi's blindness and his (masked) "facelessness" combine to enable him to hide his "true" identity from her. Subsequently, both You Tanzhi's face and Ah Zi's gaze are restored, although in each case the gaze and the face have been fundamentally transformed by the circuitous route that they have traversed. You Tanzhi dons a mask made from human skin to hide his badly scarred face, and Ah Zi's gaze is restored when You Tanzhi volunteers to deface himself further by literally giving her *his own eyes* so that she may see again. Finally, at the end of the novel, this dialectics of gaze and face comes full circle when Ah Zi throws away "her" eyes (which were originally You Tanzhi's) precisely in order not to have to continue to give him "face."

Ironically, this entire plotline of transplanted gazes and dislocated faces originated in an actual instance of facial masking and borrowed gazes. At one point while Jin Yong was writing the original novel, he had to leave Hong Kong for an extended trip and, so as not to interrupt the serialization, he asked his friend and fellow novelist Ni Kuang 倪匡 (1935–) to fill in for him. Although Jin Yong subsequently omitted Ni Kuang's ghostwritten text when he revised the novel for republication in book form,[16] he was nevertheless constrained by Ni Kuang's plot developments when he recommenced the serialization. For instance, one of Ni Kuang's plot twists was to blind Ah Zi (a character Ni Kuang did not like).[17] Consequently, all the subsequent discussions of Ah Zi's blindness, including her relations with the masked You Tanzhi during this period, derive directly from Ni Kuang's previous act of borrowing both Jin Yong's public "face" as well as his creative "gaze."

Granted, the *wugong* picture manuals are, by definition, visual documents, but a recurrent theme in the novel's discussions of the *wugong* principles is that a nonvisible plane of existence underlies the visible. A persistent concern in all the instances of visual representation in *Tianlong ba bu* discussed above involves a tension between appearance and interiority, resemblance and authenticity. On one hand, *wugong* "picture

16. Jin Yong, *Tianlong ba bu*, 1973–74.
17. Li Yijian, "Canonically 'Rewriting' Jin Yong's Novels."

manuals" such as the *Dainty Steps* scroll are presented not only as quintessentially representational (in the sense that the realistic nudity of the images of the Goddess Immortal makes Duan Yu exceedingly uncomfortable) but also as, in a sense, *beyond* representation (insofar as the images contain such information as the location of acupoints and *jingmai* vessels normally not visible to the naked eye). Similarly, although the picture manuals function pedagogically by encouraging imitation and corporeal mimicry, their ultimate emphasis is the acquisition of a more intangible mental or spiritual state.

A comparable tension between visible and nonvisible factors seems to be implicit in the cases of mistaken identity discussed above: there are assumed to be certain intangible factors relevant to one's ethnic or familial identity that transcend everything that one thinks one knows about oneself at any particular time. Recognizing the authority of these intangibles, if and when they make themselves known (even if they contradict everything one thought one originally knew about oneself), is similar to recognizing the authority of the delocalized "gaze" in the theory of screen-mediated identification and subjectivity I have been developing in this study. In fact, I would take this line of analysis a step further and suggest that Jin Yong's texts themselves function in a way comparable to the "picture manuals" they describe insofar as they provide a sort of metaphorical sociocultural "screen" against which vast numbers of diasporic and nondiasporic Chinese readers can reaffirm and retrospectively reconstruct their sense of being "Chinese."

Contemporary Global Chinese Diasporas

> The next work of Jin Yong's that I read was during the period in which the television series adaptation of *Tianlong ba bu* was casting both heaven and earth into darkness. . . . The novel was seven volumes long, and I was able to get through the first volume only by holding my nose, but for the life of me I was not able to read the second volume. Do you need to eat an entire dish in order to be able to determine whether the food is good or spoiled?
>
> —Wang Shuo, "My Views on Jin Yong"

> Mr. Wang Shuo says that he bought a seven-volume set of *Tianlong ba bu*, but after having read only one volume found that he could not read on. However, the Hong Kong, Taiwan, and Mainland editions of the novel have only five volumes each; so I have no idea where his seven-volume edition could have come from.
>
> —Jin Yong, "Undeserved Recognition and Destructive Perfectionism"

On November 1, 1999, the Beijing novelist Wang Shuo 王朔 incited an uproar when he published an article sharply critical of Jin Yong in the popular newspaper *Zhongguo qingnian bao* 中國青年報 (China youth daily).[18] Among other points, Wang Shuo suggested that Jin Yong's novels could be grouped with Hong Kong's celebrity actors, the "four kings"; the Taiwanese romance writer Qiong Yao's 瓊瑤 various television series; and Jackie Chan's martial arts movies—a collection of pop-cultural figures whom Wang Shuo refers to collectively as the "four great vulgarities," troping ironically on the "four great evil men" in Jin Yong's own novel. Three days later, Jin Yong responded with an essay answering Wang Shuo's critique point-for-point.[19] The posting of both essays on *China Youth Daily*'s website generated an avalanche of spirited missives from Chinese readers worldwide. In the first week and a half following the publication of Jin Yong's article, for instance, more than fifty such letters were posted on the website,[20] and several hundred more were posted on the electronic bulletin board linked to Wang Shuo's own homepage.[21]

Most relevant to the concerns of this chapter is a series of remarks Wang Shuo made in the middle of his essay:

> I believe that Jin Yong very unwisely fabricated the image of a large group of Chinese people. Through the widespread dissemination of Jin Yong's movies and television programs, this group [of fictional Chinese] has, to a certain extent, come to replace Chinese people's true image. As a result, the world has been given a very serious misunderstanding, *believing* [this image] *to be the Chinese people's original face*.[22]

This appeal for a return to the Chinese people's "original face" (*benlai de mianmu* 本來的面目, literally "original face and eyes") is highly ironic

---

18. Wang Shuo, "Wo kan Jin Yong."

19. Jin Yong, "Letter to the Editor."

20. See http://www.cyd.com.cn/ztzl/wsyjy/wsyjy-index.htm (accessed on Nov. 21, 1999).

21. At the end of 1999, this bulletin board contained over 2,500 individual postings dated between June and mid-November 1999, a significant portion of which were explicitly concerned with the Wang Shuo–Jin Yong debate. This file, however, is no longer accessible.

22. Wang Shuo, "Wo kan Jin Yong."

given the degree to which *Tianlong ba bu*, in particular, emphasizes the transferability of both face and gaze and questions the "originality" of both. Furthermore, Wang Shuo himself, as I discuss in Chapter 9, is concerned in his own writings with issues of self-representation and of the duplicity of the image. It is thus particularly odd that he should criticize Jin Yong precisely for not producing a *more faithful image* of China to be disseminated to the rest of the world.

At the same time, I would argue that this issue of (visual) representation is at the heart of the contemporary "Jin Yong phenomenon." At stake is not so much the manner in which Jin Yong represents the image of China to the "rest of the world" (as Wang Shuo asserts), but the degree to which he represents the image of China to those, both in China and throughout the world, *who already regard themselves as Chinese.* There is currently a vast, and still-growing, body of Chinese-language writings on Jin Yong's works. In the 1990s, for example, the Mainland critic Chen Mo 陳墨 alone published more than eight book-length studies of Jin Yong's works (with each of them running between 300 and 600 pages long).[23] Although literary scholars have recently begun to take a serious interest in Jin Yong, the majority of these secondary writings are of a more popular sort, consisting primarily of long quotes, straightforward plot summaries, and largely uncritical affirmations of Jin Yong's roots in traditional Chinese culture. Rather than examine this vast body of secondary literature in detail, in the following I focus on some claims and statements that appear in the Taiwan edition of Jin Yong's complete works.[24]

On the rear cover-leaf of each volume in the Taipei series, there is a reaffirmation that Jin Yong's novels constitute "the common language of Chinese around the world." The cover-leaf also proudly proclaims:

From Taipei to New York, from Hong Kong to London, from Tokyo to Shanghai, Chinese people everywhere may speak different dialects of Chinese,

---

23. And this does not include four other book-length works he wrote on the same topic (but was unable to publish) between 1987 and 1990; see Chen Juntao, "Dalu 'Jinxue' diyi jia," 2.

24. Published by the *Yuanliu* (literally, "flowing widely") publishing company in 1987.

may eat different cuisines, and may have different political views, but all nevertheless read *Jin Yong's Collected Works*.[25]

Similarly, the front cover-leaf attempts to advance this process of specular identification by noting:

In order to help Jin Yong fans from around the world communicate with one another and share the insights each has gained from reading his works, Yuanliu [the publisher of the edition] has specially set up a "Jin Yong teahouse" website, in order to collect, supply, bring together, and disseminate all information and news relating to Jin Yong's works. The website is located at http://www.ylib.com.tw/jinyong.[26]

The Taiwan edition further attempts to reinforce Jin Yong's status as a literary Rosetta stone linking together mutually alienated, diasporic Chinese by appending, at the beginning of each volume of his collected works, a series of illustrations depicting an assortment of images associated with Chinese culture, most of which have only a tangential relationship to the novels they accompany.

The contemporary Chinese global diaspora can be seen as a rough inverse of the multicultural Northern Song "Greater China" that Jin Yong mobilizes as a historical backdrop to *Tianlong ba bu*. Jin Yong presents ethnic categories (Han, Khitan, Tangut) as having a certain degree of relevance, but their importance is ultimately overridden by a form of culturally grounded Sinocentrism. The implication seems to be that, as long as people are familiar with Chinese culture and behave in ways consonant with "Han" interests and ideals, they are for all practical purposes "Chinese" whether or not they are ethnically Han. In the contemporary Chinese global diaspora, by contrast, as more and more diasporic Chinese become assimilated into "foreign" cultures (and,

---

25. Jin Yong, *Jin Yong zuopin ji*. Compare, also, the statement on the cover of each volume of Yuanjing publishing company's Jin Yong Critical Anthology (Jin Yong yanjiu congshu): "As big as the world is, it is only in China that there can be *wuxia* novels. . . . Jin Yong's collected works are made up of fourteen titles and thirty-six volumes in all, and its readers are spread out throughout every corner of the world. Chinese readers read them over and over again; and regardless of which way you look, left or right, all you see are Jin Yong['s works]."

26. This URL currently leads to an empty site.

conversely, as these foreign, especially "Western," cultures make more inroads into "Greater China" itself), an "ethnic" heritage is increasingly disassociated from the cultural trappings to which it is ostensibly linked.

The implication of the argument I develop here is that Jin Yong's novels may, indeed, function as the "the common language of Chinese around the world." However, just as the social suturing facilitated by texts such as Jin Yong's "picture manuals" is ultimately grounded on the necessary contingency and fluidity of the visual signifiers they contain, similarly his texts provide diasporic "imaginary communities" of expatriate Chinese with a common discourse precisely because the Chinese cultural signifiers they contain are *not* stable, self-evident signs. Instead, these cultural signifiers are effective because they may be uprooted from their "original" referents and reattached to a fluid range of new imaginary signifieds.

Coda

In Jin Yong's epilogue to *Tianlong ba bu* (pp. 1973–74), the author recalls an incident in which the literary critic T. A. Hsia happened on a Christmas card that reminded him of the novel's "four great evil men" (*si da eren* 四大惡人). Hsia wanted to send this card to Jin Yong, but because they were not directly acquainted, he entrusted it to their mutual friend, the scholar of Chinese literature Chen Shih-hsiang 陳世驤. Chen misplaced the card, however, and as a result it never arrived at its intended destination. This anecdote not only brings together the themes of elite and popular culture in the misdirected interaction between the academic scholar and the popular writer but also points to the role played by the visual image in mediating these sorts of identificatory relationships. The efficacy of the representational image in this anecdote lies not so much in its ability mimetically to recreate an object and faithfully convey it to another observer as in its ability to become detached from its original yuletide referent and reattached to a new imaginary signified in Jin Yong's novel.

In the following chapter, I turn to Eileen Chang, who, like Jin Yong, has a vast and enthusiastic readership both within China and among

Chinese-speaking readers around the world. In one of her essays, she, too, invokes a Christmas-related figure to summarize a position central to my own discussion of her works: "The contrast between red and green, on the other hand, can evoke a quite pleasing stimulus. But too straightforward a contrast, such as between bright red and bright green, will turn out only looking like a Christmas tree, lacking sufficient aftertaste (*huiwei* 回味)."[27] My reading of Eileen Chang starts from this theme of "contrastive colors" and the related topic of the retrospective "aftertaste" a particular visual image may invoke.

27. Eileen Chang, "Tongyan wuji," 11.

6

Eileen Chang and Photographic Nostalgia

She sat looking over the photographs before she passed them on to him. They were good clear snapshots, dark in tone, with an air of authenticity. The first picture showed a soldier with hands on hips standing beside a tree. He was visibly blond. A half-naked woman was tied to the tree. . . .

Liu turned the picture this way and that, in the lamplight, examining it closely. If there were signs of faking, he could not see them.

— Eileen Chang, *Naked Earth*

At one point in Eileen Chang's 張愛玲 (1920–95) putatively anticommunist novel, *Chidi zhi lian* 赤地之戀 (Naked earth), the protagonist Liu Quan, who is working for a Shanghai newspaper, is assigned to alter a photo of a blonde woman being ravished by a Nazi soldier so that it appears to depict an American soldier molesting a Korean woman, in order to draw attention to alleged American atrocities during the Korean-American war.[1] Liu Quan first examines the photograph that he has been given to alter, admiring its "air of authenticity." It is precisely this air of authenticity that makes the hoax plausible in the first place, allowing the photograph to be used as a propagandistic "quilting point" on which nationalist aspirations may be stitched. In fact, the proposed alteration is presented to Liu Quan as constituting not a subversion of photography's presumptive authenticity but a reaffirmation of it, on the grounds that the "essence" of American brutality

1. Eileen Chang, *Naked Earth*, 115–20; *Chidi zhi lian*, 104–8. For a discussion of this scene, see David Der-wei Wang, *The Monster That Is History*, 180.

is already known, and therefore the altered photograph will merely supply concrete corroboration.

This proposed fakery underscores an instability within photography itself. Despite the common perception of photography as a quintessentially and transparently mimetic medium, this mimeticism nevertheless actually relies on a set of contingent, and even arbitrary, representational conventions to create the *illusion* of visual verisimilitude. Although a photograph is an indexical trace of light striking a photosensitive surface, the specific configuration of the resulting image is at best a very rough approximation of the way in which we would perceive the same scene directly with our own eyes. As John Tagg argues in a related context, "We have to see that *every* photograph is the result of specific and, in every sense, significant distortions which render its relation to any prior reality deeply problematic."[2] At the same time, the hoax appears to reinforce Liu Quan's faith in the inherent "authenticity" of the photographic medium itself. Furthermore, Liu Quan's assignment ironically anticipates his own fate—insofar as he is subsequently sent to fight in Korea, where he is captured by the Americans and, ultimately, volunteers to return to China as an infiltrator, which is to say, as a "fake." Liu Quan's eventual position as an anticommunist agent working for the United States mirrors that of Eileen Chang herself, who composed *Naked Earth* as an explicitly anticommunist work on assignment from the United States Information Service. This chain of substitutions—from photograph to Liu Quan to Eileen Chang—suggests that Eileen Chang is positioning *herself* as a displaced photograph, whose underlying authenticity is ironically reaffirmed through its susceptibility to being "faked."

This chain of politically driven reversals and inversions running from the photograph to Liu Quan to Eileen Chang herself underscores Chang's own complicated and paradoxical attitude toward the question of photographic realism and visual representation in general. In the following discussion, I begin by considering some of Chang's early writings, specifically how they draw attention to a process of internalization of specific modes of visual perception. Then, I turn to how these issues

2. Tagg, *The Burden of Representation*, 2.

inform her autobiographical photo-essay, *Duizhao ji: kan lao zhaoxiang bu* 對照記：看老照相簿 (Mutual reflections: looking at old photographs). Published only a year before her death in 1995, this autobiographical volume uses annotated photos as a way of looking back over Chang's life, as well as anticipating how she would be remembered after her death.

Traveling Incarceration

> Traveling incarceration. Immobile inside the train, seeing immobile things slip by. What is happening? Nothing is moving inside or outside the train. . . .
>
> Between the immobility of the inside and that of the outside a certain *quid pro quo* is introduced, a slender blade that inverts their stability. The chiasm is produced by the windowpane and the rail.
>
> —Michel de Certeau, *The Practice of Everyday Life*

Born in Shanghai in 1920, Eileen Chang left China in 1952, moving first to Hong Kong and then to California in 1955, where she lived until her death in 1995. Her current reputation is built on a relatively modest collection of essentially popular texts, which are characterized by a careful attention to surface detail, a sense of historical pathos, and a complex attitude toward women that defies facile categorization.[3] A bilingual writer, Chang composed several of her essays and fictional works in English and also translated several of her own works into either English or Chinese. Chang was also "bilingual" in another respect—she moved comfortably between "literary" writing and the more specifically "visual" work of writing film scripts. Toward the end of her life, she had acquired something of a cult status; at one point a tabloid journalist even rummaged through the reclusive Chang's garbage for morsels to satisfy her insatiable fans.[4] Like the journalist attempting to piece together Chang's life via the indirect evidence of the discarded refuse of her everyday existence, in *Mutual Reflections* we can similarly see Chang attempting to piece together *her own past life* via the indirect evidence provided by an assortment of photographs that she cannot bring herself to discard.

Before considering the way in which Eileen Chang's *Mutual Reflections* uses photographs to figuratively *look back* on her own life, I turn first to

3. For an authoritative overview of Chang's life and oeuvre, see Zhou Fenling, *Yanyi*.
4. David Der-wei Wang, "Foreword," in Chang, *The Rice-Sprout Song*, iv.

another volume published five years later, which ironically makes the reverse gesture of using an early twentieth-century photograph as a pretext *to look ahead* to Chang's life. The volume in question is a photo album entitled *Lao Shanghai* 老上海 (Old Shanghai), with accompanying text written by the Shanghai author Wu Liang 吳亮. Near the beginning of the work is a reproduction of an anonymous 1914 photograph of a brightly dressed Shanghai woman boarding a tram. The accompanying text begins provocatively: "At the time of this photograph, Zhang Ailing [Eileen Chang] did not yet exist."[5] After discussing the photograph itself, Wu Liang returns to the counterfactually anticipatory tone with which he initially opened his commentary: "The woman boarding the tram could not have imagined that, thirty years later, another woman by the name of Zhang Ailing would also frequently board similar trams and furthermore would include trams in her fiction" (75). One of the literary works Wu Liang probably had in mind is Chang's short story "Fengsuo" 封鎖 (Shutdown), first published in 1943, which recounts an abortive romantic encounter between two strangers on a Shanghai tram during the Sino-Japanese War.[6] The entire encounter is contained within, and in fact is framed by, the suspension of service in response to the threat of an air raid.

After the air raid brings the tram to an abrupt halt, two strangers— a young, educated woman by the name of Wu Cuiyuan and a married man by the name of Lü Zongzhen—strike up a conversation that becomes increasingly intimate—to the point that they appear to seriously consider the possibility that the woman will become the man's concubine. Their shared reverie, however, is shattered when the shutdown ends and the tram ride resumes. Thinking that the man has disembarked from the tram, Cuiyuan is initially displeased: "Cuiyuan closed her eyes in annoyance. If he phoned her, she would not be able to control her voice. She would be very eager, because he would be a dead person come back to life" (236/100). The irony behind this moment of hyperbolic pique is made clear in the next paragraph: "The tram lights

5. Wu Liang, *Lao Shanghai*, 71.

6. Eileen Chang, "Fengsuo"; idem, "Shutdown." Subsequent references to these two works are cited in the text; the first number shown refers to the Chinese version; the second, to the English.

were switched on. She opened her eyes and saw him sitting far away in his old seat! She was shocked—he had not gotten off after all! She understood now. Everything that had taken place during the shutdown hadn't happened at all. The whole of Shanghai had fallen asleep and dreamed an absurd dream" (236/100).

Since Eileen Chang's story starts with Cuiyuan already on the tram, the moment in the narrative corresponding most closely to the *Old Shanghai* photograph occurs when Zongzhen recounts to Cuiyuan *his memory* of having seen her in the act of boarding:

> He remembered now, he had watched her get on the tram. It had been a very dramatic moment, but the drama was purely accidental, not of her doing. He said softly to her, "You know what? I saw you getting on the tram. The advertisement on the glass at the front of the tram has a strip torn off it. I saw part of you through the tear, just the chin." It was an ad for milk powder, with a baby's plump face on it. And then suddenly, beneath the baby's ear, a woman's chin had appeared. Thinking back on it, it had actually been quite startling. "Then you bent your head to look for change in your purse and I got to see your eyes, your brows, your hair." *Taken part by part, she did have a kind of charm to her.* (230/97; italics added)

This remarkable passage underscores the visual dimension of these advertisements, particularly the way in which the man is forced to view the world (and, specifically, to view the woman) quite literally *through* the screen of the advertisement.

Furthermore, the contents of the advertisement are significant in their own right. During this period powdered milk was predominantly a Western import, but one that, by definition, was uniquely effective in insinuating itself into the most private regions of the Chinese family sphere (inserting itself, quite literally, into the intimate space between the mother's naked breast and the infant's sucking mouth). As such, baby formula stands as a particularly evocative metonym for the pervasive colonizing effect of Western capitalism in general, and of Western-influenced scopic regimes in particular (including, for instance, the role of visual imagery in commodity advertisements). In addition to connoting foreign influence, Chang's description of the advertisement also produces the uncanny visual effect of juxtaposing different maturational stages within the same figurative frame, when she notes that "beneath the baby's ear, a woman's chin had appeared." The projection of these maturational concerns onto the female body in the "Shutdown" passage anticipates the theme of maternal/pedophilic attractions I explore in the following chapter on the contemporary Taiwan author Li Yung-p'ing (there are, for example, several explicit discussions, in Li's two most recent novels, of Taiwanese prostitutes in their early teens taking estrogen supplements to give themselves "a baby's face and the body of a woman"). In both cases, woman and child come to share the same visual space, just as visual signifiers and their referents similarly come to occupy a comparable ontological space.

This reading of the milk-powder advertisement scene can be viewed as a particularly poignant illustration of what Walter Benjamin calls the "optical unconscious"—the degree to which modern technologies of visual reproduction such as photography have conditioned the way in which we unconsciously parse the visual world.[7] With its ability to temporally parse our visual world environment in revolutionary new ways, for instance, photography has helped open our eyes to a previously invisible dimension of the world we inhabit, with the result that we often find ourselves imagining a scene as it would appear through a photographic lens, even when no camera is present. In this particular case, it is not the intersection of Cuiyuan and the advertisement in Zongzhen's line of sight *in and of itself* that produces the image he sees; rather, he needs to have first been unconsciously trained to *see* the world in certain ways.

A more explicit example of this sort of phenomenon can be observed in another, bitingly ironic scene a couple of pages earlier in "Shutdown." There, we are told that the tram also contains a medical student doing his homework:

In the tram, a medical student had taken out his sketch-book and was diligently revising a drawing of the human anatomy. The other passengers thought he was sketching the person dozing across from him. With nothing better to do, they began to gather round to watch in twos or threes, hand on hips, or behind their backs. The man holding the smoked fish said to his wife,

7. Walter Benjamin addressed this concept first in his "Small History of Photography" (1931) and then again in his "Work of Art in the Age of Mechanical Reproduction" (1936). I, however, am using the term in a sense rather different from that which Benjamin originally intended. See Krauss, *The Optical Unconscious*, 178–89, for a useful critical discussion of this concept of the "optical unconscious."

"I really have no patience for this modern cubist school or the impressionists." She whispered back, "Your trousers!"

The medical student carefully labeled every bone, every nerve and tendon. One of the homeward-bound businessmen whispered behind his open fan to his colleagues, "Influenced by Chinese painting. It's fashionable these days to add a few lines of poetry to Western paintings. It's now a case of 'the East wind blowing to the West'!" (228/95–96)

The irony here, of course, lies in the fact that the tram passengers are not merely sophisticated viewers but perhaps even overly sophisticated, in the sense that they not only recognize and comment on modern art (cubism, impressionism) but even see it where it doesn't exist.

It is not coincidental, furthermore, that both of the preceding anecdotes revolve around a figurative disarticulation of the human body. The medical student, of course, dismembers the body in a quite literal sense, as he "carefully labeled every bone, every nerve and tendon" in his anatomical diagram. Somewhat more figuratively, Zongzheng recalls how Cuiyuan originally entered his field of vision in a piecemeal fashion: first her chin and then "your eyes, your brows, your hair." He concludes with a sort of quiet satisfaction, "Taken part by part, she did have a kind of charm to her." Both the medical student's use of the anatomical diagram and Zongzheng's perception of the tram advertisement suggest that one of the components of this emerging modern optical unconscious involves a tendency to view images and subjects not as holistic unities but as always already fragmented. In the second half of this chapter, I turn to a much more recent work in which Eileen Chang, shortly before her death, used a similar process of visual fragmentation and reassimilation to reflect on her own past life.

Uneven Contrasts: Photography and Death

Contemporary with the withdrawal of rites, Photography may correspond to the intrusion, in our modern society, of an asymbolic Death, outside of religion, outside of ritual, a kind of abrupt dive into literal Death. *Life/Death*: the paradigm is reduced to a simple click, the one separating the initial pose from the final print.

—Roland Barthes, *Camera Lucida*

One term for "taking a photograph" in Chinese is *zhaoxiang* 照像, which constitutes a synthesis of two earlier terms, both of which have largely fallen out of use. The first term, *xiaozhao* 小照, was conventionally used to refer to portraits drawn or painted while their subjects were still alive; the second, *yingxiang* 影像, originally referred specifically to portraits of the deceased.[8] The neologism *zhaoxiang*[9] finds itself straddling these same mortal coils, giving posthumous life to the deceased while uncannily anticipating the future deaths of the living. This etymology term is reinforced by a well-known tradition of associating photography and death in Western writings. For instance, Roland Barthes, in his incomparably morbid monograph on photography, *Camera Lucida*, argues that "each photograph always contains this imperious sign of my future death" (97). In his own textual commentary on another photo album, Jacques Derrida made similar observations about the spectral nature of the "photographic medium": "I like the word 'medium' here. It speaks to me of specters, of ghosts, and phantoms, like these images themselves. From the first 'apparition,' it's all about the return of the departed. It is there in black and white, it can be verified after the fact. The spectral is the essence of photography."[10] Although both Barthes and Derrida are speaking about attitudes toward photography in Western culture, their comments resonate with some of the early attitudes toward photography in China, as well as thinking about representational media ("I like the word 'medium' here") in general. For instance, as discussed above, the initial mortuary connotations of photography in China fed off similar connotations, which were already associated with certain traditions of portrait painting.

These mortuary connotations of early Chinese photography (and of photography in general) also build on the rather ambivalent status women's *portraiture* came to assume in late imperial Chinese culture, an ambivalence due in large part to the conventional linkage of female portraiture with death in Chinese fiction and drama. As I discussed in the Introduction, a socio-aesthetic tradition in late imperial China dictated that a young woman's act of self-portraiture was often perceived

8. Ma Yunzeng et al., eds., *Zhongguo sheying shi*, 18.

9. Lydia Liu (*Translingual Practice*, 277) lists the term (or, more specifically, its compounds: "photography" [*zhaoxiang fa* 照像法] and "photographic camera" [*zhaoxiang jing* 照像鏡]) under the rubric "Neologisms Derived from Missionary-Chinese Texts."

10. Derrida, *Right of Inspection*, iv.

as a symbolic act of auto-effigy, linking the woman directly to her own imminent demise while uncannily anticipating her own spectral return. A striking contemporary example of this sort of female auto-effigy can be found in Eileen Chang's photo-essay, *Mutual Reflections*,[11] which she completed in 1993, in preparation for the sixteen-volume edition of her "complete" works to be published the following year by the Huan-guan publishing company. A cross between a photo album and an auto-biography, *Mutual Reflections* turned out to be the last major work Chang completed before her death in Los Angeles two years later. The essay looks back to Chang's youth even as it implicitly anticipates how she would be remembered after her death.

One entry near the end of *Mutual Reflections* begins with the remark, "In 1950 or 1952, not long after the Mainland changed color; I don't remember what permit I was applying for that needed a photograph" (74/21). She recounts how, when she approached the "big man in green fatigues" sitting at a "yellow-painted desk," his first question was whether she knew how to read. Far from being offended, the well-educated Chang was secretly pleased that the soldier had not perceived her as an intellectual. She further reflects that his assumption that she might be illiterate could not be attributed to her own political correctness in actively trying to pass as a common worker or peasant; rather, it was the result of the demystifying power of the camera lens itself:

> I believed in learning, but I did object to the distant ponderousness of some intellectuals, their inability to sit loosely to things. In fact, I lacked both "qualities" myself, they were simply something I aspired to. *Sometimes when I had my picture taken, this aspiration was unintentionally let slip under the inhuman gaze of the lens.* (74/22; italics added)

A recurrent theme in Chang's volume concerns her habit of coming back to these old photographs of herself and her loved ones and attempting to perceive in them certain qualities that have been "unintentionally let slip under the inhuman gaze of the lens."

---

11. Eileen Chang, *Duizhao ji*. Selected excepts of this work can be found in English translation in idem, "Reflections: Words and Pictures." Hereafter references to these two works are cited in the text. The first page number given refers to the Chinese text; the second, to the corresponding passage in the English translation (if available).

In the following discussion of Chang's final work, I begin by borrowing this conceit of focusing on the unconscious qualities that unintentionally slip out under the gaze of the camera lens. In particular, I will read her autobiographical text through the figurative lens of her colorful euphemism, introduced at the beginning of the passage cited above, of "color change" (*bianse* 變色) to describe the founding of the People's Republic of China in 1949. Wumingshi used the same expression in the second volume of *Golden Night of the Serpent* (itself composed shortly after the founding of the People's Republic): "These several years the map of the world was continually changing color (*bianse*)" (2: 149)—with the theme of "color change" being used here not only to refer metaphorically to changing ideological affiliations but also to designate quite literally to the contrasting colors used to distinguish between different nation-states on a map. In another passage from the same volume, Yin Di explicitly compares this metaphorical theme of chromatic regime change to the question of the representation and perception of women: "I think that it is just like this: women will always be a bloodless region, a kind of security buffer. No matter how the universe changes color (*bianse*), or whether the sun shines black or red, there will be no earthshaking changes projected onto her body" (2: 223). In this passage, Wumingshi uses "changing color" to signal the transformative implications of political revolution to evoke the way in which the figure of woman is located on the margins of these same political transformations. In Chang's case, this reference to changing color suggests a sort of cyclical, seasonal change (evoking perhaps the image of leaves changing color in the fall); it can also be understood as connoting an essentially exterior and superficial transformation that does not necessarily extend to the level of internal content (a reading consistent with Chang's notoriously cynical attitude toward political orthodoxies).

At the same time, the trope of "changing color" assumes another, very literal significance in Chang's *Mutual Reflections*. Chang's interest in her old photographs frequently revolves around issues of color and color change. For instance, in the paragraph following the description of her interview with the army officer, Chang describes how, due to cloth rationing, she was forced to wear an outfit consisting of "a length of *aquamarine* cotton and a piece of *violet* gauze" (74/21; italics added). This attention to color not only is characteristic of this particular passage (the "yellow desk" and "green fatigues") but also pervades the volume as a whole. For example, in the text accompanying the second photograph in the volume—a cute black-and-white image of a young girl sitting on a stool, which has been carefully colored by hand—Eileen Chang notes that, although she is in fact the girl depicted in the photograph, she nevertheless feels profoundly alienated from the image itself. What she *is* able to identify with, however, are the colors that were artificially (and, to some extent, inaccurately) added to the image many years later:

> The little round face doesn't ring a bell, even with me. Who else could it be, though? I've gone through all the other little girls among the relatives in my mind, and it doesn't look like any of them. It's that rattan stool that's familiar, and the dress—but the dress I remember was of pale blue silk patterned with puffs of white cloud. The T-shaped collar of white silk makes me look a bit silly. I really don't like the picture all that well, it just strikes a chord. *And it reminds me how happy I felt the day I watched my mother color it.* It was a typically gloomy northern afternoon, quite dark. I stood to one side, looking on at the cluttered desktop with the black ironwood box of watercolors, the thin brush with its black shaft, the cup of water. She painted my mouth with thin red lips and my dress she made the brightest turquoise. It was her turquoise period. (6/13; italics added)

The affective response this photo inspires in Chang is not only *not* strictly mimetic ("the little round face doesn't ring a bell, even with me"), but indeed can even be seen as *anti*mimetic—in the sense that Chang identifies most strongly with the memory of her mother *inaccurately* coloring the dress in the photograph dark turquoise rather than the light blue it should have been.

Chang notes that it is precisely these various shades of blue that not only provide a bridge linking her present self to her own childhood memories but also supply one of the most tangible connections between her and her deceased mother:

> When my first book was published, the cover I designed for it was a field of unbroken peacock blue; no artwork other than black lettering. It was so intense that it took your breath away. Only later did I hear from auntie that my mother too had liked this color and all her clothes had been various shades of turquoise. I remember that one of her oil paintings, a still life study that always hung on the wall, was predominantly aquamarine too. Heredity is just this mysteriously unpredictable—it's in these trivial things that I resemble her, and in none of her strengths. How maddening. (6/13)

This is the same mother who, we learn in another entry, handcolored all her photographs herself, was herself an oil painter, and moreover "was a great friend of [the prominent Chinese painters] Xu Beihong 徐悲鴻, Jiang Biwei 蔣碧微, and Chang Shuhong 常書鴻" (20/16). This is also the same mother who, as we learn in Chang's essay "Tongyan wuji" 童言無忌 (The guileless words of a child), allegedly advised Eileen Chang that girls who aspire to marry well should take the money they would have spent on college tuition and spend it on clothes and cosmetics instead.[12] This essay notes, furthermore, that one of Chang's earliest memories is of her mother standing in front of a dressing mirror trying on clothes (10). The irony is that her mother provides a figurative locus for Chang's own self-perception, even as Chang herself implicitly resists some of her mother's reductive stereotypes about women and visual appearance.

At one point Eileen Chang had dreamed of becoming a painter,[13] and a survey of her written works would suggest that she not only "inherited" an affinity for the color turquoise from her mother but would also appear to have inherited a fascination with colors in general. For instance, Chang once translated an essay by Yanying 炎櫻 (Fatima) entitled "Female Fashion, Female Colors" ("Nüzhuang, nüse" 女裝女色), which includes a discussion of the connotations of different colors and their effects when juxtaposed with one another:

> And another thing we should be grateful for is the contrast of colors. Currently, we have already nominally accepted the color combinations prevalent since antiquity. The eye of the new era is more accepting and meticulous as compared with that of the past; for instance, red and grey, or yellow and green, which used to be considered very compatible, are now seen as hackneyed.[14]

In her "Guileless Words" essay, Chang expressed a strikingly similar interest in color combinations:

12. Eileen Chang, "Tongyan wuji," 10; subsequent references to this essay are cited in the text.

13. As related in her autobiographical essay "Tiancai meng" (Dream of genius), written in 1949, when she was 29.

14. Yanying, "Nüzhuang, nüse" 女裝, 女色 (Female fashion, female colors); cited in Zhou Fenling, *Yanyi.*

As for the matching of colors, Chinese have only recently learned from the West the roles of "contrast" and "harmony." To oversimplify, "contrast" is red with green, and "harmony" is green with green. One would hardly imagine that, in the case of two different shades of green, their conflict and internal strife would be very apparent. The smaller the separation between two different shades of green, the greater their capacity to evoke a sense of discomfort in the viewer. The contrast between red and green, on the other hand, can evoke a quite pleasing stimulus. But too straightforward a contrast, such as between bright red and bright green, will turn out only looking like a Christmas tree, lacking sufficient aftertaste. (11)

In this essay, Eileen Chang recognized that color sensitivity is not a transhistorical constant, but is strongly conditioned by the sociocultural context in which it is embedded. Color, in this context, is found to be inherently relational, deriving its identity from the ways in which it interacts with a wider chromatic environment.

Moreover, in this same autobiographical essay, precisely in the context of a discussion of the matching of colors, Chang introduces one of her most celebrated aesthetic formulations—"uneven contrasts" (*cenci de duizhao* 參差的對照):

Modern Chinese are always saying that the people of antiquity didn't understand how to match colors; however, in the past, people didn't rely on absolute contrasts, but rather on uneven contrasts. For example, using sapphire blue to match apple green, or pine green to match scarlet red, or scallion green to match peach red. We have already forgotten everything that the ancients knew. (11)

Used here to discuss actual color combinations, the concept of "uneven contrasts" is deployed more metaphorically in another essay to describe Chang's own writing technique:

Sadness is like the combination of true red and true green, an absolute contrast. Yet it is better at stimulating than inspiring. Desolation leaves an even longer aftertaste because, like the green of scallions and the red of peaches, it is an *uneven contrast.*

I like writing that uses *uneven contrasts* because it is close to reality. . . .

The era in which I write is precisely the kind of era for which, I believe, using the technique of *uneven contrasts* is quite appropriate. I use this technique to describe the memories lived by mankind in all eras and to offer a revelation to the whole world. . . .

> . . . Beautiful things are not necessarily great, but great things are always beautiful. It is just that I don't place falseness and reality into stark contrast in my writing, yet I still use the method of *uneven contrast* to show the reality in the emptiness, the simplicity in the ornamentation, of contemporary people. . . .
>
> Also, because I use the method of *uneven contrast,* I don't like adopting those classical methods that show stark conflicts between good and evil or the spirit and the flesh. Therefore, the main theme of my works sometimes isn't clear.[15] (Italics added)

Indeed, this lack of "clarity" not only appears to be an artifact of the technique of uneven contrasts, but seems to be imbedded within the very core of the concept itself. The compulsion with which Chang repeatedly returns to this single concept in her short essay, developing it from a variety of different angles, suggests that the concept itself necessitates an unevenly contrastive mode of explication. It cannot be understood in isolation but must be developed in relation to a variety of different contexts.[16]

In the preceding discussion, I began with the concept of indirect maternal inheritance (of color affinities) and proceeded via a chain of associative links to the compositional formula of uneven contrasts, which Chang herself locates at the core of her own writing process. Of the various black-and-white photographs in *Mutual Reflections* that appear to have been retrospectively colored by hand (many presumably by Chang's mother), people's faces appear to have received the most careful attention: a touch of blush on the cheeks, some coloring on the lips, perhaps even a touch on the eyes as well.[17] By far the most striking instance of facial coloration can be found in photograph no. 33. This image, which is paired with a second black-and-white one below it, features a slightly out-of-focus view of Chang's meditative face, depicting her staring downward so that we are unable to see her eyes. Her face, however, has been stained a dark shade of turquoise. The fact that the

---

15. Eileen Chang, "Ziji de wenzhang"; translation, modified, from idem, "My Writing."

16. For a further discussion of the concept of *cenci duizhao* and its chromatic and artistic implication, see Leo Ou-fan Lee, *Shanghai Modern,* 281–84.

17. I have already discussed photo no. 2 above. See also photos no. 5 (of a strikingly effeminate younger brother), 13, and 15 (very subtle shading of the cheeks).

turquoise coloring has also left its mark on her (originally white?) undershirt, as well as bleeding into the orange-yellow of her dress, makes it safe to assume that we are seeing an artifact of careless coloring and not a reflection of Chang's unique temperament.

The turquoise photo appears with the minimalist caption "Photos nos. 33, 34: A flowery silk fabric serving as a shoulder-baring scarf" (61) (Fig. 7). This caption clearly refers to the second of the two images, leaving the chromatically startling one completely unaccounted for. This lack of commentary is partially compensated for a few pages later in the discussion of another photograph, which, like the earlier turquoise one, speaks as much to the vagaries of the developing process as it does to the image's ostensible referent. The photograph is no. 45, and consists of a rather out-of-focus head-and-shoulders shot of a tranquil and pensive Eileen Chang. The caption reads:

> This photo is too blurry, and therefore I didn't make any duplicates, just this one copy. When my mother returned to China after the war and looked over my photographs, she picked this one to take back with her, probably because this photo reminded her of her mental image[18] of her daughter. When she passed away in England in the late fifties, I collected this photo from the possessions she left behind and took it back with me. (72)

In this commentary, Chang claims to have little interest in the image itself, which is "too blurry"; instead, she is attracted to the photograph as a physical artifact bearing tangible traces of her dead mother's presence. We saw a similar pattern in the case of the handcolored photograph discussed above: Chang identified not with the actual image of herself as a young girl but with the chromatic traces her mother had inscribed onto the photo.

These interrelated themes of colors, maternal inheritance, and nostalgic recuperation come together most evocatively in the theme of masks—which, like photographs, can be seen as facial images reduced to the status of mere physical artifacts. The theme of masks is developed most strikingly in photograph no. 51, which shows Eileen Chang's face in the lower left-hand corner of the photo uncannily mirrored by a

18. *Xinmu zhong* 心目中, literally, "in her heart/mind's eye."

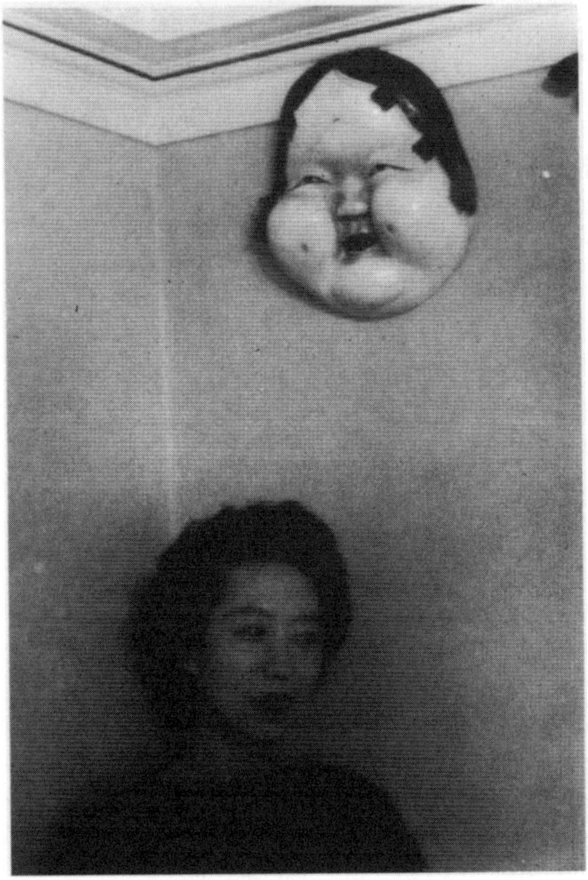

Fig. 8 Eileen Chang, photograph with a Noh mask, from *Mutual Reflections*. © Eileen Chang Estate.

Japanese Noh opera mask in the upper right-hand corne (Fig. 8); this ironic juxtaposition encourages us to see her own bemused expression as itself a "mask." This theme of figurative masking can also be retrospectively read into many of the other photos as well, in that they typically depict Chang and her relatives in highly stylized poses.

These masked poses imply a disassociation of oneself from one's own image, an act of seeing oneself *as if a stranger*, as an Other. The resulting fracturing of the myth of self-portraitive transparency results in the necessity of textual captions, which function as supplementary traces, linking the subject to the errant image like a textual umbilical cord. In a passage near the end of *Mutual Reflections*, Chang explained that her selection criteria were ultimately grounded on a consideration whether the image was one she would regret losing. Therefore, she created a self-described "confusion of image and text," out of which she hoped that one might possibly be able to "discern a self-portrait":

> The criterion for selecting which photographs to include in the preceding album is whether or not I was afraid that they would be lost. The captions are also quite disordered, but nevertheless it is my hope that, amid this confusion of image and text, it will be possible to dimly discern a self-portrait. (88)

Upon encountering this last line, the reader might be prompted to ask: for *whom* would it be possible to "dimly discern a self-portrait"? In this respect, the Chinese original is as ambiguous as my English translation. Is Chang saying that it is her hope that *she herself* be able to discern *her own* self-portrait? Or that an *outside reader* will recognize the volume as Chang's own self portrait? Or, perhaps, and most evocatively, that Chang *herself* will be able recognize it as her own self-portrait *only if* she views it from the perspective of an *outside reader*?

I use the term "outside reader" rather than "outside observer" deliberately, in accordance with Chang's own suggestion that the act of "dimly discerning" a self-portrait is as much an act of interpretive *reading* as it is one of direct *observation*.[19] As Derrida observed in a similar context:

> In all cases of the self-portrait, only a nonvisible referent in the picture, only an extrinsic clue, will allow an identification. For the identification will always remain indirect. One will always be able to distinguish the "signatory" from the "subject" of the self-portrait. . . . This is why the status of the self-portrait of the self-portraitist will always retain a hypothetical character. It always depends on the juridical effect of the title, on this verbal event that does not belong to the inside of the work but only to its parergonal border.[20]

19. Cf., e.g., the line from Wumingshi's *Siren of the Sea*: "After reading (not seeing) (*du* [*bu shi kan*] 讀 [不是看]) this woman's face, Yin Di felt as if he had lived out an era" (14).

20. Derrida, *Memoirs of the Blind*, 64.

Just as Derrida stressed the notion that self-portraiture is necessarily a product of the interaction between image and the accompanying text, similarly Chang herself, in the preceding passage, emphasized the "confusion of image and text" that simultaneously obscures and enables the perception of the self-portrait. In Chang's discussion of the inherent disorder of image and textual captions, the term she uses for "captions" is *fuji* 附記. *Fuji* was probably intended to mean "appended notes," but could also be read more literally as "appended memories."[21] This ambiguity at the level of the lexical signifier is reinforced by a comparable ambiguity at the level of the signifier's referent. That is, although it is likely that with *fuji*, Chang was probably referring primarily to the reflective commentary that she compiled for the 1994 publication of the photos, the term could also conceivably refer to the original textual inscriptions in the margins and on the backs of these old photographs themselves.

For instance, a good example of the multiple layers of commentarial *fuji* can be seen in Chang's discussion of photograph no. 49 in the collection. Chang's 1993 commentary to that image notes that the reverse side of the photograph records the name of the company that took the photograph as well as the date (1954) the photograph was taken. Furthermore, it also contains the following poem she wrote ten years before the *Mutual Reflections* compilation:

> Disappointedly looking back on thirty autumns,
> I cry a single tear;
> The desolation of a bygone era,
> And of different times. (79)

Chang describes how she had written this poem in 1984 when she ran across the photograph while moving and, realizing that it was the photograph's thirtieth anniversary, had decided to pen this poem to commemorate the occasion. The *Mutual Reflections* commentary is less a reflection on the photograph itself and more a doubly displaced rumination on the original photograph via this nostalgic poem written a full three decades after the fact.

---

21. *Ji* can mean both "to remember" and "to write down, or record."

Chang recognized many of the photographs included in her album, but often had no recollection of the specific historical circumstances under which the photographs were taken and produced. It is with a constant sense of uncanny alienation that she rereads the photographs and their respective inscriptions. For instance, referring to another photograph, she remarks, "On the back of this photo, it says *in my own handwriting*: 'August, 1946,' otherwise I would not have remembered when it was that Fatima took it at my house" (70/21; italics added). Viewing another photo, she notes, "Thus the stamp on the back of this photo. It looks completely strange to me; I have no impression of it" (85/23). This paradoxical function of alienated identification occasioned by the *fuji* brings us back to the theme of masking, discussed above, in the sense that the textual captions not only are made necessary by the sense of alienation occasioned by the self-portraitive mask but also themselves come to assume a similar self-alienated quality. That is, the *fuji* come to function as a kind of "mask," necessarily mediating between the observer and the photographs "themselves."

This theme of masking is also an important concern in Roland Barthes's *Camera Lucida*. Barthes stressed the importance of masks in performative theater ("the whitened bust of the totemic theater, the man with the painted face in the Chinese theatre, the rice-paste makeup of the Indian Katha-Kali, the Japanese Noh mask"; 31) and pointed to the mask as one of the enabling conditions of photography itself:

> Since every photograph is contingent (and thereby outside of meaning), Photography cannot signify (aim at a generality) except by assuming a mask . . . *the mask is the meaning, insofar as it is the absolutely pure* (as it was in the ancient theatre). . . . Yet the mask is the difficult region of Photography. Society, it seems, mistrusts pure meaning. . . . Hence the photograph whose meaning (I am not saying its effect, but its meaning) is too impressive is quickly deflected; we consume it aesthetically, not politically. (35–36; italics added)

For Barthes, then, the photograph represents a curious hermeneutical paradox: it simultaneously represents a uniquely direct instantiation of meaning (a "language without a code") and relies for its effect on a process of "masking," understood as a radical *defacement* of signification.

Using language strikingly similar to Eileen Chang's discussion of the unveiling function of the "inhuman gaze of the lens," Barthes also noted:

> Once I feel myself observed by the lens, everything changes: I constitute myself in the process of "posing," I instantaneously make another body for myself, I transform myself in advance into an image. . . . In front of the lens, I am at the same time: the one I think I am, the one I want others to think I am, the one the photographer thinks I am, and the one he makes us of to exhibit his art. In other words, a strange action: I do not stop imitating myself, and because of this, each time I am (or let myself be) photographed, I invariably suffer from a sensation of inauthenticity, sometimes of imposture (comparable to certain nightmares). (10, 13)

As Barthes went on to explain, this state of "imposture" and the process of "posing" for the camera are, for him, equivalent to a miniature death:

> In terms of the image-repertoire, the Photograph (the one I *intend*) represents that very subtle moment when, to tell the truth, I am neither subject nor object but a subject who feels he is becoming an object: I then experience a micro-version of death (of parenthesis): I am truly becoming a spectre. . . . Ultimately, what I am seeking in the photograph taken of me . . . is Death: Death is the *eidos* of that photograph. (13–14, 15)

At the heart of this metonymic chain linking together the acts of masking, posing, imposture, and finally death itself is Barthes's attempted recovery of the memory of his own dead mother, who had passed away shortly before he wrote *Camera Lucida.*

In fact, Barthes's text can be seen as revolving around a specific maternal photograph he deliberately chose not to include. This photograph is the "Winter Garden Photograph" of his mother as a young child, which Barthes had recently rediscovered shortly after her death:

> Something like an essence of the Photograph floated in this particular picture. I therefore decided to "derive" all Photography (its "nature") from the only photograph which assuredly existed for me, and to take it somehow as a guide for my last investigation. (26)

The Winter Garden Photograph reassured Barthes of the referential immediacy of photography—suggesting that photography differs from other semiotic systems insofar as "every photograph is a certificate of presence."[22] This assertion of the referential transparency of the photograph is highly unusual coming from a poststructuralist semiotician such as Barthes, and it is almost as if the loss of his mother led him to desire to ascribe to the figure of the photograph a kind of semiotic transparency and immediacy that might perhaps have served to counter that very real maternal loss.

What Barthes found most evocative, but at the same time most painful, about these maternal photographs was not so much their mimetic *resemblance to* his mother but their *departures from* that original maternal model:

> And here the essential question first emerged: did I *recognize* her? According to these photographs, sometimes I recognized a region of her face, a certain relation of nose and forehead, the movement of her arms, her hands. *I never recognized her except in fragments.* (65)

The focus on deceased mothers and referential authenticity in both Chang's and Barthes's works is reinforced by the fact that both works uncannily anticipate the (unexpected) deaths of their respective authors (as noted above, Eileen Chang passed away only one year after the publication of *Mutual Reflections*; Barthes was struck by a laundry truck in February 1980, shortly after the publication of *Camera Lucida,* and died a month later).[23] Therefore, both texts figure as uncanny acts of autoeffigy, themselves not only obsessed with death but also, like Du Liniang's self-portrait in *The Peony Pavilion*, ominously presaging their authors' own deaths.

In an insightful reading of *Camera Lucida*, Elisabeth Bronfen notes Barthes's remark that "a sort of umbilical cord links the body of the photographed thing to my gaze" (81), together with his earlier observation that, in the course of nursing his dying mother, he had engendered

22. Barthes, *Camera Lucida*, 87. Cf. his statement that "photography's referent is not the same as the referent of other systems of representation. I call 'photographic referent' not the *optionally* real thing to which an image or a sign refers but the *necessarily* real thing which has been placed before the lens, without which there would be no photograph" (76).

23. Jay, *Downcast Eyes*, 450.

the inversely procreative fantasy that his mother was actually his infant child: "I, who had not procreated, I had, in her very illness, engendered my mother" (72). Bronfen brings these two observations together to argue for a connection between photography's links to maternity, on one hand, and its anticipatory recuperation of death, on the other:

> In this scene [in which Barthes imagines his mother as his own child], the image serves as a surplus signifier to fill the gaping void within representational reality; loss is compensated by an image of male progeny, even as the dead mother leads him to discover the essence of photography. Seeing the image of his mother before his birth, before his own history, he images his own death; the mother who gave birth to him also becomes a harbinger of his "total, undialectical death." This trajectory from losing the maternal body, recovering it as an image, to reading not only the mother's but also one's own mortality in that same image—traces a series of narcissistically recuperative gestures.[24]

For Eileen Chang—who, like Barthes, died childless—the image of her mother similarly functions as a temporal interregnum, foreclosing the possibility of her own death before it has even come to pass, and opening a space for textually mediated modes of procreative dis/semination.

In the remaining chapters of this study, I consider several authors writing in the same *fin-de-siècle* period in which Chang composed her *Mutual Reflections* and examine the ways in which each pushes the conceptual limits of this notion of metaphorical reproduction. I argue that each borrows themes of sexual desire and visual reproduction but remobilizes them to provide a metaphorical ground for considering the reproduction of abstract structures of sociocultural identity. More specifically, I explore the ways in which four contemporary authors have attempted to come to terms with a paradoxical relation to their "own" individual and collective pasts. For each of these contemporary figures, visual images such as photographs function both as concrete links to the past and as reminders of the rupture that inevitably separates these images, as autonomous signifiers, from their ostensible referents. The

24. Bronfen, *The Knotted Subject*, 94.

visual image, in these works, functions less as a transparent window to a concrete visual referent and more as a site of projection and transformation. In this way, the image emerges as an object of perception in its own right, but one that helps to bring into question the specular and spectatorial logics that ostensibly underlie it.

PART III

Screened Projections

To the extent that the orientation of the mirror-face in Su Hanchen's Song dynasty fan painting is taken as an accurate, *inverse* reflection of the lady's own gaze, we may infer that the lady herself would be looking not *down* at the mirror on the dressing table before her but *up* in the direction of the freestanding screen positioned behind the mirror. Decorated with an abstract pattern of wavy lines, this screen, art historian Wu Hung suggests, "is also a 'mirror.' But instead of reflecting the woman's physical likeness it 'mirrors' her mind."[1] Like the tripartite screen in Cixi's mirror photograph, the screen in the background of Su Hanchen's painting represents a space of imaginary projection—a visual surface onto which a variety of cultural ideals and sensibilities may be projected. This physical screen does not merely displace but rather contains folded in within itself *both* the specular and the spectatorial perspective discussed in the first two parts of this volume. That is, the screen is at once the literal object of the lady's (presumptive) gaze and the site of the imaginary projection through which she hopes to view herself (Fig. 9).

Su Hanchen's thirteenth-century screen captures, I would argue, a conjunction of specularity and spectatoriality that has subsequently emerged as the dominant scopic mode of the contemporary, late twentieth-century era. In this period, technologies of visual reproduction

1. Wu Hung, *The Double Screen*, 22–24.

Fig. 9 Su Hanchen, *Lady at Her Dressing Table in a Garden* (detail). Photograph © 2008 Museum of Fine Arts, Boston.

have achieved such a ubiquity that concrete images no longer carry an aura of presence and authenticity as they did during the early modern period; rather, they come to function as sites of fantasy and projection. In contrast to the mirror as a figure of specular involution during the late imperial period or the camera as a figure of the external gaze during the early twentieth-century period, I argue that the visual figure par excellence of the contemporary period is that of the screen. Functioning as a site of either literal (for example, cinematic) or figurative projection, the screen represents a space of illusion, in which a projection is made visible only as a result of the elision of the material surface underneath.

Whereas the late imperial period was characterized by a backward glance toward China's cultural tradition and the early twentieth century by an outward glance to how China was perceived from abroad, during the contemporary period these respective specular and spectatorial gazes have become increasingly intertwined. The space of China itself has become more and more contested, as a combination of transnational and diasporic forces has demanded a reconsideration of the boundaries between China and an outside world, and as the deaths of Chiang Kai-shek 蔣介石 and Mao Zedong 毛澤東 in 1975 and 1976, respectively, led to the loosening of the strict sociocultural regimes that had dramatically constrained cultural production on both sides of the Taiwan Strait during the post-1949 period. As a result, the 1980s and 1990s witnessed a remarkably eclectic environment of cultural production on both sides of the Taiwan Strait and throughout Greater China.

All four authors I consider in Part III, Li Yung-p'ing, Gao Xingjian, Wang Shuo, and Chu T'ien-wen are writing in direct response to these twin tendencies of national and cultural decentering. Hailing from a variety of points throughout the global Chinese cultural sphere (they are a Mainlander based in Beijing, a Taipei-based author from a Mainland heritage, another Taipei-based writer originally from Malaysia, and an expatriate from Mainland China who is now a naturalized French citizen), each focuses on politically and culturally provocative issues that would have been virtually unthinkable during the immediate post-1949 period. Each of these authors, furthermore, shares an interest in using visual imagery not so much for its strict denotational status but as a space of imaginary projection. Whether it is Li Yung-p'ing using the figure of a city map to explore dynamics of cultural nostalgia in Taiwan, or Gao Xingjian and Wang Shuo using the memory of a destroyed or impossible photograph as an imaginary nodal point around which a personal history may be recreated, or Chu T'ien-wen using a kaleidoscopic fragmentation of the visual world as a metaphor for the "homosexualization" of a contemporary society in which sociocultural reproduction increasingly takes the form of a decentered process of textual production, in each case the significance of the visual image lies not so much in its actual denotational function as in its status as a figurative screen onto which an assortment of concerns and anxieties may be projected.

If the dominant scopic logic of the late imperial period was one of specular reflection and that of the early twentieth century was one of spectatorial observation, the dominant scopic regime of the contemporary period could be said to be that of screened projection, characterized by a constant double awareness that the image both is and is not what it appears to be. The screen, in other words, occupies a space of the fetish and is dictated by the logic of disavowal: "I know, but nevertheless . . . ." That is, the contemporary viewer consciously knows that the screen image is intangible and ephemeral but nevertheless continues to use it as a fulcrum around which to structure his or her own self-conception.

This logic of disavowal, furthermore, extends not only to visuality, but also to issues of gendered identity. Each of the contemporary works considered here is written from a very explicitly masculine perspective, while at the same time expressing a deep-rooted ambivalence about the self-sufficiency—and, indeed, the very identity—of that same masculinity. Like screened projections, however, the gendered identities at the heart of these fictional works are ultimately reaffirmed—reaffirmed, not *despite*, but rather precisely *because* of, the works' implicit recognition of the ephemeral and contested nature of those same identities.

The resulting conjunction of visual and gendered concerns brings us back full circle to a perspective already anticipated in the texts examined in the first two parts of this study. Whereas the works in Part I take the figure of the mirror as a symbol of the self-sufficiency of (gendered) identity, but then proceed to explore the processes of circulation and transvaluation that lie embedded within that moment of mirroring itself; and the works in Part II take a process of spectatorial identification and complicate it by interrogating the specific (gendered) perspectives of that spectatorial gaze itself; the works in Part III, by contrast, take as their starting point a persistent anxiety about the reliability of gendered identity, only to deliberately reconstruct the precarious specular and spectatorial foundations on which that (gendered) identity is presumed to rely.

7

Li Yung-p'ing and Spectral Cartography

In that Empire, the Art of Cartography attained such Perfection [in time] the Cartographers Guilds struck a Map of the Empire whose size was that of the Empire, and which coincided point for point with it.

—Jorge Luis Borges, "On Exactitude in Science"

Near the end of the fourth chapter—or "wandering" (*manyou* 慢遊), as Li calls his chapters—of Li Yung-p'ing's 李永平 (1947–) 1998 novel *Zhu Ling manyou xianjing* 朱鴒漫游仙境 (Zhu Ling's wanderings in wonderland), the suggestively named vice principal Tang Baoguo 唐保國 (literally, Tang "protect the nation") lectures a group of girls from the National Middle School on the question "When should pubescent girls wear their first brassiere?"[1] After citing some pseudo-scientific Japanese research on sexual maturation, Tang points to the sagging breasts of older women to illustrate the dangers of not providing maturing breasts with adequate support. He then launches into an impassioned diatribe about the general importance of breasts and buttocks:

Breast peaks and buttock mounds, the former protruding in the front and the latter uplifted behind: these are, after all, two prominent landmarks of the female body. At the same time, they also constitute an allusion to the two towering beacons that can lead voyagers astray on their way home! I am sure that

1. Li Yung-p'ing, *Zhu Ling manyou xianjing*, 242. Subsequent references to this work are cited in the text.

you must have all heard of the Greek epic poem *The Odyssey*, whose protagonist Odysseus sails off course in the Mediterranean, leading him to drift for ten years, after which— (242; final dash appears in the original)

Tang Baoguo breaks off his lecture at this point to entertain a question from the young protagonist of the novel, Zhu Ling. When she asks what he means by the term "landmark" (*dibiao* 地標), Tang replies: "A landmark is the most representative and the most striking symbol (*biaozhi* 標誌) of a city." This passage is grounded on the figure of the map—which is held up as a direct transposition of geopolitical reality into semiotic text. Here, however, the map explicitly occupies a space of fantastic projection, and it is precisely that fantastic dimension that allows it to serve as a fulcrum between the geopolitical concerns of contemporary Taipei, on one hand, and the protagonist's sexual-maturational obsessions, on the other.

Insofar as women's breasts can be seen, in Tang Baoguo's miniature allegory, as metaphorical landmarks, they have the paradoxical function of both orienting people and potentially leading them astray (like the legendary breasts of the Homeric Sirens). Tang, moreover, appears to equivocate on whether he intends these metaphorical landmarks to be taken topographically (mis/orienting the viewer with regard to the spatial layout of the female body) or temporally (mis/orienting the viewer with respect to the chronological course of the female body's sexual maturation). Finally, the explicitly nationalist connotations of Tang's name and that of the middle school, combined with Tang's reference to the city in his explication of the meaning of the term "landmark," raise the question of whether these breasts and buttocks, figurative landmarks of the female body, might also be seen as symbolic landmarks of the Taipei/Taiwan body politic.[2]

Tang Baoguo's discourse on women's breasts can itself be used as a heuristic "landmark" to help orient a reading and exegesis of Li Yung-p'ing's novel. To begin with, Tang's discussion points to the way

2. In this respect, Li Yung-p'ing is drawing on a long tradition in Taoism, dating back at least as far as the fourth century BCE text *Zhuangzi*, of seeing "the human body [as] the image of a country." For a discussion of the genealogy of this trope, see, e.g., Schipper, *The Taoist Body*, 100–112.

the novel overlays temporal teleologies onto metaphorical spatial topographies. More specifically, the passage evocatively points to the novel's thematization of female sexual maturation as both a literal subject and a rather ambiguous metaphorics for historical development. These issues of political schism and geographic dislocation are, moreover, particularly relevant to Li Yung-p'ing, given his own diasporic background: he was born in Malaysia, educated in Taiwan, received a postgraduate degree in the United States, and currently resides in Taiwan.

In this chapter, I consider the interrelated themes of spatial and temporal dislocation as they are developed in Li Yung-p'ing's 1992 novel *Haidong qing* 海東青 (The giant eagle) and its quasi-sequel, *Zhu Ling's Wanderings in Wonderland.* Both are vast enterprises, essentially plotless, and featuring a daunting linguistic and symbolic complexity.[3] A central trope in both works involves the figurative status of the Taipei road map, specifically the manner in which—given the number of streets named after mainland Chinese cities, provinces, and other placenames—a map of contemporary Taipei can be seen as a "miniature spectral reflection" of a historical map of the Chinese mainland.

Motherlands and Maternities

> According to the Trobrianders' constant affirmation, persistent in the face of all objective evidence to the contrary, children are supposed to *resemble* their fathers, while all resemblance to the mother is vehemently denied. . . . Thus children are formed *in the image and likeness* of the father, without the least recognition of his physical part in procreation; where the mother, who is the recognized *genetrix* of her children, is supposed to bear absolutely no resemblance to them.
>
> —Jean-Joseph Goux, "Sexual Difference and History"

By way of entering *Haidong qing,* I turn first to another, at first sight unrelated, text. In *The Sexual Life of Savages,* the renowned anthropologist Bronislaw Malinowski reported that the Trobriand Islanders in British New Guinea vehemently deny the existence of any physiological or corporeal link between fathers and their children; the father is viewed as a supplemental interloper into the dyadic relationship be-

---

3. Together, they total more than 1,400 pages, with *Haidong qing* alone running to nearly a thousand pages.

tween mother and child. This collective assertion of deadbeat fatherhood, however, has a curious correlate: the Trobrianders apparently deny with equal vehemence any suggestion that children bear any physical resemblance to *the mothers themselves.* For the Trobrianders, this apparent paradox is explained by the simple postulate that, although the mother supplies the material matrix out of which the child is formed, the social bond with the father nevertheless directly determines the child's subsequent image or likeness.[4]

In a discussion of the gendered connotations of tropes of visual reproduction in different cultures, Jean-Joseph Goux notes that the perspective of the Trobriand Islanders is representative of several other, more familiar, approaches to the relationship between procreation and filiation. Aristotle, for example, suggested in his writings on animal reproduction that the female of the species contributes the "matter" out of which the embryo is constituted, and the male the "form."[5] Within the Christian tradition, the trope of the virgin birth of Jesus would appear to articulate a similarly gendered dichotomy of form and substance. All three examples illustrate ways in which reproductive and progenitive tropes can be mobilized to assert and perpetuate metaphysical binary oppositions between matter and form, structure and content. Although these stark oppositions between matter and form often appear most dramatically in the sorts of progenitive paradigms cited above, they frequently exert a considerable degree of influence on other domains of social and intellectual consciousness. I argue that Li Yung-p'ing's novel *Haidong qing*, for example, draws on comparable metaphorical oppositions in its fictional reflections on contemporary Taiwan's collective cultural and political identity, particularly with respect to Taiwan's relationship to Mainland China.

Haidong qing begins with the protagonist Jin Wu's return to Taiwan after eight years teaching literature in the United States. The novel uses a rather elaborate linguistic and symbolic structure to portray Jin Wu's and the other characters' "aimless wanderings" through the city of

4. See Malinowski, *The Sexual Life of Savages*, 140–79; discussed in Goux, *Sexual Economies*, 218–19.

5. Aristotle, *Physics* I.9.192a23; cited and discussed in Goux, *Sexual Economies*, 213.

Taipei, with special attention being given to the seamier sides of the city—particularly the burgeoning industry of child prostitution. Eclipsing the figure of Jin Wu is his young companion, the seven-year-old Zhu Ling. Zhu Ling generally represents a state of idealized purity, which serves as a powerful counterpoint to the rather degenerate social practices of the adult world that surrounds her, even as she herself stands at the figurative threshold of that same adult world.

In the tradition of high literary modernism, *Haidong qing* abandons the conveniences of a traditional, linear plotline and instead functions more as a patchwork of interrelated themes and concerns, woven together around the directionless meanderings of the main protagonists. Replete with streets and avenues named after cities and provinces from the Chinese Mainland, the urban cartography of Taipei the characters traverse is explicitly described as a "miniature reflection of Great China" (*da Zhongguo de suoying* 大中國的縮影).[6] A recurrent theme concerns the different contributions to contemporary Taiwanese society and identity made, on one hand, by the founding "father" figure of Sun Yatsen 孫逸仙 (known conventionally in Taiwan as *guofu* 國父, or "father of the nation") and, on the other hand, by "Great China" (*da Zhongguo*)—what we would call in English the historical Chinese "motherland" (although the equivalent term in Chinese, *zuguo* 祖國, is closer to "ancestral homeland). The implication would appear to be that Taiwan has inherited the bulk of the raw "material" of its cultural identity from the Chinese "motherland," while it ostensibly derives its specific political and social "form" from its "founding father," Sun Yatsen.

The final chapter of the novel presents this opposition between maternal substance and paternal form in a symbolically stark manner. Standing outside the Lanling Girls' Middle School as it is letting out for the day, Jin Wu and Zhu Ling suddenly hear some middle school students singing a song commemorating the revolutionary contributions of the "national father," Sun Yatsen. Jin Wu's first thought is that "today must be the anniversary of some important event in the life of the *guofu* [Sun Yatsen], which would explain why [the schoolchildren] are

6. Li Yung-p'ing, *Haidong qing*, iv. Subsequent references to this work are cited in the text.

singing this song." Zhu Ling corrects him, pointing out that the date, May 11, is in fact a holiday of sorts, but one entirely unrelated to Taiwan nationalist politics or the "national father." May 11 is, rather, the eve of "Mother's Day" (931–32).

Even as *Haidong qing* presents this contrast between a "maternal" cultural continuity connecting Taiwan and the Mainland and a "paternal" rupture at the level of political, social, and national consciousness, the novel also contests and complicates this apparent dichotomy. While borrowing familial and progenitive tropes to comment metaphorically on the political/national relationship between Taiwan and the Mainland, Li's novel simultaneously uses these same tropes in a much more "literal" and direct way—but one that ultimately turns the apparent linearity of these progenitive tropes on their figurative heads. One of the recurrent themes of *Haidong qing*, for instance, concerns the frequently severed relationship between mothers and their children. This theme is best exemplified by the figure of An Lexin, who throughout is portrayed as ostensibly searching for his own mother while continually singing a popular Taiwanese ditty about longing/looking for one's mother:

> Oh! Mama,
> You are truly heartless,
> Mama, ah,
> I searched the entire courtyard without finding you.
> Oh! Mama,
> For what other ambition was it,
> That you abandoned your children?[7]

This search, however, risks losing sight of its original object and becoming an end in itself, as suggested by one of the last passages in the novel discussing An Lexin and his mother. Jin Wu hears Lexin singing and asks him, laughing, if he misses his mother. Lexin laughs as well and replies that, no, he is "merely singing the song!"[8] On the following page, Zhu Ling repeats the same question and then asks Lexin if he has

7. See, e.g., pp. 130, 214, 485, 537, 553, and 795 for passages either citing or alluding to this song.

8. Pages 794–95. There is also a similar exchange on p. 537.

a mother at all, to which Lexin replies that he "grew up in the countryside in the south and as a result never had a chance to see her" (796).

In another of the An Lexin passages, a Taipei taxi driver remarks to Jin Wu that "everyone in Haidong 海東 [literally, "East of the sea": i.e., Taiwan] is looking for their mother" (486). This particular passage is immediately preceded by another episode in which Jin Wu gazes out the window of the taxi and sees that the clock on the wall on the National Parliament building reads 4:05. Jin Wu immediately looks at the wristwatch of his young female friend Ya Xing, and, seeing that it reads 4:00, he remarks that the clock on the parliament building appears to be five minutes fast. Ya Xing replies that the clock is not fast but has been stopped at 4:05 for many years (486). The fact that this particular scene occurs in the middle of a discussion of searching for missing mothers suggests that the phenomenon of searching for motherhood may be comparable to the arrested temporality symbolized by the clock. The frozen time of the clock also happens to coincide almost precisely with the time on the watch worn by the young Ya Xing; the resulting uncanny synchronicity suggests a pattern of transtemporal transferences between missing mothers and young girls.[9]

More generally, *Haidong qing* thematizes the taboo topic of older men's pedophilic attraction to young girls. The basic plot of the novel concerns the protagonist Jin Wu, a middle-aged male professor of literature, and his rather intimate relationship with a small group of young, school-age girls.[10] Although the work never suggests that there is an overtly sexual dimension to these relationships, it repeatedly demonstrates its awareness of how these relationships might be misperceived by others. In Chapter 12, for example, there is an ambiguous moment when Jin Wu squeezes Zhu Ling's shoulders. She immediately jumps back and asks him what he is doing. He replies, "Nothing, I just

---

9. Cf., e.g., the most famous work about pedophilia in twentieth-century Western literature: Nobokov's *Lolita*. In that novel, Humbert's attraction to young girls is explicitly explained in terms of arrested temporalities, in that his "first love" was killed suddenly while both were still children, leaving his libido stranded at an earlier developmental stage.

10. The girls range in age from seven (Zhu Ling and Ya Xing) to fourteen (Zhang Tong).

wanted to stroke you a little," whereupon Zhu Ling's face "flushed bright red as she stared up at him with a strange expression on her face, not knowing whether to laugh or not" (819). In another scene, Jin Wu attempts to take Ya Xing out of school in the middle of the day. The female instructor who greets him obviously suspects his intentions. He immediately tries to justify himself by explaining defensively that he is a professor in the foreign language department at Hai-tung University (that is, he is a respected member of the community) and that he needs to inform his neighbor's child, Ya Xing, about a "family emergency." This rather conventional excuse ironically points to the novel's theme of the deterritorialization of nuclear-family kinship structures (481–82).

If the theme of pedophilia implicates the novel's main protagonists only through a series of innuendoes and misprisions, the same taboo topic is an explicit and dominant concern throughout much of the work. At the very beginning of the novel, for instance, Jin Wu remarks to the taxi driver who picked him up at the airport at 3:00 A.M. that there are a lot of young girls out in the street for that time of night. The taxi driver replies that "as of late, when it comes to playing with women, men's tastes have changed" (29), a reference to Taiwanese men's increasing sexual interest in ever-younger girls.

This theme of pedophilia is elaborated most explicitly in Chapter 11. There, several professors discuss, among other things, the increasing prevalence of underage prostitution in Taiwan and Hong Kong. A certain Professor He Jiayu proffers the following observations:

> Today I read a report from the Republic of China Women's Rescue Foundation (中華民國婦女救援基金會), which noted that surveys reveal that there are a hundred thousand prostitutes in the city, and that the average age at which the girls enter prostitution is between twelve and fourteen. . . . Furthermore, the Republic of China Women's Rescue Foundation also reports that as the availability increases, and as men's tastes change, the age of prostitutes in the city will drop precipitously. Right now, what is deemed most desirable are those girls who are still in first or second year of middle school, or even fifth or sixth grade of primary school. (695)

This discussion of underage prostitution in Taiwan and Hong Kong is followed by an extended reflection on pedophilia in contemporary Japanese culture and society. A Professor Chen Bule remarks, for example, that the theme of "older men sexually obsessed with youth" is an established motif (*muti* 母題, literally "mother topic") in Japanese movies and literature (727). Professor Chen uses the term "motif" in a strictly academic sense, even apologizing for his use of overly technical terminology. Nevertheless, his use of this specific phrase (with its allusion to the figure of motherhood to describe the cultural phenomenon of pedophilia) coincidentally points us to one of the more intriguing dimensions of the theme of pedophilia in Li's novel—one that provides a potential link between the treatment of pedophilia and the equally prominent theme, discussed above, of missing motherhood. Specifically, these two chains of misdirected identifications and projections (children straying from their mothers and men's libidinal impulses straying from their generational peers and onto their figurative daughters) come full circle with the novel's reflections on a curious phenomenon wherein a young girl's sexual attractiveness allegedly, and paradoxically, lies in her embodiment of a certain "maternal quality."

This paradoxical generational conflation is presented most explicitly in the novel's discussion of contemporary Japanese culture and society. The professors in Chapter 11, for example, following their discussion of pedophilia, eventually turn to popular Japanese cinema. Of particular interest to them is the prominent Japanese teenage actress Miyashino Yuko. Although already sixteen or seventeen, she looks as though she were only twelve. She is also described as embodying "that sort of motherly love men are always searching for." Professor He Jiayu follows up on his earlier remarks, cited above, by observing,

> Professor Chen, what are you saying? That old Japanese men have an obsession with young girls (*you liannütong zhi pi* 有戀女童之癖)? Oh, it generally seems that way. When I was studying in the United States, I had a chance to see the documentary on the Rape of Nanjing filmed by American missionary John Magee. In it, there was one scene in which a group of Japanese soldiers raped a seven-year-old Chinese girl. I think that this represents the most specific, most bare-boned, and most horrid manifestation of this Japanese obsession with young girls. Returning to our earlier topic of discussion—although Miyashino Yuko is actually sixteen or seventeen years old, she looks as if she were only twelve or thirteen. Yet, at the same time she possesses the sort of motherly love which men are perpetually seeking. . . . This sort of maternal girl actress is something Japanese male audiences have always loved the most. (741)

These specific comments about the Sino-Japanese War and Japanese cinema make it clear that in *Haidong qing* young women occupy a rather curious libidinal and temporal interstice. On one hand, they are eroticized precisely because of their (comparative) sexual immaturity. On the other hand, they are presented as the objects of a "future perfect" eroticization because they embody maternal qualities that presumably pertain to the other end of the figurative incest taboo—a taboo against sleeping, not with one's potential daughter, but rather with one's potential mother. This maturational chiasmus—in which girls are erotized simultaneously for both their sexual *im*maturity and their apparent (super)maturity—is seen perhaps most clearly in the theme of young Taiwan girls' taking estrogen supplements to hasten their sexual development, resulting in "a baby's face and the body of a woman."[11] Not only do the hormones facilitate the pedophilic ideal of simultaneous sexual maturity and immaturity, but they also point to a reification of both maturation and femininity. This enables both qualities to be artificially separated from the individual herself and to become objects of investment in their own right.

The last allusion to female hormones in the novel is juxtaposed with another, closely related, discussion. Throughout much of the novel, there are regular references to the practice of eating "turkey kidneys" (*huoji yaozi* 火雞腰子).[12] Not until the final chapter, however, does it occur to Zhu Ling to ask Jin Wu what, exactly, *yaozi* are. When informed that they are avian gonads, Zhu Ling is horrified, but she develops an even greater sympathy for the live rooster she happens to be holding in her lap at the time (901). This rooster is one of a large group of birds deliberately liberated to protest America's dumping of unwanted turkey testicles on the Taiwan market, where they are an expensive delicacy. Having initially acquired the rooster out of a somewhat abstract sympathy for its predicament, Zhu Ling grows even more attached to the bird when she realizes that she may be protecting it from caponization. With both the female hormones and the turkey "kidneys," then, we have a symbolic distantia-

11. Page 927; see also pp. 665 and 669 for two other references to this practice.

12. See, e.g., pp. 290, 598, 605, 795, and 885. In the novel, the delicacy is invariably prepared with sesame oil and shredded ginger.

tion of the essence of masculinity and femininity from the actual bodies they help to bring to maturity.

In his second discourse on pedophilia, cited above, Professor He Jiayu moves from a remark about Japanese soldiers raping Chinese girls during the Sino-Japanese War to a more extended discussion of pedophilia in contemporary Japanese culture. Although, in this specific context, the precise relationship between these two themes may be somewhat ambiguous, the Rape of Nanjing is, nevertheless, a central theme in the novel. For example, in Chapter 6 there is an account of an interview with a member of the Japanese Diet, published in that paragon of pedophilic fantasies: the American edition of *Playboy*. In this interview, the Japanese assemblyman calmly denies that the "Rape of Nanjing" ever occurred and instead claims that it was a hoax staged by the residents of Nanjing to tarnish the reputations of the Japanese invaders (313). If the assemblyman's historical blindness in this scene can be seen as an example of Freudian displacement, then its precise inverse can perhaps be seen in another Rape of Nanjing scene in Chapter 11, one grounded on a similarly Freudian logic of overdetermined condensation. In this latter scene, the group of college professors featured in that chapter give the fourteen-year-old girl Zhang Tong a series of dates and ask her to identify the important event in modern Chinese history associated with each. To every date, Zhang Tong invariably advances the same guess: the Rape of Nanjing (699).[13]

These various allusions to the Rape of Nanjing can be related to two distinct themes in *Haidong qing*. On one hand, all are explicitly bound up with the issue of historical commemoration. How are historical events to be remembered? What is their status when viewed through the lens of retrospective commemoration? As noted above, the novel forsakes the structuring conveniences of a conventional teleological plot. Just as the plot of the novel itself doesn't really go anywhere, this plotlessness finds a parallel in the major theme of "wandering." Amid all this aimless wandering, official and traditional holidays come to substitute, in large part, for the absent topographical landmarks. The Rape of Nanjing functions as an example of this sort of "temporal landmark," providing a concrete,

13. See pp. 296 and 765 for other prominent discussions of this historical event.

if rather overdetermined, historical ground against which the novel's characters can orient themselves.

At the same time, these allusions to the Rape of Nanjing can also be seen from the perspective of the theme of temporal discontinuity. Throughout the novel, the seven-year-old protagonist Zhu Ling repeatedly shocks her interlocutors by voicing thoughts and observations (typically dealing with either sex or politics) that suggest a much more mature consciousness. Examples of this sort of diaglossia include her reflections on the Rape of Nanjing, on accelerated maturation through the use of female hormone supplements,[14] on the Japanese practice of taking "sex vacations,"[15] and on the use of the term *biqin* 避秦 (fleeing from Qin Shihuang, the notoriously autocratic emperor of the Qin dynasty) to describe Mainlanders who fled the communist regime.[16] One of the most striking instances of this double-voicing can be found near the end of the novel. Zhu Ling recounts to Jin Wu a mysterious recent dream of hers. All the bronze statues of Sun Yatsen in front of Taiwan elementary schools suddenly come to life and search out those officials who had vandalized Sun's banners and carried off his placards. In addition, the living statues make a point of hunting down and beheading all the adults who had sexually taken advantage of young girls. Jin Wu is stunned that the young, supposedly innocent, Zhu Ling could have such a dream:

> "Girl, how old are you? 'Vandalizing the banners of the National Father' (*dazhe Guofu de qihao* 打著國父的旗號), 'bringing calamity to the nation and its people' (*huoguo yangmin* 禍國殃民), 'violating young girls' (*zaojian xiao nühai* 糟踐小女孩)—this kind of talk doesn't sound like something a seven-year-old little girl would say." (924)

Jin Wu appears to be somewhat reassured when she informs him that this is only a story her father told her. She nevertheless hastens to add, however, that she had also dreamed the same dream herself (924).

Just as the perverse, hormone-laden girls with a "baby's face and a woman's body" are portrayed as appealing to at least a portion of adult

14. See, e.g., p. 927.
15. See, e.g., p. 791.
16. See, e.g., p. 292.

males in Taipei, similarly we might speculate that Zhu Ling's (and, to a lesser extent, her friends, Ya Xing's and Zhang Tong's) diaglossic combination of childlike innocence with parodic adult precocity partially accounts for Jin Wu's own emotional attachment to them. The resulting Janus-like approach to temporality can, moreover, be observed in one of Jin Wu's bizarre behavioral quirks: his habitual, almost obsessive, practice of checking the watches on the wrists of his young female friends, Zhu Ling, Ya Xing, and Zhang Tong, to determine the time.[17] So egregious is Jin Wu's temporal parasitism that at one point his female student Gong Qing asks him in exasperation, "Don't you *yourself* ever wear a watch?" (471). This seemingly innocent gesture of telling time from young girls' wristwatches can be seen as metonymically endowing the girls with precisely the same temporal continuity that their own intellectual precocity, and potentially sexualized bodies, would appear to threaten.

I suggest above that one recurrent theme of the novel concerns the temporal disjunction arising between Taiwan and its figurative "mother," the Chinese Mainland, with Taipei both constituting a spectral reflection of Mainland topography and serving as a prophetic anticipation of the Mainland's possible future. This theme of maternity "out of joint" is echoed within the novel itself by a series of references to the Chinese custom of having postpartum mothers undergo a month of symbolic quarantine after giving birth. Known as *zuo yuezi* 坐月子, or "sitting out the month," this practice generally dictates that new mothers remain indoors and away from open air and running water. Interspersed regularly throughout *Haidong qing* are references to a Mixin *zuo yuezi* Center 彌馨坐月子中心.[18] Typically short and highly repetitive, these passages focus on spectral figures of new mothers standing silently at their windows,

17. See pp. 87, 782, 786, 792, 806, 811, 895, 903, 914, and 936 for examples of Jin Wu's looking at Zhu Ling's watch; pp. 315, 358, 746, 842, 857, 864, and 869 for examples of his looking at Ya Xing's watch; and pp. 421, 423, 424, 445, 696, and 712 for examples of his looking at Zhang Tong's watch.

18. The term *mixin*, a proper name with no clear semantic value, is also a nearly precise homophone for the Chinese term *mixin* 迷信, meaning "superstition." Other references to the practice of "sitting out the month" may be found on pp. 291, 308, 323, 550, 554, 661, 668, 682, 691, 696, 699, 707, 712, 713, 733, 744, 782, 786, 792, and 922.

peering down at the street below. The following account is fairly typical and repeated virtually verbatim countless times:

> Across from the hot-pot restaurant there is the Mixin *zuo yuezi* Center. Upstairs, there is a secluded red shrine, and behind the virtually silent curtained windows, there stand twenty or thirty postpartum mothers, both large and small, all nursing their infants and with their hair combed flat against their heads. Wearing nightgowns, they peer down with bright eyes at the street below. (782)

This temporal interregnum between the moment of birth and the mother's re-entry into normal society reproduces in miniature the historical aporia in which the novel implicitly locates the Chinese Mainland. Holding their newborn babies in their arms, the mothers stand silently at the windows of the center, enjoying a bird's-eye view of the city streets stretching out below them. This maze of roads and alleys, together with its implicit cartographic representation, is in turn one of the central tropes of the novel.

Haidong qing contains several explicit discussions of the spectral reflection of Mainland China's historical geography in Taipei's urban cartography. At one point, for example, the new, aboriginal female parliamentary representative, Jianxu Yugui, comments on this phenomenon:

> "Japan and China kill each other; Japan is defeated and China wins, so the Chinese come over here to loot and plunder! The KMT and the Communists kill each other; the Nationalists are defeated and the Communists win, so the Nationalists come over here to build a presidential mansion! They haphazardly change all our street names without any justification. Really hilarious! Huayin Road, Hanyang Road, Lishan Road, Tianshui Road, Nanjing Road, Guilin Road, Emei Road. Really hilarious! They pretend that this little island of ours represents all of China! Sham immortal, sham immortal!" (495)

Earlier in the same chapter, Zhu Ling's father elaborates somewhat more concisely the relationship of Taiwan to Japan and China, as well as the way in which "this little island of ours represents all of China." He explains to Jin Wu that, when the Japanese invaded Taiwan, they gave all the streets and other landmarks Japanese names. Later,

> when the Japanese surrendered, the 70th Regiment of the Nationalist army crossed the strait to accept the surrender, and the commanding officer of the [provincial] administrative office had some lower-level clerks from the vanguard commanding post take some large maps of China and lay them down on

the table next to some Taipei maps the Japanese had printed up. Putting them together and comparing, and then a wave of the pen, and Hah!, they renamed every street and road in the entire city with Chinese names, [as if they had] returned to their own homeland. (460)

Just as the story of the Rape of Nanjing persistently haunts the narrative of the novel, similarly the cartography of Taipei points to how, hidden between the cartographic image and its own spectral reflection, lie imbedded half-hidden traces of Japanese military aggression.

Finally, Li Yung-p'ing, in his preface to the novel, makes yet another reference to the specular dimension of Haidong's spectral topography. Li's remarks come in the context of his suggestion that the novel's self-consciously "allegorical" structure might be read as having a "prophetic" significance, in that the novel's allegorical observations about Haidong might in the future come to apply to the Chinese Mainland. Because of its centrality to both Li's novel and my own argument here, I quote the relevant passage at length:

Look, the novel describes that great city, located in the dynamic waves of the bright and magnificent Eastern Sea—an impregnable fortress and a base for the renaissance of the "Three People's Principles." But notice that all the street names and road names of that city *are nothing more than miniature reflections of the Great China* [*da Zhongguo de suoying*]: Xuzhou Zhengzhou Zhangzhou Jingzhou Gangzhou Liangzhou, Luoyang Nanyang Hengyang, Huayin Hanyin Huaiyin, Kunlun Hami Xichang Andong. Each of these roads crosses toward the Republic of China's presidential palace in the center of the city. North and south of the Yangzi, above and below the Great River, the thousand-year-old imperial palace, the city of the five ethnicities, they are like a myriad of stars that shine resplendently on the road map of the temporary capital of the Republic of China—*but doesn't it bear an uncanny resemblance to a map of the Chinese Mainland, quiet and at peace, eternally young through the ages? For this reason,* Haidong qing, *in addition to being an allegory, is also a prophecy.* The city described in this novel, with its countless local conditions and customs, multitudinous bustling atmosphere, is all brought together in this miraculous place that is the immortal Isle of Penglai; in another ten, twenty, or maybe even fifty years, might it not also appear, under the banner of the Three People's Principles, in every city and every corner of that ancient Chinese Mainland, resting place of the one billion descendents of [the two legendary Chinese emperors] Yan and Huang?

Zhu Ling, I hope that you will grow up well. (iv–v; italics added)

I would agree with Li Yung-p'ing that this cartographic figure has a temporal valence in addition to the obvious spatial one. However, I would suggest that, *pace* Li himself, this chronological cartography is more melancholic than prophetic. To borrow from the terms of the preceding discussion, we might say that the maps of "Donghai" (Taipei) mirror the assortment of young women that populate the novel, and the spectral and specular resemblance they bear to the Mainland evokes more the young girls' resemblance to the mothers from whom they have been separated than it does suggest a prophetic premonition of what the figurative absent mothers will develop into.

Relatively early in the novel, Jin Wu casually quizzes An Lexin on his carto-geographic knowledge, asking him to identify the historical referents of the various names on a Taiwan road map (122–24). In a similar scene in Chapter 12, the roles are inverted as Zhu Ling playfully tests Jin Wu's knowledge of historical geography by similarly asking him to identify the historical origins of Taipei cartographic landmarks (806–7). Although it occurs only once in the novel, Zhu Ling's quizzing of Jin Wu on his carto-geographic knowledge could be seen as a precise inverse of Jin Wu's compulsive habit of checking Zhu Ling's, Ya Xing's, and Zhang Tong's wristwatches. In both cases, Zhu Ling and Jin Wu take figures that best represent (for them) nodes of temporal instability (namely, the city maps and the precocious, prepubescent girls, respectively) and "neurotically" redirect them into symbols of the same (unstable) temporal continuity itself.

We could even take this reading a step further and suggest that Li's own systematic pattern of cartographic allusion lends the novel's preface—and, by implication, the entire novel—a similar quality of neurotic temporal denial. Just as Jin Wu's habit of checking the young girls' watches can be read as an effort to deny and repress the temporal challenge they themselves represent, Li Yung-p'ing's own cartographic allusion could be seen as a figurative act of watch-checking. Through this allusion he attempts to see the novel in terms of general types of teleological historical trajectories, when, in fact, the novel is arguably most concerned with presenting an emphatic questioning of the rationality and tenability of precisely those same trajectories.

In Chapter 7, the young Zhang Tong tells Jin Wu that "the most unbenevolent aspect of this model 'Three People's Principles' precious island of ours is that it doesn't let young girls grow up properly" (431). A slightly different version of this statement is repeated in Chapter 11: "The most inhuman aspect of this society of ours is that it doesn't let young girls grow up properly" (744). Similarly, in the final line of the work Jin Wu exhorts Zhu Ling, "Girl, don't grow up so quickly," and Zhu Ling promptly breaks into tears (941).[19] Given the intimate imbrication, and mutual transference, of national and sexual developmental trajectories in the novel, we might even invert these claims and exhortations about girls growing up in Taiwan. That is, the novel's focus on the topic of Taipei's spectral cartography can arguably be read as a form of transference and as having the effect of forestalling the "proper development" of the novel's own deconstructive implications regarding Taiwan's own historico-developmental status.

Paternities and Expatriatisms

> The emperor of the South Sea was called Shu, the emperor of the North Sea was called Hu, and the emperor of the central region was called Hundun. Shu and Hu from time to time came together for a meeting in the territory of Hundun, and Hundun treated them very generously. Shu and Hu discussed how they could repay his kindness. "All men," they said, "have seven openings so they can see, hear, eat, and breathe. But Hundun doesn't have any. Let's try boring him some!"
>
> Every day they bored another hole, and on the seventh day Hundun died.
>
> —*Zhuangzi*

By way of suggesting a point of entry into a reading of Li Yung-p'ing's 1998 novel, *Zhu Ling's Wanderings in Wonderland*, I first turn to the evocative passage from *Zhuangzi* 莊子 cited in the epigraph to this section. This miniature creation myth of the role of bodily penetration in Hundun's symbolic entry into the mortal world[20] suggests a useful approach to the themes of maturation and transition in Li Yung-p'ing's novel. *Zhu Ling* explicitly and emphatically thematizes the role of corporeal perforation as a symbolic rite of passage into maturity and mortality. Specifically, I have in mind the use of ear-piercing as a

19. See also pp. 391, 598, 780, and 885 for other passages to this effect.

20. For similar discussions of this passage, see Giradot, *Myth and Meaning in Early Taoism*, 77–112; and Zito, *Of Body and Brush*, 208.

symbol for a girl's maturation into womanhood. This theme is initially introduced in *Haidong qing* (374), but it is developed more systematically in *Zhu Ling*. Near the beginning is an explicit discussion of how the act of piercing a young girl's ears symbolizes the ruptured hymen that conventionally represents her own loss of innocence. As An Lexin explains to Zhu Ling's friend Lian Mingxin, "If a young girl wants to grow up, then she must first be shot by a man with a gun, pierced with a hole, and bleed a drop of red, red blood" (74).[21]

When Zhu Ling herself has her ears pierced, the instrument used to perform the procedure is referred to as an ear-piercing "gun" (*qiang* 槍) and more specifically a "Japanese gun."[22] The novel's repeated emphasis on this "Japanese gun" suggests an uncanny juxtaposition of the trajectories of individual sexual maturation and of collective national development. The reason Zhu Ling's use of this particular term inspires such surprise and shock in her interlocutors is obviously because it immediately evokes memories of Japanese aggression against both Taiwan and the Chinese Mainland. The confusion this terminology initially elicits in the novel's own characters is itself emblematic of one of the dominant levels of symbolic significance of both *Haidong qing* and *Zhu Ling*—the symbolic coupling of individual and collective maturational trajectories as projected onto the bodies of the young female protagonists, on one hand, and China's own body politic, on the other. In other words, the novel suggests that the symbolic violence imposed on the girls' bodies by means of the Japanese ear-piercing gun is mirrored by the violence historically imposed on the Chinese body politic by Japanese aggression. Japan's military aggression, Li is saying, contributed to Taiwan's symbolic development and maturation in much the same way that the practice of ear/hymen-piercing contributes symbolically to a girl's personal and physical maturation.

Further reinforcing this association between these individual and national historical trajectories are the rough parallels drawn between Zhu Ling's ear-piercing and one of the most famous historical acts of Japa-

---

21. In an uncanny echo of the "seven holes" of the *Zhuangzi* allegory, An Lexin speaks specifically of giving Zhu Ling and her six friends a group discount for all "seven shots" (82).

22. See, e.g., pp. 73, 94, and 159, among others.

nese aggression against China, the Rape of Nanjing. Although the Chinese term for this incident (*Nanjing da tusha* 南京大屠殺, or "the great Nanjing massacre") is not as explicitly evocative of sexual transgression as the conventional English translation, Li Yung-p'ing's treatment of the incident in both novels stresses the rapes performed by the Japanese soldiers on Chinese women. Furthermore, references to ear-piercing in both novels frequently occur in close proximity to evocative discussions of sexual violence during the Rape of Nanjing. On pages 373–74 of *Haidong qing*, for instance, Jin Wu discusses with Zhu Ling and Ya Xing the prospect of having their ears pierced; this discussion is followed about 25 pages later by a scene in which Zhu Ling and Ya Xing, while riding on a train, read a newspaper report about gang rapes during the Rape of Nanjing (401–2). Similarly, the account of Zhu Ling's ear-piercing in *Zhu Ling* (159) is immediately preceded by a scene in which she recollects having watched a television documentary on that same historical event (152–53). The parallel between sexual and national transgression is drawn even more clearly a few lines later, when Zhu Ling's friend He Lishuang adds that, while selling flowers at the bars along Zhongshan Road, she would occasionally have as customers old Japanese men who would grope under her skirt while reminiscing about the WWII-era competitions they used to hold—competitions involving the piercing of young girls' "private parts" (*michu* 祕處) with bayonets. This moment, therefore, marks a striking conflation of narratives of sexual and military transgression, with the old men's groping of the girls' private parts marking a stark displacement of their earlier sexual violence during the war.

He Lishuang's bars are located in the alleys adjoining Zhongshan Road 中山路, named after Sun Yatsen, who is more commonly known as Sun Zhongshan 孫中山 in Chinese. This allusion to Taiwan's *guofu* follows directly on the heels of Zhu Ling's account of a dream that she had after watching the television documentary on the Rape of Nanjing, a dream in which "the *guofu* [Sun Yatsen] was pointing angrily at Chiang Kai-shek's nose and cursing him."[23] I argue below that Sun Yatsen and

23. Page 153. This dream is reminiscent of Zhu Ling's dream about Sun Yatsen at the end of *Haidong qing*, discussed above.

Chiang Kai-shek represent two opposing ways in which a figurative "word of the father" or "touch of the father" is juxtaposed with an allegorical understanding of female maturation. Schematically speaking, I suggest that they represent, respectively, a form of superficial, cosmetic continuity versus a more violent, penetrative rupture.

For the moment, however, I return briefly to the theme of female "maturation" in Li Yung-p'ing's novel. In the novel's discussion of child prostitution, the colloquial equivalent of the symbolic ear-piercing discussed above is the expression "opening the jug" (*kaiguan* 開罐). Near the end of the novel, however, a character mentions that he prefers the term "dressing one's hair" (*shulong* 梳攏) as a more elliptical and euphemistic term for the process of losing one's virginity (379). This term resonates not only with the tradition of courtesanship in Chinese history but also with the sociocultural happenstance that, in contemporary Taiwan, hairdressing salons (*lifating* 理髮廳) frequently function as sites of prostitution.[24] Furthermore, insofar as *shulong* connotes a more cosmetic, continuous view of female "maturation," and *kaiguan* its more abrupt, violent side, then the *shulong/kaiguan* dichotomy can be seen as representing the individual, maturational equivalent of the Sun Yatsen / Chiang Kai-shek dichotomy alluded to above.

These two euphemisms for loss of virginity and (implicit) sexual maturation come together in a passing comment made by Zhu Ling in *Haidong qing*. One day (coincidentally, it happens to be "daughters' day" in Japan), Jin Wu notices that Zhu Ling's braid has been cut off. He asks her about it, and she explains that her mother cut it because she "is not a little girl anymore" (773–74). Here, the surface, cosmetic alterations connoted by the term *shulong* intersect with the violently transgressive connotations of *kaiguan*. Moreover, the act of cutting one's braid is serendipitously evocative of the practice of cutting men's queues—one of the more potent symbols of China's "maturation" from an antiquated, imperial system into a "modern" republic. When the topic of ear-piercing as a symbol of young girls' sexual maturation is discussed in *Haidong qing* and *Zhu Ling*, both novels pose the question of the

24. See the discussion on p. 54, to cite just one of many passages discussing this phenomenon.

equivalent rite of passage for young boys. In each case, a parallel is drawn between female ear-piercing and male circumcision.[25] However, the relationship between ear-piercing and hairdressing suggests another point of entry into this question of the masculine equivalent of this maturational metaphor.

Near the beginning of Chapter 6 of *Zhu Ling* is a short passage that bears on this question. Zhu Ling and her friend Lian Mingxin are using a small telescope to watch the comings and goings of the president. They discover that, after work, the president and his motorcade do not go home; rather they proceed to Changchun (Everlasting Spring) Road—a district the novel repeatedly describes as renowned for its abundance of hairdressing salons–cum–sex shops. Zhu Ling asks in surprise, "How could the president go to that kind of hairdressing salon (*lifating*) to have his hair done? In those kinds of hairdressing salons, it is so dark inside, that he could very easily accidentally have something else snipped off while having his hair cut" (317). Lian Mingxin finds this prospect rather amusing and suggests, "If things were to go wrong, the hairdressing lady might even cut off his two balls (*liang li dandan* 兩粒蛋蛋)." Zhu Ling agrees and notes that the newspapers once reported such an incident (317). Given that the hairdressing salons (operating as fronts for underage brothels) mark a topographical site of girls' premature developmental transition into sexual "maturity," one is tempted to ask whether the joke about accidental presidential emasculation might be related to the theme of female sexual maturation—and how both themes, in turn, may be related to the novel's larger political symbolics.

We might begin by positioning Lian Mingxin's rather salacious joke within a larger discussion of severed male gonads in both *Haidong qing* and *Zhu Ling*. For example, the last chapter of *Haidong qing* features the rather peculiar image of Zhu Ling running around disconsolate with a live turkey grasped closely to her bosom. Similarly, the first chapter of *Zhu Ling* begins with a closely related discussion of young girls' culinary interest in turkey testicles (35). Both novels refer to this delicacy rather delicately as *yaozi* 腰子 (kidneys), but when Zhu Ling's friend Lin Xiangjin asks what they are, Zhu Ling explains that they are *gaowan* 睪丸

25. See, e.g., *Haidong qing*, 374; and *Zhu Ling*, 77.

(testicles). When Xiangjin still fails to understand, Zhu Ling reverts to the same terminology she and Lian Mingxin previously used to refer to the presidential "balls" (*dandan* 蛋蛋). As the *Zhu Ling* passage makes clear, it is believed that eating turkey testicles and rooster rumps will help young girls to "grow up quickly" (35).

These (avian) male gonads, standing in isolation from the actual male bodies from which they originated, can also be related to the theme of political paternity in both novels. In the preceding discussion of *Haidong qing,* I addressed the novel's explicit thematization of the "national father," Sun Yatsen, and particularly the degree to which it draws on prevalent progenitive metaphors to describe how the "maternal" Chinese motherland (the Mainland) is perceived as having given Taiwan its basic cultural "matrix," and the "paternal" Sun Yatsen is perceived as having contributed its distinguishing sociopolitical "form." Here, I expand on that discussion by pointing to the way in which both of Li Yung-p'ing's novels elaborate a discussion of metaphorical political paternity by devoting comparable attention not only to Sun Yatsen but also to Chiang Kai-shek. Both of these historical figures are regarded as having played paradigmatic roles in shaping modern Taiwan, although there are salient differences between the specific roles each played.

Both novels explicitly compare Chiang Kai-shek's role in the founding of Taiwan to Moses's act of leading the Israelites out of Egypt and across the Red Sea into Israel. In *Haidong qing*, this Biblical symbolism is prominently and explicitly foregrounded in the preface to the novel itself (i–iii). If Chiang Kai-shek's role in the establishment of present-day Taiwan is grounded in his role as a military leader during the period of civil war and Japanese aggression, then Sun Yatsen's political paternity is elaborated on a rather more abstract and idealized plane. His thought and writings from the 1911 revolution and early Republican period are retrospectively held up as cornerstones of the political identity of the Republic of China. Although the historical grounds for this move are somewhat questionable, the political and ideological ones are unmistakable—turning to 1911 and Republican-era political rhetoric makes it possible to elaborate a political ideology that in theory embraces the Mainland in a way that merely looking to a military figure like Chiang Kai-shek would be unable to do.

The continuity between the themes of paternity and procreation in the two novels' discussions of rooster gonads and founding fathers is further strengthened by the fact that the vast majority of the references in *Zhu Ling* to Sun and Chiang are not references to the historical individuals themselves; rather, they focus on plaques, statues, portraits, inscriptions, and other assorted physical and symbolic memorials commemorating their existence and achievements. Just as Zhu Ling and Lian Mingxin joke about separating the president from the symbolic seat of his phallic authority (his "balls"), similarly the "paternal" national-political authority of both Sun Yatsen and Chiang Kai-shek is, in effect, disassociated from those original historical individuals and cathected onto a series of symbolic substitutes.

Moreover, in both of Li Yung-p'ing's novels, these themes of disassociated and cathected paternity resonate ironically with the novels' explicit thematizations of pedophilia. As discussed above, in *Haidong qing* the pedophilic allure of having sex with young girls is associated in part with the way in which their immature bodies are sometimes perceived by the adult men as paradoxically embodying "that motherly sort of love which men are always searching for" (741). Therefore, their sexual attraction partially derives from their location at a rather peculiar temporal interstice, simultaneously straddling the double incestuous prohibition against sleeping with one's figurative daughter, on the one hand, and with one's figurative mother, on the other. *Zhu Ling* offers its own, somewhat related, analysis of the allure of pedophilia. Here, the same allure is portrayed as being related to the urban myth that by having intercourse with a young virgin, a man infected with an STD can "pass" the disease to the girl (392). In this manner, it is believed, not only will the girl acquire the disease, but the adult man will be able to rid himself of it and thus symbolically regain a sort of prelapsarian innocence. This phenomenon has ambivalent and paradoxical implications for the significance of "paternity"—having sex with one's own figurative daughter simultaneously leapfrogs her into a symbolic, if not actual, sexual maturity and supposedly enables the adult man to erase the ravages of his own history of sexual conquests and return to a state of symbolic sexual purity. This symbolic exchange of sexual contamination and innocence can be seen as comparable to the temporal inversion previously observed in *Haidong qing*, in which the prepubescent girl is refigured as the adult pedophile's symbolic mother.

These temporal paradoxes played out in the arenas of sexual politics and pedophilic transgression have an evocative parallel in the way both *Haidong qing* and *Zhu Ling* elaborate the symbolic relationship between Taiwan and the Chinese Mainland. Both novels' evocative juxtapositions of discussions of girls' sexual maturation with reflections on Taiwan's own political and historical "maturation" suggest that Taiwan constitutes a symbolic embodiment of Mainland China's own (potential) future.[26] Both novels, furthermore, make the almost identical claim that "Taiwan's today is the Mainland's tomorrow."[27] In this respect, *Zhu Ling* picks up on one of the dominant images of *Haidong qing*: that of Mainland China staring out across the Taiwan Strait and seeing in Taiwan a spectral image of its own (potential) future self, thus producing an uncanny mirroring reinforced by the observation that Taiwan's (and in particular Taipei's) urban cartography is merely a "miniature reflection" of the political topography of the Chinese Mainland.[28]

I began this section with a discussion of the themes of diaspora and expatriatism and their relationship to Li Yung-p'ing's oeuvre. The sense of topographical ungroundedness evoked by the theme of expatriatism is reflected nicely by a concept central to both of Li's two most recent novels: that of *zhitu* 迌迌. *Zhitu* is a Taiwanese term meaning roughly "to roam, wander, or stroll." The term, together with various synonyms (including *piaobo* 漂泊, *liulang* 流浪, *youguang* 遊逛, *liuda* 溜達), is explicitly and repeatedly used in the novels to describe the various protagonists' characteristic means of moving through space. Like the figurative expatriate, most of the two novels' characters are never in a place where they can feel truly at home; instead, they are constantly on the move with no real topographical telos in mind.

Beyond its actual meaning of "wandering" or "roaming," *zhitu* is also a homonym of another binome, which in Mandarin is pronounced *titou* 剃頭 and has a range of potential meanings, including "to cut one's

26. See, e.g., *Zhu Ling*, 333.

27. *Haidong qing*, iv–v; *Zhu Ling*, 333.

28. "Da Zhongguo de suoying"; *Haidong qing*, iv.

hair," "to shave one's head," or even "to decapitate." Both novels have a passage in which the characters hear the Taiwanese term and mistake it for its Mandarin homonym.[29] This fortuitous pun brings together many of the various themes discussed in this chapter, in the sense that the literal meaning of the term suggests the bodily dislocation from a topographic point of origin, such as one's "motherland," characteristic of the expatriate condition.

The range of potential meanings of the Mandarin homonym traverses the array of connotations suggested by the *shulong/kaiguan* dichotomy discussed above. For example, understood in the sense of "haircutting," *titou* shares the surface, cosmetic connotations of *shulong*. At the other extreme, understood in the sense of "decapitation," the term comes to approximate the violently transgressive connotations of *kaiguan*. Furthermore, this pun on *titou*, in the sense of decapitation, is further reinforced by a series of references throughout *Haidong qing* to the Biblical story of Salome and the beheading of John the Baptist. A Hong Kong pop song on this same subject, for instance, is one of the first sounds Jin Wu hears at the beginning of the novel (10), and this passage is followed by suggestions that Jin Wu's young female friends themselves stand as miniature Salomes.[30] Finally, these two connotations of the Mandarin *titou* (hairdressing and decapitation) are brought into juxtaposition in the presidential hairdressing anecdote. That anecdote uses *titou* first to denote conventional, cosmetic haircutting, and then, in Zhu Ling's elliptical formulation, to suggest a symbolic "beheading" or emasculation.

The various different meanings of *titou* come together to express what I would argue is one of the implications of *Zhu Ling* as a whole for the question of the relationship between symbolic paternity and expatriatism. The original Taiwanese meaning of *titou/zhitu*, "to roam" or "wander," is suggestive of a certain rootless diasporic or expatriate condition. The two meanings of the Mandarin *titou*, "hairdressing" and "decapitation," are suggestive of the same cosmetic continuity / violent rupture dichotomy I have argued is shared by the *shulong/kaiguan* and

29. *Haidong qing*, 124; *Zhu Ling*, 322.
30. See David Der-wei Wang, "Shalemei zhitu/titou," 95–99.

Sun Yatsen / Chiang Kai-shek dyads. Moreover, Zhu Ling's salacious innuendo (which Lian Mingxin makes explicit) draws on the castrative dimension of *titou*, which I have suggested can be linked to the process of positing an idealized model of individual or collective development thought to be located outside of oneself.

I have argued that a central theme in Li Yung-p'ing's recent novels concerns the way in which fantasies of femininity are used to help imagine a post-national Taiwanese identity. Maternity provides a model for the progenitive continuity between the Mainland and Taiwan, even as girls' premature maturation implicitly represents a site of radical rupture between one's origins and current identity. In the following chapter, I look at another diasporic author who similarly uses the ambiguities of femininity to help explore some of the issues of a "post-national" Chinese identity. This author, Gao Xingjian, was born and grew up in Mainland China, but in the late 1980s he left for France and eventually became a naturalized French citizen. Like Li Yung-p'ing, Gao Xingjian's recent writings seek to deconstruct an essentialist, unitary Chinese identity, although he does it from the perspective not of Taiwan's relationship with Mainland China but of a broader Chinese diaspora. Like Li, however, Gao repeatedly uses tropes of femininity to help explore these issues of post-national identity. In particular, Gao's narrator's various heterosexual relations come to stand for his idealized freedom from any fixed ideological or familial ties, even as his highly equivocal relationship with the figure of his mother comes to represent his ultimate *inability* to separate himself entirely from these same cultural origins.

8

Gao Xingjian and Maternal Photographs

Mama, how is it that you have come here? Oh, no, don't leave! I haven't seen you for a very, very long time, and now I almost don't even recognize you.

— Gao Xingjian, "Mother"

Gao Xingjian's 高行健 (1940–) 1983 short story "Muqin" 母親 (Mother) opens with the first-person narrator's memory of his dead mother and his poignant appeal that she not leave him again, quoted in the epigraph above.[1] The narrator observes that he last saw his mother twenty years earlier, during the summer following his sophomore year in college. He quickly qualifies this statement, however, by noting that he subsequently glimpsed her in a dream—a dream in which her appearance, though hazy and indistinct, closely resembled an old, yellowing photograph of her that once hung in the entryway to their home. In that particular photograph, taken shortly after the narrator's birth, the mother is leaning against a railing and wearing an elegant *qipao* 旗袍 (cheongsam) dress.

Later in the story, the narrator reflects back on an even earlier photograph of his mother in a *qipao*—a photo taken when she was only nineteen, shortly after her marriage to the narrator's father. The narrator had accidentally rediscovered the photograph at the beginning of

1. Gao Xingjian, "Muqin," 155.

the Cultural Revolution (1966–76) as he was burning all his papers for fear of political persecution:

> As I was tearing up these notebooks, your photograph slipped out. I picked it up off the floor and, without hesitation, thrust it into the stove. The photograph curled up in agony and instantly turned brown. I wanted to pull it back out again, but within an instant it had already exploded into flames. (160)

The destruction of his last remaining image of his mother stands as a potent symbol of the narrator's own highly ambivalent relationship not only with his memory of his mother but also with *his own* past. Throughout the story, he agonizes over the degree to which he has distanced himself from her memory; he has even misplaced her cremation papers, and forgotten the location of the crypt where her ashes are stored.

This self-ascribed lack of filial piety, however, appears to reflect more an implicit denial of the reality of the mother's death than an inherent lack of affection for her on his part. Gao's story takes primarily the form of a displaced dialogue between the narrator and this absent maternal presence, with the narrator seeking to come to terms with his own highly equivocal attitudes toward both his mother's memory and his own past. The narrator's life is mirrored quite evocatively in this (repressed) memory of his mother's death, in that he is now roughly the same age as she was when she passed away (although he claims not to be able even to remember her age at death).[2] The figure of the mother here becomes a crucial locus for the subject's self-understanding, as well as a limit point for his own personal memory. It is only by working through this maternal memory that the narrator is finally able to begin to come to terms with his own identity.

In the following discussion, I focus on the relationship between visuality and representations of maternity and femininity in Gao's novel *Yi ge ren de shengjing* 一個人的聖經 (One man's bible). I argue that the figure of the maternal photograph, together with its ensuing destruction and imaginary reconstruction, points to a way in which the novel's nar-

2. Ibid. From dates and ages provided in the story, we know that the narrator's mother was roughly 40 when she died, this being roughly the same age as the narrator at the time of the story (Gao Xingjian himself was 43 at the time he published the work).

rator appears to be haunted by the figure of the absent mother—or, more abstractly, by an abstract fantasy of an idealized maternal space. More specifically, the cluster of anxieties revolving around these fantasies of maternal origins has important implications for our understanding of the position of the female body and of erotic desire in Gao's novel. The narrator repeatedly seeks to position himself in a space of diasporic freedom—in the sense not only of social, intellectual/artistic, and national freedom, but also of a sexual freedom unfettered by the ties of family and household. This "freedom," however, is rooted quite directly in a series of transferences and displacements that lead the narrator to postulate, retrospectively, an imaginary maternal ground against which he subsequently strives to define himself.

Photography and Memory

> Everything should be beautiful: beautiful people, beautiful clothes, as well as a beautiful heart—all of this is a kind of out-of-date sorrow, like a photograph that has been burned up.
>
> —Gao Xingjian, *One Man's Bible*

Gao Xingjian was born in 1940, in Jiangxi province. He initially studied French at the Beijing Foreign Languages Institute but in 1970 was sent down to the countryside for "re-education" during the Cultural Revolution. In 1975 he was permitted to return to Beijing, where he began to work as a playwright for the Beijing People's Art Theater. In 1987, Gao went to Germany for a conference, and from there he proceeded to France and subsequently became a naturalized French citizen. In this age of increasing disciplinary and professional specialization, Gao represents something of a throwback to an earlier ideal of the Chinese literatus (or Western "Renaissance man"), in that his creative work spans the categories of fiction, drama, criticism, and the graphic arts. As a playwright, Gao is recognized as a leading figure in China's modernist drama movement in the early and mid-1980s and was influenced by such European modernists as Brecht and Beckett. As a critic and a theorist, he has written a number of influential pieces on modernism, drama, painting, and social critique. His 1981 monograph, *Xiandai xiaoshuo jiqiao chutan* 現代小説技巧初探 (A preliminary exploration of the techniques of modern fiction), for instance, was particularly influential. As a fiction writer, Gao is currently best known for his two full-length novels, *Lingshan* 靈山 (Soul mountain) and *One Man's Bible*, though he is also quite accomplished as a painter. In addition to his involvement with the Chinese modernist movement, Gao has come to be known for his motto of being "without isms," a slogan that alludes to his ideal of freedom from traditional ideological, national, familial, and other ties. The idealized fluidity of this notion of being without isms is reinforced by a narrative technique in which the quasi-autobiographical narratorial voice is splintered into a variety of individual voices located at differing degrees of removal from the enunciative space of the narratorial "I." Gao began to experiment with this technique in his stories from the early 1980s, developed it in several of his plays, and ultimately used it to greatest effect in his two novels.

Although Gao has been an influential presence in Chinese literary and artistic circles for nearly two decades, he received relatively little critical attention after leaving China in 1987. As a result, the announcement that he had won the Nobel prize in 2000 surprised many observers, since Gao had not been one of the handful of Chinese writers who were regarded as being on the short list for the prize. In addition, the significance of Gao's being the first Chinese-language writer to win the prize was complicated by the fact that he is not only a naturalized French citizen but also endeavored to distance himself from the nationalistic subtexts that informed many subsequent discussions of his receipt of the prize. The official announcement of the prize singled out Gao's first full-length novel, *Soul Mountain*, for special attention. Completed in 1989, the novel was inspired in part by Gao's experience of having been mistakenly diagnosed in 1983 with terminal lung cancer (the same disease that took his father's life) and details the quasi-autobiographical protagonist's journey through Sichuan in southwest China as he searches for a spiritual "soul mountain." The work focuses on his relationships with a variety of women (especially a handful of ethnic minority women) whom he encounters along the way.

Like the short story "Mother," *One Man's Bible* opens on a melancholic note, with an allusion to an old, yellowed family photograph poignantly counterpointing the narrator's own sense of alienation from these memories of his own past:

It was not that he didn't remember that he had once had a different kind of life, the memory of which made him feel a certain sense of sorrow, just like that old family photograph which had not yet been burned up or turned yellow with age. These memories are so distant as to seem almost unreal, like another world that had already disappeared forever.[3]

The narrator (referring to himself here in the third person) then recalls that in his old Beijing home, which the police subsequently searched and sealed off (*chafeng* 查封), there was an old family portrait, which comprised no less than thirteen of his relatives, including even his senile grandfather. The narrator, the only child in the photograph, appeared wearing a pretty sailor's cap and "split-bottom" pants (ubiquitous among Chinese toddlers during that period, and still popular today), which inadvertently revealed his tiny penis (*xiao ji* 小雞, literally "little chicken") to the camera. Although this detail is mentioned only in passing, I will argue that it is of crucial importance to our understanding of the novel as a whole.

This memory of the family portrait precipitates a chain of recollections of the narrator's childhood and family, concluding with his mother's death during the Great Leap Forward (1958–61). He immediately notes, however, that it was his mother who taught him how to read and write and, later, encouraged him to keep a diary. The narrator's mother, therefore, represents a limit-point of his own personal memory, while also standing as one of the crucial conditions of its very possibility. Similarly, this focus on her visual image suggests that, within the novel, she both occupies a fantasy space beyond conventional language and represents the narrator's own entry-point into language and literacy.

Later in the novel, Gao returns to this figure of the family photograph and specifically its relation to his mother in a scene that is a close copy of the description of the maternal photograph in his story "Mother" from almost fifteen years earlier. Like the narrator in the earlier story, the narrator in the novel accidentally runs across the photograph as he is

3. Gao Xingjian, *Yi ge ren de shengjing*, 1; idem, *One Man's Bible*, 1. Subsequent references to this work are cited in the text; the first number shown refers to the Chinese version, the second, to the corresponding passage in the English version. All translations are my own.

destroying all his papers, notes, diaries, and stories at the beginning of the Cultural Revolution. As he is about to toss a notebook into the flames, an old and forgotten photograph slips out from between its pages—a photograph that turns out to be a childhood picture of himself with his parents. In the photo, he notes, his mother is wearing a *qipao*. He distinctly remembers having seen that same colorful silk dress in a chest when he was young, although now the photograph itself is so old that the colors have already started to fade:

> Without hesitation, he thrust the photograph into the stove, and its edges crackled as they started to burn. The images of his parents had already started to wrinkle up before it occurred to him to try to retrieve the photograph from the flames, but by then it was already too late. As he watched, the photograph curled up and then straightened out again, as the images of his parents were reduced to black and white ashes, and that skinny boy standing between them was already starting to turn brown. (72/69)

As in the earlier story, the narrator watches helplessly as his own image follows those of his parents into fiery oblivion. Unlike the earlier story, however, here the narrator and his father appear in the photograph along with the mother, and the destruction of the family image literally presages, at a visual level, the destruction of a part of the narrator himself.

This immolation of the maternal image represents the most direct link between these two fictional works, and it suggests that the novel may be seen as an attempt to work through some of the concerns the earlier story raised but left unresolved. Both scenes, moreover, appear to be partially autobiographical, since Gao Xingjian, like many other authors, found it necessary to destroy all his writings, diaries, and other papers during the early years of the Cultural Revolution for fear of political persecution (he noted in a later interview that he destroyed several dozen kilograms of documents and secretly buried others).[4] Whether this specific detail of the family photograph is based in reality, however, is less certain (indeed, the fact that the two works present us with two slightly different photographs suggests that memory of the

4. Gao Xingjian, "Lun wenxue xiezuo," 62–63.

Fig. 9 Su Hanchen, *Lady at Her Dressing Table in a Garden* (detail). Photograph © 2008 Museum of Fine Arts, Boston.

Fig. 10 Chuchu's tattoo, in *Red Cherry* (Ye Daying, dir., 1995)

Fig. 11

Fig. 12

Fig. 13

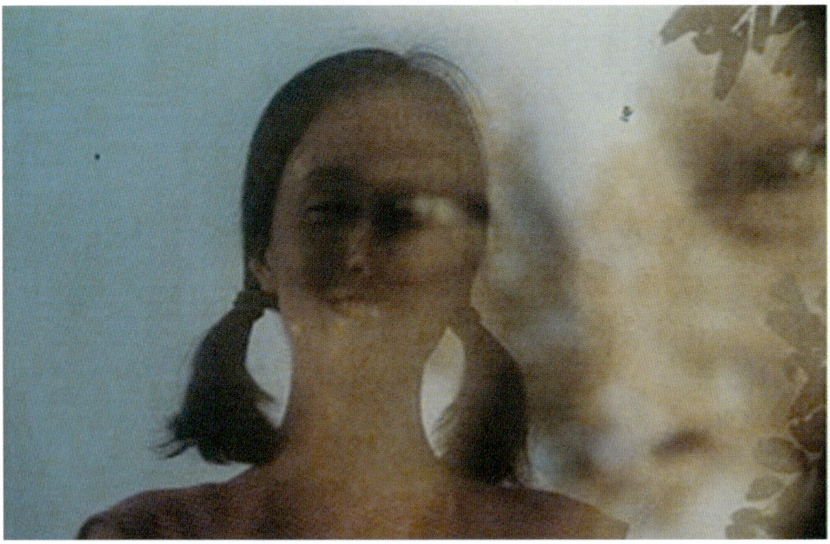

Fig. 14

Figs. 15–16 Free-standing exterior movie screen in *Heat*.

Fig. 17 Advertisement for *Heat*.

Fig. 18 Mao portrait at the end of the "narrative meltdown" sequence in *Heat.*

Fig. 19 Mao rearview mirror ornament, from the final credits sequence in *Heat.*

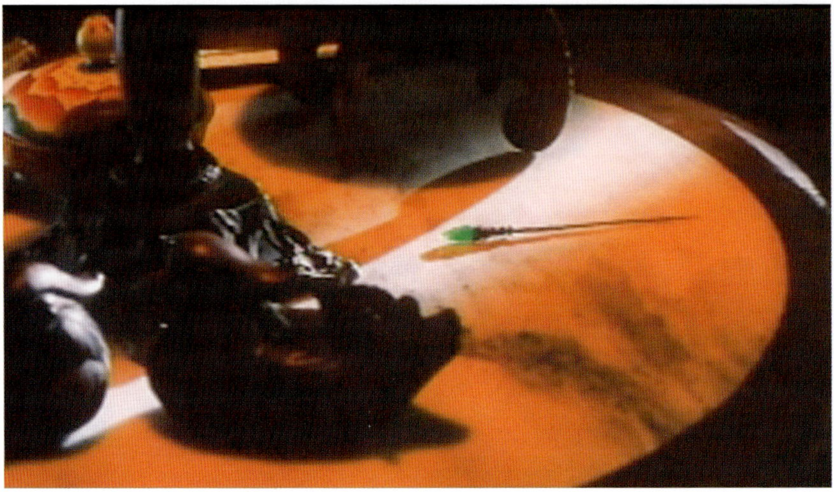

Fig. 20 Dressing table with jade hairpin, from *Shanghai Flowers* (Hou Hsiao-hsien, dir., 1998).

photograph itself may be strategically overdetermined). Nevertheless, the recurrence of these nearly identical scenes in the two works, separated by nearly two decades, does point to a recurrent attempt in Gao's fiction to use figures of visuality and maternity as symbols both of the subject's nostalgic return to the past and of the same subject's repeated denials of the relevance of that same past as he strives to anchor himself in the present.

One Man's Bible is structured as a series of chapters that alternate loosely between the present and the narrator's past, with the present-day chapters set in Hong Kong, Paris, and New York, among other places, and the retrospective ones gesturing back to the period of 1950s and 1960s Maoist China in which the narrator grew up. In the first half of the book, many of the chapters set in the present feature an ongoing discussion between the male Chinese "narrator" and a young Jewish woman named Marguerite (Magelite), whom he had met in China several years earlier.[5] As mentioned above, the novel also builds on a narratorial technique Gao developed in some of his previous fictional works, wherein the quasi-autobiographical "narratorial" voice is splintered into a variety of voices located at differing degrees of removal from the enunciative space that would have been occupied by the narratorial "I" in a traditional first-person narrative. More specifically, the narrator generally refers to himself in the second-person "you" in the chapters set in the present, and in the third-person "he" in the chapters set in the past (with occasional cross-references that make clear this is a single individual). Furthermore, this symbolic fracturing of the subject is also played out in the narrator's relationship to the other characters in the novel, in the sense that all the women who populate the work (and it is significant that the vast majority of the characters whom the narrator encounters are women) could be seen as embodying different dimensions of the narrator's own subjectivity. Therefore, to the extent that the bulk of the novel

5. Kwok-Kan Tam ("Language as Subjectivity in *One Man's Bible*") suggests that the name "Marguerite" may be an allusion to Marguerite Duras, the author of the novel on which Alain Resnais's celebrated 1959 film, *Hiroshima mon amour*, was subsequently based—with Duras's novel also featuring, like Gao's novel, a disjunctive play of projection and identification between a German woman and her Asian (Japanese) lover.

focuses on the narrator's encounters with a variety of women from both his present and his past, these romantic encounters and reminiscences can be seen as an illustration of the narrator's highly ambivalent attitudes toward his own identity, as well as toward his own past.

The imbrication of visuality, femininity, and personal memory that we find in the descriptions of the family photograph and of the photograph of the mother is repeated again in the second chapter of the novel, although from a radically different perspective. This chapter, like the first, opens with an evocative visual *mise-en-scène.* The narrator is in a Hong Kong hotel room having just made love to Marguerite. He becomes intrigued by the "postmodernist" façade of the building across the street from his hotel window and observes that he can even make out a couple kissing in the glass elevator as it scales the side of the building. He then translates this voyeuristic fantasy into a scopic paranoia: he suggests to Marguerite that there might be hidden cameras in their own hotel room, able to record the intimate scenes of their lovemaking. Marguerite laughs away his concern, noting that they are, after all, not in Mainland China, but he responds that the hotel was recently purchased by a group of Mainland businessmen.

The narrator then redirects this paranoiac concern with being the potential object of a voyeuristic external gaze by appropriating a similar transgressive voyeuristic gaze for himself. Specifically, he asks Marguerite, who is sitting naked on the bed beside him, to spread her legs, explaining that he wishes to etch this particular moment deeply in his memory (*shenshen yinru jiyi* 深深引入記憶) (11/11). She replies that she, however, does *not* want to remember this moment but merely to experience it for what it is. The narrator then asks her whether she is able to feel the power of his gaze (*muguang* 目光); she answers that what she is able to feel is the weight of his body on top of her. A moment later he enters her, and her first question is, "Have I sucked you in deeply?" (*shenshen xiyin ni?* 深深吸引你), and he agrees that, yes, "there is now no memory, just the present" (11–12/12). Here, Marguerite's "deep" (*shenshen*) corporeal absorption of the narrator is counterposed precisely to the narrator's attempt to inscribe her "deeply" (*shenshen*) in his own memory. This male narrator represents the preserve of the visual gaze and nostalgic recollection; his female lover, tactile corporeality and contemporaneity. The narrator is drawn to her because of the challenge she poses to everything he values, because she represents the potential negation of the power of his memory and gaze—a visual and mnemonic power he simultaneously desires and fears.

Underlying these considerations of vision and memory are Marguerite's and the narrator's diasporic conditions; each has been displaced from a homeland that, in a sense, never really existed. In the narrator's Hong Kong hotel room, both he and Marguerite find themselves in a state of doubled exile—removed not only from their original "motherlands" but also from their surrogate homes in France and Germany, respectively. The chapter concludes with an explicit reflection on how the narrator (as an "overseas Chinese") and Marguerite (as a displaced German Jew) lack direct access to a "motherland." However, whereas the narrator seeks to use his memory to reconstruct a motherland he no longer inhabits, Marguerite wishes merely to abandon herself in the present moment, even as she recognizes the impossibility of escaping from memory and the past altogether. Marguerite also suggests a key distinction between herself and the narrator is that she is ultimately *unable* to escape from her memory, precisely because she is a woman (17/16).

What is it about being a woman that both makes it necessary for Marguerite to attempt to ground herself firmly in the present moment and at the same time makes it impossible for her to "escape from memory"? What is the nature of the symbolic trajectory traced from the narrator's dead mother in the first chapter to his very-much-alive foreign lover in the second? Finally, what is the relationship between the narrator's underdeveloped boyish penis, which inadvertently peeks out from his split-bottom pants in the family portrait from the opening chapter, and his mature, phallic gaze in the second chapter—a gaze that seeks to use the sight of his lover's genitals to anchor his rootedness in the present moment? To address these questions, I return first to my earlier discussion, in the chapter on Eileen Chang, of Roland Barthes's visual hermeneutics in *Camera Lucida*, and then proceed to a more direct reflection on the status of photography in Gao's own novel. More specifically, I argue that photography in the novel is associated with a fantasy of nostalgic immediacy, which holds up the tantalizing ideal of a direct, unmediated access to the past, only to have that ideal dissolve, mirage-like, upon closer inspection.

Roland Barthes, in *Camera Lucida*, posited a contrast between the "studium" and the "punctum" of a photograph. For Barthes, the "studium" is the dimension of a photograph that succeeds in evoking emotion via "the rational intermediary of an ethical and political culture" (26). Opposed to the studium is the "punctum," which Barthes suggests constitutes a stain in the photograph that violently disrupts the viewer's gaze:

> A detail that overwhelms the entirety of my reading; it is an intense mutation of my interest, a fulguration. By the mark of *something*, the photograph is no longer "anything whatever." This *something* has triggered me, has provoked a tiny shock, a *satori*, the passage of a void (it is of no importance that its referent is insignificant). (49)

Extending Barthes's concepts to Gao Xingjian's novel, we can see that the glimpse of the narrator's tiny penis peeking out of his split-bottom pants in the family portrait clearly functions as a punctum. It draws the viewer's eyes away from what is ostensibly the main focus of the portrait—the family members' faces—and eerily anticipates the novel's fascination with (hetero)erotic desire, of which this initial photograph stands as a silent prelude.

Underlying Barthes's contrast between the studium and the punctum is an attempt to retrieve and come to terms with the absent figure of the mother. As noted above, Gao Xingjian's *One Man's Bible*, like Barthes's text, appears to be haunted by the figure of the absent mother, and it is precisely this maternal specter that leads the narrator to reflect on the apparent referential immediacy of specific photographs. Furthermore, even in passages not directly concerned with the memory of his mother, the narrator nevertheless explores the referential and epistemological implications of photographic images. One of the most revealing discussions of photography in the novel can be found in Chapter 48, where the narrator (referring to himself in the second person) reflects back on the black-and-white photographs he took while undergoing labor-reform in the countryside in the late 1950s. The chapter opens with a reflection on the aesthetisizing and distantiating effects of photography:

> When seen through the lens [of a camera], the world becomes immediately transformed, and even the most ugly scenes come to possess a certain beauty. During those years you spent in the countryside, you had an old camera that you would always take with you whenever you went into the mountains. This camera served as your substitute eye. (363/363)

The narrator follows this discussion of photography with a description of three photographs preserved from his period in the countryside, each of which illustrates in a different way this theme of the alienating effects of photography.

The preceding metaphor of the camera functioning as a "substitute eye" is neatly mirrored in the first of the three photographs, which depicts a black chicken on a wooden bridge. The narrator notes that he particularly liked to photograph this chicken:

> And in front of your camera, this black fellow would raise its head and look around after it was finished eating. It didn't understand what a camera was and would just stare at it with its eyes wide open, with those black eyes, which had the power to take your breath away. When it raised its head to gaze ahead, you could see in those eyes a limitless reservoir of meaning. (364/364)

The chicken's black eyes are both oblivious to the significance of the camera and a locus of significance exceeding that of the narrator's own gaze. The chicken's eyes thus represent a precise inversion of the narrator's gaze and are comparable to the limited omniscience of the camera lens—"limited" in the sense that, although the camera lens, like the chicken's eyes, constitutes an ultimate repository of meaning and signification, it nevertheless remains oblivious to its own significance.

The second photograph depicts an image of an old, dilapidated village. The narrator notes that, merely looking at the photograph itself, one would never guess that behind it lie the horrors of the Great Leap Forward (1958–61), an economic stimulus policy gone awry that resulted in the deaths of up to 30 million Chinese from famine. The narrator describes some of the scenes of suffering he knows lay behind the gaze of the camera but adds, "All of this is merely based on what your [the narrator's] students have told you, and in the photograph itself, of course, none of this can be discerned. The scene in the photograph appears desolate, yet at the same time beautiful" (364/364). Further underlying these concerns with the paradoxical beauty and desolation of this visual memory is the unstated fact that the photograph also dates from approximately the same period as the death of the narrator's mother (who passed away during the period of the Great Leap Forward).

The third photograph is of two girls, fifteen and eighteen years old, respectively. The older girl had been sent down to the countryside because her grandfather had been a landlord, and the younger girl is the daughter, interestingly enough, of an optometrist. Unlike many youth from the countryside during that period, these two girls appear to have no reservations about being photographed. What is of particular interest to the narrator here, though, is the miniature transformation of one girl's appearance at the precise instant that he opens the shutter of the camera. As the narrator prepares to take the picture, both girls are smiling and posing for the camera. When he subsequently develops the print, however, he notices that "the older girl's eyes were avoiding the camera, besides which, she had such a melancholy expression" (365/365). Here, it is only via the photograph that the narrator is able to discern the passive resistance on the part of this female subject, a resistance he initially had been so pleased to note that both girls appeared to lack.

In each of these three photographs, there is a stark disparity between the visual shock produced by the actual image, on one hand, and the contextual information that lies beyond it, on the other. In Barthes's terms, this disparity could be understood as a tension between the punctum of each photograph (the black chicken's eyes in the first image, the older girl's eyes avoiding the camera in the third), and the narrator's own, often unsuccessful, attempts to "read" the studium of these photographs for insight into this period from his own past (an attempt confounded, for instance, by the marked disparity between the apparent contents of the second photograph and the historical realities he knows necessarily underlie it). In each case, the narrator's attention to the apparent referentiality of the photograph leads back to an interrogation of the status of the narrator's own gaze. Furthermore, just as Barthes's concern with the death of his mother underlies his own reflections on photography, a similar conjunction of concerns with maternity and visuality appears to underlie the narrator's reflections on photography here. In contrast to Barthes, however, it is not so much the loss of the mother that leads the subject to associate visual (photographic) signifiers with an idealized referential immediacy; rather, in *One*

Man's Bible, it is almost as if the narrator's desire to occupy a specifically masculine and visually empowered diasporic subject position leads him to retroactively postulate an imaginary space of lost maternity. In the following section, I develop this argument by considering how the narrator also uses his relationships with a wide variety of women (both lovers and maternal figures) in order to interrogate, and ultimately assert, the visual primacy of his own masculine subjectivity.

Lovers and Others

> When he was a child, he would secretly observe his mother's young and beautiful naked body while she bathed. Since then, he has been very fond of beautiful women.
>
> —Gao Xingjian, *One Man's Bible*

Beyond the maternal photographs featured in Chapters 1 and 9 of *One Man's Bible*, one of the most revealing descriptions of the narrator's relationship with his mother can be found at the end of Chapter 26. Here, the narrator prefaces a reflection on his childhood by remarking on his weakness for feminine/sexual pleasure and relating how, as a young boy, he once secretly spied on his mother:

> Moreover, he is also fond of women (*haose* 好色). As a child, he once secretly observed his mother's young and beautiful naked body while she bathed. Ever since then, he has been very attracted to beautiful women, and when he didn't have access to women, he would put his pen to paper and write in a quite erotic mode. (218/213)

This evocative passage suggests not only that the narrator's adult sexual relations with women are rooted in his own childhood scopophilic attraction to his mother's body, but also that he perceives the act of writing as a secondary displacement of this relationship with the mother (in the sense that his lovers appear as merely indirect substitutes for his absent mother, just as his writing functions as a substitute for those same absent lovers). This passage can also be read in the reverse, as suggesting that the specter of this eroticized maternal fantasy continues to haunt both the narrator's sexual encounters with other women and his fictional writings.

A good example of the ways in which this partially repressed memory of the mother, together with the ultimately impossible homecoming she represents, subtly reintrude into the narrator's consciousness can be found in the narrator's account of a nightmare of returning to Beijing. Unable to find his keys to his former apartment, he asks a neighbor, "old Liu," for assistance and is told that his apartment was confiscated by the government and is now rented to someone else. Liu adds that the narrator should never have come back to China and then hurries off as if they were complete strangers. In this alienated homecoming scene, the narrator essentially steps into the personal/historical space of the family photograph that opens the novel, only to find it profoundly unwelcoming. The lost key and the sealed-off apartment clearly symbolize his inability to re-enter that former familial space, even as his melancholic memory insistently draws him back toward it.

The narrator then searches for somewhere to spend the night and finally finds a place in a rural area outside the city. The accommodations are quite rudimentary—the beds consist simply of bare concrete slabs, and the narrator explicitly compares the size of the bunks to the double crypt in which the urns containing his parents' ashes are stored. In this fantasy, the narrator not only attempts to step back into the space of his childhood but also finds that in order to do so he must *work through* a displaced identification with the memory of his dead parents. The nightmare concludes with the narrator observing that if he were to rent one of the bunks, he would want one of the soundproofed bottom ones, because of his wife's fondness for singing karaoke. The narrator appears to do a double take, remarking, "Who would have known that he had even brought a woman with him?" (34/33). Then he wakes up. This final, last-minute appearance of the narrator's wife illustrates the way in which throughout the novel his female lovers function as potential bridges to his own past. It is extremely suggestive that the sudden presence of this wife, at the moment the narrator contemplates sleeping in the crypt-like bunk, neatly parallels the cremated remains of his own mother—with the narrator's sharing of the bunk with his karaoke-singing wife uncannily mirroring the two urns in the double-crypt holding the cremated remains of his mother and father.

After waking up and realizing that it had all been merely a dream, the narrator notes that he rarely dreams about China anymore and proceeds to compare his current diasporic condition to being a "free bird":

> Now, he is a free bird. This kind of heartfelt freedom, without any fetters, is like the clouds and wind. . . . In addition, he also now no longer allows himself to be tied down to any woman, because for him, a household and children constitute too heavy a burden. (35/34)

What is interesting here, beyond the suggestive segue from being freed from the burdens of his motherland to being freed from the burdens of women and a family, is the term the narrator uses to describe himself: "a free bird" (*ziyou de niao* 自由的鳥). The term *niao* 鳥 (bird) also happens to be a popular euphemism for the male sex organ and is semantically related to the term *ji* 雞 (chicken), used to refer to the narrator's own boyish penis in description of the family photo at the opening of the novel (as discussed below, the same avian euphemism is also used at the end of the novel to refer to the adult narrator's flaccid member). The narrator's self-description here can thus be seen as suggesting the image of an emancipated phallus, flying freely through the world, unbound by ties to either homeland or family. At the same time, this self-conceived bird/phallus is not truly "without fetters," in that it (that is, the narrator) has a very specifically gendered perspective on the social landscape it traverses, one that oscillates between seeing women as hypersexualized objects of desire, on one hand, and as "maternal" limit-points of both desire and self-knowledge, on the other.

The narrator then notes that only when he closes his eyes is he able to experience this sense of free flight and that it is only when his eyes are closed that he is able to avoid the gaze (*zhushi* 注視) and visual supervision (*jiandu* 監督) of others. When he closes his eyes, he gains a feeling of freedom and is consequently able to "travel into the miraculous space of women's caves (*dongxue* 洞穴)" (35/34). Here, a *negation* of vision (the act of closing one's eyes) becomes a crucial enabling condition for achieving a sense of untethered freedom. It is, however, a paradoxical freedom, insofar as it leads the narrator symbolically to enter the quintessentially confined space of the maternal womb.

The suggestive metaphor of the female vagina/uterus being a "cave" immediately assumes a life of its own, as the narrator launches into a sexually charged description of a recent trip to see limestone caves in central France. Here, the latently erotic etymological overtones of his description of the dripping wet stalactites and stalagmites (*zhongru* 鐘乳 and *rutu* 乳突, in Chinese, literally meaning "bell nipples" and "protruding nipples") of the French caves draw him into a singularly bizarre erotic fantasy of being merely a minuscule sperm swimming within a vast maternal uterus:

> Leaning against the railing, all around him the orange light of the lamps illuminated the enormous cave. The entire wall was filled with layer upon layer of crevices, and the hanging stalactites and the countless stalagmites were all soaking wet. This naturally created cave was like an enormous uterus, unfathomably deep. In the darkness of this natural cave, he was as insignificant as a single sperm—an impotent sperm content to swim around inside the womb, relishing a kind of carefree attitude, which only becomes possible after one has freed oneself from desire. (35/34)

This curious fantasy, in which the narrator's sense of diasporic unrootedness is translated into an image of himself as a sperm swimming within a maternal uterus, quite precisely echoes, and inverts, his earlier fantasy of being a free-flying bird—with the difference that the bird is explicitly imagined as independent of women, whereas the sperm is embedded within the quintessentially female space of the womb. This parallel between the figures of the bird and of the spermatozoon in these two juxtaposed passages reinforces the phallic connotations implicit in the Chinese term for bird, as used in the earlier passage.

This stark juxtaposition of the images of the free-flying bird and the free-swimming spermatozoon—together with their diametrically opposed connotations with respect to feminine and maternal attachment—is immediately followed by a striking reminiscence that essentially deconstructs the conventional notion of maternity itself. This reminiscence concerns the nursemaid who effectively raised the narrator as a young boy:

> He still remembers that his first taste of feminine warmth came not from his mother but from a nanny named Mama Li employed by his family, who would always bathe him. He would play naked in the bathtub, and then Mama Li would grasp him close to her warm chest and carry him to his bed. (35/34–35)

In an ironic echo of the young narrator's glimpsing of his mother's naked body as she emerged from the bath, this nanny from the countryside functioned as a quasi-maternal figure who was the object of his unformed scopic desires—insofar as she not only bathed him but also bathed herself and changed her clothes in front of him. This figure of the nursemaid thus represents an important conflation of the novel's apparent dichotomy of the figure of the (absent) mother and that of the eroticized lover. In the eyes of the young narrator, Mama Li stands as an evocative site of sexual maturity, but, viewed retrospectively from the perspective of the narrator's position in the present, she becomes a metonymic figure for the narrator's own prepubescent naïveté.

The narrator's use of the double fantasy of being a free-flying bird / spermatozoon to characterize his own diasporic condition is premised on a double gesture of retrospectively positing an imaginary site of maternal origins and then immediately renouncing it by asserting his symbolic independence. Similarly, the narrator explicitly notes that "his first taste of feminine warmth" came from his nanny, Mama Li, and *not* from his more distant mother—thus suggesting that, for him, it is the nanny who effectively occupies a site of "maternal" origins, even as her impact on the young narrator challenges the classical psychoanalytic category of a naturalized "maternity" itself.[6] Furthermore, the nursemaid's status as a family servant ironically draws attention to the (largely unacknowledged) class considerations implicitly underlying the adult narrator's subsequent use of an idealized fantasy of maternity to underlie his self-identification as a globally free-flying, diasporic subject.

To the extent that Mama Li represents the youthful narrator's entry into sexual maturity, the apparent inverse of this trajectory can be found in the figure of a high school student by the name of Xiaoxiao, whom the narrator seduces one night during the Cultural Revolution. Xiaoxiao unexpectedly visits him at his apartment one night, and as they are chatting, she removes her outer shirt because of the heat. She then spontaneously lifts her inner shirt to show him a fresh scar right

6. As Anne McClintock (*Imperial Leather*, 87) has observed, "Classical Freudian psychoanalysis has, for the most part, steadfastly refused to grant any theoretical status to the maidservant other than as a temporary intruder into the family romance, or as a parental surrogate." Cf. also Gilles Deleuze and Félix Guattari's (*Anti-Oedipus*, 253) early 1980s remarks along similar lines: "For those looking for a thesis topic on psychoanalysis, one should not suggest vast considerations on analytic epistemology, but modest and rigorous topics such as the theory of maids or domestic servants in Freud's thought."

below the nipple of her right breast. Although the narrator is intensely curious how she acquired such a peculiarly located wound, he keeps his questions to himself and instead abruptly begins to fondle her small breasts and, as she moans softly, leads her to his bed. Although his subsequent recollections of what happened next are a blur, he does remember pulling her pants down to her knees and fondling her moist and hairless genitals. All the while, Xiaoxiao lies there with her eyes closed, neither resisting nor reciprocating. Apparently amazed by his own actions, however, the narrator stops short of sexual intercourse, ostensibly because he is afraid that she might become pregnant (228–29/226–27). Xiaoxiao does not reappear until near the end of the novel, when the narrator unexpectedly runs into her one day in the street (Chapter 55). Many years have elapsed since that winter night, and the delicate, pubescent beauty he had known has now matured into a robust, country woman. In fact, even after she calls out to him, he almost fails to recognize her. He accepts her invitation to go to her room but almost immediately regrets having done so, because he finds his treasured memories of her youthful beauty shattering under the cold weight of contemporary reality.

The narrator's re-encounter with Xiaoxiao can also be seen as marking a point where the novel's general displacement of maternal attachments onto the eroticized bodies of young women comes full circle. In the second encounter, Xiaoxiao is technically not yet a mother, although she has had two abortions. It is also no coincidence that Xiaoxiao has returned to the city because of *her own* ailing mother, who is suffering, ironically enough, from breast cancer. The narrator, for his part, focuses on the transformation of Xiaoxiao's once-pert breasts—which have become the solid, fleshy breasts of a mature woman—as marking one of the most tangible signs of her physical maturation. The breast, therefore, becomes a quintessential site of maternal displacement, functioning as a synecdoche for maternity as well as, in its diseased, cancerous form, a symbol of its ultimate somatic negation. The mysterious scar below Xiaoxiao's breast similarly marks a point of rupture between her former, presexualized pubescence and her current state of "post-maternity."

The narrator's conflicted relationships with these women from his past (his mother, his nursemaid, and Xiaoxiao, among others) are paralleled by his relationships with his adult lovers. For instance, the narrator's relationship with his feminine alter ego, Marguerite, plays out many of these same themes of scopophilia, nostalgia, and amnesia examined above in relation to the narrator himself. To the extent that the narrator is obsessed with returning to his past, Marguerite seeks to *avoid* hers by burying herself in the present moment. Like the narrator, Marguerite is haunted by her past, specifically by a sexual trauma she experienced when she was only thirteen at the beginning of puberty. At the time, her parents had separated. Her father had returned to Germany, and she was living in Venice with her mother. A local painter offered to give her and a young friend lessons, but when she went to his studio, he insisted that she pose naked for him and then raped her. He continued to rape her over the next two years:

> At the time, I was still too young to understand what was going on, and I didn't know what he was doing on top of my body. Therefore, I simply lay there staring up at the gray sky, and all I remember is that the flagstones beneath me were very cold. It was not until two years later that I began to notice the changes in my body, and it was only then, upon becoming a woman, that I finally understood what had transpired. As a result, I now hate this body of mine. (122/117)

Later, as Marguerite was leaving the painter's studio one day, she ran into another young girl and knew immediately from the way in which the other girl examined her body that the painter had been sleeping with her as well. As the adult Marguerite explains to the narrator, the gaze of her figurative double emblematized all her own frustrations with herself:

> No, you can't possibly understand the look (*muguang*) she gave me. I'm referring to that gaze (*yanguang* 眼光) with which that girl examined my body—I hate myself, and not just that girl. It was only by looking into her eyes that I was finally able to see myself. I hate him and also hate this body of mine, *this body that prematurely became that of a woman.* (124/119; italics added)

The other girl's gaze represents both Marguerite's own alienated perception of her own body and, indirectly, the moment of *visual* violation that immediately preceded the physical rape (the painter's demand that she pose naked for him). That gaze also represents the transtemporal paradox that Marguerite initially "witnessed" her own rape before she was able to understand what she was seeing and experiencing, but the memory of that same transgressive event would later dominate the way she subsequently came to view her own mature body.

Positioned at a seminal moment of the translation of flesh into image, Marguerite's sexual encounter with the Italian painter plunges her into a peculiar temporal loop. Although she did not appreciate the full import of this event until several years after the fact, it nevertheless left an invisible scar in her psyche. This pattern of rape extending over the course of two years is one reason Marguerite wishes to drown herself in the present moment and also precisely the reason she, like the narrator, remains haunted by her past. This moment, as she describes it, "made her a woman," but later makes her, as a mature woman, despise her own body. The rape thus marks a moment of premature maturation but simultaneously ensures that she is never able to completely emerge from the shadow of that pubescent temporal fold.

The psychological echoes of this childhood trauma can be seen in Chapter 16, in which Marguerite asked the narrator to "rape" her. She insists that what she wants is not merely some sadomasochistic "sex play" but a genuine rape. The narrator begins with a halfhearted attempt to tie her up and beat her but is unable to carry through with it. To the same extent that we see the narrator, throughout the novel, using a variety of feminine figures as foils against which to develop his own identity, in this scene we see Marguerite ironically struggling against *her own* femininity, vainly attempting to use simulated sexual violence as a way of exorcising the memory of the sexual violence that prematurely "made her a woman."

This interpenetration of maternal fantasies and (hetero-)erotic desire comes together explicitly near the end of the novel, in Chapter 57. The narrator is making love to a French woman named Sylvie, and he ends up ejaculating on her chest because neither of them brought a condom. Shortly afterward, he starts crying on her moist breasts, which perversely remind him of his mother's. Addressing himself in the second person, he reflects:

> You want to cry, and then proceed to place your face in her firm and ample chest, crying on those breasts that are not only sweaty but furthermore have been smeared with semen. You sob uncontrollably, like a child that needs its mother's warmth. (427/427–28)

In this startling scene, Sylvie, with her sweat- and semen-stained breasts, is figuratively conflated with the figure of the maternal memory that has persistently haunted the narrator's sexual encounters throughout the novel, and the narrator imagines himself in the position of an infant crying at its mother's breast.

After this suggestive conflation of maternal affection and adult sexuality, the narrative immediately shifts to a series of memories of his mother herself and specifically returns to the seminal scene (already described once in Chapter 26) in which the narrator accidentally caught sight of her naked body as she was bathing:

> The first naked body of a woman you ever saw was that of your mother, whom you glimpsed through the lamplight of the half-open door. In the middle of the night you were sleeping on your bamboo bed, when you heard the sound of water running. You wanted to go and take a look and lifted yourself up on your elbows, as the bamboo bed creaked in protest. [Upon hearing this sound, y]our mother came out to take a look, her body covered with soap, and you immediately buried your face in your pillow, pretending to be asleep. When she returned to the bathtub, however, she happened to leave the door partially ajar, and you were able to glimpse those breasts that had nourished you, as well as that dark patch from which you had emerged. At first you held your breath, and then you began to breathe very rapidly, before finally falling back asleep in the throes of desire and confusion. (427–28/428)

The narrator then recalls that his mother would gently stroke his naked body, including his tiny penis, which she would refer to as her "little bird" (*xiao niao*) (428/428). As discussed above, *xiao niao* is a colloquial term for the male organ, often used to refer to that of young boys, and is semantically related to the expression *xiao ji* (little chicken) used to refer to the narrator's own boyish penis at the beginning of the novel. This latter scene, therefore, not only returns the narrator to a memory of his own fantasy of a presexualized relationship with his mother but also ironically echoes the phallic punctum that partially compromised the idealized visual nostalgia of the same family photographs the narrator later uses to attempt to retrospectively (re)construct this idealized figure of the mother.

This process of erotic displacement, in which the narrator's adult lover effectively dissolves into a tangled web of maternal memories, mirrors the more general phallic perspective of the novel, whereby the narrator repeatedly uses women's erotized bodies as a way of simultaneously positing an imaginary maternal ground for his own self-identity and employing this maternal ground as a foil against which to elaborate a fantasy of diasporic freedom. One of the clearest illustrations of this fantasy can be found in the description of the soaring bird / spermatozoon near the beginning of the novel, in which the narrator's current diasporic condition is articulated as an independence from the ties of women and family, even as this diasporic space is itself immediately translated into that of the female womb. The "masculinist" subtext of this fantasy of the free-floating, diasporic subject and its complicity in the narrator's perception of his status as an author are evocatively brought together in a slightly different version of this avian fantasy earlier in Chapter 57, in a discussion of the narrator's relationship with Sylvie: "You [the narrator] float lightly, having lost all your weight. You travel between different nations, different cities, and different women, not wanting to find a resting place. Floating along, you merely chew playfully on words, thus leaving behind traces of life just like drops of ejaculated semen" (426/426). From viewing the act of writing as a secondary displacement of a prohibited erotic desire for the mother to fantasizing oneself as being a free-floating spermatozoon within a vast maternal womb, this final passage brings us back full circle to imagining the act of writing itself as sexual ejaculate.

Language and Subjectivity

> "These are only different pronouns, to change the point of view of the narrative. This can't replace the portrayal of characters. These pronouns of yours—even if they are characters—don't have clear images and can barely be said to have been described."
>
> He says that he isn't painting portraits.
>
> —Gao Xingjian, *Soul Mountain*

In the previous section, I suggest that the narrator's attempt to occupy an idealized space of diasporic freedom independent from fixed subject positions is elaborated by using the various women in his life as figurative screens onto which different facets of his own subjectivity may be projected. This technique is mirrored, at a more formal level, by the novel's use of shifting personal pronouns to designate different facets of the narrator's persona as well as the varying degrees of alienation from the different perspectives each represents. This technique is not unique to *One Man's Bible*; in fact, it is one of the characteristics for which Gao Xingjian's fiction is best known. Pronouns belong to a class of words the linguist Emile Benveniste has labeled "shifters," which have no absolute, predetermined referent but derive their meaning and function from the contingent conditions of relational reference. In Gao Xingjian's works, the shifting space of pronominal signifiers disorients the reader while providing a shifting tableau across which negotiations with the novel's narrator/protagonist are developed. The author uses the multiple pronouns not only to explore different facets of his narrators' subjectivities but also to mask the degree to which his decentered narrators continue to be marked by a variety of gender- and class-specific assumptions.

The pronominal subject of *One Man's Bible* generally alternates between the contemporary *you* of the present and a nostalgic *he* firmly embedded in the past. At several key points in the narrative, however, these two voices explicitly enter into a dialogue, illustrating the tensions underlying the narrator's consciousness. Although *One Man's Bible*, unlike Gao's earlier *Soul Mountain*, does not use the female third-person pronoun to refer directly to the narrator, many of the women who appear in the novel effectively function as projections of the narrator's anxieties and desires. Throughout much of the first half of the work, for instance, Marguerite functions as the narrator's alter ego, mirroring his own diasporic condition and eliciting his narratives of his past while providing an ironic counterpoint to his own obsession with personal origins. By denying her own past, Marguerite serves as a catalyst for the narrator's nostalgic reverie. Similarly, her dissatisfaction with her female body mirrors the narrator's erotic infatuation with it. In Chapter 22, soon after Marguerite leaves him in Hong Kong to return to Germany, the narrator's two voices first come into dialogue with each other—as if Marguerite's status as a displaced projection of the author's consciousness is momentarily replaced by the spectral appearance of the narrator's own youthful incarnation.

Chapter 22 begins with the narrator's description of the letters Marguerite writes him (in Chinese) from Germany, and the torment these letters cause him (among other reasons, because she apparently does not write Chinese as well as she speaks it). This is followed by a curious dialogue between the narrator's two pronominal voices:

> *His* experiences have accumulated in the interstices of *your* memory, but how can *you* separate them layer by layer in order to inspect them individually and then use a cold, disinterested gaze to regard those events he has experienced? *In the end, you are you, and he is he.* It is also very difficult for *you* to return to the state of mind *he* had at the time, because *he* has already become so alien to *you.* Don't attempt to use *your* current sense of self-satisfaction to try and go change *him. You* must preserve *your* distance, let *your* heart sink, and be even more observant. (188/182; italics added)

The narrator then stresses the need to allow his younger alter ego to preserve a certain degree of autonomy from his "own" mature consciousness:

> You must let him, that child, that youth, that boy, who has not yet become a man, that daydreaming, happy-go-lucky fellow, . . . that past version of yourself, you must let him emerge from your memory, and you mustn't make excuses for him or repent for him. But while you observe and listen to him, you may naturally feel a sense of profound sadness, but you mustn't heed this emotion and allow it to develop into true sorrow. When you remove his mask to observe him more carefully, you must also transform him back into fiction, into a character unrelated to yourself waiting to be discovered. (188/182–83)

Here, *pace* Benveniste, language does not produce the "possibility of [singular] subjectivity" but instead explicitly allows for the fragmentation of a multiplicity of potential subject positions within the same "individual." At the same time, this fantasy of a linguistic plurality of diverse subject positions masks the degree to which those subject positions are invisibly informed by a cluster of unacknowledged (gender-specific) assumptions.

The theme of demasking is crucially important in the work as a whole. At one point early in the novel, for instance, the narrator remarks that "all Chinese live behind masks, masks that are very difficult to remove" (46/45). In the following chapter, the narrator (this time in the third person) repeats this sentiment, noting, "In order to survive, one has no alternative but to wear a mask" (56/56). Here, the narrator equivocates whether this reliance on masks is a culturally or socially specific phenomenon ("All *Chinese* live behind masks") or whether it has more universal implications ("*one* has no alternative but to wear a mask"). This equivocation, in turn, is related to a deeper ambivalence within the novel over the gender, class, and ideological implications of the narrator's attempt to identify with an allegedly "unmarked" position of diasporic consciousness.

The most detailed discussion of the theme of masks can be found at the beginning of Chapter 56:

> It is with considerable difficulty that he finally removes this mask, this fake skin, covering his face. This mask consists of a plastic covering made to precise specifications and has considerable flexibility, able to expand and contract. When worn on the face, it always creates the appearance of being a personage with a correct (*zhengque* 正確) and respectable (*zhengjing* 正經) façade (*zhengmian* 正面 [literally, "correct face"]). (418/418)

After elaborating at length on the various sorts of masks found in contemporary society, the narrator fondles his own metaphorical "mask," which he now holds in his hands, and reflects on how, by removing it, he has managed to relieve himself of the most salient of his social ties; indeed, his only remaining tie is to language itself:

> Because he doesn't have any leaders, he therefore is not managed by the Party or other organization; without a motherland, he therefore does not care about a homeland; and, with both parents dead, he does not have a family, and therefore does not have anything tying him down. . . . As always, the only ties he has not severed are those of language. He *could*, of course, write in a foreign tongue, and therefore the only reason he continues to preserve his native language becomes largely an issue of convenience. (419/419)

These masks thus have two interrelated meanings. On one hand, they are a convenient shorthand for the ways in which subjects are interpellated into different social positions. On the other hand, they also seem to operate on a more abstract level, functioning as metaphors for the process by which the narrator allows his subjectivity to become fragmented into several quasi-autonomous voices. They also implicitly signal the degree to which this idealized fantasy of a fragmented subjectivity "masks" the degree to which these various narratorial personas continue to be informed by a cluster of unacknowledged gendered assumptions and prejudices.

This apparent linkage between the themes of masking and of pronominal differentiation is further reinforced by the fact that it is precisely at the end of Chapter 56, which began with the extended reflection on the theme of masks and demasking, that the novel's two pronominal subjects finally come "face to face." The last line of the chapter reads: "He sat in front of you, gazing at you, and laughing in the mirror in front of him" (420/420). After this displaced mirror scene at the end of Chapter 56, the narrator's two "voices" intersect again in Chapter 60, the penultimate chapter of the novel. There, the second- and third-person voices—*you* and *he*—finally come together, as a third-person narrative voice tells the second-person "narrator" that "you" are no longer needed:

> Enough! He said.
> Enough of what! You ask.
> He says, enough. Finish him!
> Who? Who is supposed to finish whom?
> Him, the character you are writing about. Finish him up.
> You say that you are not the author.
> Then, who *is* the author?
> Isn't it clear to you yet? It's he, himself. You are only his consciousness.
> Then what about you? Once he is finished, wouldn't you be finished as well?
> You say that you can also become a reader, just like an audience watching a drama. The "he" in the text does not have any significant relationship with you. (439–40/440)

This passage begins as a dialogue between the two narratorial voices in the novel: the third person *he* and the second person *you*, with the *he* speaking of the character in the novel (and, by implication, himself) as "he," while at the same time addressing the *you* in the second person, as "you." The situation, however, is complicated by the fact that the *you* also uses the second person pronoun to refer to himself, despite the fact that, in the context of the dialogue, the antecedent of this personal pronoun would appear to refer instead to his (i.e. *you*'s) interlocutor, the *he*. For instance, in the line "You say that you are not the author" (你說你不是作者), both "you's" ostensibly refer to the speaker, *you*, though grammatically speaking one or both could also theoretically be read as referring to the *he* (e.g., parsing this unpunctuated line of dialogue as meaning either: "*You* says, 'You [*he*] are not the author,'" or, instead, as, "[*You* says,] 'You [*he*] say that you [*he*] are not the author.'") This grammatical blurring of subject positions is then developed more explicitly in the following lines, as Gao Xingjian suggests that it is actually the *he* who is authoring the *you* subjectivity, rather than the other way around.

In the following, and final, chapter of the novel, the narrator is in the city of Perpignon in the French Pyrenees, when he suddenly discovers that he is carrying with him an old photograph from his stint of labor "re-education" during the Cultural Revolution:

> You don't know how, at that time, you managed to insert this photograph into a book and bring it out with you. In the photograph, he is thin and has a shaved head. You carefully examine this old photograph, which you still keep close at hand. It was taken more than thirty years ago at that so-called 57 Cadre School farm for labor re-education and has already begun to turn yellow. You hope to be able to discover something in his gaze (*muguang*). He has raised his shaved, gourdlike head, which visibly marks him as a prisoner. He appears to have a certain sense of pride, which is probably what ultimately saved him. . . . But now, that pride is no longer necessary. Now, you are a free bird (*ziyou de niao*) and can fly wherever you wish. You feel that before you lies a stretch of virgin land, which, for you at the very least, is new. (443/444)

This passage brings together a number of the themes structuring the novel as a whole. On one hand, the narrator's mirrored dialogue with his own past self is here realized most explicitly in his examination of an actual photograph of himself from more than three decades earlier. The fantasy of the narrator's being an autonomous free bird also recurs at the end of this passage and is once again accompanied by a surprisingly direct metaphor of sexual conquest: in this case, the implicit exploration and cultivation of "virgin land" (*yi pian chunü di* 一片處女地).

One Man's Bible as a whole is structured as a series of mirrored displacements, whereby the narrator seeks to assert his personal and ideological independence via a series of identificatory and antagonistic mirrored projections with a variety of alter egos (either pronominal or copulative). It is a central contention of the present chapter that this assertion of identity and quest for self is played out against the backdrop of a narrator's imaginary reconstruction of his memory of his mother—wherein the resulting maternal space functions as both an imaginary ground for his own subjectivity and a site of resistance. In the final section, I take these conclusions from the novel and consider their relevance to Gao Xingjian's status as a diasporic writer.

"Without [Femin]ism"

> "When your mother gave birth to you, she didn't have any 'isms,' and therefore why can't you, this last son of a fallen lineage, also live outside of 'isms'?"
>
> —Gao Xingjian, *One Man's Bible*

Gao Xingjian's notion of being "without isms" (*meiyou zhuyi* 沒有主義) is, on the surface, a call for the potential independence of aesthetics from ideology, a call for an autonomous "art for art's sake." For a Mainland Chinese author writing and working in the wake of the Communist aesthetic orthodoxy of socialist realism, this call for the independence of writing and politics has an obvious appeal. At the same time, it is important to recognize that Gao, in his advocacy of a pure "art for art's sake," is implicitly relying on a rather specifically Western concept of Romantic aesthetics, one deeply conditioned by what Terry Eagleton has called "the ideology of the aesthetic."[7] Eagleton's argument is that the attempt to articulate a pure space of aesthetic production outside conventional ideological currents is itself a thoroughly ideological act. What is important, therefore, is not so much which ideologies the work of art advocates but what sorts of ideological currents it attempts to suppress.

The contemporary critic Ma Sen 馬森 has observed that "if many people espouse a doctrine of 'without isms,' it itself may become an 'ism' in itself: a 'nonismism.' This, of course, was not Gao Xingjian's original intention."[8] Regardless of what Gao Xingjian's "original intention" might have been, I would argue that his notion of being "without isms" is indeed an "ism," not because it has attracted a group of followers (as Ma Sen suggests), but because this position inevitably carries a tangible ideological baggage. In *One Man's Bible*, this notion of being "without isms" not only constitutes an idealized return to a presexual moment of union with the figure of the mother (as discussed above), but also is used as part of a systematic denial of the claims of feminism. Near the end of the novel, for instance, the narrator, speaking to himself in the second person, remarks of his lover Sherry [Xi'erwei]:

7. Eagleton, *The Ideology of the Aesthetic.*

8. Ma Sen, "Taowang," 80. David Der-wei Wang also makes reference to this argument in his article "Meiyou [xiandai]zhuyi."

> Do not mistake her for a feminist (*nüquan zhuyizhe* 女權主義著), because she is, like you, without "isms." . . . You[, like her,] also do not dare to rashly contribute your own opinions on feminism, and neither have you personally experienced masculine oppression. If you are not a woman, you therefore cannot truly understand the unspoken difficulties of being a woman, and therefore what point is there in rebelling? (390/389)

Revolving around an abstract ideal of being "without isms," this passage illustrates two of the opposing tendencies within the novel. On one hand, the work is structured around a series of projective identifications with the various women in the narrator's life, including not only his mother but also, among others, Marguerite, Sherry, Xiaoxiao, and Mama Li. These women embody different dimensions of the narrator's consciousness, even as they stand as imaginary foils against which he develops his own self-understanding. On the other hand, this ventriloquistic denial of the claims of feminism can be seen as paralleling the narrator's partial erasure of gender difference in the novel. Beyond specifying that Sherry is not a "feminist," the narrator also positions *himself* against feminism on the ironic grounds that, not being a woman, he is in no position to "rebel" against women's oppression. In a work revolving around a series of projective identifications, this suggestion of the ultimate impossibility of "truly understand[ing]" the condition of another subject appears to be rather disingenuous even as it gestures toward a more fundamental problem with the novel's model of projective identification.

Even as Gao's narrator seeks to use Marguerite and the other women in the novel as figurative screens onto which he may project his own anxieties and concerns, these same women are consistently reduced to the status of mere sexual objects. A recurrent fascination throughout the book is the eroticism of these women's naked bodies, and several of the narrator's conversations with the women take place while he is caressing, or even physically, entering their bodies. Although an attention to the erotic dimension of women's bodies is not, in and of itself, necessarily misogynist (indeed, there is a well-established tradition in feminist literature and criticism that takes the eroticized feminine body as its own explicit starting point), I would nevertheless argue that the way in which Gao Xingjian develops this theme suggests a more systemic "blindness" to the gendered dimensions of his own position.

In a post-Maoist social and cultural field, Gao Xingjian's narrator (as well as the author Gao Xingjian himself) is emphatic in wanting to position himself outside the visible constraints of "isms" and ideology. At the same time, he appears to be less sensitive to the degree to which even the act of denying ideology may itself constitute an ideological act in and of itself. More specifically, the novel's narrator appears blinded to the degree to which his sociopolitical stance involves a degree of systematic misogyny. Gao Xingjian's "misogyny" does not, however, necessarily entail an overt disparagement of the women around him; rather, it resides precisely in the ways in which these women are paradoxically *overvalued* (as lovers and mothers) in his text. Indeed, I would argue that the central problem with the novel is not so much that the women in it are portrayed as straightforward sex objects but that they are frequently located within a chain of displacements ostensibly rooted in the narrator's own early scopophilic interest in his mother.

In *One Man's Bible*, the narrator repeatedly posits the figure of the mother as the imaginary ground against which he seeks to assert his own identity, and the destruction of her memory is, similarly, one of the conditions of possibility of his current self-understanding. At the same time, this figure of the mother never really disappears; instead, it returns repeatedly in a variety of guises. In fact, even the act of writing itself can also be seen as a displaced working out of the sexual prohibition the figure of the mother represents. The narrator's relationship with his mother is riddled with paradoxes: although he was apparently never close to her as a young child and was forced to destroy one of his last remaining photographs of her during the Cultural Revolution, nevertheless her memory, together with more abstract notions of maternity and femininity, continues to exert a profound influence on him. This figure of the mother is placed in the position of being the origin of a process of doubled displacement. The erotic attraction that the narrator, as a young boy, is imagined to have originally felt for his mother is first displaced onto other young women toward whom he feels attracted, and this desire is subsequently partially sublimated into the act of writing itself. At the same time, this act of writing becomes one of the prime means by which the narrator's conflicted attitudes toward maternity and femininity are played out, to the extent that the act of writing itself is designated in sexually explicit metaphors (drops of semen, etc.). The narrator/author of *One Man's Bible*, in his attempt to locate a space for himself on the margins of conventional national and ideological structures, continually returns to this imaginary maternity as a locus of self-identity. Ultimately, however, he fails to acknowledge or address the ways in which this imaginary and idealized vision of maternity, together with its various eroticized displacements, condition his gendered identity in very determinate and consequential ways.

Both Gao Xingjian and Li Yung-p'ing use figures of the mother and the female lover to explore the limits of the cultural impact of Mainland China in conditioning the identities of postnational Chinese subjects. In contrast, the contemporary Beijing author Wang Shuo uses images of women to elaborate the paradoxical inverse of this issue—the way in which the figure of woman also comes to link a recent Chinese past, not to contemporary postnational Chinese identities but to the contemporary reality of China's capital, Beijing itself.

9

Wang Shuo and Historical Portraiture

History decomposes into images, not into narratives.

—Walter Benjamin

In 1998, as part of its "Hundred most important people of the century" project, *Time* magazine published a list headed "Leaders and Revolutionaries: Twenty people who helped define the political and social fabric of our times."[1] Of these twenty individuals, two were Chinese. One, inevitably, was Mao Zedong, whose own political power was very much grounded in his attempted control over the dissemination of his own image. The other figure, however, was more of a surprise: it was the "unknown rebel" in the ubiquitous video clip of a solitary man standing in front of the line of tanks in Tiananmen Square on June 4, 1989. If Mao's identity has, in many respects, been reduced to that of his own two-dimensional image, the "identity" of the "lone protester" (and to this day, he remains publicly unidentified), by contrast, is in a sense entirely an artifact of the original, endlessly reproduced, image itself.[2]

1. "Time 100."

2. The man was identified in some sources as Wang Weilin 王维林, but the Information Center of Human Rights and Democratic Movement in China (HRDMC) has since reported that he was incorrectly identified and now would reveal himself only after the reputation of the Chinese pro-democracy movement has been restored ("1989 Tiananmen Tank Protester").

This juxtaposition of the images of Chairman Mao and the anonymous lone protester—with the protester standing under the ironic eye of the enormous Tiananmen Square Mao portrait, which had itself been defaced with paint by the student protesters several days before—represents a symbolic intersection of two different scopic regimes. On one hand, there is the Maoist faith in the manipulation and consolidation of power through the widespread dissemination of identically reproduced images and texts; on the other hand, there is the post-Maoist treatment of the visual image as a mere simulacrum, infinitely reproducible but lacking an ultimate referent and always susceptible to intentional or unintentional deviations from that which it seeks to reproduce. At the same time, just as the Cultural Revolution constituted an attempt by Mao to consolidate the political power he had, in a sense, already lost; similarly, the Maoist faith in the exercise of power through the dissemination of identically reproduced images can be seen as a profoundly melancholic gesture, a silent denial of the extent to which this utopian "reproduction without difference" is necessarily always-already lost. In this chapter, I examine how several works by contemporary Beijing novelist Wang Shuo 王朔 (1958–) explore how both history and personal memory can be condensed into, and refracted through, a single visual image and, conversely, how a single image can provide the seed out of which an entire history or personal memory is (spuriously) unfolded.

As the pictures of Mao and of the Tiananmen protester illustrate, visual images may function as nodal points onto which historical or personal narratives are anchored, even though, as signifiers, they inevitably have the potential of becoming separated from their ostensible referents. In the following discussion, I consider how this potential dissociation of signifier and referent makes photographs, in Wang Shuo's novels, powerful loci onto which individual identities may be anchored and reconstructed.

Flies in the Ointment

Bodiliness, above all, is put up for grabs. Hence the presence, in Eastern as well as Western trompe l'oeil, of a fly, a fly motionless in a corner or on someone's nose. Like trompe l'oeil itself, the fly is obsessed with our minutiae, Christian or Confucian. The fly moves between the cracks of houses and bones, waiting upon feasts and misfortune; it generates—it was long thought—spontaneously, coming from nowhere to live briefly on that which we leave behind. It is the afterimage of the flesh.

—Hillel Schwartz, *The Culture of the Copy*

Wang Shuo emerged on the Chinese literary scene in the late 1980s, and his work constitutes an ironic response to an earlier literary equivalent of this Maoist reproduction without difference. Cultural production in China from 1949 through the late 1970s was dominated by socialist realism, which relied on a tight control over both content and structure to ensure that literary work supported Communist ideals. Following the death of Mao and the official end of the Cultural Revolution in 1976, a wider range of literary and cultural production became possible. Among the literary movements during this period were "scar literature" (which sought to bear witness to the horrors suffered during the Cultural Revolution), "seeking roots" (which turned to rural subjects in an attempt to affirm an intangible quintessence of Chinese culture), the "experimentalists" (who used radical deviations from conventional narrative structure to defamiliarize the reading process), and the "new realists" (who sought to preserve "realistic" narrative conventions but to disassociate them from the overtly ideological connotations of socialist realism). Wang Shuo represents a cynical variant on these previous literary traditions. His novels and novellas, set in contemporary Beijing, rely on an acerbic sense of humor and intimate familiarity with contemporary Beijing slang to convey his distinctive perspective on the axiological rootlessness of China's urban "Cultural Revolution generation" (most of his protagonists are people, like himself, who came of age during China's Great Proletarian Cultural Revolution, between 1966 and 1976). Wang's works not only comment on this sense of rootlessness and alienation but can themselves be seen as enthusiastic participants in a related process of commercialization and cultural commodification.

Wang Shuo was remarkably prolific during the late 1980s and early 1990s, producing, in the eight years from 1984 to 1992, a total of 24 medium- and full-length novels, as well as screenplays for seven movies and three television series.[3] His works were, and remain, immensely popular, quickly becoming best-sellers (and inspiring a flurry of illegal pirated editions). Wang's ability to achieve this market success despite deliberately distancing himself from the professional Chinese Writers' Association, is commonly referred to as the "Wang Shuo phenomenon" (*Wang Shuo xianxiang* 王朔現象).[4] His dual status as an author and a writer of movie and television screenplays has further contributed to a complex perspective, in several of his works, regarding the relationship between textuality and visuality, specifically the ways in which a text or an image may function as the site of nostalgic or historical investment.[5]

Wang Shuo's novels *Wo shi "lang"* 我是"狼" (I am the "wolf"; 1988), *Wan'r de jiu shi xin tiao* 玩兒的就是心跳 (Playing for thrills; 1989), and *Dongwu xiongmeng* 動物凶猛 (Ferocious animals; 1991) share a similar structure. Each begins with the systematic reconstruction of a series of events from a decade or two earlier—events that appear to lead to a murder committed by the protagonist himself. Moreover, roughly two-thirds or three-quarters of the way through each work, this reconstructive narrative is brought to an abrupt halt by the revelation that there was no murder. The last portion of each work then returns to the earlier narrative but from a different perspective—this time, with the explicit realization that the murder in question, as well as many of the related details, are all fabrications. This realization of the patent ficticity of the original narrative does not, however, lead to a straightforward process of disillusionment; rather, it leaves the reader with a profound skepticism regarding the truth-value of even the latter, supposedly veridical, account.

In each of these three works, the fabricated narrative revolves around a visual image. In the last two works (*Animals* and *Thrills*), this visual image is a photograph; in the first (*I Am the "Wolf"*), the embed-

3. Wang Shuo et al., *Wo shi Wang Shuo*, 227–28.

4. Jing Wang, *High Culture Fever*, 261–86.

5. With the added twist that the striking foregrounding of visual imagery in several of his novels is always-already mediated by textual narrative.

ded story is somewhat more abstractly framed by allusions to the act of figuratively walking into a picture or mirror, and incorporates complex tropes of visual observation into the narrative proper. At issue in each work is the relationship between the concrete visual image and the emplotment of historical and personal narratives.

I begin my reading of Wang Shuo by considering the figure of a fly. Sun Quan 孫權 (r. 222–52), the king of Wu, asked the painter Cao Buxing to paint a screen in his palace. Cao accidentally spilled a drop of ink on the unpainted screen and, realizing he would be unable to remove the stain, he covered his tracks by transforming the inkspot into the image of a fly. Sun Quan's response to the screen illustrated Cao's success: Sun tried to brush what he took to be a real insect off the canvas![6] Wu Hung, in his discussion of this anecdote, observes:

> The merit of the image [of the fly] was found in its deceptive power, and it gained this power from its interaction with the surface, since what Sun Quan saw was not just a fly but *a fly landing on the white silk*. To Cao Buxing the screen had no mystery; it simply bore a painted fly against an empty background. Sun Quan, on the other hand, was not only confused by the fly but was also deceived by the screen, which appeared to him "unpainted." Although the artist and the spectator had entirely different interpretations of the screen, they both acknowledged the concept of a surface and approached the screen as a medium for painting.[7]

Wu Hung is arguing here that the concept of the screen, as an independent paintable surface in its own right, is a historically specific one, one that emerged in China only during the Han dynasty. However, I would like to borrow his analysis to point to how the figure of the fly functions both as the stain that challenges the potential mimeticism of the screen and as a supra-mimetic aporia that threatens the screen's mimetic potential from the other direction by giving the screen's images the appearance not of mimetic representation but of "reality" itself. The spot of ink, in other words, is a stain on the blank screen; dis-

6. Zhang Yanyuan, *Lidai minghua ji*, *juan* 4, 165–66. Cf. Pliny's account of Zeuxis's grape painting and Norman Bryson's (*Vision and Painting*, 1–2) discussion of the status of this anecdote in the Western art-historical tradition.

7. Wu Hung, *The Double Screen*, 16.

guised as the image of a fly, it becomes another kind of stain, a point of transcendental, unquestioned realism that, in effect, frames the representational screen on which it appears.

This chapter extends this concept of the "screen" to indicate the cultural or ideological horizon against which individual memories and histories are sketched. Specifically, I am interested in how subjects locate themselves within these sorts of personal and historical narratives ("screens"), as well as how these narratives frequently are elaborated out of a need to explain incongruous "stains" on the "screens" themselves. These stains-cum-flies constitute the greatest threat to the truth-effect of these narrative "screens"; at the same time, they can be seen as the catalysts for the re/writing of these narrative screens in the first place. Finally, I am particularly interested in the specifically visual resonances of this historical emplotment-as-screen metaphor: how the process of constructing personal and historical narratives within which to place oneself often involves a figurative act of *viewing oneself* as if from outside.

We see another image of a fly serving a similar function in a more modern text, from 1941. In Ding Ling's 丁玲 (1904–86) short story "Zai yiyuan zhong shi" 在醫院中時 (While in the hospital), two descriptions of these unsanitary flying insects represent a stain in what should ostensibly be a hygienic medical environment. However, as the contemporary literary critic Huang Ziping's 黄子平 discussion of an early (1942) critique of the story demonstrates, this detail does not, as one might expect, reinforce the fundamental realism of this May Fourth text; instead, it represents a moment of hyper-realistic excess, a point at which the story's realism starts to fold in upon itself. Huang sensibly observes that one could not reasonably expect to see flies anywhere, outdoors *or* indoors, on the sort of cold, snowy December day on which the story is set.[8] This moment of mimetic overcompensation ironically draws attention to the inherent fictionality of the narrative itself. One final anecdote illustrating the ironic relationship between flies and mimetic representation can be found in Jia Pingwa's 賈平凹 1993

8. Huang Ziping, *Geming, lishi, xiaoshuo*, 146–47. The earlier critique Huang is discussing is Liao Ying's "'Ren . . . zai jianku zhong shengzhang.'"

novel *Feidu* 廢都 (Fallen capital), which notes that the most effective way of distinguishing male and female flies is to see which ones land on the face of a mirror, because "the ones landing on a mirror will be the female ones, since female flies also love beauty."[9] Just as Lévi-Strauss's hooded egret allegory (see Chapter 2) suggests that the birds may be trapped by a visual reproduction of the immaculate purity they themselves can only aspire to, Jia Pingwa's account of the narcissistic flies similarly suggests that the insects (hardly paragons of beauty themselves) are attracted not so much by their own reflections as by the idealized reflexivity inherent in the mirror itself.

These fly anecdotes help to provide a frame within which we may consider a series of intriguing fly references in Wang Shuo's short novel *I Am the "Wolf."* The first such allusion occurs near the beginning of the work, as the protagonist complains about the Big Brotherly familiarity his police investigator seems to have with respect to the events of his own past:

> "You make me think that you are one of those shameless little people who, with the rim of their hat folded down and holding a little notebook in their hands, run around eavesdropping on other people's conversations while carefully writing everything down word for word. You even know exactly what I said in those casual remarks I made a decade ago while at the far corners of the earth, could it be that you were already observing me even back then? . . ."
>
> "I myself am too insignificant to merit mention, but you should have some awareness of the giant eye of the people."
>
> "The structure of this giant eye should probably resemble that of a fly's compound eye?"[10]

This initial evocation of a fly serves to distinguish between the localized, individual "eye" of the investigator himself and the delocalized "gaze" of the "people" whom the investigator indirectly represents. The protagonist gives this second, highly abstract, concept a concrete visual correlate: a fly's compound eye.

9. Jia Pingwa, *Feidu*, 65.

10. Wang Shuo, *Wo shi "lang,"* 170. Subsequent references to this work are cited in the text.

In the very next line, however, the investigator picks up on the protagonist's fly metaphor, and neatly—even viciously—inverts its significance:

> "If you have any understanding of your present situation, then you need not entertain any illusions and aspire to use deception to finagle your way out. Right now, you are nothing more than a fly trapped under the lens of a microscope, and not even that tiny particle of filth stuck to your paws will escape detection." (170)

The same figurative insect that, in the preceding line, was used to evoke the ubiquitous, panopticon-like surveillance powers of the modern state, is used in the following line to suggest the isolated individual trapped under that same gaze.

A few pages later, as the interrogation proceeds, the narrator's attention is distracted at one point by a fly's perambulations through the room:

> A fly buzzed as it soared downwards from the high ceiling, flying rapidly around the spacious room. It tried to fly out into the sunny garden, but instead merely bumped its head on the pristinely transparent glass of the window. . . . It laboriously flew into the glass again and again until finally, exhausted, it fell to the floor and lay there without moving. Its inability to fly out resembles the outside flies' inability to fly in; and even though they are separated by a pane of glass, they can still understand one another (*huxiang dongxi* 互相洞悉) without any difficulty at all. (178)

This final fly is inserted, without any transition, directly into the psychoanalytic police interrogation, just as the narrator is finding himself getting stuck more and more tightly under the investigator's discursive gaze. The concluding image of two flies gazing at each other across a pane of transparent glass condenses the two earlier references, in which the fly was made to symbolize, at different points, both the oddly omniscient *observer* (the "compound eye of the people") as well as the powerless *observed* (the "fly trapped under the lens of a microscope"). These three fly images in *I Am the "Wolf,"* each mentioned only in passing and then apparently forgotten, provide an evocative figuration of the narrative dynamics of the novel. Like two flies staring at each other across a pane of transparent glass, the entire novel revolves around the face-to-face epistemological battle between the protagonist and the investigator, as each struggles to assert his right to view and narrate the protagonist's own personal past.

I Am the "Wolf" narrates the protagonist's discussion with a police investigator, who introduces himself as Shan Liren. The investigator informs the protagonist that a woman (whom he claims is a former acquaintance of the narrator's by the name of Zhou Yao) was found drowned that morning, and that next to her body was a slipper with the name of the guest house where the protagonist is currently staying as well as his room number. Although the protagonist adamantly proclaims his innocence of any involvement in the woman's demise, Shan proceeds methodically to demonstrate to him that he had both the opportunity and the motivation to drown the woman. The exchange culminates in a variation of the title line, when the protagonist complains that Shan must have concrete proof, rather than mere circumstantial evidence, that he committed the murder: "It is one thing to say that I am the wolf, and quite another to say that I actually ate the sheep." To this argument, Shan promptly replies,

> "Is it hard to come up with proof? . . . No, not hard at all. For us, the hardest task lies in identifying who is the wolf disguised as a human. If we want to prove that the wolf ate the sheep, that is very easy. Even the question of how it ate the sheep is merely a technical issue." (188)

This contrast between "identifying the wolf" and "prov[ing] that the wolf ate the sheep" anticipates the relationship between visual images and discursive narrative, which is foregrounded in the two Wang Shuo novels I discuss below. The moment of "recognition" can be compared to the apparent transparency of the mimetic image, and the process of "proof" can be compared to the discursive narrative that is elaborated on the basis of that initial (visual) "identification."

In the "coda" to the novel, Shan Liren and another police officer who is referred to as Xiao Ding pay a visit to Zhou Yao and inform her that earlier that morning a man turned himself in to the police and confessed to having drowned her. Of course, the investigators add cheerfully, it is clear that she is still very much alive. They further explain that someone pretending to be Shan Liren had confronted

"Wolf"[11] with the evidence of the drowned corpse and strong-armed him into believing that he was the murderer (the body, it is revealed, was actually that of a love-sick suicide). Zhou Yao tells the investigators that she had, at one time, known Wolf, but that they hadn't spoken for years until he called her up the night before to ask her out to dinner, an invitation she declined.

The coda ends with Zhou Yao remarking that Wolf should be locked up in a mental institution, to which the investigators respond that he has already been committed. In the hospital, Xiao Ding adds, "he sometimes pretends to be a policeman, and sometimes pretends to be the criminal." On his way out the door, Shan Liren asks Zhou Yao why she had turned Wolf down the preceding evening. She responds, "I just didn't want him to see what I look like now. And, by the way, how did he know your name?" The first "he" in her remark clearly refers to Wolf, but the second one would appear to refer back to the police imposter who cross-examined Wolf throughout the first two-thirds of the novel (as Xiao Ding observes three pages earlier, "[we] don't know how he [the imposter] learned about comrade Lao Shan's ["old Shan," viz., Shan Liren] name" [196]).

In response to Zhou Yao's final question, Xiao Ding speculates that "he" probably learned Shan's name because "that day the television news had announced the arrival of our Lao Shan" (199). However, Zhou's final remark/question is, itself, somewhat confusing, with its abrupt shift in the referent of the pronoun "he." Perhaps she is simply being careless, or assuming that the context of her remarks will make the referent of each "he" unambiguously clear to the listener. However, if we reconsider the preceding conversation, another, even more intriguing, possibility suggests itself. Xiao Ding had just told Zhou that, in the mental hospital, Wolf alternates between pretending he is a policeman and a criminal. Perhaps, therefore, Zhou's subsequent pronoun conflation reflects her unstated realization that there was never a "police imposter" to begin with; rather, that it was Wolf himself who, already mad, was assuming the positions of both investigator and

11. We are never told the protagonist's actual name; for convenience, I refer to him simply as "Wolf."

accused throughout the entire bizarre interrogation recounted in the first two-thirds of the novel. The resulting scenario gives new significance to Wolf's vision, discussed above, of two flies mutually observing each other across a transparent pane of glass (178).

Wang Shuo's novella also elaborates this interrelationship between observer and observed in a more concrete manner, through the metaphor of "entering a picture." At the beginning of *I Am the "Wolf,"* for instance, the narrator relates that, when he went to a particular island on vacation, it was "like walking into a painting" (158). Roughly three-quarters of the way through the novel, at the end of the "inner narrative" of the story, we return to a similar trope of walking into a visual image, although in this instance the visual image is not a figurative painting but a hall of mirrors in a fun house:

> Amid the incessant sound of explosions, *I walked into a hall of "funny mirrors"* (*haha jingzi* 哈哈鏡子), making me suddenly as thin as a willow, or as short and squat as an earthen jar. One instant I'm just a pair of legs without a body, and the next instant I'm a legless torso. Eyes protruding like a goldfish, mouth grinning like a blood basin. (194; italics added)

This sense of having "walked into a painting" is developed even further when, later on the same page, all the lights of the dance hall are described as being projected onto the four walls, thus creating an "enormous, circular screen" (*yi ge juda huanxing yinmu* 一個巨大環形銀幕), onto which a series of moving "tableaux" (*huamian* 畫面) are projected in succession (194).

Just as the inner narrative of *I Am the "Wolf"* is framed by this trope of "walking into a picture," *Playing for Thrills*, one of Wang Shuo's best-known works, features a comparable moment in which the protagonist, Fang Yan, feels as if he has entered a picture. Fang Yan discovers a packet of photographs ostensibly showing him with a circle of friends from several years earlier. One of the photos, he is told, depicts Liu Yan, his former beloved and a potential alibi for the murder he is accused of having committed a decade earlier: "A girl is standing in the dim light, everything behind her a blur, and her mouth is open as if she is about to say something. . . . Although the quality of the photo was quite poor, making it difficult to see the person clearly, I nevertheless knew it was her. I recall removing the photograph and pocketing it before heading back to the restaurant."[12] At the restaurant, Fang Yan finds himself surveying

> the scene like a movie director with a zoom lens moving in for close-ups, I discovered [my companions] weren't who I thought they were. The distinct, familiar features and magnified pores of all those faces began to fade and evolve into unfamiliar noses, eyes, and mouths, forming shapes I couldn't recognize, layers of alien faces. A graceful girl stood by watching me, and it was as if I'd taken out the photograph and laid it on the table beside me. *I wasn't sure if it was I who had entered the photograph, or she who had emerged from it.* (262/91; italics added)

As the novel progresses, however, it becomes clear that the paradigmatic visual trope in the work is not so much this act of "walking into a picture" as it is that of the photographic image itself. Fang Yan carries the blurry photograph of Liu Yan with him nearly everywhere he goes, and it provides him with an external instantiation of the (spurious) personal history he can no longer recall. At the same time, the photograph helps to lead him to the "truth" behind the complex ruse within which he has become ensnared.

Like the protagonist in *I Am the "Wolf,"* Fang Yan finds himself implicated in a murder. The ostensible victim, in this case, is Fang Yan's onetime acquaintance Gao Yang, whose corpse allegedly has recently been found in Yunnan. Only a partial skeleton remains (*sans* skull), but the neck vertebrae were severed in such a way as to suggest that he was beheaded. The murder is said to have occurred during a specific week a decade earlier, but the problem is that Fang Yan has no memory of what he did that week. His only potential alibi, it turns out, is a woman by the name of Liu Yan. He was apparently with her at the time, but he currently has absolutely no recollection of her. His sole link to this mystery woman is a blurred photograph that ostensibly represents her. It bears an uncanny resemblance to his current friend, Li Jiangyun. Fang

---

12. Wang Shuo, *Wan'r de jiu shi xin tiao*, 262. Goldblatt, trans., *Playing for Thrills*, 91. Subsequent references to these works are cited in the text; some of the English translations have been modified.

Yan spends the first portion of the novel hiding from the police while he painstakingly attempts to track down Liu Yan and reconstruct his own personal life history. As Li Jiangyun perceptively tells him, the resulting detective work is less an attempt to exonerate himself than it is a means to discover himself:

> I can tell by the extent of your concern that there's more to this than just clearing your name. It's mainly self-knowledge. Your anxiety comes from not understanding some aspect of yourself, as if you've lost something, as if your image of yourself were somehow incomplete. (271/106)

Given the importance, for Fang Yan, of the photographic image of Liu Yan, it is significant that Li Jiangyun metaphorically expresses Fang Yan's own lack of self-knowledge in terms of the incompleteness of his own "visual image" (*xingxiang* 形象) of himself.

Roughly two-thirds of the way through the novel, it is finally revealed that Gao Yang (like Zhou Yao in the preceding novel) is actually alive and well, his head still securely attached to his shoulders. Several years earlier, Gao Yang and his friends found themselves bored with their lives and decided to "stage" a murder to liven things up a bit. In order to make the game even more interesting, they decide to pin the murder on Fang Yan. As Gao Yang subsequently explains to him:

> When we decided to include you in our plan, Feng Xiaogang warned us to be careful, saying that you might turn our elaborate scheme to your own advantage and have a good time at our expense. I didn't believe him, because you were running around with your head in the clouds over some girl, and couldn't be distracted. (348/222)

As it turns out, Fang Yan proves true to both expectations, plunging wholeheartedly (if unwittingly) into the "game" precisely *because* his "head [is] in the clouds over some girl"; energetically attempting to reconstruct the fictional past of which he has no distinct memories, even as the (real) police are turning his apartment upside down looking for clues.

Somewhat shockingly, at the end of the novel, it is revealed that that "staged" murder was actually a real murder that subsequently masqueraded as its own imitation. On the evening of the murder, the four conspirators were taking a bus through the mountains of Yunnan, when an accident on the highway made it necessary for everyone to get off the bus. After a while someone heard "a single scream," but it was too dark to see anything. When they finally reboard, the four friends have now been reduced to "three passengers, two men and a woman . . . their faces pale as paper" (360/240). During the entire trip home, they have the impression that the clouds in the sky have

> formed a massive human head looking majestically into the sky, showing only the whites of its eyes. As the bus rounded the lakeshore, the head followed its progress with its eyes, now happy now sad now angry now exasperated, abruptly looking straight down into the bus then abruptly cocking itself to gaze off into the distance. When the bus came to the end of the lake the head still hung in the sky, reluctant to leave. (360/240)

The cloud-head is, of course, the uncanny reminder of Feng Xiaogang's decapitated head, as well as an ironic foreshadowing of Fang Yan's "head in the clouds" that will result in his having the murder pinned on him.

When Fang Yan finally tracks down Gao Yang, who has been assuming Fang Yan's identity for some time, Fang Yan is not angry at having been deceived and set up. Rather, he is exulted by the exciting personal history their plan has allowed him to vicariously assume:

> From out of nowhere, I learned that I had been somebody once, a guy who did something important. I had both a reason and the guts to commit murder. For me that was a real high, just knowing I wasn't some mediocrity. I wish it had been true. (348/222)

In an ironic play on Shan Liren's moral in *Wolf* (regarding the relationship between "identification"/image and "proof"/narrative), vastly more attention is given in *Thrills* to working out the chain of identifications and misidentifications of the various characters (Gao Yang impersonating Fang Yan, who was framed as the murderer of Feng Xiaogang disguised as Gao Yang, and who is himself searching for Liu Yan using a photograph that actually depicts Li Jiangyun, and so forth), while the truly shocking revelation (that Gao Yang and his companions beheaded their friend Feng Xiaogang a decade earlier) remains virtually unstated.[13] These questions of which events get historicized and the processes through which they make the transition from event to personal memory or historical record are, in turn, central to the two works I discuss.

Commemoration and Personal Memory

> In this charming civilization, the female beauties trace the outlines of the collective dream with their make-up; their patterns are hieroglyphics describing an inaccessible golden age, which they extol in their ornamentation, since they have no code to express it, and whose mysteries they disclose as they reveal their nudity.
>
> —Claude Lévi-Strauss, *Tristes Tropiques*

The top film of 1995 in the PRC (as ranked by the journal *Dangdai dianying* 當代電影 [Contemporary cinema]) was *Hong yingtao* 紅櫻桃 (Red cherry), a film explicitly advertised as being a "commemoration of the fiftieth anniversary of the world's triumph over fascism." The movie portrays the experiences of three children—two of them Chinese and the third of mixed German and Chinese descent—in Russia and Belarus during World War II. The film synthesized the experiences of about twenty such children, whom the director Ye Daying 葉大鷹 interviewed as he was writing the script.[14] The central story line revolves around a single image: a large eagle and Nazi swastika tattooed onto the Chinese girl's back by a one-legged German general called Dr. von Dietricht (Fig. 10). His intention was to create a "living masterpiece," a work of art that would achieve a certain kind of immortality, aesthetically commemorating the (transitory) glory of the Third Reich. After being rescued by the Russians, the girl is ostracized because the Nazi emblem is taken as an indication of her own political orientation and ideological allegiance. In desperation, she finally takes a flaming torch and attempts to scorch the inscribed flesh off her own back. For this she is hailed as a martyr, and the Allied leaders agree to help her

13. So understated is the account of the actual murder that Jing Wang, in her authoritative discussion of the novel in *High Culture Fever* (278), seems to have overlooked it entirely when she writes that, in the novel, "no real blood is spilled."

14. Ye Daying, "Wo he *Hong Yingtao*," 48–50.

have the image surgically removed, on the condition that they be allowed to keep the flesh on which it was inscribed as a morbid commemoration of Nazi atrocities. The movie itself ends with a black-and-white shot of the actual piece of skin, reputedly on display in a museum in Moscow. This image of the severed fragment of flesh constitutes a potent reminder of the ways in which images of women, and by implication women themselves, may be mobilized and appropriated for the purposes of nationalist historiography.

The figurative inverse of this reductive use of women's images can be found in the film *Contemporary Cinema* ranked as the *second*-best movie of 1995: Jiang Wen's 姜文 *Yangguang canlan de rizi* 陽光燦爛的日子 (In the heat of the sun), based on Wang Shuo's 1991 novel *Ferocious Animals*. Released in the autumn of 1995 almost immediately after *Red Cherry*, *Heat* can also be seen as a commemoration of sorts; a commemoration, moreover, that also revolves around a single, ontologically ambiguous image. This image, as in *Playing for Thrills*, is a photograph, which is dislocated from its original referent and itself becomes productive of a series of new, vicarious identifications. Both the novel and the film versions of *Heat* also succeed in problematizing many of the same assumptions about history, memory, and imagery that tacitly underlie a straightforward reading of *Red Cherry* as an unproblematic historical "commemoration."

Heat portrays the narrator's recollection of a series of events from his childhood in Beijing twenty years earlier. Both the movie and the novel specify that the events in question took place near the end of the Cultural Revolution in the mid-1970s, thus implicitly locating the movie's narrative voice in the contemporary "present." Given that 1995 marked not only the fiftieth anniversary of the end of World War II but also the eve of both the thirtieth anniversary of the commencement of the Chinese Cultural Revolution and the twentieth anniversary of its official conclusion, it is tempting to ask to what extent *Heat* can also be seen as a sort of historical commemoration. At first glance, the film would not appear to be commemorative in the traditional sense of the term. The sorts of politicized images of struggle sessions and mass gatherings characteristic of so many cinematic portrayals of the Cultural Revolution (particularly in its earlier period) are largely absent from this film, which instead concerns itself with the mundane and quotidian adventures of a group of teenagers in Beijing during this period. On the other hand, *Heat* (both the film and the novel versions) can be seen as presenting a rather more subtle commentary on the notion of historical "commemoration" itself.

Told retrospectively by an adult narrator looking back on his youth in Beijing in the mid-1970s, *Heat*[15] details the teenage protagonist Ma Xiaojun's[16] various violent escapades and amorous infatuations. The narrator relates that, at one point, he became obsessed with keys and locks and taught himself to be an amateur "locksmith." At first, he opened doors for friends and neighbors who had inadvertently locked themselves out of their apartments, but after a while he began performing this service without being asked. During one of these solitary, voyeuristic visits to a stranger's apartment, he found himself in the bedroom of an unknown young lady (her name is later revealed to be Mi Lan) only a few years older than himself. He immediately falls in love with her lingering scent, as well as with her photograph, which hangs on her bedroom wall.

A few weeks later, Xiaojun happens to meet the same young lady in the street and recognizes her from the photograph (as well as from an encounter in a police station where both had recently been detained for loitering). Although she repeatedly rebuffs his advances, he ultimately succeeds in ingratiating himself and talks her into letting him be her "younger brother." They end up spending a great deal of time together, and their relationship becomes increasingly (though platonically) intimate. He convinces her to let him introduce her to the other, predominantly male, members of his little "gang" (he, of course, wants to show her off to them). The meeting, however, does not go exactly as Xiaojun planned. Mi Lan, while remaining friendly with him, becomes increas-

15. Although there are several important points of divergence between the novel and film versions of the work, much of my initial discussion is generally relevant to both versions. Therefore, I refer to them as simply *Heat* when my comments would apply equally well to either version and refer to each version by its full name when I need to distinguish the two.

16. The name is from the movie version; the character remains unidentified in Wang Shuo's original novel.

ingly interested in Gao Jin (Liu Yiku, in Jiang Wen's film)—the informal leader of their little gang, who is slightly older than Xiaojun and is presented as being unusually handsome.

The narrator becomes intensely jealous, and the narrative culminates in a birthday banquet held some time later for both Gao Jin and the narrator (who, though of different ages, happen to share the same birthday). By the time of the banquet, Mi Lan and Gao Jin have already started "dating," but she still remains on good terms with Xiaojun. At the banquet, she gives each of them a present, but Xiaojun reciprocates by publicly mocking her. The climax of the scene occurs when the narrator and Gao Jin get into a fight, which quickly escalates. Xiaojun smashes a wine bottle against the table and starts stabbing Gao Jin in the stomach with the broken shards.

This rather striking scene clearly marks the apogee of the work, not only because of the violence of the attack itself but, more important, because of the violence that is imparted onto the narrative structure of the work itself. In Wang Shuo's novel, this narrative meltdown is signaled by the interjection of the narrator's voice, speaking retrospectively from the 1990s, as he presents the problem of memory and commemoration in specifically linguistic and literary terms:

> My mind is now as clear as a bright moon, and I realize I am once again fabricating. At the beginning of this work I swore that I would tell this story truthfully and present it as it really happened. All along, I thought that I was faithfully following the drops of memory as I truthfully narrated my story, and I even discarded a few impressions that struck me as unreliable, no matter how important a role they may have appeared to play in the events and continuity of the plot.
>
> . . . When I decided to use the structure of the novel to try to tell the truth, I committed a fundamental mistake: the stronger my original intentions to tell the truth, the more I was obstructed by the text itself. To my sorrow, I discovered that, from a technical point of view, it was impossible to return to the original truth. The meaning of each of the words that I used always exceeded the specific feeling that I had intended for them to express. Even in the case of the most specific and accurate adjective, when I use it, it always still retains some of its meaning with respect to other objects; it is like a hat that, regardless of how accurately you measure it to fit snugly your own head, will always be separated from your head by a tiny gap. When all these tiny gaps add up, they open up an enormous

space and have the effect of forming a vast gulf between myself and the actual truth, thus in turn creating a new world. I have never seen anything as fond of flaunting itself and such a compulsive liar as is a text. (481–82)

Jiang Wen's cinematic adaptation of Wang Shuo's work, by contrast, leaves out much of the novel's deconstructive ruminations on textuality, semantics, narrative structure, and the like, and instead foregrounds (either explicitly or implicitly) cinematic themes such as those of the image, the gaze, and of cinematicity itself. As a result, the "narrative meltdown" scene is figured rather more dramatically in the film by having the film reel itself appear to sputter back and forth before finally grinding to a halt, as the narrative voiceover steps in with the following meta-textual commentary:

Narrator: (*laughs*) You mustn't believe any of this. I could never have gotten up the courage to do something like this. I keep swearing that I will tell this story as honestly as possible, but no matter how great my desire to tell the truth, the obstructions to that truth are even greater. I therefore realized, with regret, that it was impossible to adhere to reality. My memory is constantly being twisted around by my emotions, torturing me until I am completely confused. I now suspect that the first time I met Mi Lan was actually a fabrication. Actually, I never did meet her in the street. The afternoon Liu Yiku invited her over and Big Ant and I waited at the gate for him was actually the first time that I met Mi Lan. That also explains why that day I went to play Vasily[17] with Big Ant, rather than staying to chat with her: because Mi Lan and I were not close at all at that point. In fact, I never really knew her. Oh God! Was Mi Lan the person in that photograph after all? And what about [Xiaojun's other young female friend] Yu Beipei? Why has she suddenly disappeared? Maybe, maybe they were actually the same person after all? I simply can't bear to consider the implications of that.

The story that I had with such truthful intentions begun to tell has come to be such a bundle of distortions and lies. Maybe I should just give up right here? No, and you wouldn't want me to, either. Now I understand how those compulsive liars must feel—if they want to become a truthful person, it is simply impossible.

17. From the Soviet film *Lenin in 1918*, which is projected on the outdoor movie screen (see discussion below), and which Xiaojun himself acts out at another point in the story, when he (allegedly) first met Mi Lan.

> Look! Sometimes a certain sound, or a certain smell, can bring you back to reality.
>
> My mind is as clear as a bright moon. OK, let me return to telling my story, not caring anymore whether it is true or false.
>
> I remember that the day of our birthdays passed uneventfully. Liu Yiku and I were very happy and shared many toasts with Mi Lan. Oh, yes, Yu Beipei was also there; I had almost forgotten. Everyone brought many presents, and Mi Lan was very friendly with me. And later, we all got drunk.[18]

As this narrative voiceover is progressing, the images on screen begin to rewind back through the banquet and the preparations for the banquet and then proceed to present a glimpse of a "new" perspective on the banquet scene itself. The result is that, even as the narrative voiceover is advising us what to believe, the image on the screen is simultaneously using purely visual cues to express a similar point.

Postmodernist theorists working in various disciplines have critically interrogated the role of narratives and imagery in our understanding of both history and subjectivity. One general continuity in these discussions is a recognition of the role played by narrative or visual schemata in conditioning the subject's understanding of its position within a larger social and cultural environment. At the same time, however, the postmodern critiques of meta-narratives and visual simulacra differ in at least one crucial respect: namely, that narrative schemata operate, almost by definition, by placing the subject within a chronological trajectory of some sort (spurious though this trajectory may be). By contrast, the visual image or simulacrum is frequently viewed as having the effect of contesting and subverting these same chronological boundaries. Film can, perhaps, be seen as occupying the intersection of these two tendencies. Its temporal format makes it almost inevitable that it will rely on narrative structures of some sort or another, and the visual quality of its medium suggests that it will always retain the possibility of crystallizing into myriad frames of atemporal, individual images. Because of cinema's position as mediating between the roles played by both narratives and visual simulacra in structuring our understanding of history

18. Transcribed from the movie; my own translation is used in place of the movie's original English subtitles.

and personal memory, I next look at two crucial scenes that director Jiang Wen introduced into Wang Shuo's text while translating the novel's original textual and narrativistic concerns into the more explicitly visual medium that is cinema.

In the first scene, Xiaojun has used his skeleton key to let himself into a stranger's apartment and is lying on the bed eating dumplings when he suddenly notices a telescope on the wall. He uses the telescope voyeuristically to watch his high school teacher urinate behind a wall visible from the apartment window. Then he proceeds to spin around and around while continuing to peer through the lens. During one dizzying rotation, he catches sight of a momentary, blurred image of a young woman, which turns out to be a photograph of Mi Lan. Continuing to use the telescopic lens as a prosthetic eye (Fig. 11), he slowly gropes forward, until finally reaching the actual photograph (Fig. 12). At the end of the scene, the photographic image of Mi Lan fades into a "live" image of Yu Beipei,[19] a young female member of Xiaojun's little gang and also, it turns out, the person who first mentioned Mi Lan's name to Xiaojun (Figs. 13–14). This cinematic morphing of one young woman's face into another has the effect of planting the suggestion, developed later in the work, that there is probably a considerable degree of transference between Xiaojun's memories of the two figures.[20]

This scene with the telescope is not found in the original novel,[21] but its insertion into the film follows logically from the novel's concerns

---

19. The second character in Beipei's 北蓓 given name should technically be pronounced "bei" (this particular character being typically found, in modern Chinese, in the compound *beilei* 蓓蕾, meaning, interestingly enough, "unopened flower bud"). However, the text observes that everyone calls her "Yu Bei*pei*," and further notes at one point that even she herself is not entirely certain of the correct pronunciation of that particular ideograph.

20. Cf., e.g., the convergence of Li Jiangyun and the photograph of Liu Yan in *Thrills*.

21. Compare, however, the photograph scene in *Thrills*, cited above, in which Fang Yan suddenly has the impression that he is seeing his companions as if he were "a movie director with a zoom lens moving in for close-ups" (262/91).

with the constructivity of visual experience. In the novel, the evanescent quality of Xiaojun's first sight of the photograph is narrated directly, and is further reinforced by the narrator's implicitly retrospective commentary that he later came to doubt that the photograph had actually existed. The film is somewhat more subtle on this point. Rather than contributing further to a potential polarity between the cinematic image (which implicitly presents the world from Xiaojun's point of view but also happens to coincide with what the audience sees) and the narrative voice (corresponding to Xiaojun as an adult), this particular scene manages instead to use the lens of the miniature telescope to integrate both sides of this schizophrenic duality *back into the cinematic image itself.* This scene, therefore, presents an early hint that the cinematic image (that is, what the film audience perceives via the prosthetic eye of the camera) itself may be somewhat less than completely reliable. At the same time, in allowing the image to convey its own unreliability directly, the film simultaneously, and paradoxically, allows the same image to retain a certain degree of authenticity (a paradoxical situation reminiscent of the proverbial Cretan who states that all Cretans are liars). This move, moreover, has the effect of shifting some of the "meta-narrative" concerns away from the narrativizing "voice" (i.e., the narrator's voiceover) onto the cinematic image itself. This has the double effect of, on one hand, helping the film move away from the novel's binary dichotomy between the "unreliable" narrative and the implicitly "reliable" meta-narrative voice, and, on the other hand, of producing a certain "split" in the position created for the spectator. This "split" is created by drawing the viewer both into the child's gaze, in all of its unreliability, and by inscribing the meta-narrative commentary onto that very gaze itself.

Although this first scene interpolated by Jiang Wen is concerned with the relationship between voyeurism and the image, the second interpolated scene deals with the relationship between voyeurism and spectacle. The latter scene opens with a rather stunning view of a standalone outdoor movie screen (Figs. 15–16). Immediately preceding a quintessentially voyeuristic sequence in which Xiaojun and his other teenage friends sneak into an adjacent moviehouse where many of the adults in the community are watching a pornographic Soviet film, the youngsters watch, and play around, the outdoor screen. At times, the stand-alone movie screen's image coincides precisely with the image that we ourselves see (thus placing us precisely in the position of the movie's own interior spectators); at other times the camera takes a step back and allows us to see the outdoor movie screen enframed by its immediate surroundings. Most dramatic, however, is when Xiaojun (and the camera) swings around *behind* the free-standing movie image, producing a scenario in which we see exactly the same image that the movie's internal audience is seeing (it is a mirror image, of course), although spatially the site of our, and of the camera's, gaze is that of the *object* of the internal movie audience's own gaze.

The movie version of *Heat* is particularly explicit in developing how this figurative "screen" of contemporary cultural productions (and particularly films) functions as a tertiary "mirror stage" through which the subject perceives himself. Repeatedly throughout the film, we glimpse Xiaojun peering at his own reflection in a mirror. Significantly, many of these specular moments feature Xiaojun *watching himself act out various roles, particularly ones from other movies.* Most dramatic, in this respect, is a scene (subsequently edited out of some versions of the film) that follows shortly after the narrative meltdown scene described above. It begins with Xiaojun riding his bicycle along a dirt road, with Mi Lan sitting behind him. She requests that he stop, saying that she will walk the rest of the way. Her departure is followed by an extended nightmare sequence, in which Xiaojun sees himself, Mi Lan, and many of the other youngsters in his little clique parodically acting out scenes from popular war films.

This nightmare sequence presents a particularly evocative illustration of the ways in which Xiaojun's self-perception is mediated through cultural images such as those of popular cinema, while at the same time introducing an interesting twist—it is actually *the woman's gaze* that plays a crucial role in the construction of the psycho-cultural "screen." For instance, after Xiaojun appears to awake from his war-film nightmare, he finds himself with Mi Lan in the middle of a large field. Suddenly stricken with a painful stomachache, Xiaojun attempts to hide behind some bushes to relieve himself but is repeatedly frustrated by a deviously voyeuristic Mi Lan, who pursues him through the field with a bicycle bell and continually peeks at him when he squats down to relieve himself. Eventually, Xiaojun wakes up for real and realizes that the second vision was a nightmare as well and that the bicycle bell belongs to an old man who found him lying by the side of the road and is currently standing over him to see if he is okay.

Although this particular sequence does not appear in the novel, the novel *does* explicitly acknowledge the ways in which Ma Xiaojun continually finds himself haunted by the intrusive and destabilizing power of Mi Lan's female gaze. For instance, the narrator remarks at one point:

> She [Mi Lan] stared at me [Xiaojun], looking into me with those eyes sharp as a drill and deep as a dark pool. Often she would look at me such that my words would melt as they reached my mouth, and I would stand there smiling stupidly without knowing what to do. Often I would try to use the same sort of gaze to stare back at her. At times like those our face-off would become a test of willpower, and nine times out of ten I would be the one stared down, forced to avert my eyes. Even today, I consider myself to have rather good bearing and self-control, and yet I still have not gotten used to being the object of her gaze. An overly concentrated gaze will often cause me to begin to doubt myself, and in this gaze is always contained a bundle of overly complicated emotions. Even a completely careless glance can have the effect of causing the person who has been glanced at to feel uneasy, even to the point of feeling the need for self-examination. This can have the effect of destroying tacit understandings, and I consider it a personal affront.
>
> She was very pleased with the power of her eyes, and although this might be seen as her way of strengthening her own sense of self-fascination, at the same time I couldn't deny the possibility that she was purposefully using her gaze as a way of belittling and humiliating me. (448)

This same dialectics of vision and displaced voyeurism, finally, are brought together in one of the posters used to advertise the movie (Fig. 17). The top half of the poster contains an image of Xiaojun and Mi Lan, both smiling sweetly as they gaze out at the (implicit) viewer. In the lower right-hand corner of the page (Fig. 17, detail) are four stills depicting scenes from the movie. Most intriguing, however, is the image in the lower left-hand corner of the poster, which consists of a large photograph of Mi Lan wearing reflective sunglasses, staring, as it were,

Fig. 17 Advertisement for *Heat* (detail).

directly at the poster's viewers.[22] Reflected in her shades are two separate images of Xiaojun and Liu Yiku (Gao Jin), respectively—suggesting that Xiaojun's subjectivity and self-conception are already mediated through the displaced "mirror stage" of Mi Lan's own enigmatic gaze.

This film poster mirrors the scene in the film in which Ma Xiaojun first speaks to Mi Lan on the street—a scene in which the reflection of his face is clearly visible in the dark lenses of her sunglasses. Mi Lan's reflective sunglasses, therefore, provide an evocative parallel of the outdoor film screen discussed above. In both cases the process by which the subject's self-perception is produced through a double identification with/against both externalized images, on one hand, as well as with/against the invisible gaze (in this case, a very explicitly gendered gaze) that is imagined as lying behind those same images.

22. This latter image is itself a miniature version of the same poster most commonly used to advertise the movie when it first came out in Beijing.

Mao II

> Mao Zedong. She liked that name all right. But it is funny how a picture. It is funny how a picture what?
>
> —Don DeLillo, *Mao II*

In the narrative meltdown scene in Wang Shuo's original novel, the line "My mind is now as clear as a bright moon" occurs at the beginning of the supposedly lucid commentary of the narrative voiceover. In the movie version of the work, by contrast, the same line marks the conclusion of the schizophrenic interjection and the recommencement of the narrated story itself. Furthermore, in the film the line about the narrator's head being like a bright moon coincides with the visual image of a mural depicting Mao's portrait with bright rays radiating out from his head (Fig. 18). This Mao portrait, which reappears hanging from the rearview mirror of the limousine in the movie's coda (Fig. 19), presents a suggestive parallel with the other semiotically ambiguous fetishized image in the work: namely, the photograph of Mi Lan. The movie stops short of making the connection explicit, but implies that the conventional historical view of the Cultural Revolution may be compared to Xiaojun's spurious reconstruction of his own childhood. In both cases, an entire narrative ends up being grounded on, and inspired by, a single iconic image—here, the portraits of Mao Zedong and Mi Lan, respectively—an image, moreover, that shares with postmodern simulacra the potential to be infinitely reproduced, as well as to become dissassociated from its original referent.

Wang Shuo's novel presents the linkage between Mao's and Mi Lan's portraits even more explicitly. When Xiaojun recalls, at the beginning of *Ferocious Animals*, his first sight of Mi Lan's photograph, he remarks, "With the exception of the great Chairman Mao and his closest comrades in arms, that was the first time in my life that I had seen a color photograph capable of producing a true mimetic effect" (413). Similarly, in *Playing for Thrills*, there is a comparable linkage between the photographic image of Liu Yan (Li Jiangyun) and the ubiquitous Mao portrait. At one point, while looking at the old photograph, Fang Yan finds himself speculating:

"But there was someone, a royal consort, I think, though her face is blurred and her name escapes me. But then we knew our dear Chairman Mao better than anyone, didn't we? And still if I don't head over to Tiananmen Square for a look once in a while, I can never remember how the old fellow combed his hair, straight back, or parted." (267/100)

Like Cao Buxing's fly, the portraits of Mao represent points of transcendental, unquestioned verisimilitude that condition the perception of the entire ideological screen in which they are embedded. Conversely, the strength of the narratives that develop out of these sorts of images (both the Mao portraits and the women's photographs), in turn, help to buttress the truth-effect of these spurious images. Whether looking at the photograph of Mi Lan or at Mao's portrait, Jiang Wen's film foregrounds the ability of images to structure individual or collective identities in subtle, and largely unconscious, ways. I therefore conclude by turning to some additional uses of these same Mao portraits, which directly subvert their conventional significance.

The circulation of Mao imagery in modern Chinese society provides a powerful node onto which various sorts of cultural and national identity may be projected. Similarly, the global dissemination and circulation of the image of the anonymous 1989 "lone rebel" provides an equally convenient figurative node onto which a bewildering range of political and ideological aspirations are projected. In the latter half of the twentieth century, Maoist iconography enjoyed several periods of impressive popularity. The most familiar and politically influential such period was, of course, the Cultural Revolution, which was characterized by a ubiquitous reproduction and dissemination of Mao's distinctive mug through virtually every corner of Chinese society. More recently, however, the post-1989 period has witnessed an explosion of Maoist imagery that frequently verges as closely on the sacrilegious as the original Maoist era iconography approached the hagiographic.[23] The limousine's "Mao portrait" rearview mirror ornament at the end of *In the Heat of the Sun* is one example of this phenomenon, as are such veritably postmodernist cases as the Beijing native and current New York resident conceptual artist Zhang Hongtu's 張宏圖 "Chairmen Mao series,"

23. See Barmé, *Shades of Mao.*

which presents various parodic renditions of the famous Mao portrait, as well as New York fashion designer Vivienne Tam, who has designed a line of clothing incorporating several of Zhang's parodic images.

An excellent illustration of the simultaneous centrality and invisible transparency of Mao's portrait can be seen in Wang Jinsong's 王劲松 1990 painting *Taking a Picture in Front of Tiananmen*,[24] which presents a group of Chinese tourists assembled for a photograph in front of the Tiananmen Square portrait of the Great Helmsman. Ironically, the portrait itself (ostensibly the reason the tourists decided to pose in that particular location in the first place) is almost completely obscured by the tourists' heads, particularly by the spectral, faceless figures in the second tier. Here, Mao's image has been literally reduced to an empty signifier, but one that plays a central role in anchoring the social fabric woven around it. Similarly, the "lone rebel" photograph has inspired its own philosophico-parodic riffs. For example, in his "Reasons of State" photography series (exhibited in Houston in 1999), the Peruvian native and current Houston resident artist Fernando Castro uses imaginative restagings of the Tiananmen photograph to explore visually some of the ethical, political, and philosophical implications of the image.[25]

In Wang Shuo's first novel after he started writing fiction again in 2000, *Kanshangqu hen mei* 看上去很美 (It looks really beautiful), these themes of Maoist hagiography and iconoclasm intersect momentarily with the theme of figurative flies with which I opened my discussion of Wang's works. The scene in question occurs in the latter portion of the novel and describes the beginning of the Cultural Revolution. The young protagonist Fang Qiangqiang and his friends are singing revolutionary songs, while laughing at their school's principal: "Both singing and laughing at each other; what we were laughing at was the school's principal, standing up on the stage. He was also beating his clapper with a single hand, [seeming to grab] one handful after another, as if there were a fly flying around in front of his eyes."[26] Here, the intended

24. See Minglu Gao, *Inside Out*, plate 36, and discussion on p. 156.

25. Johnson, "Photos Tell of Courage, Defiance."

26. Wang Shuo, *Kanshangqu hen mei*, 231. Subsequent references to this work are cited in the text.

sublimity of the mass political gathering comes full circle with the explicit absurdity of the school principal gesticulating on stage; mediating between these two extremes is the image of a figurative fly. This "fly," invisible in and of itself, represents a tiny imperfection in the choreographed reality of the demonstration that, in turn, conditions and reinforces how the children view the truth-value of the (screen of the) political gathering itself.

It Looks Really Beautiful, published in 1999, was Wang Shuo's first literary work since his public announcement in 1992 that he was giving up the writing of fiction. The novel, set in the years (1961–66) leading up to the Cultural Revolution, describes the childhood of Fang Qiangqiang, who is the same Fang Yan featured in *Playing for Thrills* and several of Wang Shuo's other works. Most of the other children who populate the novel will also be familiar to readers of Wang Shuo's fiction. Just as many of Wang Shuo's novels feature a character's archaeological reconstruction of his own past, similarly this latter work is portrayed as an archeological descent into Wang Shuo's own literary past. As Wang Shuo writes in the preface:

> This novel of mine is simply a reminiscence of life from years past. A beginning. . . .
>
> All along, this novel has been fermenting in my mind. Or, you could say that, all along, I have been using my brain cells to write it. The actual first day of composition can be traced back to twenty years ago, when I first thought of pursuing this writing career. When I worked out the plot of my first novel, I simultaneously mapped out the plot of this one. (5–6)

At the same time, just as Wang Shuo, in many of his works, attempts to distinguish between subjective or reconstructive histories, on one hand, and objective, factual histories, on the other, in the preface to this most recent work, he similarly warns readers that "one's own memory cannot be trusted" and that the novel is nothing more than a "work of fiction" (8).

Given the degree to which many of Wang's earlier novels explicitly thematize the infinite reproducibility of simulacra and question discourses of authentic origin, it is particularly ironic that this 1999 novel was published under the shadow of Wang's concern with issues of textual authenticity in relation to contemporary copyright law. The final page of the book contains an unusually elaborate legal disclaimer, beginning with several lengthy quotes from relevant statutes of Chinese copyright law. The disclaimer goes on to note that each "authentic" copy of the new novel contains a CD with the complete text of Wang Shuo's four-volume "selected works" (*Wang Shuo wenji* 王朔文集) (which, in fact was precisely the edition of Wang Shuo's earlier works most widely pirated to begin with).[27] The irony here surely lies in the fact that the "authenticity" of the printed document is being validated by means of a CD, which is, if anything, even more easily copied than a printed book (as evidenced, for example, by the scores of Wang Shuo's compatriots who cheerfully sell bootleg CDs on the streets of Beijing and other major Chinese cities).

Just as Fang Yan's and Ma Xiaojun's attempts to reconstruct their own personal histories are stimulated, and complicated, by the existence of photographic simulacra, similarly Wang Shuo's most recent, semi-autobiographical novel delves into his own literary and personal origins against the backdrop of the uncontrolled dissemination of pirated editions ("print simulacra") of his own earlier literary traces. These (pirated/piratable) literary traces, just like the photographs that abound in them, are truly "afterimages of the flesh" that contaminate, but also catalyze, the screen/narratives in which they are embedded.

---

27. Each volume of my set of Wang Shuo's *Selected Works* (itself a pirated edition) contains a warning on the last page stating: "Recently it has been noticed that a large number of pirated editions of *Wang Shuo's Selected Works* have appeared on the market. Our company solemnly declares: All of these who are not entrusted by our company to distribute this book . . . ."

10

Chu T'ien-wen and Cinematic Shadows

When we escape the logic of words, abandoning even their semiotic functions, they become shards of colored glass in a kaleidoscope that forms magnificent visual scenes.

—Chu T'ien-wen, *Notes of a Desolate Man*

In a curious echo of the thematic linkage of flies, vision, and representation in Wang Shuo's works, Taiwan novelist Chu T'ien-wen 朱天文 (1956–) concludes the paragraph from which the epigraph above was taken by describing the sense of entering the gaze of a fly's compound eyes: "I lost myself in this color garden of pure sensation, as if flying in a world seen through the compound-lens eyes of a fly, and forgot to return to the real world."[1] A similar fly metaphor is used in the following chapter to evoke the spectral presence of the narrator's deceased friend, Ah Yao: "Turning-to-dust red, old folks are partial to turning-to-dust red. I recited my own sutra to get through the days and brave the storm of loneliness, in the fashion of Ah Yao, the human Fly, who telephoned for my help from the other side of the world" (93/67).

Chu T'ien-wen's prizewinning 1994 novel, *Huangren shouji* 荒人手記 (Notes of a desolate man), describes the narrator Xiao Shao's attempts

1. Chu T'ien-wen, *Huangren shouji*, 89; idem, *Notes of a Desolate Man*, 65. Subsequent references to these two works are cited in the text; the first number refers to the Chinese edition; the second, to the corresponding passage in the English translation, which has occasionally been modified here.

to work through his sense of loss following the death of his close friend Ah Yao from complications resulting from AIDS.[2] This comparison of Ah Yao to a human fly, accordingly, refers to the use of a fly's compound eyes to describe a splintered kaleidoscope that is a world in which lexical terms have become disassociated from their ostensible referents. At the same time, it gestures back to an earlier discussion in which the narrator invokes an image from the horror film *The Fly*[3] to describe Ah Yao's dehumanized status as someone who is living abroad and dying of AIDS:

> I later realized too that [Ah Yao] would call for no other reason than to hear my voice, which connected him with his past, like a safety rope thrown just in time to prevent him from falling into an abyss. Our conversations preserved for him the feeling that he was a human being, not an animal. Cowering in a phone booth on some street in a foreign land, cradling the receiver in his ear, he was like the tragic protagonist in *The Fly*, who, after finally finding his girlfriend, begs her to help change him back into a human being. (42/27)

Here, Chu T'ien-wen uses the figure of the fly (eye) both as a trope for the reconstitutive act of recovering Ah Yao's splintered memories and as a symbol for the figure of Ah Yao himself.

In the following discussion, I examine the ways in which Chu, in *Notes of a Desolate Man* and other texts, uses the explosion of visuality featured above to re-examine issues of perception, commoditization, and desire. I argue that she ultimately uses a "homosexualized" model of nonreproductive desire to describe a specific postmodern condition wherein the visual image comes to function as the quintessential commodity fetish. I then conclude by turning to a specific scene (of eye licking) from Hou Hsiao-hsien's 侯孝賢 1998 film *Haishang hua* 海上花 (Flowers of Shanghai)—for which Chu T'ien-wen wrote the screenplay—and use it as a starting point for recapitulating the central conclusions of this project.

---

2. The original, Chinese version of *Notes of a Desolate Man* received the first-place prize in *Lianhe wenxue*'s prestigious annual literary competition. Howard Goldblatt and Sylvia Lin's 1999 English translation was also reviewed very favorably and was ranked by both the *New York Times* and the *Los Angeles Times* as one of the best works of the year.

3. It is unclear whether the reference is to Kurt Neumann's 1958 film or to David Cronenberg's 1986 remake.

Bodily Traces

She [Eileen Chang] also said that colors are a kind of language.

—Chu T'ien-wen, "A Flower Recalls Its Previous Lives"

Chu T'ien-wen has been a prominent figure on the Taiwan literary scene for the past three decades, producing an impressive oeuvre of novels, stories, memoirs, and film scripts. Her early work from the 1970s and early 1980s is often regarded as characterized by a sentimental nostalgia for mainland Chinese culture.[4] However, her 1990 collection of short stories, *Shijimo de huali* 世紀末的華麗 (Fin-de-siècle splendor), consists of startling and subtle explorations of the complexities of contemporary "postmodern" existence and marks an important turning point in her career. In 1994, Chu published *Notes of a Desolate Man*, which developed some of the aesthetic and intellectual directions begun in works like *Fin-de-Siècle Splendor.*

As its title suggests, one of the central concerns of *Fin-de-Siècle Splendor* is precisely a kind of postmodern, and specifically visual, culture. For instance, in her short story "Yidian bu zai" 伊甸不再 (Eden no more), Chu addresses the question of the fetishistic potential of the disarticulated photograph that Wang Shuo was simultaneously exploring in his own fiction. Chu's female protagonist Zhen Sulan is described as gazing endlessly at an old, black-and-white family photograph. For Zhen, this image not only provides a nostalgic link to her own past but also performs the equally important role of *framing* that same memory, preventing it from being contaminated by the stark, unpleasant reality within which it is embedded. Combined, therefore, with this interest in framing is a parallel concern that the photographic image might somehow manage to escape the confines of its original frame:

Her three sisters stood next to her father. When the wind blows hard, it seems as if the six people [in the photograph] are crowded into the right corner of the photo frame as if they were about to be released from the frame. Sulan would perpetually stare at it, transfixed; and asking herself if they actually did

4. See discussion in Yvonne Sung-Sheng Chang, "Chu T'ien-wen and Taiwan's Recent Cultural and Literary Trends."

succeed in being released from the picture frame, what would the world be like? Where would they be released to?[5]

This family photograph represents not only a specific physical artifact but also Sulan's attempt to impose a certain kind of ontological order on her own life. Confronted with emotional adversity, one of Sulan's primary defense mechanisms is to pull back and attempt to frame the emotionally unpleasant scene as though it were a still picture. As Ban Wang has observed, this use of pictures as empty nodes of imaginary nostalgia is a recurrent device in Chu's fiction, and many of her film scripts incorporate still photographs in a comparable manner.[6] The photograph functions here almost as a symbol of its own mimeticism—a meta-metaphor for nostalgia itself.

Chu T'ien-wen's use of the photograph as a symbol of imaginary nostalgia is also arguably a symptom of her melancholic relation to her own literary development. As she was growing up, Chu was explicitly and profoundly influenced by Eileen Chang's works; similarly, Chu's personal tutor was none other than Eileen Chang's first hus-band, the prominent philosopher and literary critic Hu Lancheng 胡蘭成. Chu T'ien-wen herself acknowledges her use of Hu Lancheng as an intermediary to Eileen Chang when she remarks, in the preface to a recent compilation of her works, "Because my 'love for a person's house extends to the crows on the roof,' therefore since I could not meet Eileen Chang, I settled for seeing Hu Lancheng."[7] Chu's close personal and intellectual relationship to Hu Lancheng can thus be seen as an ironic attempt to recuperate the (literary) relationship with Eileen Chang she had never had. Furthermore, as I discuss below, Chu's recent literary works, particularly *Notes of a Desolate Man*, constitute a similarly nostalgic attempt at once to recuperate and to defer her earlier relationship with Hu Lancheng.

At one point in the novel, the narrator, Xiao Shao, recalls a time when "the only thing I was able to read was an article on color, some research on the visual imagery of red and green in Chinese poetry"

5. Chu T'ien-wen, "Yidian bu zai," 118.
6. Ban Wang, "Re-enchanting the Disenchanted Image."
7. Chu T'ien-wen, "Huayi qianshen," 43.

(89/64). Xiao Shao intersperses discussions of this article—which is described as consisting primarily of "names for reds and greens from several color systems" (89/64)—with more abstract discussions of the epistemology and ontology of visual perception. For example, Shao cites Goethe to the effect that "the key to the study of color lies in strictly separating the subjective from the objective" (90/65) and then follows up this allusion with a brief discussion of the epistemology of visual perception:

> Do the colors of the natural world exist by themselves or through our seeing eyes? Or is it in between, like with Monet, who developed cataracts in his later years and had to rely on labels to choose colors for his paintings? After painting lilies for over twenty years, were what he painted the colors in his memory after his eyesight dimmed, or were they the colors he saw in the absence of vision, light, and color? (90/66)

This passage echoes not only Wumingshi's earlier ruminations on the epistemology and ontology of color perception, but also the concerns with the relationship between color and memory found in some of Eileen Chang's texts (Eileen Chang passed away the year following the publication of *Notes of a Desolate Man*).

In fact, Chu may be said to have inherited from Chang a peculiarly *visual* writing style that uses rich imagery as a figure for a frozen slice of time, a final bulwark against the looming tides of historical contingency.[8] More specifically, just as Eileen Chang claimed to have inherited her color sense from her mother, similarly Chu T'ien-wen could be seen as having inherited her fascination with colors from her literary "mother," Eileen Chang. Compare, for instance, Chang's discussion of "unevenly contrastive" colors in her essay "The Guileless Words of a Child" ("for example, using sapphire blue to match apple green, or pine green to match scarlet red, or scallion green to match peach red") with Chu's famously virtuosic display of visual brilliance at the end of the chapter containing the Goethe discussion, which consists of nearly two pages of a kaleidoscopic display of lexical variations on the color terms for red and green (of which I cite only a small fraction here):

---

8. See, e.g., Ban Wang, "Re-enchanting the Disenchanted Image."

> Whale fin red, the red color of whale fins shining over the city.
>
> Lips just turning red, the young red beak of a house parrot.
>
> Red under the water, the round morning sun turns the water red. Barbarian brocade red, a narrow blouse with short sleeves in barbarian brocade red. Spoiled peach red, putting on make-up in spoiled peach red. Flapping fish red, startling drumbeats make the fish jump and flap its red fins. Cut flower red, light fragrance from red cut flowers caressing the sleeve. . . .
>
> Peeking undergarment red, five-foot red, a window of red, a speck of red, . . .
>
> A whole window of clamorous red.
>
> Redlike, floating green and redlike, but nothing happens.
>
> Chaotic red, someone submerged in chaotic red and terrifying green. Terrifying green, startling green, pallid green, decadent green, fatigue green, . . .
>
> . . . .
>
> Vermilion from jade, complexion vermilion, two-ribbed vermilion, cannot vermilion, twice-proscribed vermilion, powder vermilion, lip grit vermilion, cold water vermilion. (90–92/66–67)

As I argue below, it is significant that this disassociation of color terms (*se* 色) from any concrete anchor occurs precisely in the context of a larger discussion of the disassociation of sexual desire (*se* 色) from any concrete concern with reproduction and progenation.

First, however, I begin my reading of *Notes of a Desolate Man* by considering a specific use of a photograph. At one point, the protagonist is traveling in Italy with his lover at the time. There they visit the residence of a mutual friend: an Italian by the name of Momo. Momo's apartment is adorned with a variety of China-related souvenirs and other memorabilia that he collected as an international student in China in the mid-1970s. These mementos consist predominantly of various sorts of visual artifacts, including:

> Zhen Banqiao's bamboo painting and calligraphy, woodblock prints from Suzhou. . . . Paper puppets for shadow shows hung from a lamp; there was a movie poster for *Woman Basketball Player No. 5*; and above his bed hung two framed calligraphic scrolls in the flowing cursive style, both ghastly. (74/53)

Occupying a privileged position at the beginning of this chain of visual signifiers is a 1974 photograph of the Italian Momo, as a foreign student at Liaoning University,

> [dressed] in his Mao jacket, crouching in a vegetable field, but it wasn't clear if he was actually planting anything. The photo was black and white, but you could almost see the Mediterranean blue in his eyes transported in the Great Northern Wasteland, where the sky's edge hung so low. (73–74/52–53)

Although this initial photograph is presented without authorial commentary, its semi-parodic significance is clearly suggested by the iconic company it keeps (e.g., the "ghastly" calligraphic scrolls, the propagandistic movie poster).

The photograph of Momo has a curiously ambivalent status in this passage. On one hand, it is virtually "beyond representation"—despite its status as a mere black-and-white photo, it almost comes to assume the status of a transcendental signifier for the "reality" that lies behind it ("you could almost see the Mediterranean blue in his eyes transported to the Great Northern Wasteland"). On the other hand, the photograph, in conjunction with the other visual signifiers in Momo's apartment, functions for Xiao Shao as a figurative Lacanian mirror, with the key difference being that it does *not* give him a jubilant impression of corporeal integrity, but instead leads him *backwards* to the other side of the figurative Lacanian looking glass, to the state of being once again a "body in bits and pieces." As the narrator observes at one point, "When I looked at this [collection of visual images], I couldn't help feeling that I was witnessing the carcass of my own youth scattered all over the place" (74/53).

Momo's kaleidoscopic array of visual images constitutes for him a sort of "artificial nostalgia," in the sense that the "past" it preserves is one from which he was (always-)already self-alienated as a foreigner in China in the latter years of the Cultural Revolution period. Ironically, however, this same visual array also inspires a similarly displaced sense of nostalgia on the part of the novel's narrator, Xiao Shao. Being from Taiwan, Xiao Shao himself could not have visited Mainland China in the 1970s, but it is quite possible that he shared the author Chu T'ien-wen's own "nostalgic" obsession with Mainland China during that same period. In any event, the narrator's sense of viewing his own fractured past ("the carcass of my own youth") is grounded on a chain of multiply displaced imaginary identifications (Xiao Shao → Momo → Mainland China), which simultaneously gives rise to *both* the nostalgic "form of . . . totality" that serves to anchor his sense of self *and* the "fragmented body image" to which it is imaginatively opposed.

The identificatory calculus on which this particular scene is grounded is, in turn, one of the structuring principles of the novel as a whole. *Notes of a Desolate Man* developed out of an earlier, aborted work written in the voice of a heterosexual woman.[9] Finding herself unable to complete this version of the work, Chu decided instead to start over again, using the voice of a gay Taiwanese man of her acquaintance. The resulting protagonist of *Notes of a Desolate Man*, Xiao Shao, is himself engaged in a similar process of alienated self-narration, as he attempts to perceive himself through the figurative lens of a series of lovers and intimate acquaintances he has had over the years. The most prominent of these acquaintances is clearly Ah Yao, and the novel both opens and concludes in a melancholic mode, mourning Ah Yao's premature death due to complications resulting from AIDS. In fact, Chu's entire work can be seen as an extended elegy for the deceased Ah Yao, since it appears that his death has served as the primary catalyst for the narrator's extended reflections on mortality, solitude, and desolation that constitute the core of the novel.

In the novel, Xiao Shao "narrates himself" through the mediated identification with his former lovers, just as Chu T'ien-wen is finally able to narrate *herself* through the ventriloquistic identification with the story of her unnamed gay friend. This chain of mediated identifications is brought full circle when it is revealed that it is precisely in this novel—arguably one of Chu's least autobiographical works to date—that Chu comes closest to addressing the issue of her adolescent relationship with Hu Lancheng and Eileen Chang: an issue, up to that point, she had never addressed publicly. I return to Chu's retrospective essay on Hu Lancheng below, as the issue of mediated self-perception on which it is grounded is central to my discussion.

Notes of a Desolate Man is a reflection on both a contemporary transnational gay subculture and the postmodern fracturing of linear narratives. In fact, the narrative modes of these dimensions of the work are themselves closely interrelated. First, the novel is not only about queer

9. See the discussion in Kim-chu Ng, "Shenji zhi wu," 277–81.

individuals and their lifestyles but also seeks to use the *concept* of homosexuality as an ur-trope of modern existence, emphasizing its lack of procreative teleology and the manifest fluidity of the social relationships on which it is grounded (as, for example, with the constitution of the transnational gay "subculture" itself). Second, the novel mirrors this rejection of teleological imperatives at the level of its own narration—it makes no attempt to present Xiao Shao's personal history and cultural milieu in a linear fashion; rather, it tantalizes the reader with bits and pieces of that history, as if refracted through a prism. Similarly, the work details the "postmodern" quality of Xiao Shao's cultural environment, not so much through direct narration as through an illustrative mélange of references to high and low culture. Finally, these parallel themes of homoeroticism and postmodernity are explicitly brought together in the novel's contention that postmodern culture is characterized by a generalized "homosexualization of heterosexuality." Below, I consider each of these dimensions in more detail, looking first at the novel's treatment of homosexuality and then proceeding to the closely related issue of postmodern culture.

"Homosexualization" of Heterosexuality

> I'll never forget, when the nurses pulled back the bedsheet, how Ah Yao looked when dead—there was nothing left of him. All that remained on that naked bag of bones, eaten away by AIDS, were two bony knees and a superfluous, rumpled penis. As the only fleshy part of his body that remained, it looked abnormally, even shockingly big.
>
> —Chu T'ien-wen, *Notes of a Desolate Man*

In Chapter 3, I discussed two fictional passages that implicitly comment on the theme of the desublimation of the phallus: the first appears in Chen Sen's nineteenth-century homoerotic novel, *Precious Mirror for Evaluating Flowers*, and the other in the contemporary Taiwan author Wu Chi-wen's 1996 rewriting of that same work. In both cases, I suggest that the penis is paradoxically fetishized at precisely the moment its symbolic significance as the "phallus" is most explicitly challenged. In the epigraph to this section, I cite a similar moment in Chu T'ien-wen's homoerotic novel (published two years before Wu Chi-wen's), in which the narrator's memory of the shriveled body of his deceased friend Ah Yao is oddly dominated by the figure of his "superfluous, rumpled penis." In all three cases, a careful examination of the penis has the effect of ironically "dephallicizing" it, of stripping it of the sociocultural connotations of gendered privilege with which it is frequently associated.

Beyond this basic similarity of Chen's, Wu's, and Chu's works, however, there are several important differences. In both Chen Sen's and Wu Chi-wen's novels, a crucial issue is that of the phallus's signification of "masculine privilege," together with the ever-present danger that the anatomical penis may cease to denote the abstract "phallus." In the parallel scene from Chu T'ien-wen's work, by contrast, the penis/phallus's status as a marker of sexual difference is arguably less important than its allusion to a general system of sexual reproduction. A recurrent theme in Chu's novel is the so-called homosexualization of contemporary (Taiwan) society; that is, sexual desire ceases to be yoked to mere procreative imperatives and thereby assumes a more fluid, "textual" existence. In this respect, the penis marks a figurative transition point mediating between its conventional status as a metonym for sexual reproduction and its potentially sublimated significance as a figure for a "homosexual" regime of asexual "textual" reproduction. At the same time, the specific context of the epigraph is that the narrator is viewing Ah Yao's body one last time before it is cremated (217/165)—thus marking the symbolic end of Ah Yao's life and, at the same time, signaling the beginning of his postmortem existence in Xiao Shao's memory and writing. In this sense, the penis also marks a transition point between mortal existence and the nostalgic, textual existence that Ah Yao assumes in Xiao Shao's memory and writings.

The epigraph stands as ample evidence that Chu's novel does not shy away from frank descriptions of sexual organs, nor from discussions of sexual acts and sexuality in general; yet, at the same time, the narrative does not simply revel in them either. In fact, it often seems as if the narrator values the sexual act less for its own sake and more for the opportunity it creates for melancholically savoring the traces and vestiges that it subsequently leaves in his memory. This nostalgic approach to desire is further illustrated in the novel's discussion of the phenomenon of "secondary virginity" popular among young girls in Japan, which happened to coincide with a period during which polls revealed that girls were losing their virginity at earlier and earlier ages.[10] The public discussion of these same polls, meanwhile, reveals that the reason for this phenomenon is that many girls were deciding to lose their virginity to someone "relatively experienced," in order to "let the experience be preserved in their memories." The narrator concludes that this attitude of valuing the memory more than the act itself can be regarded as an example of the "homosexualization of heterosexuality" (115/84).

For Xiao Shao, "homosexuality" connotes the sort of "finality without end" that Kant famously attributed to pure aesthetics. That is, in homosexuality the "finality" of the sex act is disassociated from the (ostensible) procreative "end" of heterosexual copulation. One of the more explicit discussions of this issue can be found in a scene in which Xiao Shao moves from a discussion of the young boy he has just met (whom he refers to as *FIDO*, after the *Fido-Dido* logo on the boy's T-shirt) to a consideration of Xiao Shao's own androgynous nature. In the resulting discussion, Xiao Shao sees himself as being located not only between two different biological sexes but also between two different modes of visualization. He reinscribes femininity and masculinity within the asymmetrical axes of the gaze, referring specifically to the way in which "the *femininity that is gazed upon* and the *masculinity that gazes* coexist in us" (97/70; italics added). From this theme, Xiao Shao then turns to the Lévi-Straussian quandary concerning the relationship between history and myth:

> Ah, where does myth end? Where does history begin? Lévi-Strauss said, In a society with no writing system or records, myth exists to ensure the insulation of society, so that the future will be the same as the present and the past.
>
> Perhaps all myths describe an upheaval that occurred more than ten thousand years ago.
>
> Myth reveals secrets, nature created woman, and woman created man. But man created history. Yes, history. Man (*nanren* 男人) wrote the story of mankind (*renlei* 人類) based upon his conceptions. (98/71)

---

10. Cf. the discussions of Japanese "secondary virginity" and teenage prostitution in Li Yung-p'ing's *Haidong qing*.

Here, the familiar stereotype of man as the possessor of the gaze is rearticulated metaphorically, with man now becoming the symbolic viewer of history. At the same time, it is suggested that this privileged "view" of history may itself be a form of blindness, in that the (male) viewer is ultimately unable to see history as anything other than a mediated version of his own self-image, of his own "conceptions."

In a fortuity of Howard Goldblatt and Sylvia Lin's English translation of the novel, this final use of the term *conceptions* to describe the narcissistic ground of "man's" logorrheic historicizing connotes not only *idea* (the literal meaning of the original Chinese term, *yisi* 意思) but also *procreation* (in the sense of the "conception" of a child). Although this double entendre is not present in the Chinese, Chu's text *does* move directly from this earlier theme of androgyny to the related consideration of the nonprocreative dimension of homoerotic desire:

> I dissected myself, the bud of a feminine soul trapped in a masculine body. My mental activities were full of feminine characteristics, but my body, this body that carried the DNA of reproduction, could never escape its biologically determined state. A fate of blood and iron.
>
> DNA blindly moves around to create more DNA. The male and female have different strategies of reproduction. The male is a competitor, while the female a selector. . . .
>
> Our feminine qualities include favoring concrete feelings, appreciating the physique, and a fondness for outward appearance. The material is existence, the only kind of existence. *There is mediation and no metaphysics, for what the subjective eye sees is the only thing that exists.* Double vermilion red, rosy red, shell red, persimmon red, agate red, gray lily red, ivory red, pink oyster red, silver star cherry-apple red. I recite my own sutra: Streaming red, Bright sun steamed the small peaches red.
>
> Yes, feminine qualities. But we lack the nature to reproduce or the virtue to improve human life. *And so the idea that what we see is what exists is pushed to the limit.* It is like a Victorian woman howling: I am amazed by the beauty of my own body. I want to create this statue! But how shall I proceed? Marriage is the only answer. (99–100/72–73; italics added)

This passage begins with the same fascination with androgyny that had characterized the preceding discussions but then transitions to the theme of DNA and genetics. At first, genetics is introduced in contraposition to the narrator's perceived androgyny, in the sense that "his" body still remains genetically male in spite of his hermaphroditic inclinations. In the next paragraph, however, DNA is attributed a procreative function that effectively transcends gender distinctions: "DNA blindly (*mangdong* 盲動) moves around to create more DNA"—evoking Richard Dawkins's thesis in his influential 1976 book *The Selfish Gene*, which resituates the reproductive imperative at the level of the autonomous gene rather than that of the organism. In this sense, the figure of DNA in this passage can be seen as a metaphor for textuality itself, insofar as text is not merely a medium for transmitting meaning but an autonomous object in its own right.

Furthermore, Chu's use of the term *blindly* to describe the movement of DNA brings us back to the *visual* metaphors permeating this particular passage, as well as the novel. Femininity, for instance, is explicitly associated with a "fondness for outward appearance" and a skepticism toward "mediation and metaphysics," with the conclusion that "what the subjective eye sees is the only thing that exists." This generalization reinforces the conventional association of women with surface appearance—as discussed, for instance, by Naomi Schor in *Reading in Detail: Aesthetics and the Feminine*. Similarly, the narrator's "feminine" voice is also said to be "amazed by the beauty of my own body," even as it expresses frustration that "we lack the nature to reproduce . . . *And so the idea that what we see is what exists is pushed to the limit.*" Here, the rhetoric of sexual reproduction is brought full circle with that of visual reproduction; the inability to produce biological progeny ironically suggests a "return" to the visual plenitude ("what you see is what exists") posited to have existed *before* the advent of what Benjamin calls "mechanical reproduction." In this way, a postmodernist attention to the materiality of the visual image itself (whereby "the image has become the final form of commodity reification," as Guy Debord has famously observed)[11] returns ironically to what might be described as a "premodern" fascination with the materiality of surface appearance. In the following section,

11. Debord, *Society of the Spectacle*, 21.

I take this "postmodern" attention to the potential autonomy of the visual image and use it as a starting point for rereading the themes of imagery and commodification in Chu's novel.

Postmodern Graveyard

So, in postmodern culture, "culture" has become a product in its own right; the market has become a substitute for itself and fully as much a commodity as any of the items it includes within itself: modernism was still minimally and tendentially the critique of the commodity and the effort to make it transcend itself. Postmodernism is the consumption of sheer commodification as a process.

—Fredric Jameson: *Postmodernism, or, The Cultural Logic of Late Capitalism*

Chu's visual/literary indebtedness to Eileen Chang is not limited to their mutual interest in color combinations; it also extends to their shared attention to the visual quality of textuality itself, and specifically the position of textuality within modern capitalism. For instance, in a passage from near the beginning of Eileen Chang's short story "Shutdown," the male tram passenger, Zongzhen, is snacking on some *mantou* buns that were wrapped in newspaper:

> Some of the newspaper was stuck to the buns, so he carefully peeled it off. The print had come off on the buns, in reverse, a mirror image. Zongzhen had the patience to bend his head and try to make out the words one by one: 'Obituary . . . Classified . . . Chinese Stock Market News . . . A Grand Performance . . .' Serious words all, but somehow risible printed in reverse on the buns. (226/94)

This momentary fascination with the textual vestiges of the newspaper marks a symbolic escape from the commodity culture within which Zongzhen is embedded; at the same time, it signals the degree to which contemporary print capitalism permeates virtually every facet of contemporary urban existence.

This image of an urban modernity perfused with the visual imagery of (capitalist) textuality, as memorably illustrated in the preceding passage, is developed even more explicitly in *Notes of a Desolate Man*. One of the most striking illustrations of the intersection of capitalism and visual culture in Chu's novel, for instance, can be observed in a curious passage that reflects ironically on the theme of Taipei cartography as developed in Li Yung-p'ing's *Haidong qing*. Here, Xiao Shao finds himself "reading" a map of Taipei:

> Then I started reading the map of the city, made up of numerous shop names, interpreting them with no clear understanding, mixing and matching them at will. . . .
>
> KISS LA BOCCA offered the trendiest red wine, Test Tube Baby, originally called KAMAKAZE, now bottled in red, white, and yellow test tubes. . . .
>
> FRIDAY, CIRCUS, TOP, The Vendor, VINO VINO, Southern Comfort, Butterfly Feeds the Cat, Summer Blossom, Tricks, SOMETIMES, The Rest Stop, Rooster, Sunflowers, Hide and Seek, 4T5D, *Postmodern Graveyard.*
>
> [. . . the text continues for another five paragraphs consisting entirely of brand names . . .]
>
> Sitting at my desk, I saw the features and construction of the city composed by the arrangement of words materializing in front of me like icebergs rising out of the water, where the clouds and ocean met. *The city appearing under my pen existed only in words, and when the words disappeared, so would the city.* (163–44/121–22; italics added; the words printed here in capitals appear in English in the original).

This insight into the textual grounding of the (post)modern city (a "Postmodern Graveyard," to borrow Chu's term) is closely linked to Xiao Shao's observation that his own existence is also grounded on textuality. Just as "the city appearing under my pen existed only in words," similarly Xiao Shao himself, as I discuss below, sees himself as existing only through the process of his own writing.

The "postmodern" quality of *Notes of a Desolate Man* not only is exemplified by the lack of a unitary linear narrative at the level of the novel's plot but also is visible in the complex pastiche of allusions making up the work. In addition to the discussions of Goethe's work on color perception, Chu T'ien-wen's novel also incorporates a wide range of other cultural allusions, both Asian and Western. Many of these allusions are to elite intellectual figures, such as Fellini (the text cites his *Eight and a Half*), Lévi-Strauss (*Tristes Tropiques*), and Foucault (*History of Sexuality* and *Power/Knowledge*), as well as, among others, Ingmar Bergman, Montaigne, Rodin, D. H. Lawrence, Schopenhauer, Buñuel, and Heraclitus. At the same time, the novel is also replete with cultural allusions of a more "popular" nature, such as to Mel Gibson's *Hamlet*, Ridley Scott's *Blade Runner*, *Starlight Twins*, and familiar brand names such as Hello Kitty, Winki Pinki, and Sanrio.

Although apparently random, some of these cultural allusions, I would suggest, contain within them clues to a reading of the novel that helps explain the functions of these allusions themselves. Specifically, in Chapter 4 Xiao Shao reads aloud a celebrated passage from Lévi-Strauss's *Tristes Tropiques* concerning the Brazilian Caduveo Indians and their practice of covering their own bodies with elaborate tattoos of abstract designs:

> The more Caduveo Indians' present circumstances deteriorate, the more they seek to preserve some distinguishing qualities from the past—a tendency which is exhibited most clearly in their art of body-tattooing. They believe that, to be human, it is necessary to decorate one's body—because if one allows one's body to remain in an undecorated state, then there will be nothing to distinguish one from mere beasts. . . . In the first place, facial patterns confer human dignity on the individual; they insure the transition from nature to culture, from 'stupid' beast to civilized man. Next, since they vary in style and pattern according to caste, they express differences in status within a given society. This means that they have a sociological function. As for the distinguishing characteristic of Caduveo art, it may be found in the male/female dichotomy—whereby men are sculptors, and the women painters.
>
> . . . In the last resort the graphic art of the Caduveo women is to be interpreted, and its mysterious appeal and seemingly gratuitous complexity to be explained, as the phantasm of a society ardently and insatiably seeking a means of expressing symbolically the institutions it might have, if its interests and superstitions did not stand in the way. In this charming civilization, the female beauties trace the outlines of the collective dream with their makeup; their patterns are hieroglyphics describing an inaccessible golden age, which they extol in their ornamentation, since they have no code in which to express it, and whose mysteries they disclose as they reveal their nudity. (43–44/28–29)

The length and specificity of this passage (Chu/Shao even specifies the page number of the Chinese edition from which it is ostensibly quoted)[12] suggests its relative centrality among the mobile army of

12. Howard Goldblatt and Sylvia Lin, the translators of the English version of the novel, however, note that they were unable to match the quoted passages in Chu's novel to any existing Chinese translation of Lévi-Strauss's work. The above translation incorporates relevant passages of John Weightman, trans., *Tristes Tropiques*, 188–97.

metaphors, metonymies, and anthropomorphisms that populate the novel's pages. In addition, I would argue that the Caduveo example suggests a way of making sense of the assortment of other allusions out of which the fabric of the novel is woven.

The Caduveo reassure themselves of their own humanity by wrapping themselves in tattooed decorations—with these tattoos functioning simultaneously as signifying structures and visual art forms. Similarly, we could read *Notes of a Desolate Man* as an attempt by the narrator, Xiao Shao, to metaphorically wrap himself in cultural allusions—allusions that, like the Caduvean tattoos, can be appreciated both for their significatory potential and for their paralingual plasticity and texture. As with the Caduveo tattoos, the very plasticity of the signifying systems in which the novel's narrator envelops himself has a functional utility over and above the meanings of the signs themselves. If the Caduveo cloak themselves in tattoos in order to distinguish themselves from "stupid beasts" and mere "nature," then the "desolate man" similarly cloaks himself in cultural and philosophical allusions in order to fend off and contain the specters of "desolation" and "death"—in short, of his own mortality. For instance, at one point in Chapter 8, it is remarked that "the body is sacred attire, your first and last piece of clothing"—this, in a sense, brings us back full circle to the original Caduveo example, even as, in a sense, the original visual emphasis is transmuted into a purely tactile one.

This general compulsion to cloak oneself in writing (metaphorical or otherwise) is perhaps summed up most succinctly by Shao's paraphrase, at the end of Chapter 3 of the novel, of the famous Cartesian formula: "I *write*, and therefore I am" (italics added). And then—as if satisfying the dictum's logorrheic imperative even while subverting its original implications—Shao rushes on to elaborate, "When I can no longer write, I will throw down my pen, and to hell with it, for I'll no longer be able to lay claim to emotions, consciousness, or form" (38/25). Appropriately enough, the final lines of the novel, following Ah Yao's cremation, return once again to this theme: "Time cannot be turned back, nor can life. However, in the process of writing, I am able to turn back everything that otherwise couldn't be. So my writing, it continues" (218/166).

One of the underlying themes of Chu's novel concerns the narrator's search for closure: his attempt to come to terms with the death of Ah

Yao. It is therefore ironically appropriate that the novel itself suffered from problems with "closure." Specifically, a series of events in the years immediately following the work's original publication led Chu to revisit the novel and explicitly address some of its implicit points of "incompletion." First, *Desolate Man*'s concerns with homoerotics, queer identity, death, and writing were uncannily realized in an unexpectedly concrete way when, a year after the publication of *Notes of a Desolate Man*, the young and openly lesbian Taiwan writer Qiu Miaojin 邱妙津 wrote her own novelistic epitaph: *Mengmate yishu* 蒙馬特遺書 (Montmartre suicide note). Like Chu's novel, Qiu's work also uses a diary format to grapple with the significance of death. In contrast to the multiple levels of mediation that characterize Chu's work (i.e., her ventriloquization of the life story of an unnamed friend, who in turn is remembering his own former lover), the "death" Qiu is attempting literarily to "work through" is, quite literally, *her own*. The entire work constitutes an extended elegy on the act of suicide, and Qiu took her own life soon after its completion (the novel was published posthumously). Second, the publication of Chu's novel was followed by an influential reading of the work by the critic Kim-chu Ng 黄錦樹 that stressed the spectral presence, in *Notes of a Desolate Man*, of Chu T'ien-wen's childhood tutor, Hu Lancheng. Chu T'ien-wen apparently followed these discussions with interest. When asked to contribute a preface to a 1998 anthology of her work, entitled *Huayi qianshen* 花憶前身 (A flower recalls its previous lives), she began by acknowledging the influence of Qiu's death and Ng's review and then proceeded to use the occasion to embark on a long and detailed reminiscence of her relationship with Hu Lancheng—the first time that she had ever publicly addressed this important topic in print.

In both Kim-chu Ng's article and Chu's response, one of the most visible sites of Hu Lancheng's personal/intellectual influence on Chu's work (particularly on her *Notes of a Desolate Man*) relates to Hu's polemical theory of "feminology" (*nüren lun* 女人論), which he developed most directly in his book *Jinri heri xi* 今日何日兮, and continued to draw on in many of his subsequent essays as well.[13] Explicitly *not* a

13. For a detailed discussion of this issue, see Kim-chu Ng, "Shenji zhi wu."

theory of "feminism," Hu's cultural-philosophical "feminology" foregrounds the formative role of women/femininity in culture in general and in Chinese/Asian culture in particular. As such, the theory is partially grounded on a paradox, insofar as Hu is attributing a creative and foundational role to "woman," even as his theory arguably necessitates the reduction/sublimation of actual "women" to the aesthetic ideal of a timeless "woman."

My primary concern here is with the (hidden) influence of this theory of "feminology" on Chu's own writing, and I begin my discussion of her relationship to Hu by turning directly to her own summary of this theory in her introduction to *A Flower Recalls Its Previous Lives*, which repeats Hu's account virtually verbatim, silently bringing together relevant passages from several of his writings on the subject:

> Teacher Hu believed that, historically speaking, it was woman[14] that first created civilization. This civilization was one ["one body"] with nature, and it also served as the mold for the creation of concreteness. After this, man integrated it into a theoretical academic system. Woman is responsible for the "investigation of things" (*gewu* 格物), and man is responsible for "acquiring knowledge" (*zhizhi* 致知). With these [contributions], civilization can progress and expand. If, for example, a woman manages unwittingly to write a good initial ideograph, then the rest of the literary work will follow naturally; this is something no man can match. But when a man is able to specify and explain with precision the reason for a woman's beauty, she is then truly happy. On one hand, the woman is delighted with man, who inspires in her a sense of modesty; on the other hand, she looks up to him and desires to compete with him, as if they were mutual enemies.[15]

C/Hu's[16] major point in this ventriloquistic manifesto is that women are responsible for having created the substantive basis for "civilization," and that it was on this ground that men proceeded to elaborate a

14. Chu's Chinese here is ambiguous on whether the subject is singular or plural. Given the mythological tone of the passage, I use the singular throughout, with the understanding that in many cases it could just as well be talking about wo/men in the plural.

15. Chu T'ien-wen, "Huayi qianshen," 71.

16. I use "C/Hu" here as an unfortunately unaesthetic graphical convenience, given that the ventriloquistic embrace Chu and Hu find themselves in in this passage makes it unproductive to attempt to distinguish between them.

theoretical system. It is therefore ironically fitting that Chu T'ien-wen, in her own essay (as well as, arguably, in *Notes of a Desolate Man*), is in effect inverting this symbolic order—by taking Hu's theoretical system as a figurative "ground" on which she elaborates her own (personally) "substantive" poetic edifice.

In this passage, C/Hu takes the Confucian formula "acquiring knowledge through the investigation of things" (*gewu zhizhi*) and explicitly bifurcates it along gendered lines. The apparent "materialism" of *gewu* (investigating things) is coded as feminine, and the abstraction of *zhizhi* (acquiring knowledge) is coded as masculine. In Chapter 1, I sketched a schematic genealogy of this same phrase and suggested that under Song-Ming Neo-Confucianism, the *gewu* formula largely lost its (apparent) "materialist" connotations and came to signify not so much an inquiry into the nature of actual "things," but rather the use of "things" as a foil for a more abstract consideration of issues of "mind" (*xin* 心) or "principle" (*li* 理). As I discussed, there was an apparent backlash, during the Qing dynasty, against the "abstraction" of Neo-Confucianism—a backlash that is best exemplified by the Qing dynasty *kaozheng xue* school of evidential scholarship, which stressed a close attention to the physical appearance of social and natural phenomena, as well as a literal-minded return to Han dynasty canonical texts. Furthermore, in Chapter 2, I noted Stephen Roddy's argument that the gendered dichotomies in *Flowers in the Mirror* are symptomatic of contemporary scholarly debates between the (Song-Ming) tradition of Neo-Confucian "philosophy" and the "evidential" mid-Qing philological *kaozheng xue* school, with the former being coded as masculine in the novel and the latter as feminine.

At first glance, Roddy's reading of *Flowers in the Mirror* might appear to be consonant with C/Hu's gendered reading of Chinese intellectual history, insofar as the "feminine" *kaozheng xue* movement is grounded in a Han dynasty philosophical tradition that literally antedates the "masculine" Song-Ming Neo-Confucian "philosophy." However, the relationship between these two gendered chronologies (i.e., both positing a "feminine" base that ostensibly *antedates* the subsequent masculine elaboration) is somewhat more complicated. Roddy's reading of *Flowers* suggests that the "feminized" *kaozheng xue* position was not a straightforward antecedent of the "masculine" abstraction of Qing Neo-Confucianism; rather, it was born out of a cultural-intellectual *backlash against* the latter—a retrospective construction inspired by intellectual debates in the same nineteenth-century period in which the novel was written. The view of temporality suggested by this reading of Li Ru-zhen's novel is grounded not on progressive linearity but on a pattern of recursive return. In his reading of Chu's novel, Kim-chu Ng argues that *Notes of a Desolate Man* is itself structured by a similar temporality of the "future perfect," of reconstituting the past from the perspective of an anticipated futurity. In particular, Ng argues that *Notes of a Desolate Man* borrows from Hu Lancheng's theory a trajectory of double sublimation—with an initial aestheticization of eros (desire) being accompanied by a parallel eroticization of aesthetics.

Ng's description of Chu's double "sublimation" is itself strikingly reminiscent of Lévi-Strauss's description of the Caduveo women—who first translate institutional and societal tensions into abstract significatory systems and then proceed to invest those same significatory systems with a tangible corporeality by inscribing them onto their own bodies. Furthermore, the "tensions" visually inscribed, in sublimated form, on the faces of Caduveo women are, Lévi-Strauss argues, precisely concerned with the perceived conflict between the Caduveo's (imagined) "golden age" and the present "deterioration." Just as the young women in *Flowers in the Mirror* are imagined to be retrospective embodiments of Han dynasty philosophical/literati ideals, the Caduveo women are similarly perceived as embodying the ideal of a bygone Golden Age—a golden age that, it is suggested, becomes visible only from the retrospective perspective of the imperfect present.

Shanghai Flowers

> A study of dreams, phantasies and myths has taught us that a morbid anxiety connected with the eyes and with going blind is often enough a substitute for the dread of castration.
>
> —Sigmund Freud, "The 'Uncanny' "

The future anteriority of Lévi-Strauss's Caduveo women provides a useful perspective not only on Chu T'ien-wen's relationship to *Notes of a Desolate Man* but also on the late imperial courtesans featured in Hou Hsiao-hsien's 1998 film *Flowers of Shanghai*, for which Chu adapted the screenplay from Han Bangqing's 韓邦慶 late nineteenth-century courtesan novel, *Haishang hua liezhuan* 海上花列傳 (Biographies of Shanghai flowers, 1894). Courtesans' idealized expectations for the future (in the form of their hopes that the matrimonial charade they play out on a daily basis will eventually be realized through an actual romance that enables them to be purchased out of servitude) ironically intersect with their own status as sites of *nostalgic investment* on the part of the literati who cultivate their services (as well as of the twentieth-century figures who subsequently use them as tropes for late imperial decadence). The courtesans' dream of emancipation is found repeatedly in nineteenth-century works such as *Flowers in the Mirror* and *Precious Mirror for Evaluating Flowers.* At the same time, as we saw in our readings of those two early works, this promise of emancipation is frequently presented as double-edged, in that it merely substitutes one form of symbolic servitude for another. In this concluding section of my study, I use the future anteriority of the courtesans in *Flowers of Shanghai* not only to link my discussion of Chu T'ien-wen back to my earlier discussions of Li Ruzhen and Chen Sen but also more generally to bring together the central concerns of this volume.

Although specifically grounded in late Qing courtesan culture, Han Banqing's original novel *Biographies of Shanghai Flowers* has nevertheless acquired a timelessness that generally eluded many of its now-forgotten *fin-de-siècle* contemporaries. In the mid-twentieth century, for instance, Eileen Chang found herself fascinated by the novel and completed not one, but two translations of the work—one rendering its Shanghai dialect into standard Mandarin Chinese, and the second translating it again into English. Coincidentally, at around the time of the release of Hou's film, the manuscript of Eileen Chang's English translation, which had been feared lost since her death, was suddenly discovered in the archives of the University of Southern California library.[17] Like *Peony Pavilion*'s uncanny return in the late 1990s, Han Bangqing's manuscript about late imperial prostitutes can be seen as having made a similar

17. A revised version of Chang's translation has been published by Columbia University Press under the title *The Singsong Girls of Shanghai.*

spectral "return" from textual oblivion, coming back to haunt the present with the shattered ideals of another era.

Hou Hsiao-hsien's cinematic adaptation of *Flowers of Shanghai* is a visually stunning cinematic tour de force, in which the richness of the visual display often deliberately takes precedence over more conventional cinematic concerns with character development and narrative progression. For instance, about half an hour into Hou's film there is a fifteen-second still shot of a green jade-tipped hairpin lying amid other knickknacks on a small circular table (see Fig. 20). Not only is this one of the only long takes of the film that does not contain any visible human being, but it is also here that the male voiceover (spoken by Master Wang) articulates what is arguably the central theme of the work: "When I began calling on Crimson, she told me that a really good gentleman caller is every flower-girl's dream." Hou's film, together with the novel on which it is based, is centrally concerned with a group of Shanghai courtesans and their dreams of being able to meet, fall in love with, and marry an eligible patron. This ideal, ventriloquized here by one such gentleman caller, is visually instantiated in this scene by the jade hairpin, a visual metonym for the traditional practice of married women of wearing their hair bound up rather than letting it hang straight down (appropriately enough, among the other knickknacks on the table is a pair of wooden "mandarin ducks," traditional Chinese symbols of matrimonial bliss).

The ensuing scene points to an additional wrinkle in the significance of this particular hairpin. First, Master Wang complains that, even though Crimson indicated that it was her dream to be loved and married, now that he, Master Wang, has paid off her debts and offered to marry her, she comes up with excuse after excuse for not doing so. Second, the hairpin, which Crimson fiddles with throughout the following scene, is on loan from a jeweler. Crimson is considering paying the rather steep price of sixteen foreign dollars for it—not because she wants or needs it but because she wants to "waste" Master Wang's money on it. He, in turn, encourages her to take the money but to "waste" it on something else. Thus the hairpin scene is oriented around a cycle of dialectical opposition and sublimation. Crimson begins by appealing to the ideal of matrimony as a possible escape from the cycle of commoditization and exchange (i.e., prostitution) in which she finds herself. However, she apparently (according to Master Wang) subverts that same ideal even before it has been realized; subverting it, moreover, precisely through an *excess* of commodification (i.e., wanting to waste Master Wang's money on an expensive "matrimonial" hairpin). He, in turn, attempts to subvert her very act of subversion, again by relying on an excess of commodification: by encouraging her to go ahead and "waste" his money as she wishes. In this scene, therefore, the jeweled hairpin oscillates between its status as a visual signifier of matrimony and as a "mere" commodity, just as Crimson oscillates between her dual status as sexualized commodity and as autonomous individual. Ironically, Crimson's most visible acts of autonomy are those that appear to defy the possibility of matrimony, which would appear to constitute her most concrete hope for escaping prostitution altogether.

One of the clearest examples of the courtesans' dual status as both "mere" performers and aspirants to the matrimonial status that they are themselves performing can be found in the opening scene of the film. The work begins with a banquet sequence in one of the courtesan houses. Several of the male patrons and their courtesans are chatting and playing drinking games. They joke that the patron/courtesan couple, Tao Yufu and Crystal (Li Shufan), are inseparable, and one character recounts that he once visited the two lovers, only to find them staring wordlessly into each other's eyes. In an attempt to distract them, he suggested several possible activities (e.g., going to the opera, riding in a horse-drawn carriage), but Crystal objected to each of them in turn. Finally he suggested that she and Yufu have their portraits taken, but Crystal again objected, claiming that "the camera will capture the beams from our eyes." The narrator concludes the anecdote by relating that henceforth Crystal began each day by licking Yufu's eyes with her tongue.[18]

Despite its lighthearted tone, this anecdote from *Flowers of Shanghai* points to a fascinating theme that has surfaced repeatedly throughout this study: namely, the act of falling back onto the reassuring concreteness of the anatomical eye as a way of responding to the

18. The scene in the film corresponds to Chapter 7 of the novel; see Han Bangqing, *Haishang hualie zhuan*, 214.

epistemological threat implicitly posed by changing technologies (and practices) of visual perception and reproduction. Among the many examples discussed in previous chapters are the Qing dynasty philosopher Yan Yuan, who drew on similar tropes of ocular physiognomy to illustrate his arguments against the vagaries of Neo-Confucian metaphysical abstraction; Old Tuo in *Flowers in the Mirror*, who counterpoints his emphasis on the tiger's ostensible ability to *see through* the indeed's beast-like exterior, with a curious emphasis on the fact that the tiger was killed by an arrow through its eye; and Wumingshi, in his *Anonymous Book*, who responded to the perceived threat of epistemological transparency posed by modern Western art by falling back onto surprisingly detailed discussions of the anatomical structure and physiognomic function of the human eye. More recently, both Wang Shuo and Chu T'ien-wen develop elaborate and multifaceted fly-eye metaphors in an attempt to defamiliarize the ostensible immediacy and reliability of visual perception. Finally, the scopic skepticism that pervades Jin Yong's *Tianlong ba bu* (a work in which few characters are who they initially appear to be, and in which a portrait does not represent the individual whom the portraitist himself thought he was painting) exists side by side with a plotline in which a character goes blind, has her sight restored when another character gives her *his* own eyes, and finally reblinds herself by gouging her new eyes out of their sockets and throwing them back at their original owner.[19]

In each instance, the concreteness of the anatomical eye is used as a displacement of the inherent ephemerality and transmutability of the decentered "gaze." Just as the attention paid to the materiality of the penis in Chen Sen's and Wu Chi-wen's novels signaled a displaced awareness of the ultimate contingency of sociocultural constructs of gender, similarly this attention to the materiality of the eye constitutes an unconscious compensation for a deep-rooted skepticism about the ultimate reliability of the visual image itself. Seen in this way, the ac-

---

19. Furthermore, these two themes of the circulation of the phallus and the circulation of the gaze are evocatively brought together in a scene from near the end of Jia Pingwa's *Fallen Capital* (a work I discuss in a different context in Chapter 9), which tropes on the canine penile-grafting scene in Li Yu's *Carnal Prayer Mat* by having a character's eyes be replaced by those of a dog.

count of Crystal's licking of Tao Yufu's eyes in Hou's film functions simultaneously on two levels—as an affirmation of the power of the gaze with which he perceives her, and as a denial of her own commodified status (which is to say, her attempt to have him perceive her as a true love, rather than as a courtesan performing *the role* of an idealized lover). These two issues of Yufu's gaze and Crystal's commodified status come together in Crystal's own metaphorical status of being a "flower" (*flower* being a common metaphor in Chinese for both women and courtesans), insofar as the expression "flowers in the eyes" (*yanhua* 眼花)—which might be used to describe Yufu's perception of Crystal, as well as her act of physically licking his eyes—is also a familiar term for "optical illusion," suggesting that his perception of her, together with her perception of herself vis-à-vis his imaginary gaze, is itself necessarily grounded on a process of illusion and misperception.

These associations of flowers with femininity and prostitution partially overlap, but they are, of course, not identical. In fact, a central theme of Chu and Hou's film is precisely the women's attempt to *escape* their social identity as courtesans by assuming the same social roles (lovers or wives) they are expected to performatively enact. Appropriately enough, Chu used the figure of the flower in the title of her quasi-autobiographical essay, "A Flower Recalls Its Previous Lives," three years earlier. Just as *Notes of a Desolate Man* uses an anonymous, external figure as a locus for self-representation, Chu's more recent essay uses the trope of the flower as a metaphor for processes of identification and self-representation. This semantic overdetermination of the term *hua* is, in turn, one of the key themes of this study. From the Buddhist "flowers in the mirror" (*jinghua*) formula to the conventional Chinese expression for visual illusion, "flowers in the eyes" (*yanhua*); from the "flower selection" (*huaxuan*) *dan* performer beauty contest in Chen Sen's *Precious Mirror for Evaluating Flowers* to Hou Hsiao-hsien's contemporary remake of Han Bangqing's *Flowers of Shanghai*; from Wumingshi's *Blooming Flowers Beyond the Stars and Clouds* to Chu T'ien-wen's autobiographical essay "A Flower Recalls Its Previous Lives"—this study has returned repeatedly, almost obsessively, to the theme of flowers, used variously as symbols of visual beauty, visual illusion, femininity, courtesanship, and prostitution, as well as the aesthetic sublimation of erotic desire.

This overdetermination of the figure of the flower suggests that, in many cases, these floral tropes function not so much as concrete signifiers as figurative "screens" onto which an array of different attitudes and beliefs may be projected. This notion of the screen is, moreover, explicitly developed in these works themselves, as, for instance, in the semitransparent "crystalline screen" mediating between external scenes and the observer's eye, in the nineteenth-century commentary on *Flowers in the Mirror*; the "mirrored screen" containing the portrait of Mei Ziyu at the beginning of *Precious Mirror for Evaluating Flowers*; the call, in Wumingshi's *Siren of the Sea*, for "illusions [to] function as a screen between one person and another"; as well as the large, freestanding outdoor movie screen in Jiang Wen's film, *In the Heat of the Sun*. I argue that the significance of these screens (figurative or otherwise) lies not so much in their ability to add "a little mistiness and ambiguity" to interpersonal relations, as suggested in the Wumingshi passage, as in the way in which they paradoxically reinforce the illusion (and even the very possibility) of *transparency* itself. For instance, even as Wang Shuo is criticizing Jin Yong for creating and circulating a "false image" of the Chinese people (and even as he is, in his own works, subjecting photography's mimetic potential to a devastating deconstruction), Wang Shuo's critique nevertheless remains grounded on the assumption that it remains possible to present "true images" of "the Chinese people's original face." I suggest that this figure of the screen provides a useful way of approaching the convergence of issues of visuality and gender represented metaphorically in the "flowers in the mirror" aphorism itself. More specifically, a central concern throughout this study has been the question of how to address the cultural and historical specificities of both gender (i.e., "flowers") and vision (i.e., "mirrors"), while abstracting them enough that it becomes possible to place texts from different periods and cultures into dialogue with one another. That is, even as I sketch a general historical progression from nineteenth-century concerns with reflection to twentieth-century interests in issues of representation and reproduction, I attempt to develop a critical vocabulary that will allow us to trace continuities and parallels among these texts—continuities which frequently cut across the specific historical moments in which the individual texts were composed. To this end, I suggest that we may see the figure of the screen as marking a point of intersection between the contingent sociocultural attitudes of specific historical moments and the gaze (both that of the individual subject and our own), which partially transcends those same sociocultural attitudes.

The themes of eyes, flowers, and screens come together in the earliest instance of the "flowers in the mirror" formula that I discuss in detail in this book: the maid Chun Xiang's observation, in the self-portraiture scene in Tang Xianzu's *The Peony Pavilion*, that it is "easy enough to sketch her aspect in hues red or dark: harder to portray the rare individual self, *when the image reflects the reality like flowers behind closed lids*, or the moon in the water." Rather than the now-standard *jinghua shuiyue* 鏡花水月 formulation, Tang Xianzu's text reads *konghua shuiyue* 空華水月, with the character for mirror, *jing*, replaced with the character *kong*, meaning "empty," "hollow," "void." Although Cyril Birch, in his authoritative translation, renders Tang's line as "flowers seen behind closed lids," a consideration of the etymology of this phrase reveals an even more specifically optical underpinning—one that not only invokes the figure of the "screen" in a very concrete sense but also points to a potential continuity between the general ocular skepticism of Tang Xianzu's late imperial period and the postmodern fetishization of visual images.

Tang Xianzu's use of the term *konghua* in this passage is somewhat unusual, and it is quite likely intended as a homophonic variant on the more popular Buddhist term, *konghua* 空華, in which the *hua* 華 means not "flower," but "visual splendor."[20] This expression locates the site of visual instability not at the material level of the mirror (as in the *jinghua shuiyue* formulation), but at the anatomical/physiological level of the human eye itself. One of the earliest usages of the term *konghua* can be found in the Buddhist sutra *Shou lengyanjing* 首楞嚴經 (Śūraṃgama-sūtra), reportedly translated into Chinese in 705, the final year of the reign of Empress Wu Zetian (whose reign provides the fictional backdrop for Li Ruzhen's *Flowers in the Mirror*):

> Take also the example of people suffering from a corneal defect—they look into empty space (*kong* 空) and see a display of visual splendor (*hua* 華). If you succeed in ridding them of their corneal defect, then the visual splendor will

20. See, e.g., the entry for *konghua* in the *Hanyu da cidian* 漢語大辭典.

disappear back into the empty space. Now there suddenly appears an ignorant person, who continues to stare into this empty space into which the fragment of visual splendor had disappeared, waiting for it to reappear. If you were to encounter such a person, would you call him ignorant or intelligent?

亦如翳人, 見空中華, 翳病若除, 華於空滅. 忽有愚人, 於彼空華, 所滅空地, 待華更生. 汝觀是人, 爲愚爲慧.[21]

In this fascinating passage, not only do we see a displacement of visual skepticism from the external surface of a (figurative) mirror to the surface of the eye itself, but also in the second half of the passage there is in effect a secondary displacement in which the visual illusion is erased from the corneal surface and transferred onto the "ignorant man's" memory. In addition, these two meanings of the phoneme *hua* ("flower" and "splendor") are figuratively brought back together again on this same corneal surface, in that, as noted above, the Chinese expression for "visual illusion," *yanhua* 眼花, literally means "flowers in the eye."

Embedded in the intertextual shadows of Tang Xianzu's *konghua shuiyue* formulation, it is possible to discern the image of this proverbial "ignorant" man, recently cured of his ocular illness but still waiting for his optical illusions to rematerialize as empirical reality. This instant of sight embedded within two moments of partial blindness suggests a potential deconstruction of the rough teleological narrative I have outlined in the preceding pages. On one hand, the "ignorant person" can be seen as gazing ahead from the "specular" late imperial period to the "modern" period, when visual concerns would be increasingly dis/functions of the optical physiognomy itself. On the other hand, he can also be seen anachronistically as a figure for our own "modern" positionality, waiting patiently for the spectral reapparition of bygone visual orthodoxies. Looking outside for what was originally an artifact of his own visual perception while looking forward in anticipation of the reappearance of a moment of "visual splendor" from the past, the ignorant/intelligent man simultaneously reflects and embodies the qualities I have attributed to the figurative "screen," which provides an uneasy point of suture, bringing together the cultural specificities of the scopic regimes of different eras and different societies.

21. *Shou lengyan jing*, T19.120c.

Reference Matter

Works Cited

Anderson, Benedict. *Imagined Communities*. London: Verso, 1991.

Balázs, Béla. *Theory of the Film: Character and Growth of a New Art*. New York: Dover, 1970.

Barmé, Geremie. *Shades of Mao: The Posthumous Cult of the Great Leader*. New York: M. E. Sharpe, 1996.

Barthes, Roland. *Camera Lucida: Reflections on Photography*. Trans. Richard Howard. New York: Farrar, Straus and Giroux, 1981.

Benjamin, Walter. "A Small History of Photography." In idem, *One Way Street and Other Writings*, trans. Edmund Jephocott and Kingsley Shorter. London: New Left Books, 1979, 240–57.

———. "The Work of Art in the Age of Mechanical Reproduction." In *Illuminations*, ed. and with an introduction by Hannah Arendt; trans. Harry Zohn. New York: Harcourt, Brace & World, 1968, 217–51.

Benveniste, Emile. *Problems in General Linguistics*. Trans. Mary Meek. Coral Gables: University of Miami Press, 1971.

Boucher, Sandy. *Discovering Kwan Yin, Buddhist Goddess of Compassion*. New York: Beacon Press, 2000.

Bronfen, Elisabeth. *The Knotted Subject: Hysteria and Its Discontents*. Princeton: Princeton University Press, 1988.

Bryson, Norman. *Vision and Painting: The Logic of the Gaze*. New Haven: Yale University Press, 1983.

Buck-Morss, Susan, *The Dialectics of Seeing: Walter Benjamin and the Arcades Project*. Cambridge: MIT Press, 1989.

Bush, Susan. *The Chinese Literati on Painting: Su Shih (1037–1101) to Tung Ch'i-ch'ang (1555–1636)*. Cambridge: Harvard University Press, 1971.

Cahill, James. "Innovation After 'Progress' Ends." In Sherman Lee, ed., *China, 5,000 Years: Innovation and Transformation in the Arts*. New York: Guggenheim Museum, 1998, 174–92.

Cao Xueqin 曹雪芹 and Gao E 高鶚. *Honglou meng* 紅樓夢 (Dream of the red chamber). 3 vols. Beijing: Renmin wenxue chubanshe, 1995.

———. *The Story of the Stone: A Chinese Novel by Cao Xueqin in Five Volumes*. Trans. David Hawkes and John Minford. New York: Penguin, 1973.

Carl, Katherine. *With the Empress Dowager of China*. New York: KPI, 1986.

Caygill, Howard. *Walter Benjamin: The Colour of Experience*. London and New York: Routledge, 1998.

Chan, Wing-Tsit. *A Source Book in Chinese Philosophy*. Princeton: Princeton University Press, 1963.

Chang Bide 昌彼得. *Mingdai banhua xuan chuji* 明代版畫選初輯 (Selected Ming woodblock prints, first compilation). Taibei: Guoli zhongyang tushuguan, 1969.

Chang, Eileen (Zhang Ailing 張愛玲). *Chidi zhi lian* 赤地之戀 (Naked earth). *Zhang Ailing quanji* 張愛玲全集 (The complete works of Zhang Ailing), vol. 2. Taibei: Huangguan congshu, 1983.

———. "Chinese Life and Fashions." Reprinted in *Lianhe wenxue* 3, no. 5 (1987): 66–67. Originally published in *The XXth Century* 4 (Jan. 1943): 54–61.

———. "Dream of Genius." Trans. Karen Kingsbury of "Tiancaimeng." In *Renditions*, no. 45 (Spring 1996): 25–27.

———. *Duizhao ji: kan lao zhaoxiang bu* 對照記: 看老照相簿 (Mutual reflections: looking at old photo albums). *Zhang Ailing quanji* 張愛玲全集 (The complete works of Eileen Chang), vol. 15. Taipei: Huangguan, 1994.

———. "Fengsuo" 封鎖 (Shutdown). In idem, *Diyi luxiang* 第一爐香 (The first incense burner). Taibei: Huangguan congshu, 1993, 223–36.

———. Honglong meng*yan* 紅樓夢魘 (Nightmare of *Dream of the Red Chamber*). *Zhang Ailing quanji* 張愛玲全集 (The complete works of Eileen Chang), vol. 9. Taipei: Huangguan congshu, 1993.

———. "My Writing." Trans. Wendy Larson of "Ziji de wenzhang." In Kirk Denton, ed., *Modern Chinese Literary Thought*. Stanford: Stanford University Press, 1996, 36–39.

———. *Naked Earth*. Hong Kong: Union Press, 1956.

———. "Reflections: Words and Pictures (Excerpts)." Trans. Janice Wickeri. *Renditions* 45 (1996): 1–24.

———. "Shutdown." Trans. Janet Ng and Janice Wickeri. *Renditions* 45 (1996): 93–100.

———. "Tiancaimeng" 天才夢 (Dream of genius). In *Zhang Kan* 張看 (Eileen Chang's perspectives). Taibei: Huangguan chubanshe, 1988, 278.

———. "Tongyan wuji" 童言無忌 (Guileless words of a child). In idem, *Liuyan* 流言 (Gossip). Taibei: Huangguan congshu, 1993, 5–16.

———. "Ziji de wenzhang" 自己的文章 (My writings). In idem, *Liuyan* (Gossip). Taibei: Huangguan congshu, 1993, 17–24.

Chang, Yvonne Sung-Sheng. "Chu T'ien-wen and Taiwan's Recent Cultural and Literary Trends." *Modern Chinese Literature* 6 (1992): 61–84.

Chen Juntao 陳駿濤. "Dalu 'Jinxue' diyi jia—Chen Mo he ta de Jin Yong ji xin wuxia yanjiu" 大陸"金學"第一家—陳墨和他的金庸及新武狹研究 (The foremost Jin Yong scholar in Mainland China: Chen Mo and his study of Jin Yong and new knight-errant fiction). In Chen Mo 陳墨, *Jin Yong xiaoshuo renlun* 金庸小説人論 (On the views of humanity in Jin Yong's novels). Nanchang: Baihua zhou wenyi chubanshe, 1993.

Chen Sen 陳森. *Pinhua baojian* 品花寶鑒 (Precious mirror for evaluating flowers). Beijing: Renmin Zhongguo chubanshe, 1993.

Chen Sihe 陳思和. "Shilun *Wumingshu*" 試論《無名書》(Exploratory discussion of *Nameless Book*). In idem, *Tanhu tantu* 談虎談兔 (Speaking of tigers and rabbits). Guilin: Guangxi shifan daxue chubanshe, 2001, 81–107.

Chow, Rey. *Primitive Passions: Visuality, Sexuality, Ethnography, and Contemporary Chinese Cinema*. New York: Columbia University Press, 1995.

Chu T'ien-wen (Zhu Tianwen) 朱天文. *Huangren shouji* 荒人手記 (Notes of a desolate man). Taibei: Shibao wenhua chubanshe, 1994.

———. "Huayi qianshen: ji Hu Lancheng ba shu" 花憶前身: 記胡蘭成八書 (A flower recalls its previous lives: remembering eight books by Hu Lancheng). In idem, *Huayi qianshen* 花憶前身. Taipei: Maitian chubanshe, 1996, 31–106.

———. *Notes of a Desolate Man*, Trans. Howard Goldblatt and Sylvia Li-chun Lin of *Huangren shouji*. New York: Columbia University Press, 1999.

———. "Yidian bu zai" 伊甸不再 (Eden no more). In idem, *Huayi qianshen*. Taibei: Maitian chubanshe, 1996, 115–34.

Clunas, Craig. *Pictures and Visuality in Early Modern China*. Princeton: Princeton University Press, 1997.

Conger, Sarah Pike. *Letters from China*. London: Hodder and Stoughton, 1909.

Cowie, Elizabeth. *Representing the Woman: Cinema and Psychoanalysis*. Minneapolis: University of Minnesota Press, 1997.

———. "Woman As Sign." *m/f* 1 (1978): 49–63.

Crary, Jonathan. *Suspensions of Perception: Attention, Spectacle, and Modern Culture*. Cambridge: MIT Press, 1999.

———. *Techniques of the Observer: On Vision in the Nineteenth Century*. Cambridge: MIT Press, 1990.

Dawkins, Richard. *The Selfish Gene*. Oxford: Oxford University Press, 1976.

Debord, Guy. *The Society of the Spectacle.* Detroit: Red and Black, 1977.

de Certeau, Michel. *The Practice of Everyday Life.* Berkeley: University of California Press, 1984.

Deleuze, Gilles, and Félix Guattari. *Anti-Oedipus: Capitalism and Schizophrenia.* Minneapolis: University of Minnesota Press, 1981.

Der Ling, Princess. *Two Years in the Forbidden City.* New York: Dodd, Mead, 1924.

Derrida, Jacques. *Memoirs of the Blind: The Self-Portrait and Other Ruins.* Chicago: University of Chicago Press, 1993.

———. *Right of Inspection.* Photographs by Marie-Françoise Plissart. New York: Monacelli Press, 1998.

Ding Ling 丁玲. "Zai yiyuan zhong shi" 在醫院中時 (While in the hospital). In idem, *Ding Ling xuanji* 丁玲選集 (Ding Ling's selected works). Chengdu: Sichuan renmin chubanshe, 1984, 2: 463–85.

Duara, Prasenjit. *Culture, Power and the State: Rural North China, 1900–1940.* Stanford: Stanford University Press, 1998.

Eagleton, Terry. *The Ideology of the Aesthetic.* Cambridge, Eng.: Basil Blackwell, 1980.

Elman, Benjamin. *From Philosophy to Philology: Intellectual and Social Aspects of Change in Late Imperial China.* Cambridge: Harvard University Press, 1984.

Fong, Grace. "Engendering the Lyric: Her Image and Voice in Song." In Pauline Yu, ed., *Voices of the Song Lyric in China.* Berkeley: University of California Press, 1994, 107–44.

Foucault, Michel. *The History of Sexuality,* vol. 1, *An Introduction.* Trans. Robert Hurley. New York: Vintage Books, 1990.

Freud, Sigmund. "Femininity." In James Strachey, ed., *The Complete Psychological Works of Sigmund Freud.* London: Hogarth Press, 1955, 22: 112–35.

———. "The 'Uncanny.'" In James Strachey, ed., *The Standard Edition of the Complete Psychological Works of Sigmund Freud.* London: Hogarth Press, 1955, 17: 217–56.

Gallop, Jane. *Reading Lacan.* Ithaca: Cornell University Press, 1985.

Gao, Minglu, ed. *Inside Out: New Chinese Art.* San Francisco: San Francisco Museum of Modern Art, 1998.

Gao Xingjian 高行健. *Lingshan* 靈山 (Soul mountain). Taibei: Lianjing, 1990.

———. "Lun wenxue xiezuo" 論文學寫作 (On the writing of literature). In idem, *Meiyou zhuyi* 沒有主義 (Without isms). Taibei, Lianjing, 2001, 31–93.

———. "Mei you zhuyi" 沒有主義 (Without isms). In idem, *Meiyou zhuyi* 沒有主義 (Without isms). Taibei: Lianjing, 2001, 3–14.

———. "Muqin" 母親 (Mother). In *Gei wo laoye mai yugan* 給我老爺買漁竿 (Buying my grandfather a fishing rod). Taibei: Lianhe wenxue, 1989, 155–64.

———. *One Man's Bible*. Trans. Mabel Lee of *Yi ge ren de shengjing*. New York: Harper Collins, 2002.

———. *Soul Mountain*. Trans. Mabel Lee of *Lingshan*. New York: Harper Collins, 2001.

———. *Xiandai xiaoshuo jiqiao chutan* 現代小說技巧初探 (A preliminary exploration of the techniques of modern fiction). Guangzhou: Huacheng, 1981.

———. *Yi ge ren de shengjing* 一個人的聖經 (One man's bible). Taibei: Lianjing, 1999.

Geertz, Clifford. *Agricultural Involution: The Process of Ecological Change in Indonesia*. Berkeley: University of California Press, 1963.

Giradot, Norman. *Myth and Meaning in Early Taoism: The Theme of Chaos (Hundun)*. Berkeley: University of California Press, 1988.

Goux, Jean-Joseph. *Symbolic Economies: After Marx and Freud*. Trans. Jennifer Curtiss Gage. Ithaca: Cornell University Press, 1978.

Hamm, John Christopher. *Paper Swordsmen: Jin Yong and the Modern Chinese Martial Arts Novel*. Honolulu: University of Hawai'i Press, 2005.

Han Bangqing 韓邦慶. *Haishang hua liezhuan* 海上花列傳 (Biographies of Shanghai flowers). *Zhongguo jindai wenxue daxi* 中國近代文學大系, vol. 3. Shanghai: Shanghai shudian, 1991.

———. *The Singsong Girls of Shanghai*. Trans. Eileen Chang of *Haishang hua liezhuan*; rev. and ed. Eva Hung. New York: Columbia University Press, 2005.

Han, Sungmii Lee. "Wu Chen's 'Mo-Chu P'u': Literati Painter's Manual on Ink Bamboo." Ph.D. diss., Princeton University, 1983.

Hegel, Robert. *Reading Illustrated Fiction in Late Imperial China*. Stanford: Stanford University Press, 1998.

Heidegger, Martin. "The Age of the World Picture." In William Lovitt, trans. and editor, *The Question Concerning Technology and Other Essays*. New York: Harper Torchbooks, 1977, 115–54.

Hinsch, Bret. *Passions of the Cut Sleeve: The Male Homosexual Tradition in China*. Berkeley: University of California Press, 1990.

Hou Hsiao-hsien (Hou Xiaoxian) 侯孝賢, dir. *Haishang hua* 海上花 (Flowers of Shanghai). 1998.

Hsia, C. T. "The Scholar-Novelist and Chinese Culture." In Andrew Plaks, ed., *Chinese Narrative: Critical and Theoretical Essays*. Princeton: Princeton University Press, 1977, 266–305.

Hu Lancheng 胡蘭成. *Jinri heri xi* 今日何日兮 (What day is today?). Taibei: Yuanliu chubanshe, 1991.

Hu Shi 胡適. "*Jinghua yuan* de yinlun" 鏡花緣故的引論 (Introduction to *Jinghua yuan*). In idem, *Hu Shi wencun* 胡適文存 (Hu Shi's collected works). Taibei: Yuandong tushu, 1965, vol. 3, book 2, 400–433.

Huang Ziping 黄子平. *Geming, lishi, xiaoshuo* 革命, 曆史, 小說 (Revolution, history, and the novel). Hong Kong: Oxford University Press, 1996.

Irigaray, Luce. "Women on the Market." In *This Sex Which Is Not One*. Trans. Catherine Porter. Ithaca: Cornell University Press, 1985, 170–91.

Jay, Martin. *Downcast Eyes: The Denigration of Vision in Twentieth-Century French Thought*. Berkeley: University of California Press, 1994.

———. "Scopic Regimes of Modernity." In Hal Foster, ed., *Vision and Visuality*. Seattle: Bay Press, 1988, 3–28.

Jia Pingwa 賈平凹. *Feidu* 廢都 (Fallen capital). Beijing: Bejing chubanshe, 1993.

Jiang Wen 姜文, dir. *Yangguang canlan de rizi* 陽光燦爛的日子 (In the heat of the sun). 1995.

Jin Yong 金庸. "*Houji*" 後記 (Afterword) to idem, *Tianlong ba bu* 天龍八部. In *Jin Yong zuopin ji* 金庸作品集 (Jin Yong's collected works). Beijing: Sanlian shudian, 1994, 25: 1973–74.

———. *Jin Yong zuopin ji* 金庸作品集 (Jin Yong's collected works). 36 vols. Taibei: Yuanliu chubanshe, 1987.

———. "Letter to the editor." *Wen Wei Po* 文匯報 (Hong Kong), Nov. 11, 1999.

———. *Liancheng jue* 連城訣 (trans. as "A Deadly Secret"). *Jin Yong zuopin ji* 金庸作品集 (Jin Yong's collected works), vol. 20. Beijing: Sanlian shudian, 1994.

———. *Sanshisan jianke tu* 三十三劍客圖 (Thirty-three pictures of chivalrous swordsmen). In *Jin Yong zuopin ji* 金庸作品集 (Jin Yong's collected works). Beijing: Sanlian shudian, 1994, 27: 665–834.

———. *Tianlong ba bu* 天龍八部 (trans. as "Demi-gods and Semi-devils"). *Jin Yong zuopin ji* 金庸作品集 (Jin Yong's collected works), vols. 21–25. Beijing: Sanlian shudian, 1994.

Johnson, Patricia. "Photos Tell of Courage, Defiance." *Houston Chronicle*, Sept. 23, 1998, 1.

Kao, Hsin-Sheng C. *Li Ju-Chen*. Boston: Twayne Publishers, 1981.

Kecskes, Lily. "Photographs of Tz'u-hsi in the Freer Gallery Archives." *Committee on East Asian Libraries Bulletin* 101 (Dec. 1993): 87–92.

Ko, Dorothy. *Teachers of the Inner Chambers: Women and Culture in Seventeenth-Century China*. Stanford University Press, 1994.

Kracauer, Siegfried, *Theory of Film: The Redemption of Physical Reality*. New York: Oxford University Press, 1960.

Krauss, Rosalind. "Notes on the Index, Parts I and II." In idem, *The Originality of the Avant-Garde and Other Modernist Myths.* Cambridge: MIT Press, 1986.

———. *The Optical Unconscious.* Cambridge: MIT Press, 1994.

Kristeva, Julia. *Powers of Horror: An Essay on Abjection.* New York: Columbia University Press, 1982.

Lacan, Jacques. *Écrits: A Selection.* Trans. Alan Sheridan. New York: W. W. Norton & Co., 1977.

———. *The Four Fundamental Concepts of Psychoanalysis.* Ed. Jacques-Alain Miller; trans. Alan Sheridan. New York: W. W. Norton & Co., 1981.

———. "The Mirror Stage as Formative of the Function of the I as Revealed in Psychoanalytic Experience." In idem, *Écrits: A Selection,* trans. Alan Sheridan. New York: W. W. Norton & Co., 1977, 1–7.

———. "Some Reflections on the Ego." *International Journal of Psychoanalysis,* no. 34 (1953): 11–17.

Lee, Leo Ou-fan. *Shanghai Modern: The Flowering of a New Urban Culture in China, 1930–1945.* Cambridge: Harvard University Press, 1999.

Lévi-Strauss, Claude. *The Elementary Structure of Kinship.* Trans. James Harle Bell and John Richard. Boston: Beacon, 1969.

———. *Structural Anthropology.* Trans. Claire Jacobson and Brooke Grundfest Shoepf. New York: Basic Books, 1963.

———. *Tristes Tropiques.* Trans. John Weightman and Doreen Weightman. New York: Macmillan, 1973.

Li Ruzhen 李汝珍. *Flowers in the Mirror.* Trans. Li Tai-yi of *Jinghua yuan.* London: Peter Owen, 1965.

———. *Huitu Jinghua yuan* 繪圖鏡花緣 (Illustrated *Flowers in the Mirror*). Beijing: Zhongguo shudian, 1985.

———. *Jinghua yuan* 鏡花緣 (Destiny of the flowers in the mirror). Shijiazhuang: Huashan wenyi chubanshe, 1994.

Li, Wai-yee. *Enchantment and Disenchantment: Love and Illusion in Chinese Literature.* Princeton: Princeton University Press, 1993.

Li Yijian 李以建. "Canonically 'Rewriting' Jin Yong's Novels: A Consideration of Jin Yong's Novels as Serialized Fiction." Trans. Carlos Rojas. In Ann Huss and Jianmei Liu, eds., *The Jin Yong Phenomenon: Chinese Martial Arts Fiction and Modern Chinese Literary History.* New York: Cambria Press, 2007, 73–96.

Li Yu 李漁 [attributed]. *Roupu tuan* 肉蒲團 (The carnal prayer mat). Taibei: Shuangdi guoji chuban, 1994.

———. *The Carnal Prayer Mat.* Trans. Patrick Hanan. Honolulu: University of Hawai'i Press, 1990.

Li Yung-p'ing (Li Yongping 李永平). *Haidong qing* 海東青. Taibei: Lianhe wenxue, 1992.

———. *Zhu Ling manyou xianjing* 朱鴒漫游仙境 (Zhu Ling's wanderings in wonderland). Taibei: Lianhe wenxue, 1998.

Liao Ying 燎熒. "'Ren . . . zai jianku zhong shengzhang'—Ping Ding Ling tongzhi de 'Zai yiyuan zhong shi'" "人 . . . 在艱苦中生長"—評丁玲同志的《在醫院中時》("Humanity . . . developing in the midst of adversity"—a critique of Ding Ling's "When in the Hospital"). *Jiefang ribao* 解放日報. 1942.

Lin Jing 林京. "Cixi sheying shihua" 慈禧攝影史話. *Gugong bowuyuan yuankan* 故宮博物院院刊 1988, no. 3: 82–88.

Lin Yü-sheng. *The Crisis of Chinese Consciousness: Radical Antitraditionalism in the May Fourth Era.* Madison: University of Wisconsin Press, 1979.

Liu Beisi 劉北汜 and Xu Qixian 徐啓憲, eds. *Gugong zhencang renwu zhaopian huicui* 故宮珍藏人物照片薈萃 (Exquisite figure photographs from the Palace Museum). Beijing: Zijincheng chubanshe, 1992.

Liu, Lydia. *Translingual Practice: Literature, National Culture, and Translated Modernity—China, 1900–1937.* Stanford: Stanford University Press, 1995.

Ma Sen 馬森. "Taowang: zhuiqiu geren ziyou de bijing zhi lu: tan *Yi ge ren de shengjing*" 逃亡: 追求個人自由的必經之: 談《一個人的聖經》(Exile: seeking a canonical path to individual freedom—on *One Man's Bible*). *Lianhe wenxue* (Unitas) 2 (2001): 79–82.

Ma Yunzeng 馬運增 et al., eds. *Zhongguo sheying shi* 中國攝影史*, 1840–1937* (A history of Chinese photography, 1840–1937). Beijing, China: Zhongguo sheying chubanshe, 1987.

Malinowski, Bronislaw. *The Sexual Life of Savages.* Boston: Beacon, 1987.

McClintock, Anne. *Imperial Leather: Race, Gender and Sexuality in the Colonial Contest.* New York: Routledge, 1995.

Meijer, Marinus. "Homosexual Offenses in Qing Law." *T'oung pao* 71 (1985): 109–33.

Montrelay, Michèle. "Inquiry into Femininity." In Toril Moi, ed., *French Feminist Thought: A Reader.* New York: Blackwell, 1987, 227–49.

Mu Shiying 穆时英. "Luotuo, Ni Cai zhuiyizhe yu nüren" 駱駝, 尼采主義著與女人 (Camel, Nietzschean, and woman). In idem, *Baijin de nüti suxiang* 白金的女體塑像 (Platinum statue of a female figure). Beijing: Jiuzhou chubanshe, 1995, 189–96.

Mulvey, Laura. "Visual Pleasures and Narrative Cinema." In idem, *Visual and Other Pleasures.* Bloomington: Indiana University Press, 1989, 14–26.

Ng Kim-chu (Huang Jinshu 黃錦樹). "Shenji zhi wu—hou sishi hui? (Hou) xiandai qishilu?" 神姬之舞—後四十回? (後)現代啓示錄? (Dance of the divine concubine—the last forty chapters? (Post)modern apocalypse now?).

In Zhu Tianwen, *Huayi qianshen* 花憶前身(A flower remembers her previous lives). Taibei: Maitian chubanshe, 1996, 265–312.

"1989 Tiananmen Tank Protester Remains Unidentified." *Japan Economic Newswire*, Apr. 6, 1998.

Pang, Laikwan. "Photography, Performance, and the Making of Female Images in Modern China." *Journal of Women's History* 17, no. 4 (2005): 56–85.

Qiu Miaojin 邱妙津. *Mengmate yishu* 蒙馬特遺書 (Montmartre suicide note). Taibei: Lianhe wenxue chubanshe, 1996.

Roddy, Stephen. *Literati Identity and Its Fictional Representations in Late Imperial China.* Stanford: Stanford University Press, 1998.

Rojas, Carlos. "Wu Jiwen and the Ruins of Representation." *Journal of Modern Literature in Chinese* 5, no. 1 (2001): 29–64.

———. "Wumingshi." In Thomas Moran, ed., *Modern Chinese Fiction Writers, 1900–1949.* Detroit: Thomson Gale, 2007, s.v.

Rojas, Carlos, trans. "Zheng Fuguang's *Humble Reflections on Specularity.*" *Connect: art, politics, theory, practice* 2 (2001): 71–80.

Roudinesco, Elisabeth. *Jacques Lacan.* Trans. Barbara Bray. New York: Columbia University Press, 1997.

———. "The Mirror Stage: An Obliterated Archive." In Jean-Michel Rabaté, ed., *The Cambridge Companion to Lacan.* Cambridge: Cambridge University Press, 2003, 25–34.

Schipper, Kristofer. *The Taoist Body.* Trans. Karen Duval. Berkeley: University of California Press, 1992.

Schor, Naomi. *Reading in Detail: Aesthetics and the Feminine.* New York: Methuen, 1987.

Sharf, Robert. "The Scripture on the Production of Buddha Images." In Donald Lopez, ed., *Religions in China in Practice.* Princeton: Princeton University Press, 1996, 261–67.

Shou lengyan jing 首楞嚴經 (Śūraṃgama-sūtra). Taishō shinshū daizōkyō 19.

Silverman, Kaja. *The Threshold to the Visible World.* New York: Routledge, 1996.

Smith, Ken. "Now the Epic Tale Can Be Told: After All the Political Fireworks, Chen Shizheng's Version of Ancient China's 'Peony Pavilion' Will at Last Premiere in the U.S." *Los Angeles Time*s, July 4, 1999, 5.

Sommer, Matthew. *Sex, Law, and Society in Late Imperial China.* Stanford: Stanford University Press, 2000.

Song Weijie 宋偉杰. *Cong yule xingwei dao wutuobang chongdong: Jin Yong xiaoshuo zai jiedu* 從娛樂行爲到烏邦托沖動: 金庸小説再解讀 (From recreational activity to utopian impulse: a re-reading of Jin Yong's fiction). Nanjing: Jiangsu renmin chubanshe, 1999.

Sun Yanjing 孙燕京, ed. *Wanqing yiying* 晚清遗影 (Late Qing shadows). Ji'nan: Shandong huabao chubanshe, 2000.

Tagg, John. *The Burden of Representation: Essays on Photographies and Histories.* Minneapolis: University of Minnesota Press, 1993.

Tam, Kwok-kan. "Language as Subjectivity in *One Man's Bible*." In idem, ed., *Soul of Chaos: Critical Perspectives on Gao Xingjian.* Hong Kong: Chinese University Press, 2001, 293–310.

Tang Xianzu 湯顯祖. *Mudan ting* 牡丹亭. Beijing: Renmin chubanshe, 1997.

———. *The Peony Pavilion (Mudan Ting).* Trans. Cyril Birch. Bloomington: Indiana University Press, 1994.

"Time 100: Leaders and Revolutionaries." http://www.pathfinder.com/time/time100/leaders/index.html. Accessed on Apr. 13, 1998.

Van Gulik, Robert. *Sexual Life in Ancient China: A Preliminary Survey of Chinese Sex and Society From Ca. 1500 B.C. Till 1644 A. D.* Leiden: Brill, 1961.

Vinograd, Richard. *Boundaries of the Self: Chinese Portraits, 1600–1900.* Cambridge: Cambridge University Press, 1992.

Wang, Ban. "Re-enchanting the Disenchanted Image: Reification and Nostalgia in Zhu Tianwen's Fiction." In David Der-wei Wang and Carlos Rojas, eds., *Writing Taiwan: A New Literary History.* Durham: Duke University Press, 2006, 370–88.

Wang, Cheng-hua. "Presenting the Empress Dowager to the World: Cixi's Images and Self-fashioning in Late-Qing Politics." Paper presented at the New Directions in Chinese Women's History conference, Columbia University, Feb. 16–17, 2001.

Wang, David Der-wei (Wang Dewei 王德威). *Fin-de-siècle Splendor: Repressed Modernities of Late Qing Fiction, 1849–1911.* Stanford: Stanford University Press, 1997.

———. "Foreword." In Eileen Chang, *The Rice-Sprout Song.* Berkeley: University of California Press, 1998, vii–xxv.

———. "Meiyou [xiandai]zhuyi: tan *Gei wo laoye mai yugan* ji qita" 沒有[現代]主義：談《給我老爺買漁竿》及其他 (Without [modern]ism: on [Gao Xingjian's] *Buying My Grandfather a Fishing Rod* and other matters). *Lianhe wenxue* (Unitas) 2 (2001): 71–74.

———. *The Monster That Is History.* Berkeley: University of California Press, 2004.

———. "Shalemei zhitu—ping Li Yongping *Haidong qing*" 莎樂美迠迌—評李永平《海東青》(Salome's "wandering/beheading"—commentary on Li Yongping's *Haidong qing*). In idem, *Zhongsheng xuanhua yihou: dianping dangdai zhongwen xiaoshuo* 眾聲喧嘩以後：點評當代中文小說 (After heteroglossia: reviews of contemporary Chinese fiction). Taipei: Maitian chubanshe, 2001), 95–99.

Wang, Jing. *High Culture Fever: Politics, Aesthetics, and Ideology in Deng's China.* Berkeley: University of California Press, 1996.

———. *The Story of Stone: Intertextuality, Ancient Chinese Stone Lore, and the Stone Symbolism of* Dream of the Red Chamber, Water Margin, *and* The Journey to the West. Durham: Duke University Press, 1992.

Wang Shuo 王朔. "Dongwu xiongmeng" 動物匈猛. In idem, *Wang Shuo wenji* 王朔文集. Beijing: Huayi chubanshe, 1994, 1: 406–93.

———. *Kanshangqu hen mei* 看上去很美 (It looks really beautiful). Beijing: Huayi chubanshe, 1999.

———. *Playing for Thrills.* Trans. Howard Goldblatt of *Wan'r de jiu shi xin tiao.* New York: William Morrow and Company, 1963.

———. *Wan'r de jiu shi xin tiao* 玩兒的就是心跳. In idem, *Wang Shuo wenji* 王朔文集. Beijing: Huayi chubanshe, 1994, 2: 201–416.

———. "Wo kan Jin Yong" 我看金庸" (How I see Jin Yong). *Zhongguo qingnian bao* 中國青年報 (China youth daily), Nov. 1, 1999.

———. "Wo shi 'lang'" 我是'狼.' In idem, *Wang Shuo wenji* 王朔文集. Beijing: Huayi chubanshe, 1994, 2: 158–200.

Wang Shuo 王朔 et al. *Wo shi Wang Shuo* 我是王朔 (I am Wang Shuo). Beijing: Xinhua shudian, 1998.

Wang Yingguo 汪應果 and Zhao Jiangbin 趙江濱. *Wumingshi zhuanqi* 無名氏傳奇 (The legend of Wumingshi). Shanghai: Shanghai wenyi chubanshe, 1998.

Watson, Burton, trans. *The Lotus Sutra.* New York: Columbia University Press, 1993.

Wile, Douglas. *Art of the Bedchamber: The Chinese Sexual Yoga Classics Including Women's Solo Meditation Texts.* Albany: State University of New York Press, 1992.

Wu Chi-wen (Wu Jiwen) 吳繼文. *Shijimo shaonian ai duben* 世紀末少年愛讀本 (*Fin-de-siècle* reader of young love). Taibei: Shibao wenhua chubanshe, 1996.

Wu Hung. *The Double Screen: Medium and Representation in Chinese Painting.* Chicago: University of Chicago Press, 1996.

Wu Jiwen, *see* Wu Chi-ren.

Wu Liang 吳亮. *Lao Shanghai: yishi de shiguang* 老上海：已逝的時光 (Old Shanghai: a light that has already disappeared). Nanjing: Jiangsu meishu chubanshe, 1998.

Wu, Qingyun. *Female Rule in Chinese and English Literary Utopias.* Syracuse: Syracuse University Press, 1995.

Wu Yitang 吳貽棠. *Fengyue jian* 風月鑒 (Mirror of romance). Taibei: Shuangdi guoji chuban, 1994.

Wumingshi 無名士. *Beiji fengqing hua* 北極風情畫 (A picture of an arctic romance). Shanghai: Huabei xinwen chubanshe, 1944.

———. *Chuang shiji da puti* 創世紀大菩提 (Great enlightenment of the creation of a new era). Taibei: Yuanjing chuban, 1984.

———. "Dongti ningsi" 胴體凝思 (Reflections on the body). In idem, *Shuqing yanyun* 抒情煙雲 (Expressing emotions of mist and clouds). Taipei: Wenshizhi chubanshe, 1998, 2: 389–94.

———. *Haiyan* 海艶 (Siren of the sea). Hong Kong: Xinwen tiandishe, 1977.

———. *Jinse de sheye* 金色的蛇夜 (Golden night of the serpent). Hong Kong: Xinwen tiandishe, 1982.

———. *Jinse de sheye xuji* 金色的蛇夜續集 (Golden night of the serpent: continuation). Hong Kong: Xinwen tiandishe, 1982.

———. *Kaihua zai xingyun yiwai* 開花在星雲以外 (Blooming flowers beyond stars and clouds). Hong Kong: Xinwen tiandishe, 1993.

———. *Si de yanceng* 死的岩層 (The stone strata of death). Hong Kong: Xinwen tiandishe, 1981.

———. *Tali de nüren* 塔裏的女人 (Woman in the pagoda). N.p.: Shidai shenghuo chubanshe, 1946.

———. *Yeshou, yeshou, yeshou* 野獸 野獸 野獸 (Beast, beast, beast). Taibei: Yuanjing chubanshe, 1984.

Xu Shuofang. "Notes on the Program: Tang Xianzu and *The Peony Pavilion.*" In *Lincoln Center Festival 99: Stagebill*, July 1999, 7–25.

Yan Yuan. "Learning Through Experience." In Wing-Tsit Chan, trans., *A Source Book in Chinese Philosophy*. Princeton: Princeton University Press, 1963, 707–8.

Ye Daying 葉大鷹. "Wo he *Hong yingtao*" 我和《紅櫻桃》(*Red Cherry* and I). *Dangdai dianying* 當代電影 1996, no. 1, 48–50.

Ye Daying 葉大鷹, dir. *Hong Yingtao* 紅櫻桃 (Red cherry). 1995.

Yu, Anthony, trans. *Journey to the West.* 4 vols. Chicago: University of Chicago Press, 1984.

Yu, Chun-Fang. *Kuan-yin: The Chinese Transformation of Avalokitesvara.* New York: Columbia University Press, 2001.

Zeitlin, Judith. "Making the Invisible Visible: Portraits of Desire and Constructions of Death in Sixteenth and Seventeenth-Century China." In Jane Donawerth and Adele Seerf, eds., *Crossing Boundaries: Attending to Early Modern Woman.* Baltimore: University of Maryland Press, 2001, 48–79.

Zhang Ailing 張愛玲, *see* Chang, Eileen.

Zhang Yanyuan 張彥遠. *Lidai minghua ji* 歷代名畫記 (Records of famous paintings of successive dynasties). Beijing: Zhonghua shuju, 1985.

Zheng Fuguang 鄭復光. *Jingjing lingchi* 鏡鏡詅癡 (Humble ruminations on specularity). Beijing: Zhonghua shuju, 1985.

Zhou Fenling 周芬伶. *Yanyi: Zhang Ailing yu Zhongguo wenxue* 艷異: 張愛玲與中國文學 (Colorful *différance:* Eileen Chang and Chinese literature). Taibei: Meta Media, 1999.

Zhu Tianwen 朱天文, *see* Chu T'ien-wen.

Zito, Angela. *Of Body and Brush: Grand Sacrifice as Text/Performance in Eighteenth-Century China.* Chicago: University of Chicago Press, 1997.

Žižek, Slavoj, and Alain Badiou, eds. Special issue on "Names-of-the-Father." *Lacanian Ink* 27 (2006).

Index

Harvard East Asian Monographs

(*out-of-print)

*1. Liang Fang-chung, *The Single-Whip Method of Taxation in China*

*2. Harold C. Hinton, *The Grain Tribute System of China, 1845–1911*

3. Ellsworth C. Carlson, *The Kaiping Mines, 1877–1912*

*4. Chao Kuo-chün, *Agrarian Policies of Mainland China: A Documentary Study, 1949–1956*

*5. Edgar Snow, *Random Notes on Red China, 1936–1945*

*6. Edwin George Beal, Jr., *The Origin of Likin, 1835–1864*

7. Chao Kuo-chün, *Economic Planning and Organization in Mainland China: A Documentary Study, 1949–1957*

*8. John K. Fairbank, *Ching Documents: An Introductory Syllabus*

*9. Helen Yin and Yi-chang Yin, *Economic Statistics of Mainland China, 1949–1957*

10. Wolfgang Franke, *The Reform and Abolition of the Traditional Chinese Examination System*

11. Albert Feuerwerker and S. Cheng, *Chinese Communist Studies of Modern Chinese History*

12. C. John Stanley, *Late Ching Finance: Hu Kuang-yung as an Innovator*

13. S. M. Meng, *The Tsungli Yamen: Its Organization and Functions*

*14. Ssu-yü Teng, *Historiography of the Taiping Rebellion*

15. Chun-Jo Liu, *Controversies in Modern Chinese Intellectual History: An Analytic Bibliography of Periodical Articles, Mainly of the May Fourth and Post-May Fourth Era*

*16. Edward J. M. Rhoads, *The Chinese Red Army, 1927–1963: An Annotated Bibliography*

*17. Andrew J. Nathan, *A History of the China International Famine Relief Commission*

*18. Frank H. H. King (ed.) and Prescott Clarke, *A Research Guide to China-Coast Newspapers, 1822–1911*

*19. Ellis Joffe, *Party and Army: Professionalism and Political Control in the Chinese Officer Corps, 1949–1964*

*20. Toshio G. Tsukahira, *Feudal Control in Tokugawa Japan: The Sankin Kōtai System*

*21. Kwang-Ching Liu, ed., *American Missionaries in China: Papers from Harvard Seminars*

*22. George Moseley, *A Sino-Soviet Cultural Frontier: The Ili Kazakh Autonomous Chou*

23. Carl F. Nathan, *Plague Prevention and Politics in Manchuria, 1910–1931*

*24. Adrian Arthur Bennett, *John Fryer: The Introduction of Western Science and Technology into Nineteenth-Century China*

*25. Donald J. Friedman, *The Road from Isolation: The Campaign of the American Committee for Non-Participation in Japanese Aggression, 1938–1941*

*26. Edward LeFevour, *Western Enterprise in Late Ching China: A Selective Survey of Jardine, Matheson and Company's Operations, 1842–1895*

27. Charles Neuhauser, *Third World Politics: China and the Afro-Asian People's Solidarity Organization, 1957–1967*

*28. Kungtu C. Sun, assisted by Ralph W. Huenemann, *The Economic Development of Manchuria in the First Half of the Twentieth Century*

*29. Shahid Javed Burki, *A Study of Chinese Communes, 1965*

30. John Carter Vincent, *The Extraterritorial System in China: Final Phase*

31. Madeleine Chi, *China Diplomacy, 1914–1918*

*32. Clifton Jackson Phillips, *Protestant America and the Pagan World: The First Half Century of the American Board of Commissioners for Foreign Missions, 1810–1860*

*33. James Pusey, *Wu Han: Attacking the Present Through the Past*

*34. Ying-wan Cheng, *Postal Communication in China and Its Modernization, 1860–1896*

35. Tuvia Blumenthal, *Saving in Postwar Japan*

36. Peter Frost, *The Bakumatsu Currency Crisis*

37. Stephen C. Lockwood, *Augustine Heard and Company, 1858–1862*

38. Robert R. Campbell, *James Duncan Campbell: A Memoir by His Son*

39. Jerome Alan Cohen, ed., *The Dynamics of China's Foreign Relations*

40. V. V. Vishnyakova-Akimova, *Two Years in Revolutionary China, 1925–1927,* trans. Steven L. Levine

41. Meron Medzini, *French Policy in Japan During the Closing Years of the Tokugawa Regime*

42. Ezra Vogel, Margie Sargent, Vivienne B. Shue, Thomas Jay Mathews, and Deborah S. Davis, *The Cultural Revolution in the Provinces*

43. Sidney A. Forsythe, *An American Missionary Community in China, 1895–1905*

*44. Benjamin I. Schwartz, ed., *Reflections on the May Fourth Movement.: A Symposium*

*45. Ching Young Choe, *The Rule of the Taewŏngun, 1864–1873: Restoration in Yi Korea*

46. W. P. J. Hall, *A Bibliographical Guide to Japanese Research on the Chinese Economy, 1958–1970*

47. Jack J. Gerson, *Horatio Nelson Lay and Sino-British Relations, 1854–1864*

48. Paul Richard Bohr, *Famine and the Missionary: Timothy Richard as Relief Administrator and Advocate of National Reform*
49. Endymion Wilkinson, *The History of Imperial China: A Research Guide*
50. Britten Dean, *China and Great Britain: The Diplomacy of Commercial Relations, 1860–1864*
51. Ellsworth C. Carlson, *The Foochow Missionaries, 1847–1880*
52. Yeh-chien Wang, *An Estimate of the Land-Tax Collection in China, 1753 and 1908*
53. Richard M. Pfeffer, *Understanding Business Contracts in China, 1949–1963*

*54. Han-sheng Chuan and Richard Kraus, *Mid-Ching Rice Markets and Trade: An Essay in Price History*

55. Ranbir Vohra, *Lao She and the Chinese Revolution*
56. Liang-lin Hsiao, *China's Foreign Trade Statistics, 1864–1949*

*57. Lee-hsia Hsu Ting, *Government Control of the Press in Modern China, 1900–1949*

*58. Edward W. Wagner, *The Literati Purges: Political Conflict in Early Yi Korea*

*59. Joungwon A. Kim, *Divided Korea: The Politics of Development, 1945–1972*

60. Noriko Kamachi, John K. Fairbank, and Chūzō Ichiko, *Japanese Studies of Modern China Since 1953: A Bibliographical Guide to Historical and Social-Science Research on the Nineteenth and Twentieth Centuries, Supplementary Volume for 1953–1969*
61. Donald A. Gibbs and Yun-chen Li, *A Bibliography of Studies and Translations of Modern Chinese Literature, 1918–1942*
62. Robert H. Silin, *Leadership and Values: The Organization of Large-Scale Taiwanese Enterprises*
63. David Pong, *A Critical Guide to the Kwangtung Provincial Archives Deposited at the Public Record Office of London*

*64. Fred W. Drake, *China Charts the World: Hsu Chi-yü and His Geography of 1848*

*65. William A. Brown and Urgrunge Onon, translators and annotators, *History of the Mongolian People's Republic*

66. Edward L. Farmer, *Early Ming Government: The Evolution of Dual Capitals*

*67. Ralph C. Croizier, *Koxinga and Chinese Nationalism: History, Myth, and the Hero*

*68. William J. Tyler, tr., *The Psychological World of Natsume Sōseki,* by Doi Takeo

69. Eric Widmer, *The Russian Ecclesiastical Mission in Peking During the Eighteenth Century*

*70. Charlton M. Lewis, *Prologue to the Chinese Revolution: The Transformation of Ideas and Institutions in Hunan Province, 1891–1907*

71. Preston Torbert, *The Ching Imperial Household Department: A Study of Its Organization and Principal Functions, 1662–1796*
72. Paul A. Cohen and John E. Schrecker, eds., *Reform in Nineteenth-Century China*
73. Jon Sigurdson, *Rural Industrialism in China*
74. Kang Chao, *The Development of Cotton Textile Production in China*

75. Valentin Rabe, *The Home Base of American China Missions, 1880–1920*
*76. Sarasin Viraphol, *Tribute and Profit: Sino-Siamese Trade, 1652–1853*
77. Ch'i-ch'ing Hsiao, *The Military Establishment of the Yuan Dynasty*
78. Meishi Tsai, *Contemporary Chinese Novels and Short Stories, 1949–1974: An Annotated Bibliography*
*79. Wellington K. K. Chan, *Merchants, Mandarins and Modern Enterprise in Late Ching China*
80. Endymion Wilkinson, *Landlord and Labor in Late Imperial China: Case Studies from Shandong by Jing Su and Luo Lun*
*81. Barry Keenan, *The Dewey Experiment in China: Educational Reform and Political Power in the Early Republic*
*82. George A. Hayden, *Crime and Punishment in Medieval Chinese Drama: Three Judge Pao Plays*
*83. Sang-Chul Suh, *Growth and Structural Changes in the Korean Economy, 1910–1940*
84. J. W. Dower, *Empire and Aftermath: Yoshida Shigeru and the Japanese Experience, 1878–1954*
85. Martin Collcutt, *Five Mountains: The Rinzai Zen Monastic Institution in Medieval Japan*
86. Kwang Suk Kim and Michael Roemer, *Growth and Structural Transformation*
87. Anne O. Krueger, *The Developmental Role of the Foreign Sector and Aid*
*88. Edwin S. Mills and Byung-Nak Song, *Urbanization and Urban Problems*
89. Sung Hwan Ban, Pal Yong Moon, and Dwight H. Perkins, *Rural Development*
*90. Noel F. McGinn, Donald R. Snodgrass, Yung Bong Kim, Shin-Bok Kim, and Quee-Young Kim, *Education and Development in Korea*
*91. Leroy P. Jones and Il SaKong, *Government, Business, and Entrepreneurship in Economic Development: The Korean Case*
92. Edward S. Mason, Dwight H. Perkins, Kwang Suk Kim, David C. Cole, Mahn Je Kim et al., *The Economic and Social Modernization of the Republic of Korea*
93. Robert Repetto, Tai Hwan Kwon, Son-Ung Kim, Dae Young Kim, John E. Sloboda, and Peter J. Donaldson, *Economic Development, Population Policy, and Demographic Transition in the Republic of Korea*
94. Parks M. Coble, Jr., *The Shanghai Capitalists and the Nationalist Government, 1927–1937*
95. Noriko Kamachi, *Reform in China: Huang Tsun-hsien and the Japanese Model*
96. Richard Wich, *Sino-Soviet Crisis Politics: A Study of Political Change and Communication*
97. Lillian M. Li, *China's Silk Trade: Traditional Industry in the Modern World, 1842–1937*
98. R. David Arkush, *Fei Xiaotong and Sociology in Revolutionary China*
*99. Kenneth Alan Grossberg, *Japan's Renaissance: The Politics of the Muromachi Bakufu*
100. James Reeve Pusey, *China and Charles Darwin*

101. Hoyt Cleveland Tillman, *Utilitarian Confucianism: Chen Liang's Challenge to Chu Hsi*
102. Thomas A. Stanley, *Ōsugi Sakae, Anarchist in Taishō Japan: The Creativity of the Ego*
103. Jonathan K. Ocko, *Bureaucratic Reform in Provincial China: Ting Jih-ch'ang in Restoration Kiangsu, 1867–1870*
104. James Reed, *The Missionary Mind and American East Asia Policy, 1911–1915*
105. Neil L. Waters, *Japan's Local Pragmatists: The Transition from Bakumatsu to Meiji in the Kawasaki Region*
106. David C. Cole and Yung Chul Park, *Financial Development in Korea, 1945–1978*
107. Roy Bahl, Chuk Kyo Kim, and Chong Kee Park, *Public Finances During the Korean Modernization Process*
108. William D. Wray, *Mitsubishi and the N.Y.K, 1870–1914: Business Strategy in the Japanese Shipping Industry*
109. Ralph William Huenemann, *The Dragon and the Iron Horse: The Economics of Railroads in China, 1876–1937*
*110. Benjamin A. Elman, *From Philosophy to Philology: Intellectual and Social Aspects of Change in Late Imperial China*
111. Jane Kate Leonard, *Wei Yüan and China's Rediscovery of the Maritime World*
112. Luke S. K. Kwong, *A Mosaic of the Hundred Days:. Personalities, Politics, and Ideas of 1898*
*113. John E. Wills, Jr., *Embassies and Illusions: Dutch and Portuguese Envoys to K'ang-hsi, 1666–1687*
114. Joshua A. Fogel, *Politics and Sinology: The Case of Naitō Konan (1866–1934)*
*115. Jeffrey C. Kinkley, ed., *After Mao: Chinese Literature and Society, 1978–1981*
116. C. Andrew Gerstle, *Circles of Fantasy: Convention in the Plays of Chikamatsu*
117. Andrew Gordon, *The Evolution of Labor Relations in Japan: Heavy Industry, 1853–1955*
*118. Daniel K. Gardner, *Chu Hsi and the "Ta Hsueh": Neo-Confucian Reflection on the Confucian Canon*
119. Christine Guth Kanda, *Shinzō: Hachiman Imagery and Its Development*
*120. Robert Borgen, *Sugawara no Michizane and the Early Heian Court*
121. Chang-tai Hung, *Going to the People: Chinese Intellectual and Folk Literature, 1918–1937*
*122. Michael A. Cusumano, *The Japanese Automobile Industry: Technology and Management at Nissan and Toyota*
123. Richard von Glahn, *The Country of Streams and Grottoes: Expansion, Settlement, and the Civilizing of the Sichuan Frontier in Song Times*
124. Steven D. Carter, *The Road to Komatsubara: A Classical Reading of the Renga Hyakuin*
125. Katherine F. Bruner, John K. Fairbank, and Richard T. Smith, *Entering China's Service: Robert Hart's Journals, 1854–1863*

126. Bob Tadashi Wakabayashi, *Anti-Foreignism and Western Learning in Early-Modern Japan: The "New Theses" of 1825*
127. Atsuko Hirai, *Individualism and Socialism: The Life and Thought of Kawai Eijirō (1891–1944)*
128. Ellen Widmer, *The Margins of Utopia: "Shui-hu hou-chuan" and the Literature of Ming Loyalism*
129. R. Kent Guy, *The Emperor's Four Treasuries: Scholars and the State in the Late Chien-lung Era*
130. Peter C. Perdue, *Exhausting the Earth: State and Peasant in Hunan, 1500–1850*
131. Susan Chan Egan, *A Latterday Confucian: Reminiscences of William Hung (1893–1980)*
132. James T. C. Liu, *China Turning Inward: Intellectual-Political Changes in the Early Twelfth Century*

*133. Paul A. Cohen, *Between Tradition and Modernity: Wang T'ao and Reform in Late Ching China*

134. Kate Wildman Nakai, *Shogunal Politics: Arai Hakuseki and the Premises of Tokugawa Rule*

*135. Parks M. Coble, *Facing Japan: Chinese Politics and Japanese Imperialism, 1931–1937*

136. Jon L. Saari, *Legacies of Childhood: Growing Up Chinese in a Time of Crisis, 1890–1920*
137. Susan Downing Videen, *Tales of Heichū*
138. Heinz Morioka and Miyoko Sasaki, *Rakugo: The Popular Narrative Art of Japan*
139. Joshua A. Fogel, *Nakae Ushikichi in China: The Mourning of Spirit*
140. Alexander Barton Woodside, *Vietnam and the Chinese Model: A Comparative Study of Vietnamese and Chinese Government in the First Half of the Nineteenth Century*

*141. George Elison, *Deus Destroyed: The Image of Christianity in Early Modern Japan*

142. William D. Wray, ed., *Managing Industrial Enterprise: Cases from Japan's Prewar Experience*

*143. T'ung-tsu Ch'ü, *Local Government in China Under the Ching*

144. Marie Anchordoguy, *Computers, Inc.: Japan's Challenge to IBM*
145. Barbara Molony, *Technology and Investment: The Prewar Japanese Chemical Industry*
146. Mary Elizabeth Berry, *Hideyoshi*
147. Laura E. Hein, *Fueling Growth: The Energy Revolution and Economic Policy in Postwar Japan*
148. Wen-hsin Yeh, *The Alienated Academy: Culture and Politics in Republican China, 1919–1937*
149. Dru C. Gladney, *Muslim Chinese: Ethnic Nationalism in the People's Republic*
150. Merle Goldman and Paul A. Cohen, eds., *Ideas Across Cultures: Essays on Chinese Thought in Honor of Benjamin L Schwartz*
151. James M. Polachek, *The Inner Opium War*
152. Gail Lee Bernstein, *Japanese Marxist: A Portrait of Kawakami Hajime, 1879–1946*

*153. Lloyd E. Eastman, *The Abortive Revolution: China Under Nationalist Rule, 1927–1937*

154. Mark Mason, *American Multinationals and Japan: The Political Economy of Japanese Capital Controls, 1899–1980*

155. Richard J. Smith, John K. Fairbank, and Katherine F. Bruner, *Robert Hart and China's Early Modernization: His Journals, 1863–1866*

156. George J. Tanabe, Jr., *Myōe the Dreamkeeper: Fantasy and Knowledge in Kamakura Buddhism*

157. William Wayne Farris, *Heavenly Warriors: The Evolution of Japan's Military, 500–1300*

158. Yu-ming Shaw, *An American Missionary in China: John Leighton Stuart and Chinese-American Relations*

159. James B. Palais, *Politics and Policy in Traditional Korea*

*160. Douglas Reynolds, *China, 1898–1912: The Xinzheng Revolution and Japan*

161. Roger R. Thompson, *China's Local Councils in the Age of Constitutional Reform, 1898–1911*

162. William Johnston, *The Modern Epidemic: History of Tuberculosis in Japan*

163. Constantine Nomikos Vaporis, *Breaking Barriers: Travel and the State in Early Modern Japan*

164. Irmela Hijiya-Kirschnereit, *Rituals of Self-Revelation: Shishōsetsu as Literary Genre and Socio-Cultural Phenomenon*

165. James C. Baxter, *The Meiji Unification Through the Lens of Ishikawa Prefecture*

166. Thomas R. H. Havens, *Architects of Affluence: The Tsutsumi Family and the Seibu-Saison Enterprises in Twentieth-Century Japan*

167. Anthony Hood Chambers, *The Secret Window: Ideal Worlds in Tanizaki's Fiction*

168. Steven J. Ericson, *The Sound of the Whistle: Railroads and the State in Meiji Japan*

169. Andrew Edmund Goble, *Kenmu: Go-Daigo's Revolution*

170. Denise Potrzeba Lett, *In Pursuit of Status: The Making of South Korea's "New" Urban Middle Class*

171. Mimi Hall Yiengpruksawan, *Hiraizumi: Buddhist Art and Regional Politics in Twelfth-Century Japan*

172. Charles Shirō Inouye, *The Similitude of Blossoms: A Critical Biography of Izumi Kyōka (1873–1939), Japanese Novelist and Playwright*

173. Aviad E. Raz, *Riding the Black Ship: Japan and Tokyo Disneyland*

174. Deborah J. Milly, *Poverty, Equality, and Growth: The Politics of Economic Need in Postwar Japan*

175. See Heng Teow, *Japan's Cultural Policy Toward China, 1918–1931: A Comparative Perspective*

176. Michael A. Fuller, *An Introduction to Literary Chinese*

177. Frederick R. Dickinson, *War and National Reinvention: Japan in the Great War, 1914–1919*

178. John Solt, *Shredding the Tapestry of Meaning: The Poetry and Poetics of Kitasono Katue (1902–1978)*
179. Edward Pratt, *Japan's Protoindustrial Elite: The Economic Foundations of the Gōnō*
180. Atsuko Sakaki, *Recontextualizing Texts: Narrative Performance in Modern Japanese Fiction*
181. Soon-Won Park, *Colonial Industrialization and Labor in Korea: The Onoda Cement Factory*
182. JaHyun Kim Haboush and Martina Deuchler, *Culture and the State in Late Chosŏn Korea*
183. John W. Chaffee, *Branches of Heaven: A History of the Imperial Clan of Sung China*
184. Gi-Wook Shin and Michael Robinson, eds., *Colonial Modernity in Korea*
185. Nam-lin Hur, *Prayer and Play in Late Tokugawa Japan: Asakusa Sensōji and Edo Society*
186. Kristin Stapleton, *Civilizing Chengdu: Chinese Urban Reform, 1895–1937*
187. Hyung Il Pai, *Constructing "Korean" Origins: A Critical Review of Archaeology, Historiography, and Racial Myth in Korean State-Formation Theories*
188. Brian D. Ruppert, *Jewel in the Ashes: Buddha Relics and Power in Early Medieval Japan*
189. Susan Daruvala, *Zhou Zuoren and an Alternative Chinese Response to Modernity*
*190. James Z. Lee, *The Political Economy of a Frontier: Southwest China, 1250–1850*
191. Kerry Smith, *A Time of Crisis: Japan, the Great Depression, and Rural Revitalization*
192. Michael Lewis, *Becoming Apart: National Power and Local Politics in Toyama, 1868–1945*
193. William C. Kirby, Man-houng Lin, James Chin Shih, and David A. Pietz, eds., *State and Economy in Republican China: A Handbook for Scholars*
194. Timothy S. George, *Minamata: Pollution and the Struggle for Democracy in Postwar Japan*
195. Billy K. L. So, *Prosperity, Region, and Institutions in Maritime China: The South Fukien Pattern, 946–1368*
196. Yoshihisa Tak Matsusaka, *The Making of Japanese Manchuria, 1904–1932*
197. Maram Epstein, *Competing Discourses: Orthodoxy, Authenticity, and Engendered Meanings in Late Imperial Chinese Fiction*
198. Curtis J. Milhaupt, J. Mark Ramseyer, and Michael K. Young, eds. and comps., *Japanese Law in Context: Readings in Society, the Economy, and Politics*
199. Haruo Iguchi, *Unfinished Business: Ayukawa Yoshisuke and U.S.-Japan Relations, 1937–1952*
200. Scott Pearce, Audrey Spiro, and Patricia Ebrey, *Culture and Power in the Reconstitution of the Chinese Realm, 200–600*
201. Terry Kawashima, *Writing Margins: The Textual Construction of Gender in Heian and Kamakura Japan*
202. Martin W. Huang, *Desire and Fictional Narrative in Late Imperial China*

203. Robert S. Ross and Jiang Changbin, eds., *Re-examining the Cold War: U.S.-China Diplomacy, 1954–1973*
204. Guanhua Wang, *In Search of Justice: The 1905–1906 Chinese Anti-American Boycott*
205. David Schaberg, *A Patterned Past: Form and Thought in Early Chinese Historiography*
206. Christine Yano, *Tears of Longing: Nostalgia and the Nation in Japanese Popular Song*
207. Milena Doleželová-Velingerová and Oldřich Král, with Graham Sanders, eds., *The Appropriation of Cultural Capital: China's May Fourth Project*
208. Robert N. Huey, *The Making of 'Shinkokinshū'*
209. Lee Butler, *Emperor and Aristocracy in Japan, 1467–1680: Resilience and Renewal*
210. Suzanne Ogden, *Inklings of Democracy in China*
211. Kenneth J. Ruoff, *The People's Emperor: Democracy and the Japanese Monarchy, 1945–1995*
212. Haun Saussy, *Great Walls of Discourse and Other Adventures in Cultural China*
213. Aviad E. Raz, *Emotions at Work: Normative Control, Organizations, and Culture in Japan and America*
214. Rebecca E. Karl and Peter Zarrow, eds., *Rethinking the 1898 Reform Period: Political and Cultural Change in Late Qing China*
215. Kevin O'Rourke, *The Book of Korean Shijo*
216. Ezra F. Vogel, ed., *The Golden Age of the U.S.-China-Japan Triangle, 1972–1989*
217. Thomas A. Wilson, ed., *On Sacred Grounds: Culture, Society, Politics, and the Formation of the Cult of Confucius*
218. Donald S. Sutton, *Steps of Perfection: Exorcistic Performers and Chinese Religion in Twentieth-Century Taiwan*
219. Daqing Yang, *Technology of Empire: Telecommunications and Japanese Expansionism, 1895–1945*
220. Qianshen Bai, *Fu Shan's World: The Transformation of Chinese Calligraphy in the Seventeenth Century*
221. Paul Jakov Smith and Richard von Glahn, eds., *The Song-Yuan-Ming Transition in Chinese History*
222. Rania Huntington, *Alien Kind: Foxes and Late Imperial Chinese Narrative*
223. Jordan Sand, *House and Home in Modern Japan: Architecture, Domestic Space, and Bourgeois Culture, 1880–1930*
224. Karl Gerth, *China Made: Consumer Culture and the Creation of the Nation*
225. Xiaoshan Yang, *Metamorphosis of the Private Sphere: Gardens and Objects in Tang-Song Poetry*
226. Barbara Mittler, *A Newspaper for China? Power, Identity, and Change in Shanghai's News Media, 1872–1912*
227. Joyce A. Madancy, *The Troublesome Legacy of Commissioner Lin: The Opium Trade and Opium Suppression in Fujian Province, 1820s to 1920s*

228. John Makeham, *Transmitters and Creators: Chinese Commentators and Commentaries on the Analects*
229. Elisabeth Köll, *From Cotton Mill to Business Empire: The Emergence of Regional Enterprises in Modern China*
230. Emma Teng, *Taiwan's Imagined Geography: Chinese Colonial Travel Writing and Pictures, 1683–1895*
231. Wilt Idema and Beata Grant, *The Red Brush: Writing Women of Imperial China*
232. Eric C. Rath, *The Ethos of Noh: Actors and Their Art*
233. Elizabeth Remick, *Building Local States: China During the Republican and Post-Mao Eras*
234. Lynn Struve, ed., *The Qing Formation in World-Historical Time*
235. D. Max Moerman, *Localizing Paradise: Kumano Pilgrimage and the Religious Landscape of Premodern Japan*
236. Antonia Finnane, *Speaking of Yangzhou: A Chinese City, 1550–1850*
237. Brian Platt, *Burning and Building: Schooling and State Formation in Japan, 1750–1890*
238. Gail Bernstein, Andrew Gordon, and Kate Wildman Nakai, eds., *Public Spheres, Private Lives in Modern Japan, 1600–1950: Essays in Honor of Albert Craig*
239. Wu Hung and Katherine R. Tsiang, *Body and Face in Chinese Visual Culture*
240. Stephen Dodd, *Writing Home: Representations of the Native Place in Modern Japanese Literature*
241. David Anthony Bello, *Opium and the Limits of Empire: Drug Prohibition in the Chinese Interior, 1729–1850*
242. Hosea Hirata, *Discourses of Seduction: History, Evil, Desire, and Modern Japanese Literature*
243. Kyung Moon Hwang, *Beyond Birth: Social Status in the Emergence of Modern Korea*
244. Brian R. Dott, *Identity Reflections: Pilgrimages to Mount Tai in Late Imperial China*
245. Mark McNally, *Proving the Way: Conflict and Practice in the History of Japanese Nativism*
246. Yongping Wu, *A Political Explanation of Economic Growth: State Survival, Bureaucratic Politics, and Private Enterprises in the Making of Taiwan's Economy, 1950–1985*
247. Kyu Hyun Kim, *The Age of Visions and Arguments: Parliamentarianism and the National Public Sphere in Early Meiji Japan*
248. Zvi Ben-Dor Benite, *The Dao of Muhammad: A Cultural History of Muslims in Late Imperial China*
249. David Der-wei Wang and Shang Wei, eds., *Dynastic Crisis and Cultural Innovation: From the Late Ming to the Late Qing and Beyond*
250. Wilt L. Idema, Wai-yee Li, and Ellen Widmer, eds., *Trauma and Transcendence in Early Qing Literature*
251. Barbara Molony and Kathleen Uno, eds., *Gendering Modern Japanese History*

252. Hiroshi Aoyagi, *Islands of Eight Million Smiles: Idol Performance and Symbolic Production in Contemporary Japan*
253. Wai-yee Li, *The Readability of the Past in Early Chinese Historiography*
254. William C. Kirby, Robert S. Ross, and Gong Li, eds., *Normalization of U.S.-China Relations: An International History*
255. Ellen Gardner Nakamura, *Practical Pursuits: Takano Chōei, Takahashi Keisaku, and Western Medicine in Nineteenth-Century Japan*
256. Jonathan W. Best, *A History of the Early Korean Kingdom of Paekche, together with an annotated translation of* The Paekche Annals *of the* Samguk sagi
257. Liang Pan, *The United Nations in Japan's Foreign and Security Policymaking, 1945–1992: National Security, Party Politics, and International Status*
258. Richard Belsky, *Localities at the Center: Native Place, Space, and Power in Late Imperial Beijing*
259. Zwia Lipkin, *"Useless to the State": "Social Problems" and Social Engineering in Nationalist Nanjing, 1927–1937*
260. William O. Gardner, *Advertising Tower: Japanese Modernism and Modernity in the 1920s*
261. Stephen Owen, *The Making of Early Chinese Classical Poetry*
262. Martin J. Powers, *Pattern and Person: Ornament, Society, and Self in Classical China*
263. Anna M. Shields, *Crafting a Collection: The Cultural Contexts and Poetic Practice of the* Huajian ji 花間集 *(Collection from Among the Flowers)*
264. Stephen Owen, *The Late Tang: Chinese Poetry of the Mid-Ninth Century (827–860)*
265. Sara L. Friedman, *Intimate Politics: Marriage, the Market, and State Power in Southeastern China*
266. Patricia Buckley Ebrey and Maggie Bickford, *Emperor Huizong and Late Northern Song China: The Politics of Culture and the Culture of Politics*
267. Sophie Volpp, *Worldly Stage: Theatricality in Seventeenth-Century China*
268. Ellen Widmer, *The Beauty and the Book: Women and Fiction in Nineteenth-Century China*
269. Steven B. Miles, *The Sea of Learning: Mobility and Identity in Nineteenth-Century Guangzhou*
270. Lin Man-houng, *China Upside Down: Currency, Society, and Ideologies, 1808–1856*
271. Ronald Egan, *The Problem of Beauty: Aesthetic Thought and Pursuits in Northern Song Dynasty China*
272. Mark Halperin, *Out of the Cloister: Literati Perspectives on Buddhism in Sung China, 960–1279*
273. Helen Dunstan, *State or Merchant? Political Economy and Political Process in 1740s China*
274. Sabina Knight, *The Heart of Time: Moral Agency in Twentieth-Century Chinese Fiction*

275. Timothy J. Van Compernolle, *The Uses of Memory: The Critique of Modernity in the Fiction of Higuchi Ichiyō*
276. Paul Rouzer, *A New Practical Primer of Literary Chinese*
277. Jonathan Zwicker, *Practices of the Sentimental Imagination: Melodrama, the Novel, and the Social Imaginary in Nineteenth-Century Japan*
278. Franziska Seraphim, *War Memory and Social Politics in Japan, 1945–2005*
279. Adam L. Kern, *Manga from the Floating World: Comicbook Culture and the* Kibyōshi *of Edo Japan*
280. Cynthia J. Brokaw, *Commerce in Culture: The Sibao Book Trade in the Qing and Republican Periods*
281. Eugene Y. Park, *Between Dreams and Reality: The Military Examination in Late Chosŏn Korea, 1600–1894*
282. Nam-lin Hur, *Death and Social Order in Tokugawa Japan: Buddhism, Anti-Christianity, and the* Danka *System*
283. Patricia M. Thornton, *Disciplining the State: Virtue, Violence, and State-Making in Modern China*
284. Vincent Goossaert, *The Taoists of Peking, 1800–1949: A Social History of Urban Clerics*
285. Peter Nickerson, *Taoism, Bureaucracy, and Popular Religion in Early Medieval China*
286. Charo B. D'Etcheverry, *Love After* The Tale of Genji*: Rewriting the World of the Shining Prince*
287. Michael G. Chang, *A Court on Horseback: Imperial Touring & the Construction of Qing Rule, 1680–1785*
288. Carol Richmond Tsang, *War and Faith:* Ikkō Ikki *in Late Muromachi Japan*
289. Hilde De Weerdt, *Competition over Content: Negotiating Standards for the Civil Service Examinations in Imperial China (1127–1279)*
290. Eve Zimmerman, *Out of the Alleyway: Nakagami Kenji and the Poetics of Outcaste Fiction*
291. Robert Culp, *Articulating Citizenship: Civic Education and Student Politics in Southeastern China, 1912–1940*
292. Richard J. Smethurst, *From Foot Soldier to Finance Minister: Takahashi Korekiyo, Japan's Keynes*
293. John E. Herman, *Amid the Clouds and Mist: China's Colonization of Guizhou, 1200–1700*
294. Tomoko Shiroyama, *China During the Great Depression: Market, State, and the World Economy, 1929–1937*
295. Kirk W. Larsen, *Tradition, Treaties and Trade: Qing Imperialism and Chosŏn Korea, 1850–1910*
296. Gregory Golley, *When Our Eyes No Longer See: Realism, Science, and Ecology in Japanese Literary Modernism*

297. Barbara Ambros, *Emplacing a Pilgrimage: The Ōyama Cult and Regional Religion in Early Modern Japan*
298. Rebecca Suter, *The Japanization of Modernity: Murakami Haruki between Japan and the United States*
299. Yuma Totani, *The Tokyo War Crimes Trial: The Pursuit of Justice in the Wake of World War II*
300. Linda Isako Angst, *In a Dark Time: Memory, Community, and Gendered Nationalism in Postwar Okinawa*
301. David M. Robinson, ed., *Culture, Courtiers, and Competition: The Ming Court (1368–1644)*
302. Calvin Chen, *Some Assembly Required: Work, Community, and Politics in China's Rural Enterprises*
303. Sem Vermeersch, *The Power of the Buddhas: The Politics of Buddhism During the Koryŏ Dynasty* (918–1392)
304. Tina Lu, *Accidental Incest, Filial Cannibalism, and Other Peculiar Encounters in Late Imperial Chinese Literature*
305. Chang Woei Ong, *Men of Letters Within the Passes: Guanzhong Literati in Chinese History, 907–1911*
306. Wendy Swartz, *Reading Tao Yuanming: Shifting Paradigms of Historical Reception (427–1900)*
307. Peter K. Bol, *Neo-Confucianism in History*
308. Carlos Rojas, *The Naked Gaze: Reflections on Chinese Modernity*